Contents

Contents

Contents

Preface

By folklore we mean the fictional narratives in poetry and prose that supposedly originated in an oral tradition and were later recorded by gatherers of popular lore. We will emphasize the Danish ballads and Norwegian folktales that we believe influenced Ibsen's plays, not only the early works replete with fairy folk, or *Peer Gynt*, whose trolls have made those Norwegian demons famous throughout the world, but also the late plays, whose folk elements have not received the critical attention they warrant. The fairy folk in Norwegian folklore are called the "hidden people" *(huldre)*, and when Ibsen treated them more subtly in his later works, they effectively became hidden from scholarly eyes. We will argue, however, that they actually increased in importance when the playwright began to explore what his critics call the psychology of the individual. If the unconscious is the realm "hidden" from conscious awareness, then it is particularly appropriate that the hidden folk symbolize the place of unconscious or only partially conscious motivation.

In our research, we have tried to keep distinct the folklore that Ibsen knew; that which he was likely to have known and which internal evidence from the plays suggests he knew; variants of tales and ballads printed after his plays were written; and motifs common to world folklore. At the same time, we have drawn from all of these, not only because we think Ibsen was well versed in folklore but also because, with the folklorist David E. Bynum,[1] we believe that the variants of a folktale or ballad help fill out the larger narrative tradition to which it belongs, and that this tradition is then capable of illuminating the individual version, parts or much of which would otherwise remain obscure. The plays supply the best evidence that Ibsen recognized the multiple possibilities that emerge from different combinations of folk themes, and the diverse ways in which the fairy folk interact with the human world allowed him to express his concerns and the dilemmas of his age. We will often invoke this wider tradition without necessarily regarding the precise version that Ibsen was drawing on at the time.

We do not claim that only Denmark and Norway among Scandinavian countries provided Ibsen with folklore. Nor do we exclude as significant sources the traditions of other countries: indeed, Scottish folk narratives will prove important for our discussion, and it is noteworthy that Knut Liestøl, the expert in Norwegian balladry, has written on the folklore connections between Scotland and Norway.[2] Also the story of the white lady, particularly well known in Germany, seems to have provided a central theme in Ibsen's last play; he had spent much time in Germany during his self-exile from Norway. But on the whole we have focused on what appear to be the two main sources of folklore in Ibsen's plays. If any who follow our lead can expand our range to show that we have neglected a narrative tradition or a country that deserved more attention than we gave it, we will be pleased by this extension to our work.

Neither of us is a professional folklorist, although each is trained in a field that shares boundaries with folklore studies: anthropology and literary criticism. When we began this project, we assumed that we would conclude with a single voice blending our diverse as well as shared interests. But we soon recognized that our agendas were not identical. Our decision to keep our voices in this book distinct, however, grew out of the curiosity we each experienced with what the other was doing and the stimulation that came from the questions our own fields had encouraged us to ask. It was a logical extension of this mutual curiosity that led us to consider that our readers might want to see how two different scholarly disciplines approached the same material.

Once we had made this decision, we also agreed not to read what the other was writing until our first versions were complete. Therefore, cross-references to each other's work were added at the end. Until then, our exchanges were essentially informational, as we passed back and forth references to scholarly work the other might not be familiar with, or scenes and passages from the earlier plays that we thought the other would find useful. Our collaboration resulted in a division of labor that each found useful. Jacobsen concentrated on the Danish ballad tradition, although reading through numerous volumes of prose narratives not translated from the Danish and Norwegian. Leavy utilized many years of research on the demon lover and fairy mistress themes in folklore and literature, drawing from that part of the world's literature Ibsen was likely to have known. Because only one of us reads Scandinavian languages, we of necessity split up our reading of secondary sources, together going over those that seemed most pertinent to our ends. We also worked together on Ibsen's Norwegian text, so that although we quote passages in English, our interpretations are grounded in the plays as written. We might note here that the early works by Ibsen were much more significant for an understanding of the later ones than most critics of Ibsen seem to believe. Both of us regretted that space did not allow for more analysis of them than we found ourselves able to supply.

To allow our readers to observe us individually at work is consistent with the romantic period to which Ibsen belonged. During the nineteenth century the processes of thought rather than the product alone received increasing attention. Ibsen's plays reveal that he explored in each drama possibilities for human behavior and motivation that were implied but not developed in another—often the previous—work. Toward the end of his career, he requested that his readers "take possession of [his] works—by reading them and experiencing them—in the same order in which [he] wrote them" (8:359). To read the plays as a group is similar to reading variants of the same folktale, these yielding, again, a larger pattern than a single piece supplies. And although our emphasis is on the later plays, we view the earlier works as not only part of the pattern but, indeed, the plays in which the later concerns were first articulated and in which the relationship between the playwright's themes and folklore was most clearly established. Essentially, we have approached the last plays almost as if they tell a single story. It is a critical commonplace to view *Rosmersholm* and *The Lady from the Sea* as companion plays, the latter treating optimistically what resulted as a debacle in the former. To know both plays is to understand each better than would be possible if only one were analyzed, in whatever detail. Comparably, we intend our independent efforts to provide a perspective that neither could provide alone and that would be blurred if we tried to combine our voices. That is why we present two separate analyses of the seven plays that form the basis of this study. Our readers will find that although we essentially agree on how to read the plays, and although we both root our interpretations in folklore, there is surprisingly little overlap in what we have to say. Our discussions of each play are intended as companion pieces.

Moreover, maintaining the integrity of our individual scholarly disciplines will demonstrate how they complement each other. An interest in folk narratives provides an obvious link between departments of literature and of anthropology: one need only survey the course offerings of these departments across the country. Both literary critics and anthropologists depend upon the discoveries, theories, and methods of the professional folklorists, although the three disciplines have not always been on comfortable terms with one another. Fortunately, the gap between folklore studies and literary criticism seems to be closing, and the situation today is not the same as when Richard Dorson wrote—seriously or ironically, or both—that "the purist approach to defining and collecting folk tales by the touchstone of oral currency is gradually being refuted by poaching literary historians."[3] A willingness on the part of folklorists to "interpret" folklore (Alan Dundes)[4]—indeed, the urging by some that this be done (Bengt Holbek)[5]—is, we may hope, creating a climate in which folklorist, anthropologist, and literary critic can work together harmoniously. Meanwhile, two of us would like to demonstrate a fruitful collaboration.

One of our mutual conclusions—indeed, it was a mutual starting point for our collaboration—grants to folk narratives more than folklorists themselves seem to grant. It would seem that to study the relationship of literary works to their folk sources involves an effort toward a better understanding of the literature. We will argue that to attempt to fill out the tradition to which variants of folk narratives belong is to be increasingly impressed by the complexity of the folklore. It is difficult to argue that the more sophisticated literary forms supply insights that cannot be found already well rooted in the folklore. Thus we believe that we are approaching our subject with a respect for folk tales and ballads that they do not always receive. Two examples will make the point, both of them concerning what we will contend is the basic story type on which Ibsen based so much of his dramatic work: that of the human who forms an amorous relationship with a being from another world.

When commentators on Matthew Arnold's poetry, C. B. Tinker and H. F. Lowry, cited a Danish ballad as a source for "The Forsaken Merman," they noted that the English poet himself remained silent about his indebtedness,

> although he might well have taken pride in exhibiting the kind of material which his subtle and delicate touch could transform into poetry. It would be difficult to find a better example of the poet's power to select what is suitable to his purpose, and to light up an ancient theme with new and, indeed, original beauty.[6]

On aesthetic grounds, the commentators are right in pointing to Arnold's version as a particularly moving and beautiful one. But what Tinker and Lowry really are talking about is the supposed profundity that Arnold brought to his simple folk sources. We not only will present an analysis of "Agnete og Havmanden" that belies such a view but will place both Ibsen and Arnold against the nineteenth-century literary tradition that grew up around the ballad. Indeed, not only was Denmark the home of Arnold's poem, but this poem made its way back to its homeland during the very period that Ibsen was writing his late plays.[7] Meanwhile, a second example of how folklore can be slighted even by folklorists can be found in Richard Dorson's discussion of the roots of some American literature in popular legend. Writing of Nathaniel Hawthorne that none of his "moralistic romances" could be "mistaken for legends, although he retains local roots and supernatural phenomena," Dorson asks, conversely, what "folk transcription could reproduce the symbolism of . . . 'Young Goodman Brown'?"[8] It does not depreciate the literary genius of Arnold, Hawthorne, or Ibsen to argue that they did not so much add meaning to the themes they drew from folktales and ballads as display unique insight into how deep and far-ranging these themes were in their sources. Thus the reciprocal study of literature and folklore leads not only to an understanding of the former but to an increased appreciation of the latter.

We wish to acknowledge the help we have had from two renowned folklorists. Alan Dundes read the proposal for this book, and our enthusiasm for the project was enhanced by his encouragement and suggestions. Bengt Holbek carefully read our first draft, and not only did he help us avoid blatant errors with regard to folklore, but, as our notes indicate, his additions and suggestions became sources for our analyses.

If, despite this aid, errors or weaknesses can still be found, they are, of course, our own.

Per Schelde Jacobsen
Barbara Fass Leavy
New York, 1988

Notes

1. *The Damon in the Wood.*
2. "Scottish and Norwegian Ballads"; also see the entire April 1969 issue of the *Scottish Historical Review*, devoted to the connections between Scotland and Scandinavia.
3. "Print and American Folk Tales" 207.
4. *Interpreting Folklore* ix.
5. "Nordic Research in Popular Prose Narrative" 156; *The Interpretation of Fairy Tales.*
6. *Commentary* 132.
7. We are particularly grateful to Professor Eric Frykman, a scholar of English Victorian literature at the University of Göteborg, Sweden, for locating a Danish translation of Arnold's poem, published in Copenhagen in 1884: *Oversatte Engelske Digte: Shelley, Tennyson, Arnold, Swinburne*, trans. Adolf Hansen.
8. "Print and American Folk Tales" 214.

The authors wish to thank the following who have kindly given permission for the use of copyright material: Oxford University Press for the extracts from *The Oxford Ibsen*, translated and edited by James W. MacFarlane et al., 1970–77, and to A. P. Watt, Ltd. on behalf of Michael B. Yeats and Macmillan London Ltd., and Macmillan Publishing Co. for lines from "Sailing to Byzantium" from *The Collected Poems of William B. Yeats*.

PART
I

Barbara Fass Leavy

CHAPTER 1

Introduction

Ibsen and Folklore

Toward the end of *Rosmersholm,* Ibsen introduces a small detail that appears to receive more emphasis than was warranted even by the verisimilitude that nineteenth-century realism introduced into literature and drama. Rebecca West, faced with the collapse of her plans to become the first lady of Rosmersholm, and guilty about how she had tried to achieve her ends, decides to return to the northern regions from which she had come. Instructing the housekeeper to retrieve her trunk from the attic, she adds as an afterthought its description: brown sealskin. The exchange would probably escape the notice of anyone who was not familiar with the Scandinavian folklore concerning the seal folk, the seal maiden being a close cousin of the mermaid to whom Ibsen compares Rebecca. Only a few critics have realized that the name of the hero as well as the title of the play are derived from a group of Danish ballads concerning a merman who kidnaps a mortal woman and lives with her under the sea. It is therefore noteworthy that in Svend H. Grundtvig's scholarly notes to the ballad is described a narrative in which "Rosmer" dons a sealskin cloak; the name "Rosmer" can itself be translated as "sea lion" (*DgF* 41).

What can a recognition of this folklore element add to an understanding of the play? A fine study of Ibsen contends that "*Rosmersholm* is one of the most baffling and enigmatic of Ibsen's plays. The action of the play is very simple but the characters are so complex and their motivations so subtle and indirect that the effect of the play is likely to be bewildering."[1] The legends of the seal folk analyzed below provide a revealing paradigm for an increased understanding of the symbols Ibsen

3

derived from folklore. But it will be useful first to stress that one of the most underdiscussed and therefore underrated aspects of Ibsen's life is that he was not only a playwright who drew on folk themes but a folk-lorist.

In his *Ballad Books and Ballad Men* (1930), Sigurd B. Hustvedt introduces as an aside in his chapter on Scandinavian folklorists that "Ibsen in his earlier days enjoyed a public grant for the collecting of popular traditions. No ballad collection has come from him, but he has left a record of his occupation with these things in his essay, 'On the Popular Ballads and Their Importance for Literature.' And in one or two of his earlier plays."[2] In one of these, however, Ibsen appears to have left a very strong record of how folklore had affected him. For at about the same time he wrote the essay, he completed *Olaf Liljekrans*, a play in which the maiden Alfhild, who despite her name is an ordinary mortal, though she lives outside village life (that is, culture), reminds Olaf of how he had listened to her minstrel father's songs:

> You told me you rode one summer night along the green hillside where the river runs. And there you heard strange songs you but half understood, but which so haunt you that you will never forget them. . . . There you heard my father's songs. I have grown up with them. In truth I have never understood them fully, either. To me they were treasures beyond price, indeed life itself. Now they mean little to me—a hint only of the glory that was to come. (1: 490)

Unfortunately, Ibsen's essay on the folk ballads has been neglected by critics of his plays. Although frequent attention is paid to his statement in the preface to the second edition of *The Feast at Solhaug* that he had been reading Landstad's collection of Norwegian ballads, what Ibsen actually had to say about how ordinary people found in folk poetry a "satisfying medium for expressing their own inner life" (1: 672) has not led critics back to his early exposure to and fascination with folklore.

For English readers, a translation of the essay remains virtually buried in an appendix in volume 1 of the *Oxford Ibsen*, readily available, of course, but likely to be ignored because the essay is by chronology tied to Ibsen's early, inferior efforts in drama. True, his use of folklore later became increasingly subtle, except for the kinds of obvious references to trolls and mermaids found in plays such as *Rosmersholm, The Lady from the Sea*, and *The Master Builder*. But this very subtlety reflects the increasingly symbolic role of folklore as the playwright began to concentrate on the "inner life" of his characters. Again, Ibsen was not only a playwright who used folklore as a source for themes but a folklorist in whom traditional forms of literature sent down deep roots.

The subject of Ibsen's folklore gathering is sparsely scattered through biographies and critical literature on his works, but in the more than fifty years that have passed since Hustvedt's comments, little has been added to the account. Besides the work done on *Peer Gynt*, very few essays have addressed themselves to folklore in the later plays. One of these focuses too exclusively on trolls and ghosts and does not, in any event, apply the folklore to any new insights into the plays discussed. Another, not translated from Norwegian, surveys the folklore themes in *The Lady from the Sea*, for example, ballads and stories of revenants who return from the dead to claim their betrothed or spouses; unfortunately, this fascinating piece lacks documentation and therefore it is difficult to use it to trace the direct influences on the playwright.[3] One of the best of Ibsen's critics, Erik Østerud, has written about the influence on *Rosmersholm* of the story "Agnete og Havmanden" ("Agnes and the Merman"). But he focuses on Kierkegaard's treatment of the ballad rather than the folk poetry itself;[4] moreover, he talks of digressing into Ibsen's use of folklore, whereas we are treating it as a main road. There is also an important essay, written in French by Maurice Gravier, on Ibsen and the *ballade magique*.[5] This refers to the group of ballads whose subject is the confrontation between the human and the supernatural worlds that we will hold central to Ibsen's conceptions of this theme. Gravier argues, as will we, that it was the Danish ballads (not Landstad's collection) that constitute the main ballad influence on Ibsen, and Gravier recognizes in the distinction between two realms, that of *elfarland* (fairyland) and of *beijarland* (the so-called real world), the conflict between nature and culture that we will explore in more detail than his essay allowed. But we will also argue that the seal folk pattern reveals a structure that works against apportioning thematic elements to one of these two realms. Gravier himself, as will be seen, is forced into inconsistencies because he recognizes only two parts to this structure rather than the four we will demonstrate. We will also claim that Ibsen recognized the implications of this four-part split in the worlds of his plays and that it was the permutations achieved in juxtaposing them in differing combinations that provide his works with much of their variety and complexity.

A recent essay noteworthy for emphasizing Ibsen's contact with an oral folk tradition is particularly suggestive for studying the playwright's use of folklore. Once again, *Peer Gynt* is the main object of study, but in a context with wider application. W. M. S. Russell argues that the playwright's experiences as a folklorist had a "profound effect on Ibsen's development as a writer," and he quotes from a letter Ibsen wrote his publisher in August 1867:

> In case it should interest you, Peer Gynt was a real person who lived in Gudbrandsdal, probably around the end of the last century or the beginning of this. His name is still famous among the people up there, but not much more is known about his life than what is to be found in Asbjørnsen's *Norwegian Fairy Tales*. . . . So I haven't had much on which to base my poem, but that has meant that I have had all the more freedom with which to work on it.

The letter proving that Ibsen drew on both an oral tradition and scientific collection, Russell concludes that "Ibsen seems merely to be saying that he heard no legends about Peer Gynt besides the one Asbjørnsen had collected."[6]

But Russell also describes three separate perspectives where it comes to Ibsen and folklore. First, there was an oral tradition with which the playwright was intimately familiar from his own gathering of folklore. It is worth adding here that in the light of recent emphasis by folklorists on the performance of a narrative, Ibsen, deeply involved in the theater and his ambitions to be a dramatist, was probably particularly sensitive to how meanings in folk narratives are communicated through extra-verbal signals, such as body language and tone of voice. Thus he probably heard more in the tales than he would have apprehended had he only read them: he says as much in his essay on the folk ballad. Second, there was a growing body of published collections of folktales and ballads, and as a collector, Ibsen would have been interested in the work being done. In any event, we agree with Gravier that it is naive to believe that Ibsen was no reader. And third, Ibsen measured the potential for the imaginative re-creation of the lore he knew. Like Keats, who contemplated the mysterious, unexplained story on the Grecian urn, Ibsen seems to have recognized that heard melodies are sweet but unheard ones even sweeter for the writer who has his own tale to tell. But in this understanding, Ibsen would have been aware of the consequent tension between the creative artist and his folk material.

A study of Ibsen and folklore should include all three of these perspectives as well as, of course, any connections the dramatist could make between his own life and times and the subjects of folk narratives. Toward the end of his essay on the folk ballad, he writes that it should not be thought that the world of the ballad is a merely fictional one: "like all artistic production, it naturally seeks a point of departure in real life, in history, in first-hand experience and in the natural environment" (1: 683). Yet Ibsen's use of folk narratives is a fascinating subject that often raises puzzling questions. Why, for example, would he choose the name "Rosmer" associated with the merman of Scandinavian balladry and give it to a protagonist whose struggle is to rid himself of the bourgeois philistinism that is being challenged in his own time? Rosmersholm, the family estate that gives the play its name, stands for the very antithesis of the magic underworld into which mermen lure their female victims. Again, we will argue that it is knowledge of the folklore that makes it possible to answer such questions. This brief survey of the present state of scholarship on the subject is, again, intended to show that it has not progressed enough in the half century or so between Hustvedt and Russell and that Ibsen the folklorist is yet to be adequately examined.

Such an exploration should begin with Ibsen's own essay "On the Heroic Ballad and Its Significance for Literature" (1857), an exploration of folk poetry and a kind of manifesto by the playwright about his own artistic relationship to it. The essay has both an overt and an implied content. The former has to do not only with the interest in the ballad as a popular art form that occupied nineteenth-century Europe but also with the nationalistic claims accruing to folk art. Ibsen concludes his discussion rather abruptly, explaining his attempt to claim for Scandinavia "a large and essential part of the cultural heritage of [its] forefathers," and inviting historians to speak out in support of this claim. For those interested in the distinction between Ibsen's pan-Scandinavianism and his Norwegian nationalism, the essay would be a very provocative one. In the dichotomies he sets up—between paganism and Christianity, saga and ballad, folk and aristocracy, for example—Norway represents an older, Denmark and Sweden a more modern period. In his plays, this distinction sometimes picks up thematic significance, such as the point in *Lady Inger* [*til Østråt*] when Nils Lykke, a Danish knight, describes the Danish court to Eline much as elf knights proffer the delights of the otherworld as they seductively convince young maidens to elope with them.

Whether Ibsen's dissertation on the ballad has anything new to offer students of the popular art form is a point that need not be raised here,[7] although it can be insisted that he deserves a more prominent place in the literature on the ballad. Rather it is the covert content of his essay that is compelling for any study of Ibsen's drama, particularly his use in it of folklore. For embedded in his consideration of folk poetry can be found his concern with his role in culture as a playwright and, in effect, an "apology" (in the traditional aesthetic sense) that explains the importance for him of folk art. For in explaining why ballads more than saga literature suit the needs of dramatic literature, Ibsen also raises some significant concerns having to do with the relationship of his own audience to art, as well as the sometimes contradictory relationship between his dramas as literature to be read and as plays to be performed.

Ibsen begins with a rather invidious distinction between the folk for whom the ballads was an essential element of their psychological and philosophical life, and the audience of his own time, "who visit the theatre only when offered the opportunity of being titillated by some novel situation or excited by some novel intrigue" (1: 672). In this comparison lies an essential dilemma faced by the nineteenth-century European writer who found himself both dependent on the audience who would pay money for his art and yet alienated from what he often held to be its debased cultural tastes. That the folk thus becomes an idealized receiver of superior art forms is not an idea original in Ibsen: a similar reaction against the philistine middle class was experienced by William Butler Yeats—to cite but one example—who was also drawn as a result to the potential in Celtic folklore. But Ibsen does not appear to have retreated from this audience, toward whom he had ambivalent feelings. Rather, in the basis for folk poetry he found both a link between himself and those for whom he wrote and produced, as well as a fundamental reason for employing in his dramas the folk themes he drew on.

In describing the differences between the popular audience for the ballad and his own audience, Ibsen posits a kind of racial memory that links the two, and it will be this memory that he will address in his work:

> If the new is to appeal to the people, it must also in a certain sense be old; it must not be invented, but rediscovered (ikke *op*findes men *gen*findes); it must not appear as something strange and incongruous in the conceptual range inherited by the people from their ancestors, and in which our national strength mainly resides: it must not be presented like some foreign utensil whose use is unfamiliar and which is inappropriate for the familiar routine; it must be reproduced like some old family piece which we had forgotten but which we remember as soon as we set eyes upon it, because all kinds of memories are linked with it—memories which, so to speak, lay within us fermenting quietly and uncertainly until the poet came along and put words to them. (1: 672)

It is as dramatist that he is particularly able to evoke echoes of an older art, for Ibsen was perhaps in advance of his time in insisting on the performance element in folk literature: "In print, the ballad looks old and grey, indeed old-fashioned, if you will; on the lips of people age does not concern it. The living word . . . not only nourishes, it renews and rejuvenates" (1: 674). He adds that it is nevertheless "fortunate that these written records are being made, and it would be well if more were put in hand whilst there is still time" (1: 674). Again, there are two important elements to be noted in his discussion. First, there is the nostalgia for a culture that is fast disappearing in the modern technological world and that must be preserved as well as discovered while it is part of the conscious memories of people. Second, it is possible to find him exploring here the dual nature of his own work. Studies of Ibsen consistently point out that he was economically dependent upon the publication as texts of his plays and that he would often rush to be sure that they appeared in bookstores in time for Christmas sales. But it was on stage, as he seems well aware, that the *spoken* word reproduced the spirit of the folklore, appealing, again, to the emotional content of the ballad lore and to receptors in the memories of his audience.

It is for this reason that he finds the ballad, with its lyricism, better suited to his various needs than saga literature—although he understands the narrative relationship between the two: "If then the poet is to create a dramatic work from this epic material, he must necessarily introduce a foreign element into this given material: he must introduce a lyrical element; because, as is well known, drama is a higher compound of lyric and epic" (1: 675). Again, it is precisely this lyric element that he must depend upon to awaken in a contemporary audience the spirit of the past that will elevate their aesthetic responses: "the dramatist who draws his material from the ballads does not have to subject his material to the kind of transformation necessary when it is drawn from the saga . . . he is thereby enabled (if he is otherwise capable) to present his heroes to the beholder in the way in which they are already familiar from the folk poetry direct" (1: 676). Like elements in paganism, pieces of an old culture continue "to live in the consciousness and faith of the people, and there they have continued to live until our own days" (1: 677).

In his essay on the heroic ballad, Ibsen has of necessity little to say about the folktale, which would also feed his plays. But what he does note is nevertheless a clue, at least, to how he would thematically use folk narratives. For him, the "fairy tale" is akin to Christian mystery, having to do with "the inexplicable." He says that it is "in this that the mythic tales differ fundamentally from the heroic ballad; the former is to the latter as the fable is to the fairy tale. The fable does not know the miraculous, the fairy tale is rooted in it" (1: 677). It will be part of the final argument of this book that Ibsen's late plays not only shifted from an interest in social issues to the psychology of the individual—as many critics have argued—but to the psychology of the artist in particular. Already in his essay on the heroic ballad, Ibsen was evidencing concern with the role of the playwright in his contemporary environment. As that role became more problematic for him, the mysterious, inexplicable, miraculous world of the folk or fairy tale would become the landscape of the aesthetic realm, but one as increasingly remote from the day-to-day concerns of his world as the mysteries of religion would prove to be.

The Seal Folk Pattern

Now, let us return to Rebecca West's sealskin trunk. The seal is one of the animal forms assumed by the heroine of a widely distributed folktale, the swan maiden. Her basic story is well represented by Jon

Arnason's seal maiden tale from Iceland, which Alexander H. Krappe uses to introduce his essay "Scandinavian Seal Lore."

A man of Myrdal, in passing by a cave one early morning, noticed music and dancing going on inside, while a number of seal skins were lying outside. He took one of these home, locking it in a chest. On passing again by the grotto, he beheld a pretty girl entirely without clothes and weeping bitterly. She was none other than the seal whose skin he had taken. He gallantly consoled her and took her to his house. Taking a liking to her, he subsequently married her, and they had many children; but she was often seen sitting near the window, looking yearningly out to sea. On going out, he was always careful to take with him the key of the chest, in which the seal skin lay safely locked up. One fatal day, however, he forgot the key and, returning home, found that his wife had disappeared; she had donned the skin and swum out to sea.[8]

Although this husband and the children borne by the seal maiden often saw her in the sea, she never returned to them.

Scandinavia is also rich in swan maiden (and other bird maiden) stories, and Ibsen reflects his familiarity with these in *The Grouse at Justedal* and the plan for an opera called *The Mountain Bird*, which also relates the story of Alfhild. His last work, *When We Dead Awaken*, also reflects swan lore; he not only alludes to the legend of the Swan Knight, Lohengrin, but dresses one of his heroines, Irene, in a swansdown cloak. But unlike the swan maiden story, whose motifs, scattered throughout the world, have been described as "kaleidoscopic,"[9] the seal maiden tale constitutes a group of stories more finite in number and fairly concentrated geographically. Ibsen may, indeed, have been familiar with Arnason's version, since the Icelandic tales were translated into Danish and published in Denmark in the middle of the nineteenth century. In any event, there is a particular usefulness to isolating the seal maiden tales from the swan maiden group to which they belong, for from just a few variants of the former emerges a pattern spread more thinly and widely over the larger swan maiden tradition. It is a pattern worth describing, because it helps illuminate the relationships among the many ballads and folktales on which Ibsen drew for his plays, most of them depicting the union between a human being from the real world and a denizen of a supernatural realm who offers that human an alternative to a reality from which he or she shrinks. The seal maiden tales, however, describe the way in which each of these worlds is itself split, so that from the narratives emerge the four-part structure we referred to above.

In his *Migratory Legends* Reidar T. Christiansen deemed the seal maiden tale important enough to warrant a separate classification (4080), although he cites only one Norwegian variant. Significantly, this one can be found in the north, that region in Norway from which come those Ibsen characters—Rebecca West, Ellida Wangel, the latter's demon lover—whose origins are used to account for their strange powers or, correspondingly, their inability to live comfortably in ordinary society. It is from the north that the Finns come, those Laplanders who, again according to Christiansen, are held to possess magic powers.[10] "Finn" is a term used by Shetland islanders to designate not the nationality (Finns or Lapps) but the supernatural identity of the seal folk, although it is striking that Finmark is the place in Norway from which Rebecca West comes. At the end of the nineteenth century, a scholar deeply immersed in the folklore of the sea and the seal folk concluded that "however the Finn name may be explained etymologically," it remains the case that "Norway appears in the Shetland tales, and in the recollection of the people there, as the home of the 'Finns.'"[11]

For if Norway itself does not offer many variants of the seal maiden story, in the rich seal lore of Scotland, especially the Shetland and Orkney islands, Norway plays a prominent role. These islands were under Norwegian rule until the fifteenth century, and they still provide a link between Scottish and Norwegian folklore.

> So long as the realm of Norway extended as far as to Scotland, it was natural that ballads should travel across the Orkneys and Shetland. Trade has been carried on between Scotland and the Orkneys, and between the Orkneys and Shetland; how Scottish and Nordic meet in Shetland is seen in the ballad of *King Orfeo* (Child 19), where the refrain is Nordic and the text, otherwise, Scottish.[12]

A similar argument seems feasible concerning the seal maiden story.

David Thomson, who personally went in search of seal lore, begins the concluding chapter of *The People of the Sea* with the song of "The Grey Selchie of Sule Skerrie." It tells of a young woman who bears the child of a seal man to whom she must eventually surrender her child, and in this version, the human mother is Norwegian. Similarly, when Thomson asks one of his Scottish informants to account for the spells that have enchanted the seal folk so that they can only periodically assume their human form, he is given instead their genealogy: they are the cursed children of the King of Lochlann (that is, Norway).[13]

Among the stories Thomson recounts is that of Brita, who could easily qualify as a typical Ibsen heroine. The defiant child of a wealthy lord who rejects the suitors her father deems appropriate, she is, again, described as a "Norway lass." Brita is determined to marry one of her father's servants, but waits until her parent dies to propose marriage to him. She is, that is, not only rebellious but aggressive in her behavior toward men. But Brita "wasna happy. It wasna long afore she was vexed and disappointed wi' her man. But, being proud like, she'd said nothing to anyone, for she kent well the answer they'd give her."[14] However, all of this proves but the prologue to what is the essence of Brita's story, her eventual choice of a seal mate. Brita's discontent proves a summons to the otherworld and the sea creature who answers her. Like Ellida Wangel, Brita is drawn to the sea. There she sat

> on a rock, where she saw the black mark o' the high tide. She waited there or the tide did flow, and when the tide came high she shed seven tears into the sea. Folk said they were the only tears she ever shed. But she kent that was what she must do when she wanted speech wi' the selchie folk. "Well, as the first blink o' dawn made the waters grey, she saw a muckle selchie swimming for the rock. He raised his head out o' the water alow her, and he says to her, "What's your will wi' me fair lady?" So she likely telt him what was in her mind and says he, "Come down again to this rock at the seventh stream," says he, "and wait for me. For it's only at the seventh stream that I can come in the shape o' a man," says he to her, and away wi' him swimming.[15]

After that, Brita bore a series of children characterized by their webbed fingers and toes.

The story of the seal maiden captured by a mortal and forced to bear his children, on one side, and the mortal woman who has a seal lover on the other, depict two sides of the same narrative coin. But they also suggest a different relationship between the two worlds from which their protagonists come. For what an analysis of seal maiden tales reveals is two different views of the natural origin of the woman. Therefore, seal folk stories often prove to be complementary. Brita has periodic meetings with her seal/merman; in contrast is a tale in which a man who grants the seal maiden her freedom when he returns her skin to her is rewarded by regular intervals in which she first visits him and then returns to her natural element, the sea—a solution that Ibsen could not find a way of granting Ellida.

This tale from the Scottish Highlands seems to have combined in a single narrative three different versions of the swan maiden type story. Three brothers capture seal skins and thus the maidens to whom they belong. One forces his unwilling bride into the domestic servitude from which, like the typical swan maiden, she flees as soon as she recovers her stolen garment. The second brother belies a commentary on the story that holds that if the seal maiden's husband had destroyed rather than just hidden the skin, his wife would have been his forever:[16] for this husband does burn the sealskin, but unhappily, the fire destroys his home and burns to death his wife. In contrast to both men, the third brother proves a folk ancestor to Dr. Wangel, and shows his love for his captured wife by freely returning her animal covering so that she may leave him if she wishes. The bliss they experience when she comes to earth every ninth day to tend his home and spend the night is a happiness denied not only to his brothers but, implicitly, to the majority of mankind.[17] Again, the folktales sometimes resolve a dilemma that cannot be so easily resolved in the real world—as Ibsen's plays demonstrate.

Some versions of the seal maiden story have preserved a theme that no longer characterizes the swan maiden tale, although it can be found in what some have argued is the original version of that tale in Sanskrit sources. The thematic core of the swan maiden group concerns the capture of a supernatural being from another world, who, unsuited to woman's usual role in the world, eventually escapes to what she believes is her rightful existence. For most folklorists, this is where her story really begins, for they include the story in the tale type designated by Aarne and Thompson as the "Search for the Lost Wife." But the fairy some scholars have claimed is the first swan maiden, one of the Hindu Apsaras, Urvasi, leaves behind not only her supernatural realm but supernatural lovers when she takes a human mate, and the heavenly

Gandharvas who plot for her return eventually succeed in reclaiming her for their world.

Structurally, the Gandharvas's role can be said to be played by the bull seal who awaits his mate in the sea. The seal is thus the demon lover who, like the Stranger in *The Lady from the Sea*, asserts a prior claim to the heroine: the "Finn women were said to make good housewives. Yet there was generally a longing after some previous attachment."[18] Celtic folklore emphasizes this theme and there may be more than coincidence in Ibsen's stage direction, which dresses the Stranger who comes for Ellida in a Scottish cap (more about this below in the analysis of Ellida as seal maiden). For it is easy to find Dr. and Mrs. Wangel in this seal maiden tale from the Shetland islands:

> The Shetlander's love for his Merwife was unbounded, but his affection was coldly returned. The lady would often steal alone to the desert strand, and, on a signal being given, a large seal would make his appearance, with whom she would hold, in an unknown tongue, an anxious conference.[19]

In Jeremiah Curtin's story of "Tom Moore and the Seal Woman" the husband is, again, in love, whereas his merwife is not. When she recovers her magic garment, she prepares to meet her sea lover.

> All this time the big seal in the sea was roaring. Next day when Tom was at work his wife swept the house, put everything in order, washed the children and combed their hair; then, taking them one by one, she kissed each. She went next to the rock, and putting the hood on her head, gave a plunge. That moment the big seal rose and roared so that people ten miles away could hear him.[20]

In another version of the story, the husband battles the bull seal and kills him (at one point, Dr. Wangel is ready to fight the Stranger), although he is himself badly hurt.

> That night, his seal-woman wife comforted him to the utmost of her ability; and she confessed to him how her love for him, long years before, had tempted her to desert her seal husband—aye, and how, in a moment of forgetfulness, she had endangered his life, since the seal-

man always seeks out the seal-woman's earthly mate, when she desires to return to her own kith and kin among the Seal-folk.[21]

Once again it is possible to cite the complementary motif. In another story, a group of seal maidens "obeyed the compelling urge to return to the sea." When their husbands tried to stop them they were turned into stone. "But the seal-maidens never forgot, and can be seen," each one "keeping tryst with her own" stone.[22]

These corresponding patterns, according to which the woman is either a deviant mortal whose longing for the sea is a betrayal of her husband or a seal maiden whose stay on earth involves infidelity to her seal lover, raise the question that Ibsen asked himself when he came to write *The Lady from the Sea:* whether the world or the sea constitutes the true element of those who appear unable to remain content in either realm. An apt description of the seal folk is that those who "appear in the interchangeable shape of men and seals" are "partly more than human, partly less so."[23] Two basic versions of their shapeshifting can be found in the seal lore: either they are conceived of as humans undergoing punishment and deprived of healthy attachments in the real world, or they are seductive demons capable of assuming human shape to tempt a mortal being into their realm. Christianity explained some of these folk motifs by claiming that the demonic folk had to pay a tithe of a human soul to the devil. But the longing of the supernatural folk for mortal paramours existed in oral and written literature before this account of their motives, and in that longing is a feature of the so-called real world that scholars such as Gravier have overlooked in analyzing Ibsen's use of these folk motifs. *Beijarland* has much to recommend it, enough, at least, to make unhappy those enchanted sea folk who have been banished from it. It would seem that the need to abduct a mortal for fairyland speaks to the need for contact with the mortal realm.

The people of the Faroe Islands say "that the seal every ninth night puts off its skin and gets a human form, and then dances and sports like the 'human mortals,' till it resumes its skin and becomes a seal again."[24] Another belief among western Celts and Scandinavians is that the "seals were 'fallen angels,' condemned to live in the sea as seals, though on land they could assume a human shape. Again, they were human beings under a spell, or were originally human beings who had sinned grievously. 'Every true Norseman looks upon the seal as a kind of second cousin in disgrace.' "[25] Some accounts suggest that their human form is not so much a periodic release from their punishment, but a reminder of their previous existence "to keep them unhappy."[26]

But once again, the other side of the story holds that the seal woman belongs to the sea and that it is her human existence that deprives her of what she needs to be happy. Moreover, her life on earth may make it impossible for her to return to her natural element. In one story, baptism taints the woman so that the seal folk will no longer accept her among them. "The night of the dancing came and the seals danced heartily as of wont in the half-light of the moon. They did not touch her, for the blessed water was on her forehead."[27] Baptism in this case is comparable to the theft of the sealskin, which then becomes an ambiguous symbol in the story. It is the natural form that must be relinquished in the real world: "Anyone who gets hold of their protecting garment, has the Finns in his power. Only by means of the skin can they go back to the water."[28] One of Thomson's informants relates how in the "Faroe Islands there is a proverb—'She could no more hold herself back than the seal wife could when she found her skin.'" Baptism, the mark of culture, is but one way that the woman longing for freedom finds herself trapped in the role the world has defined for its females. How resistant she can be to her domestic bondage is depicted perhaps more starkly than usual in an Irish version of the story, in which the seal maiden legend merges with that of the mermaid. The captured maiden was with her earthly husband for seven years, and "by the will of God they had three sons, and through all that time she never spoke a word, but she laughed three times."[29]

But from the perspective of the human world, the sealskin is rather an outward form of the woman's depraved being, her rootedness in tainted nature, and hence the source of her rebelliousness. In this respect, the sealskin is the equivalent of the cow's tail that distinguishes the Norwegian *huldre* (fairy woman). A long antifeminist tradition may find in the swan maiden group of tales a manifestation of feminine evil that would justify the subjugation of this essentially aberrant member of the human species. In its most benign form, the wife becomes a pampered doll who lives a childlike existence under the domination of her husband. Ironically, however, Ibsen's Nora only confirms the basic point of the seal maiden tale: the captured wife seizes the first opportunity she has to escape (usually by means of her magic clothing—e.g., Nora's dancing dress), leaving behind not only her husband but their children.

There are, of course, the "Selchie" ballads, which tell of seal men, but again, the essential plot concerns the desire of the seal for contact with the human world and for a son, which suggests a yearning *toward* rather than *away from* culture. As this book will discuss at some length, the forsaken merman ballads involve an analogy between the abandoned human husband and the abandoned merman, both of whom can be conceived as victims of a faithless wife whose return to her own realm, be that world or sea, deprives them of that opposite realm they seek in union with her. It must be repeated, however, that seal women also reflect this yearning toward the world when they are imagined to be human beings under enchantment, and so the antifeminists could not find in every version of the story an appropriate vehicle for expressing the need to control women. Moreover, in the nineteenth century, male writers—Ibsen and Matthew Arnold are clear examples—would exploit the female perspective to express their own conflicts. Gender relationships are as important to understanding the folklore as they are to understanding Ibsen, but no simple schemes can be drawn to account for them. Sometimes critics treat as specifically feminist issues that which the writers believed were human dilemmas in general and the artist's dilemmas in particular.

In short, the seal woman is at times conceived of as a demon and at others as a pitiable being who cannot locate her true place. Both aspects of her character are implied in a Greek superstition surrounding the seal, beneath whose visible exterior was supposed to be "concealed a woman, and . . .. when a swimmer ventured too far he ran great risk of being seized by a seal and strangled. The creature then carried the lifeless body to some desert shore and wept over it, from which arose the popular saying that when a woman shed false tears she cried like a seal.[30] But in Scandinavian and Scottish lore, the seal maiden (and her cousin, the mermaid) is a truly divided being whose conflict was exploited by the nineteenth-century writer who could find in her plight a symbol for the difficulty of reconciling life and art. But folklore suggests that other storytellers recognized in her agony a human problem from which few were exempt. What one of Thomson's informants said of the seal folk provides a clue to many of Ibsen's plays, and in so doing, even more firmly establishes the connection between his dramatic themes and folklore: "it is given to them that their sea-longing shall be land-longing and their land-longing shall be sea-longing."[31]

In the swan maiden tale to which much seal lore is related, the flight of the wife and mother back to what she conceives as her true element usually involves, as we have noted, a seeming lack of concern for the children left behind. But in a variant from Iceland, the woman's conflict is focused on her children—the children born on earth and those she left in the sea. "Before the woman flung herself into the sea, it is said that she spoke these words":

> Woe is me! Ah, woe is me!
> I have seven bairns on land,
> And seven in the sea.

Nor did this seal maiden leave her earthly husband without regret. "Whenever he rowed out fishing afterwards, a seal would often swim round and round his boat, and it looked as if tears were running from its eyes."[32] Similarly, in his collection of *Scandinavian Folktales*, William A. Craigie tells how one seal maiden prepared to return to the sea by protecting her children from any harm: "she had put out the fire and laid away all the knives. Then she ran down to the beach, put on the skin and plunged into the sea, where a male seal came up by her side,—he had all the time been lying out there waiting for her."[33]

This ambivalence on the part of the swan or seal maiden is likely to have struck a powerful note in Ibsen's consciousness, given his complex treatment of the mother-child relationship in his plays. It is not, of course, necessary to argue for these stories as his main source for his characterization of the child as sacrificial victim or as another millstone around the neck of an angry parent. Rather, it is interesting to note that in addition to the symbolism inherent in the seal lore, stories derived from it also provide concrete domestic relationships useful for a playwright concerned with both the external and internal life of his characters.

But what is perhaps more important about the relationship of the seal maiden tale to Ibsen's plays as well as to the related folk ballads and tales, which never relinquished their hold on his imagination, is that, again, the seal lore does not stop at a simple opposition between two realms, what Gravier calls *beijarland* and *elfarland*. We do not deny that two worlds and thus two potentials for human life confront each other; however, it is arguable that such a formulation tends to simplify both the conflicts faced by humans caught between these realms and the folk-lore surrounding them. According to such a scheme, nature represents a powerful but regressive force that must be resisted in the name of social stability or the psychological health of the individual. This is the perspective of psychoanalytic critics who approach Ellida Wangel as the kind of woman likely to show up in a psychiatrist's office. They neatly equate the sea world with that of the trolls, the ugly beings who represent the unsocialized self. For them, Ellida's final choice of her husband over her demon lover proves that she has overcome a neurosis or gotten be-yond an arrested stage in her development toward maturity. Ironically, the folklore can be invoked to support the objections of those who regret her accommodation to bourgeois reality. Thomson's folk informant, who describes the oscillating pull of land longing and sea longing, makes no simple judgment about the superiority of one over the other, for the complementary motifs in the seal maiden story present as rival claims the opposition between two worlds. On the other side, the folklore also presents a bleaker picture than does psychoanalysis. Since each of the realms—this world and the supernatural—is itself split into antithetical elements, neither realm can satisfy its own inhabitants, who seek in the inhabitants of the other world what is lacking in their own.

Seal maiden tales thus proffer several narrative possibilities whose relationship to each other is what creates the essential themes in the tale:

1. The heroine is a seal maiden whose rightful place is the sea, and her being forced to submit to her husband's world and authority is a violation of her essential being. She is a victim rather than a demon.

2. The heroine is a mortal whose longing for the sea speaks to an aberration that must be remedied. Society views her as deviant and hence demonic, and in her frustration she is by her behavior likely to confirm its opinion.

3. The heroine is a seal maiden whose animal form represents some curse or enchantment that alienates her from the human world toward which she yearns. The pleasures of the supernatural realm

do not compensate for the loss of her soul, which may be interpreted symbolically as well as literally. She will strive for redemption on the world's terms, but often her sacrifice is rendered futile as the world has no place for her.

4. Comparably, the demon lover may be less a seducer than an otherworldly being (e.g., merman) who seeks some infusion of the real world into what would otherwise be a sterile existence. If he is not the seal lover awaiting the return of his mate, who in turn bides her time until she can escape her earthly husband and go back to the sea, then he is forced into the role of the kidnapper who must achieve his ends by kidnapping a woman from the real world.

In the nineteenth century, Matthew Arnold drew on the story of Agnete and the merman to portray the dilemma of his Margaret, who cannot choose between two worlds precisely because each of them is dichotomized into its positive and negative elements. The sea world offers her pleasures whose symbolic meaning goes beyond mere hedonism, but to enjoy them she must sacrifice her soul. In contrast, her own world offers her a joyful productivity and human fellowship that has no corresponding benefit in the sea world, but to enjoy that, she must submit to the narrow, restrictive ethical values that come along with such benefits. She is effectively stalemated. Arnold and Ibsen drew on the same folklore, and the English poet presents in a few lines the pattern that in Ibsen appears less obvious for being spread out over his plays rather than concentrated in a single work.

> She sits at her wheel in the humming town,
> Singing most joyfully.
> Hark what she sings: "O joy, O joy,
> For the humming street, and the child with its toy!
> For the priest, and the bell, and the holy well;
> For the wheel where I spun,
> And the blessed light of the sun!"
> And so she sings her fill,
> Singing most joyfully,
> Till the spindle drops from her hand,

And the whizzing wheel stands still.
She steals to the window, and looks at the sand,
And over the sand at the sea;
And her eyes are set in a stare;
And anon there breaks a sigh,
And anon there drops a tear,
From a sorrow-clouded eye,
And a heart sorrow-laden,
A long, long sigh;
For the cold strange eyes of a little Mermaiden
And the gleam of her golden hair.

Most Arnold critics have noted that this scene is depicted in the voice of the merman himself. The ironic significance of this narrative point of view is that the merman can recognize Margaret's plight only if he too experiences the antithetical pull of land and sea longing. The tragedy implied in this poem is not that two worlds cannot be reconciled, but that four cannot. The mismatching of couples would provide Ibsen with one of his major dramatic subjects, whose climax would come in the last of his plays, *When We Dead Awaken,* where it is the seemingly suitable pairing among his four characters that would most forcefully point out how the playwright had come to understand the stalemate depicted so movingly in Arnold's poem.

Notes

1. Hurt 130.
2. Hustvedt, *Ballad Books* 167.
3. Marilyn Anderson, "Norse Trolls"; Fraenkl, "*Fruen.*" Gravier draws on the work of Clara Stuyver, who recognizes in the names Ibsen gives his characters the elf world to which they are to be associated. Stuyver has noted the significance of the sealskin trunk as a sign of Rebecca's mermaid characteristics, but has nothing to say about the seal maiden stories (381, 385).
4. "Den rosmerske adelighet."
5. "Le drame d'Ibsen."
6. Russell 16.
7. Jacobsen argues in Chapter 4 that some of Ibsen's ideas are derived from

Introduction

Johan Ludvig Heiberg, the Danish writer. Ibsen's concerns were prevalent in the late nineteenth century.

8. Krappe 156.
9. Stith Thompson 92.
10. Christiansen, *Folktales* 259.
11. Blind, "Scottish, Shetlandic, and Germanic Water-Tales" 403.
12. Liestøl 15–16.
13. Thomson 167.
14. Ibid. 144.
15. Ibid.
16. MacRitchie 3.
17. Swire 265–66.
18. MacRitchie 4.
19. Croker 15.
20. Curtin 154.
21. MacGregor 113–14.
22. Benwell and Waugh 19.
23. Blind, "Scottish, Shetlandic, and Germanic Water-Tales" 399.
24. Croker 13.
25. Benwell and Waugh 17.
26. Swire 264–65.
27. Carmichael 17.
28. Blind, "Scottish, Shetlandic, and Germanic Water-Tales" 399.
29. Gregory 52.
30. Hulme 289.
31. Thomson 167.
32. Simpson 101.
33. Craigie 232.

PART
II

Per Schelde Jacobsen

CHAPTER 2

The Magic Ballads: An Analysis

Rationale

We have chosen to give the group of ballads that inspired Ibsen a chapter of their own because only by thoroughly analyzing the ballads and laying bare the signification patterns in them can we completely appreciate their influence on Ibsen.

Our basic claim is that Ibsen, like so many of his contemporaries, drew in his writings on the Scandinavian folklore tradition, notably the folk ballads. You might say that he entered into a dialogue with the folklore, using it to throw new light on themes important to him. As we have already demonstrated in the Introduction, Ibsen was keenly aware of and interested in Scandinavian folklore. In order to show exactly how Ibsen used themes from the ballads it is necessary to demonstrate what the themes are. We claim that Ibsen not only borrowed names and other formal features from the ballads but that he had analyzed them and internalized the meaning. He used these meaning structures in his plays, overtly in the early plays and covertly in the later ones.

It would of course be ideal if we had an analysis of the ballads from Ibsen's hands, but short of that we can assail the problem in a slightly different way: apply the same interpretational apparatus to readings of the ballads and of Ibsen.

I have chosen to focus my own folklore analysis on the Danish folk ballads. There are several reasons for this. The first and most important is that Ibsen knew Svend Grundtvig's ambitious and scholarly *Danmarks gamle Folkeviser* ("Denmark's Old Folk Ballads") (hereafter, in accordance with the folklore tradition, abbreviated as *DgF*). Maurice Gravier argues in his excellent essay "Le drame d'Ibsen et la ballade magique"[1] that there are important linguistic and logistic reasons that Ibsen would have been attracted to the Danish collection rather than to the Norwegian one by Landstad.[2] Second, the Danish ballad tradition is much richer than the Norwegian. There are more different ballads; the individual ballads exist in more, and, importantly, in more elaborate versions. Third, as both Grundtvig himself and later one of Scandinavia's foremost ballad scholars, Iørn Piø, point out, the ballads often came to Norway via Denmark. Since Ibsen saw the ballads as the best type of folkloric material to draw upon for a new national drama (not necessarily Norwegian national, since to Ibsen, for a large part of his career, national meant Nordic), the *DgF* collection was a logical choice. The fourth point is that Ibsen uses ballads that are not available in Norwegian—for example, the "Rosmer" ballad, which differs on all crucial points from the corresponding Norwegian ballad. Further, it is evident from Ibsen's discussion of the usage of folklore in literature ("Om Kjæmpevisen og dens Betydning for Kunstpoesien") that he had read Grundtvig's introduction to *DgF;* his argumentation is almost identical to Grundtvig's in terms of the provenance of the ballads and of how to interpret them.[3]

Although the analysis offered below is based on the ballads, indeed on a particular group of ballads, this does not mean that I assume that the ballads were the only folklore source Ibsen used or was interested in. Far from it. It is obvious both from the plays themselves and from Ibsen's articles and letters that he was interested in and versant with the rich Norwegian folktale, fairy tale, and myth tradition populated with *Huldrer,* trolls, and other supernaturals. The reason for limiting the analysis to the ballads is that they telescope the pattern of the interrelationship between humans and the (super)natural environment common to the entire Scandinavian folklore tradition. I will refer to other folklore sources where I feel it clarifies the argument or where it is obvious that Ibsen drew on a particular type of folklore other than the ballads. For instance, in "Ibsen and the *Huldre*" in the following chapter I draw on prose narratives.

Methodology

I have chosen to apply a semiotic-anthropological analytic apparatus to the ballads—and, in a following chapter, Ibsen—because it seems to fit the material to be analyzed. My main arguments with regard to Ibsen and the ballads are (1) that he borrowed story lines and moral-social themes from the ballad material and reworked it to fit his own social reality, and (2) that both the ballads and Ibsen's oeuvre reflect—as does all art—the societies of the authors who created them. With these two points in mind, it follows with regard to (1) that both the ballads and the plays are semiotic structures: they juggle and juxtapose signs—such as persons, mythical beings, epic motifs, poetic form—to create meaning-carrying structures. The methodology that is best equipped to bring out these symbolic significations is, in my opinion, the science whose very raison d'être is exactly the analysis of signs, of semiotic structures: semiotics.

About the above point (2): I find that the types of themes found in both sets of literary products being analyzed are largely social and anthropological. The Scandinavian ballads were functional: they were used on social occasions in connection with music and dance, and they were designed to teach young people the "facts of life." The cosmology of society was mapped onto ballad actors—humans, animals, and supernaturals—symbolizing "us," human society and its natural environment. Interactions between the symbolic actors signify the nature of the world and of the rules humans have to live by. In Alan Dundes's phrase, "Folklore as autobiographical ethnography, as a mirror of culture, is a natural projective test. . . ."[4]

More than any other social science, anthropology has made the analysis and description of societies its concern. The anthropologist in the field tries to understand all aspects of a culture. Anthropologists study the economic facts of interaction between a society and its environment and the interaction between members of the society, and they study how these infrastructural and structural underpinnings are projected onto the artistic outputs, the superstructure, of the society.[5] In some cases, when dealing with groups for which the infrastructural data are specious, anthropologists try to project the other way: they gain an understanding of the economic and political arrangements of a society by means of analysis of its superstructural outputs: myths, folktales, and so forth.

Anthropological interpretive strategies thus seem designed for my present purpose: the understanding of the societies that produced the two bodies of literature in which we are interested: the Scandinavian ballads and Ibsen's plays. Since Ibsen's Norway is much more of a known social, political, and moral entity than is the society that produced the ballads, my main concern is to get to know the latter. I want to understand the economic, social, religious, and moral underpinnings of that society. By combining the semiotic analysis with anthropological interpretive strategies I shall be able to describe the worldview of the people who "wrote" the ballads and locate the levels of meaning in them.

The Ballads

In 1853 Svend Hersleb Grundtvig started his project of publishing the body of Danish popular ballads. The idea of recording these originally orally transmitted works of art had originated in the sixteenth century, when it became fashionable for members, especially female members, of the nobility to make collections of popular ballads. Grundtvig wanted to make the ballads the subject of scientific study and he wanted, to that end, to have all known versions of all Danish ballads published together in one work. Grundtvig finished the first four-and-a-half volumes; the project found its completion in 1976, 123 years after its inception. The final opus contains twelve volumes comprising 539 ballads, each in several variations, constituting in totality thousands of ballads. In this chapter, I restrict myself to the ballads that Grundtvig called the *trylleviser*, the "magic ballads."

The reason for choosing this subset of ballads is that they are the ones from which Ibsen drew characters and themes. They are, incidentally, also the ones all the other romantics drew upon, from Hans Christian Andersen to the Danish national poets and playwrights Jens Baggesen, Johannes Ewald, Henrik Hertz, Johan Ludvig Heiberg, and Adam Oehlenschläger.[6] In the society that produced them, the function of the ballads was primarily educational and prescriptive; in Ibsen, the folkloric themes help illuminate the conflict between the artist and bourgeois society.

The following ballads will be the focus of the remainder of this chapter:

1. *DgF* 37. "Jomfruen og Dværgekongen" ("The Maiden and the Dwarf King"; henceforth abbreviated as "Dwarf")

2. *DgF* 38. "Agnete og Havmanden" ("Agnete and the Merman"; abbrev. "Agnete")

3. *DgF* 39. "Nøkkens Svig" ("The Deceit of the Nix"; abbrev. "Nix")

4. *DgF* 40. "Harpens Kraft" ("The Power of the Harp"; abbrev. "Harp")

5. *DgF* 41. "Rosmer"

6. *DgF* 183. "Kvindemorderen" ("The Man Who Murdered Women"; abbrev. "Elf"[7]).

The Sociohistorical Background of the Ballads

The Danish ballad scholar Ernst Frandsen says in his introduction to *Danske Folkeviser i Udvalg* that the Danish folk ballads were used at social gatherings in connection with a type of round dance. He says further that France is the home of the medieval round dance and goes on to conclude that "this dance came to Denmark around 1200 A.D. when the cultural connection to France was very lively."[8] This, then was the beginning of this particular artistic form in Denmark—and probably in Scandinavia in general.

Thirteenth-century Denmark had an estimated population of around one million inhabitants. An agrarian society consisting of scattered villages and isolated farms was slowly converting large natural areas such as forests into arable land. Christianity, which had been introduced in the ninth century A.D. was just as slowly replacing the ancient pagan beliefs in the Norse pantheon of gods.[9]

Similarities between some Danish and French ballads would suggest that the earliest ballads being sung in Denmark were loans, but we can see from the vast majority of them that the Danish farmers eventually made the ballad their own, keeping the artistic form but infusing it with their own social and religious world. The ballads were populated with Nordic gods—for example, "Thor fra Havsgaard," a ballad about the god of thunder Thor—and with local heroes and mythic beings. Once transformed into a local art form, the ballad inserted itself into the social fabric as an important social institution with its own function and social significance. As Danish society changed, so did the ballad: in order to maintain its importance in society it had to reflect the economic, social, and ideological changes that were taking place.

The ballad began as part of a social ritual, evolved into a popular art form performed by wandering troubadours in marketplaces, and, later, became a darling pastime of the nobility who recorded ballads for their "poetry" books. They then became an inspiration—billed as a poetic product of the people "when the people . . . was a, by the common bonds of the soul, united whole,"[10]—for romantic national poetry, and, finally, an object of scholarly and literary study.

Mapping out these changes lays bare the changes in the functions of the ballad and the continuing dialogue between social reality and the patterns of signification in the ballads. We see how socioeconomic changes effect cultural changes, which, in turn, are reflected in changes in the role and function of the ballad and/or textual and interpretational changes.

The ballads are, like all literature, both aesthetic products and carriers of social meanings. They are part of a cultural context. They are repositories of information about the world of the people who wrote them. Thus, the *trylleviser* are populated with mythical and magic beings that grow right out of the popular beliefs of the people who created and used them. It can be assumed that prior to the advent of the ballad in the thirteenth century these beings and their interactions with the human sphere were the subject matter of tales and myths. As the ballads became incorporated into the social fabric the local flora, fauna, and supernaturals began to move in. In other words, the ballads "tapped" right into the heart blood of a simple agricultural society: they addressed the problems of the relationship between a farming society and its natural environment.

Anthropology has found that there is indeed a special relationship between humans and their environment, between nature and culture, in simple agrarian societies. This relationship is special in all technologically simple societies, be they hunting and gathering, horticultural, or agricultural. In these simple economies humans live in a close interdependence with the environment. Because of a relatively unsophisticated technology—simple wooden plows, no irrigation, and low-yield plant varieties—humans are dependent on nature to do its part. Nature has to provide the rain and sun needed: if nature desires, it can wipe the farmer and his crops out through earth slides, attacks by insects, or drought. In short, the simpler the technology, the more dependent humans are on regularity and order in nature. As a mirror of the desired order in nature, human societies, in their turn, impose order onto themselves.

In technologically simple societies humans are constantly made aware of the enormity of nature relative to their little patch of culture. Population density is almost invariably low in such societies simply because the technology cannot support large populations. Human settlements and cultivated areas are but tiny dots totally surrounded on all sides by the enormity of nature. It becomes imperative, then, for humans to create clear boundaries between their domain and that of nature. People have carved their space out of nature and have to mark it off as different, as "culture" as opposed to "nature."

The idea that humans have to clearly mark off their space is found in all simple societies. Among the hunting and gathering !Kung of Southern Africa, for example, even temporary campsites are carefully marked off and laid out according to a general cosmological theory of the relationship between culture and nature. Camps are arranged in concentric circles so that sleeping quarters and cooking fires—the central aspects of culture[11]—are in the innermost cycle, waste is in the next cycle, and in the outermost cycle, just before nature begins, people go to the toilet, the human waste products being products of natural processes and thus marginally part of nature.[12]

The point of this boundary making is that humans perceive cultural space as a more or less permanent loan from nature. Unless humans maintain clear boundaries, nature can take back what has been loaned. Scandinavian folklore is full of stories where people do not keep the ritual boundaries. Evald Tang Kristensen tells of a *sagn*, "legend," in which people were punished for destroying hills in which the *ellefolk*, "elves," lived. The elves would destroy human crops or stage reprisals in the form of accidents and deaths on the farm.[13] I would argue that the reason the constructs of culture, such as houses, are so unnatural, so angular, hard, square, so *different* from the surrounding nature, is precisely that these qualities help mark the boundaries. Culture is the denial of nature, the reversal of nature.

Nature is dangerous. It does not submit to human (i.e., cultural) regulations: it has its own enigmatic rules, and it is full of lurking

33

dangers. The dangers are, of course, real: nature is full of dangerous animals, poisonous plants, and traps such as quicksand and precipitous hidden gorges. Because of their dependence on nature and because of its enigmatic character, people anthropomorphize nature. "Evil and destructive seemed to people most of these supernatural beings who could, in point of fact, be seen as natural forces personified."[14] They construct a mental image of the world, a cosmology, wherein nature is but one of the components. Nature becomes an actor in man's script. It would be intolerable for humans to have to have as their most powerful and important counterpart an impersonal, abstract, unpredictable force. So, humans re-create nature in their own image.[15]

The forces and most noticeable landmarks of nature become individualized and are supplied with humanlike desires and dislikes.[16] Nature becomes either one huge, throbbing consciousness (as among the BaMbuti Pygmies of the Ituri forest in Central Africa), or it becomes many individuals, each with his or her own consciousness and personality, but all subject to rules for conduct and some kind of authority just as humans are. Conceived of in this way, nature becomes "someone" you can enter into a regulated relationship with, someone you can enter into an exchange relationship with. Nature becomes an adversary who abides by a set of rules that are part of the same overriding cosmology that also encompasses humans and their sphere: culture.[17]

The relationship between humans and nature is an exchange relationship. Humans want something from nature: they carve areas out of its forests and transform them into cultivated land where plants are made to conform to human rule. They are planted in rows, weeds are removed, and the plants are bred, changed, and harvested for human consumption. The relationship between humans and supernaturals is peaceful and amiable as long as the two parties leave each other alone.

On the whole one might say that a friendly and good relationship exists between the farmer and "the hidden people" in the mountains and the woods so long, at least, as the farmer does not get in the way of the people but as a good neighbor stays on his own farm and does not harm his neighbors.[18]

Humans like to make the areas of nature that have been appropriated conform to a human, a culturally defined, order. Humans like to rep-

resent to themselves how thoroughly they have made nature their subordinate. So, for example, the formal gardens of Versailles are, among
other things, triumphant symbolic statements of human domination of
nature. People have taken a large area of nature and disfigured the plants
within it to conform to human tastes purely for artistic purposes, for
purposes of signifying to themselves how far they have come in their
effort to dominate nature. But this is an aside; simple agricultural societies like the one that produced the earliest ballads are not typically
concerned with gleeful demonstrations of their domination of nature.
They are much too busy maintaining some kind of truce with nature
and with keeping nature at bay.

In stating that the relationship between culture and nature is an exchange relationship, I obviously imply that it is a two-way street: humans
obtain things from nature and give things in return. The exchanges are
usually governed by rule; they are ritualized. Each spring humans perform certain rituals and sacrifice certain things to nature, and in the
fall, after the harvest, new rituals are performed as parts of the crop are
given back as sacrificial gifts to nature. These are the year-to-year, regular exchanges, but there are other interactions between humans and
nature where special sacrifices need to be made. People, having constructed clear boundaries between their own and nature's space, have to
face dangers each and every time they have to cross that boundary and
move through or into nature.

People have to cross the boundary when they want to submit additional
or new land to the plow. They have to enter the space of nature and
transform it into cultural space. Nature has to give up the land, and
humans have to pay a price. Usually the price is in the form of a human
product, be it a child, a young girl, or an animal. In the introduction
to his *Nordens Trylleviser,* the ballad scholar Axel Olrik recounts an old
Danish legend that states, "Where the sea had removed the coast, a
child in a barrel with a candle in its hand was set afloat at flood: it was
a sacrifice—a human sacrifice to the sea so that it would leave people
alone." This exemplifies what I have been saying, albeit in the reverse:
the sea had taken human space because people had neglected to pay the
price. They made a sacrifice, lest the sea take more.[19] An example of
this from the *Trylleviser* is *DgF* 52, "Trolden og Bondens Hustru" ("The
Troll and the Farmer's Wife"). In this ballad we are told that,

35

> There is a place by the Western Sea
> There a farmer intends to build:
> and he sends there both hawk and dog
> he intended to build something secure.
> The wildest animals and the animals of the woods.
>
> He put up posts, he laid down boards,
> he worked with great speed:
> then, asked the troll who was in the mountain:
> Why, I wonder is the farmer making a noise?

The farmer is intruding on the troll's space, and the troll comes to see what is going on. Trolls surround the farm and are about to descend on it, scaring the farmer out of his wits. But then his wife has an idea: she invites the trolls in to share food and drink with them. The biggest and *liedeste*, "most disgusting," troll says that he wants the farmer's wife, and later, all he owns. The farmer offers to give up the farm and the land if he may just keep his wife, but the troll is adamant:

> . . . she shall have me."
> He took her in his arms:
> the wife was red as blood,
> she was full of anger.

The story then changes into an enchanted-prince story. As a matter of fact, there seem to be in this, as in many other ballads, two different stories—maybe an earlier one and a later one—"sewed" together. In many cases, as in this one, the two parts seem very uncomfortable together conceptually. I do not know whether an old ballad simply was given a new ending by the noble "scribe" who committed it to paper or whether it reached the scribe in this form, but the point is that the ballad contains two different types of stories: one deals with man and nature, the farmer symbolizing ongoing human encroachment on nature, and the troll symbolizing nature whose space is being poached on. The second type of story, the second half of the ballad, is totally different. It belongs with the type of stories I call "soul" stories. The troll is no longer just nature's tough and powerfully violent representative, he is a pitiful human (in this case the prince of England, no less) who is trapped

36

inside the troll's body. From this revelation the ballad continues according to the soul-story formula: he was changed by (in the C version, the others do not care to tell us how he was changed from prince to troll) his stepmother. He becomes progressively more disgusting the first two times the farmer's wife kisses him, the third time he becomes "the most handsome knight who might put foot on the ground" (C version, but I am mixing the versions together here).

Once a prince again, he wants to marry his savior. In some versions he does, in some he does not. The second half represents a ubiquitous pattern in the ballads: Someone, usually a young man, is trapped in nature and needs the kiss, signifying the love, of a young woman to regain his soul. This type of story belongs in the age of romantic love, where the love of a woman can "tame" the wild and woolly nature of a young man. Usually the two get married and become another brick in the house of that most cultural institution: marriage. This theme is treated several times by Ibsen. Leavy deals with it in her analysis of *When We Dead Awaken*, and I use it in my discussions of *Fruen fra havet* and *John Gabriel Borkman*. The important point is that I claim that the *DgF* 52, and many others with it, is constructed from bits and pieces that have their intellectual/ideological/conceptual homes in different historical periods.

At the root of this ballad, however, there is a story about the interaction between culture and nature. A man encroaches on nature without warning and without making the proper ritual and sacrificial preparations; nature, personified by the trolls who live in the mountain, comes to demand its due: his wife.[20]

That the troll demands the wife, a woman, is no accident: "it is especially women: girls, married women, women giving birth, who are the victims of the *Höfolk* [the "haypeople"]. About fifty cases can be cited, while there are fourteen to fifteen about boys and three to four about men."[21] The logical thing for the troll to demand would, of course, be the farmer since he is the transgressor. But since we are dealing with a patriarchal culture and its image of the universe, the heads of the two realms, nature and culture, are both seen as male and they can exchange things they own, such as women, children, land, space, hunting rights, and so on.

The image of nature as a dangerous and real adversary shows up in all of the *trylleviser*. When people have to travel, to go to church, to visit a fiancé, and so forth, they have to move through nature's space. This is often expressed in the ballads through the image of traveling along "the little green path," or crossing rivers over bridges, or through sailing on the sea. Sometimes the conflict between culture and nature, between the eminently human and the nonhuman, is expressed in the image of people trapped in nature, in animals, demonic creatures, and even linden trees.

People constantly have to travel through nature, and they have to make sure that their end of the contract with nature is kept so that they will get free passage. After all, when people travel through the woods, cross rivers or oceans, and so on, they are traveling through enemy territory. If the exchange sheet is not balanced, problems may be encountered, as in the ballad of "German Gladensvend." A couple (in some versions the king and queen) are making a passage on the sea, but as there is no wind, the woman says,

> "Is there something under water,
> which holds the ship;
> I'll give you both gold and silver,
> you let me have a breeze."

> "You have neither gold nor silver,
> that might help that,
> it is under your belt,
> that which I desire."

She thinks he wants her keys, which hang from her belt, and throws them into the sea. They get a breeze and everything seems in order. But five months later she gives birth to a son, German Gladensvend (the name is ironic: "Gladensvend" means "happy man," and he is, of course, despite his naturally happy disposition, doomed to tragedy). The mother realizes that the child she was not aware of carrying under her belt five months earlier was what the monster wanted in exchange for a breeze, not her keys. German grows up, kept hidden by his parents, to become an attractive young man who wants to marry the princess of England. He travels to see her in his mother's *fugleham*, "bird's robe," only to be torn apart and devoured by the monster.[22] I show, in my analysis of *Bygmester Solness*, how Ibsen used this ballad to confront personal myth with social reality.

38

The above story suggests that when human actors realize that a price needs to be paid, when they find themselves caught in "enemy territory," they try to pay with gold and silver. But nature does not need gold and silver: it has all of that it wants (after all, nature is the source of those things).²³ What it does want is something that it does *not* have: a human child. The significance of obtaining human offspring, as I argue below, is that this is a way to get something distinctly human: a soul. Nature has power, riches, land, but it lacks a human soul. My use of the word "soul" here may be in need of comment. Later developments of this theme, influenced by Paracelsus, involve the nature spirits (i.e., Undine, later Andersen's Little Mermaid) who wed humans to earn a Christian soul. But the theme is older than this Christian or romantic emendation and suggests the movement of nature itself *toward* culture. In this sense, "soul" is symbolic. Of course, since humans, whether Christians or pagans, are the ones who anthropomorphize nature in the first place, they would make the essentially human, the soul, the goal of all things, including nature.

The group of *trylleviser* to be analyzed all deal with humans who have to make a passage through nature. This passage can be "real": riding through the woods, crossing rivers. Or it can be symbolic: young people who have to make the passage from childhood to adulthood, passing through the liminal area of puberty, telescoped into a rite de passage, or, in the ballads, a trip to meet a future spouse. It may even be something as simple as a ride, through the woods, from the security of the farm to the church.

The two bastions of Christian culture are the family farm—with all it entails in terms of patriarchal culture: a male-dominated realm, with paterfamilias on the top and everybody else arranged below in descending hierarchical order—and the church, the cosmological projection of the family on the farmstead: again, a hierarchy with a male (principle?) at the pinnacle, represented on earth by an appropriately named man, the *papa*, and having the rest of the Christian family neatly arranged below. It is not surprising that the ride from one of these to the other is considered dangerous in the ballads. The area between farm and church is governed by beings marching to a different (but also patriarchal) drummer, and they represent a threat to passers through. Or rather, they represent a threat to a certain category of passer: women, especially those not safely ensconced in marriage. Nature may steal young women or, worse still, women may find nature an attractive alternative to what awaits them in the human hierarchy.

The Demons and Christianity

Christianity proved an effective buffer between culture and nature. Humanity became the goal of nature. Humans are morally superior to nature. The demons may still be there, but people have a powerful ally in their fight against them. A person can mention God's name and render a troll or merman but a petrified rock, devoid of life and power. In a sense Christianity reversed the process that transformed natural landmarks into repositories of supernatural powers. Mentioning God's name kills the demon in the rock, and all that is left is stone.

An example of how Christianity is portrayed in the ballads as a powerful buffer against the forces in nature is *DgF* 50, "Hellig Olavs væddefart." This ballad deals with the Norwegian king Hellig Olav, "Holy-Olav." The king is in a boat race against his brother to decide who will be king. The brother cheats and starts while Olav is at mass. He finishes mass (symbolizing his strong faith and his assurance that his god will help him be victorious) and then he starts. He lays his route right through the mountains and, as was the case in "Trolden og Bondens Hustru," the trolls come running out to see what is going on,

> "Saint Olluff King with the red beard:
> how come you're sailing through our living-room wall?"

Olav answers,

> "stand you, troll, and become stone:
> and never do any harm!"

He goes on to win the race and become king of all Norway. The ballad is an allegorical way of saying he Christianized, and subjected to his rule parts of Norway that had resisted Christianization to this point. Ibsen uses this ballad, as I show below, in *Kongsemnerne*, *Bygmester Solness*, and *Lille Eyolf*.

The brother in the ballad signifies the fact that his enemies were indeed his "brothers": all Norwegians are one family. This analysis is strengthened by the fact that the brother becomes "so loath a worm." He becomes part of a mythical (read: pagan) underground army that keeps fighting the (Christian) government troops. Be that as it may, the point is that a strong Christian faith is a defense against demons.

In addition, as technology improved, the relationship between humans and their environment changed: People had more control, were less dependent on nature to give what they needed as gifts. They irrigated, fertilized, used more efficient plants, and had more land under the plow. In these ways humanity pushed the boundary between culture and nature back.[24] People were released from their fear of nature because technological-scientific progress diminished the power of nature, changing its "face," making it less enigmatic and more impersonal and mechanical.

The Danish writer Villy Sørensen makes this point, perhaps without realizing it. In the later ballads, he says, the demons are treated with some condescension. The reason, he says, is that Christianity has provided a buffer against the powers of nature, and therefore humans have a new and strong ally in the fight against nature and its demons. The demons are converted into almost pathetic or even comic creatures that can with ease be rendered powerless by invoking God's name.[25]

In the same passage, Sørensen mentions runes as tools humans can use against unsuspecting demons.[26] This fits the nature-culture opposition perfectly: Runes are cultural creations. They are similar to invoking God's name in that they render words magical. Words can be invested with power under certain circumstances, such as the invocation of God's name or by writing them. In the ballads we are never told what particular words are written, only that they *are written*. In other words, it is the ability to write itself that is magical. Writing (as the invocation of God in the form of, e.g., a formula) is a kind of chemical agent that renders mere words powerful tools. People create these tools, using them to change the balance between themselves and nature, just as the iron, mentioned in note 24 to this chapter, is symbolic of human technological ingenuity by transforming something torn out of nature's bosom into tools to be used in mastering and further transforming the environment.

It is worth noting, however, that the power inherent in runes is nature's own power, just as the power in iron is an amalgam of the material and the human process that transforms it into something even more powerful. In one ballad, "Hr. Luno og Havfruen" ("Mr. Luno and the Mermaid"), the protagonist is at sea on a boat decorated extensively with the names of the Virgin Mary and Jesus Christ when a mermaid stops the boat. He "ties" the mermaid, not with Christian formulas, but with runes. Runes are but nature's own power transformed into magic signs. What Mr. Luno has is a double insurance against demons: he has God and he has the ability to crystallize exactly the type of power of which the mermaid herself is an exponent.

It is probably not accidental that Christian and pagan imagery and symbolism coexist in ballads like "Hr. Luno og Havfruen"; the two religious systems coexisted for centuries after the introduction of Christianity as the official religion. And even after paganism was eradicated, the mythical beings it had created survived in the imaginations of the uneducated.

For, despite all buffers, nature was still there and still dangerous. The demons had crossed the boundary and moved into human society. Initially this transgression took the form of agents provocateurs. Some members of human society were spies and representatives of nature. What had happened was that nature had been reanalyzed: In a progressively Christianized society, nature had become synonymous with paganism. The agents of nature looked like ordinary people, they went to church, had husbands and children, but were just masquerading as humans: they were pagans/devils in sheep's clothing (the processed hide of a domesticated animal). The agents were called trolls or witches and had the same kinds of powers as pagan supernaturals of yore: they could take over a person and tear him or her away from family and home, and they could kill people by giving them diseases or casting spells on them. They could, because they internally did this themselves, erase the nature-culture boundary and change people to animals and trees, even rocks. In the emerging Christian culture, pagans and their mythic creations became agents of evil. They "moved" into Christian mythology as the devil and his representatives, "As *Jetter*, *Riser*, and other *Vetter* [various types of supernaturals] never had been the objects of adoration but rather of hatred and disgust, they were allowed to keep their ancient names and characteristics and now served to buttress the Christian teachings of the Devil and his spirits, amongst whom *Jetter* and most other supernatural beings were counted."[27]

42

A number of *trylleviser* are accounts of the exploits of such "secret agents." An already-mentioned group of ballads tells of individuals who have been changed into deer, linden trees,[28] birds, (were)wolves, ravens, and so on. The evil agent is almost invariably a woman, an evil stepmother. If we, for an instance, disregard the psychological implications, which certainly are there, we notice again that, according to Christian tradition, women are the preferred objects of pagan efforts to undermine human society. I will return to this point; suffice it to say here, that this has to do with a particular patriarchal conceptualization of women (intensified with the advent of Christianity), who are seen as inherently closer to nature and thus easier to convince to be, to stay with my metaphor, "double agents." In this group of ballads the person trapped in nature is saved as was our troll-*cum*-prince of England above: they are given back their soul by receiving one to three kisses from an eligible maiden or man. I read this to mean that the kiss symbolizes "romantic love," unselfish love (after all, the person has to kiss some fairly ugly apparitions). Love, especially unselfish and thus nonsexual, is a humanizing phenomenon that is capable of breaking the spell. Love is, then, in most cases where the one who bequeathes the kiss is not already married, followed by its idiomatic partner, marriage. The bequeather is regaled for his or her efforts by being presented with a gorgeous (as opposed to the original hideous) creature who in addition invariably is rich (usually the prince or princess of England).[29]

The above represents one level of signification in this type of ballad, but I do not claim that the ballads are univocal. Each ballad or tale is found in several versions collected at different times in different places. But even the individual versions of a ballad are not monosemic structures. Any ballad is polysemic and intertextual, or, to use Barthes's term, *multitextual*.[30] The ballads are, as is folklore in general, passed on from generation to generation, each generation offering a new interpretation—and often textual changes—based on its own socioeconomically and historically determined needs and understandings. Each ballad text carries within it other "texts" each of which has a different meaning. The texts are constantly sliding maps of the world placed on top of each other. There is never a single meaning. Every signification and signification fragment that ever was attached to the text remains an intrinsic part of it as a hidden—or not-so-hidden—coat of paint peeping through. Folklore relates to a synchronic dominant discourse but always carries within—that is why it is so pregnant with meaning—multiple meanings relating to other, past, discourses.

Put in the terminology of semiotics, the ballads, as an artistic form, are codes made up of the constituent signs. Teresa De Lauretis's excellent reading of Eco's discussion of codes and signs bears on this:

> A code is a significant *and* communicational framework linking differential elements on the expression plane with semantic elements on the content plane or with behavioral responses. In the same manner, a sign is not a fixed semiotic entity (the relatively stable union of signifier and signified) but a "signfunction," the mutual and transitory correlation of two functives which he calls "sign-vehicle" (the physical component of the sign, on the expression plane) and "cultural unit" (a semantic unit on the expression plane). In the historical process, "the same functive can also enter into another correlation, thus becoming a different functive and so giving rise to a new sign-function." As socially established, operational rules that *generate* signs (whereas in classical semiology codes *organize* signs), the codes are historically related to the modes of sign production; it follows that the codes change whenever new or different contents are culturally assigned to the same sign-vehicle or whenever new sign-vehicles are produced. In this manner a new text, a different interpretation of a text—any new practice of discourse—sets up a different configuration of content, introduces other cultural meanings that in turn transform the codes and rearrange the semantic universe of the society that produced it.[31]

An example would be Christianity reinterpreting the pagan myths and monsters. The contours, that is, the form—or code—of the myths or monsters remain the same, but they are infused with new meanings. As the totality is reinterpreted, so are the constituent symbols—integers given new values—changing the relationship between them while keeping the actual narrative or description intact. (See also note 35 below.)

The Psychologization of the Demons

As cities grew larger and technology more sophisticated, as population density became greater, the individual was removed further and further from direct contact with nature. The technological and conceptual buffers became so effective that nature, as the opposite of culture, became but a symbol, a distant thunder. Because nature as physical reality was so distant it became abstract, an idea: nature became "inner demons." At this remove, nature and its attendant demons even became an allure, a wistful memory of lost freedom and innocence.[32]

By "nature as inner demons," I mean that nature literally "moved in": rather than being outside forces lurking about the individual, it became the dangerous nature within that threatens to destroy him or her. The environment was disanthropomorphized as science and technology were able to explain and control it better. But as the economic underpinnings of human existence became increasingly detached from one-on-one interaction with the environment, the tightly regulated structure of society was loosened. For one of the seductive things about simple societies, especially agrarian ones, is that everything is explained and behavior is laid in a narrow groove: the individual is not faced with many choices or insecurities: everything is explained or at least explainable; the life of the individual is laid out in detail from womb to grave.

But in a society based on some social mobility and on scientific rather than solely on religious explanations, the individual is presented with many options. This brings me to the final reincarnation of the demons (before they became the tame pets of the romantics): they became psychologized.

In a Christian society the individual is presented with one paramount choice, a moral one: to be good and saved, or to be evil and condemned. Michel Foucault has examined the Christian focus on the individual and on the self. He finds that the Western notion of the "ego," of an individual and accountable soul, is rooted in the causes for the Fall as explained by Saint Augustine: man ate the apple because he wanted to obtain some of God's knowledge, he wanted to be in control. The punishment was that God took away control: he made man sexually incontinent and sex a sin. The lack of control is neatly laid out as a symbolic projection: the erectile function is not subject to control. Since sexuality, and even the thought of sexuality, is inherently sinful, this lack of control can obviously have catastrophic consequences. The only way to deal with it is to turn the gaze from God down and in. The individual has constantly to monitor him- or herself to ensure that no impure thoughts stir the genitals into unwanted action.[33]

Foucault's account points to my next argument: the demon within is sexuality. Once freed from the confines of a simple farming society and once Christianized, humans have to take responsibility for their actions. They must constantly examine their own motives. This process is symbolically mapped onto already existing symbols, as the gaze is turned inward, the old trolls and witches and demons are discovered to have moved into the psyche of the individual as raw and uncouth nature.[34]

The demonic is of course that in us which is animal nature, that which might make us rebel against the constraints of culture and sin against God. Sexuality is such a natural animal force. The sex drive makes people break the rules and become sinners in the eyes of God and outcasts in society. The "troll in the mountain" becomes rather than an outside agent that rapes innocent women, the troll inside the woman that makes her behave sexually in ways that defy the rules laid down by society and religion. This, incidentally, may be exactly what the ballad of "Trolden og Bondens Hustru," discussed above, is about, at least on one level: when the troll says, "she shall have me," the unusual wording (which is equally unusual in Danish: "hun skal ha' mig") suggests the same sentence as spoken in the first-person singular: "I shall have him." It is, after all, not customary to make yourself the object of a sentence where the meaning being expressed is that *you* want something.[35]

If an individual lets the "trolls" inside take over, the boundary between culture and nature is obliterated, rendering human society an easy prey to invasion, which, incidentally, in a roundabout way is exactly what happens in *Bygmester Solness*, as I argue below. The individual is important not only in terms of his or her own salvation but as part of a social fabric where everybody is dependent on everybody else to adhere to the rules, lest a tear in the fabric destroy the totality. One individual allowing the forces of nature within to take over becomes a danger to all the others. This theme is played up by Ibsen in *John Gabriel Borkman*. Culture is rules, and for culture to exist each member of the culture has to abide by the rules. This is why people who sin have to be either made to admit the sin, punished, and readmitted into culture or expelled from culture entirely by being killed or jailed or put in madhouses.

The next stage in the "archaeology of the demons" is their appropriation by the poets and writers of the romantic period. They became symbols of the "national spirit," of "the people's soul," a lost state of nature, and so on. This development will be discussed in Chapter 4,

"Ibsen and the Ballads." Here and now I will turn my attention to an analysis of the ballads that inspired the romantics.

Recapitulation

I have in the preceding section located three dominant themes in the *trylleviser* that can all be put under the general heading of *nature versus culture:*

(1) Humans versus the environment: The environment becomes anthropomorphized as monsters, mermen, trolls, and so forth. People have to keep up their end of what is essentially a trade relationship to be allowed to carve their space out of the enormity of nature.

(2) Christian versus pagan: When Christianity becomes the dominant religion, the pagan ogres are more easily rebuffed in their projected forms. Nature loses power as a direct adversary. But nature goes underground and infiltrates human society as secret agents (witches and trolls who look like ordinary people but really are the emissaries of paganism). Paganism is reanalyzed as the armies of evil of God's adversary, the devil.

(3) Nature becomes disanthropomorphized as a result of the combined forces of Christianity and technology. The demons become nature within: sexuality.

All through this development the nature-culture schism is also a gender schism: male versus female. This aspect has been only touched on so far, but it is the focus of the following analysis of the *trylleviser.*

(4) A fourth and final (but see note 36) version of this nature-culture dichotomy would, as is hinted above, be nature projected out again as a distant freedom far from the rules and constraints of civilization. This is the version the romantics became so interested in. It is ironic that the monsters that threatened our simple agrarian forefathers should become humanized again in their last incarnation before being committed to the communal waste disposal—of interest thereafter only to archaeologists. Their hideous faces and deformed bodies become symbolic of a lost freedom, their allure, which used to lead the seduced to their destruction and death, lending artistic flight and instant fame to the poets who took them to their hearts and pens. It is maybe even more ironic that these demons, who forever tried to seduce humans to obtain their souls, should

become for the romantics *the soul* of their people, of the folk who created them. Ibsen himself fits the romantic mold in this regard, as can be seen in Leavy's discussion of *Hedda Gabler* below. He even pokes fun of the infatuation, among Norwegian would-be artists at his time, with the *huldre* (a kind of elf with a tail). In *Sancthansnatten (The Midsummer Night)* which I discuss in my analysis of *Rosmersholm*, Ibsen introduces a character who loves the *huldre*—as a Norwegian symbol—until he discovers the tail![36]

Notes

1. Gravier 1970–71. A quotation from Gravier and a more thorough discussion of this essay can be found in my discussion of *Fruen fra havet*.
2. Landstad 1853.
3. Grundtvig's account of the origins and interpretation of the ballads can be found in Grundtvig 1847. Ibsen's account can be found below in Appendix A.
4. Dundes 1980: 37.
5. For the nonanthropologist, a discussion of these terms can be found in Harris 1980.
6. The story of the romantics and of their use of the ballads as inspirational sources is given in more detail in Chapter 4, "Ibsen and the Ballads."
7. This is not really a *tryllevise*—at least not in Danish. But the Norwegian equivalent, "Sveinn Normann," as well as the English one, "Lady Isabel and the Elf Knight," are genuine *trylleviser*. For more information about this ballad type, see Nygard 1958. The abbreviation "Elf" in the text is derived from the English title.
8. Reprinted in Bang 1972: 209.
9. The information here is derived primarily from Lund and Hørby 1980.
10. Geijer, quoted in Grundtvig 1847: 25.
11. Lévi-Strauss has argued in *Le crue et le cui* that the cooking process itself is a denaturalization process whereby the products of nature are transformed into items of culture.
12. Lee 1984.
13. Kristensen 1931: 111.
14. Faye 1948: xii.
15. Some anthropologists, beginning with Edward Burnett Tylor, claim that religion and ritual are but "primitive" science. People in technologically simple societies do not have the scientific insights of modern physics, chemistry, and biology, and they thus create a theory of the world based on the knowledge they

have at their disposal, filling in the gaps with myths and supernatural forces. See Horton 1964.

16. Kristensen (1892–1901) has a whole section devoted to *sagn* that attach named supernaturals to specific places, such as rivers, hills, or landmarks.

17. A bit farfetched, perhaps, but one could argue that the exchange relationship between humans and nature has the character of a "silent trade" partnership. The two trading partners seldom or never meet face to face. They leave items to be exchanged at designated points. When the item disappears, it is understood that the exchange is a fact and the rate agreed upon.

In Denmark, into this century, people would leave bowls of porridge in the hayloft for the *nisse*, the "dwarf" or "pixie." If the porridge was gone the next day, it was assumed that the *nisse* was happy and would not create trouble. (*Nisser* were assumed to be eminently capable of creating trouble. Anything from making people slip to falling trees could be their doing and an indication that they were dissatisfied with the way they were being treated.)

18. Feilberg 1910: 85.

19. Olrik 1934: 104. Danish folklorists recognize several categories of folklore, essentially distinguishing between whether the narrator is recounting something he or she has actually "seen" or is carrying on an oral tradition. Things observed are called *sagn* and *legender*, "legends," whereas stories are called *æventyr* (*folkeæventyr*). Since not much rides on the distinction in the present work, I use the terms roughly as they are used in the original sources, subsuming all under the heading of "folklore."

20. Feilberg (1910: 55) gives another example of the dangers involved in taking from nature without giving something in return or performing the necessary rituals. This example is perhaps more indicative than any other of the pervasiveness of the belief that nature and culture are disparate but contiguous realms: "The boy was picking berries during church service and the girl had not 'read over the berries.' Apparently they took the property of the *skovfrue*, "woodwoman," without taking ritual precautions against her." Both are punished severely. The notion of the boy's picking berries in the woods during church service suggests that one defense against the supernaturals is constant exposure to Christian ritual, constant immersion in Christianity. Another story in Feilberg suggests that Christianity is a "coating" that can be worn, or even *washed* off. The story tells of a woman who had just given birth. The *huldremand*, "*huldre*man," has stolen her and taken her into the woods. "When they came to a large stream he grabbed her by the hair and dipped her three times 'to wash the Christianity off her.'" Ibid. 55.

21. Feilberg 1910: 63.

22. There is more to the story; the above is an abbreviation. In this case I call the creature the "monster," since it is ambiguous. It changes name even within the same version of the ballad. For a discussion of this and other supernatural creatures in the ballads, see Iørn Piø 1969, 1970.

The story of German Gladensvend belongs to a very common type, stories that tell of people who derive economic gain from promising their offspring to a supernatural—either without knowing it, as in the ballad, or consciously. Qvigstad (1927) has several stories that follow the same pattern: #7 in volume 1, "Havkongen og Landkongen" (17–21), and #41 in volume 3, "Gutten som var lovet til Havfrua" (153–57). In the former, "The Merking and the Earthking," the Earthking finds himself in the same predicament as did German Gladensvend's parents: he is becalmed in the middle of a sea where not a wind moves. To get released, he promises his son as husband to the Merking's daughter. In the latter story, "The Boy Who Was Promised to the Mermaid," a fisherman is unable to catch any fish. A mermaid helps him on condition that she get what his wife carries under her belt. Like the queen in the story of German Gladensvend, he thinks all she carries there are her two keys, and he agrees to the mermaid's condition. The man becomes rich, but when the mermaid demands the son that the wife bore not long after the initial incident, he refuses. She destroys his boat and punishes him in other ways. The parents give the son, for safekeeping, to an old woman. He has certain supernatural abilities himself: he can change himself into a bumblebee and a wolf. By deceit, the mermaid captures him in wolf shape, but he escapes as a bumblebee and marries a princess to live happily ever after.

23. Feilberg (1910: 95–96) tells in great detail of the riches of the *ellefolk*, "elves." The supernaturals are perceived as being outrageously rich. I cannot help supposing that this is an antidote to the abject poverty and hardship of the peasantry who created the stories. That the supernaturals are rich and idle—they are always dancing and partying—serves as a justification of human poverty: those who are lured by the gold and glitter almost never become happy, and they seldom are able to bring any of the riches back. Individuals who have been with the elves are invariably demented or crippled and of no use in the world afterward. Feilberg also mentions that the riches of the supernaturals only seem to be gold and silver, as a result of the spell the elves put people under. A salve produced by the elves has the effect, when applied to the eyes, of showing what is hidden under the illusion: "all the glitter disappeared, she was in a chamber of hewn rocks, the gold, the silver and the silk were rough grey stones."

24. In the folklore, the advance of technology takes the form of synecdoche: iron is the defense par excellence against supernaturals. Feilberg (1910: 25) tells of a minister who was released from the elves by others who threw a knife over his head. Since supernaturals often appear in the shape of whirlwinds or tornadoes to carry off people and cattle, one can release those taken by throwing steel into the tornado or whirlwind. In one case, Feilberg says, a bundle of keys was thrown between a woman and an elf man who had taken her. Solheim (1952: 41) makes the same point: to protect yourself and the cattle against the attacks of *huldrer* while on the *sæter*, the summer grazing fields in the mountains, you had to always carry steel. Iron is found in nature, taken by people, and submitted to technological processes that render it an effective tool in the exploitation of the environment. Iron thus symbolizes human ingenuity and mastery over nature, hence its power over supernaturals.

25. Sørensen 1959: 194–201.
26. Ibid.: 197–98.
27. Faye 1948: xviii. Later in the same work Faye quotes Hans Lauridssen's *Sjelebog* ("Soulbook") from 1587:

> The Devil has many allies who are true spooks such as *Elleqvinder og El-lemænd*, "Elfwomen and Elfmen," *Dverge*, "Dwarfs," *Vetter, Natravne*, "Night Ravens," *Jordmaalere*, "Ground measurers," with red hot iron bars and *Gjenfærd*, "Ghosts," which are seen together with people who are going to die. These are all devils. (xix)

Later still he quotes Lauridssen again:

> When Lucifer with his angels—or the old serpent who is called the Devil or Satanas—was, as we have heard in The Book of Revelations, cast to earth, then some spirits fell in the woods, these the forefathers called *skovtrolle eller Skovsnabe*, "Wood Trolls or Woodsnabe." Some fell on plain fields and heathers, those they called *Gjengangere eller Spøgelse*, "Ghosts or Spooks." Some fell in the water, those they called *Jugger eller Nicker*, "Jugs or Nixes." Some fell on houses, they called those *Nisser og Gaardjugger*, "Fairies or Farmjugs." some fell in the mountains, they were called *Bjergtrolle*, "Mountain Trolls," and these have taken Christian people into the mountains, as several stories tell us. (xxvi)

28. The ballads are full of linden trees, always as ominous symbols. Linden trees seem to be *brændpunkter*, "focal points," between nature and culture, just as the mirror in *Alice in Wonderland* is a door connecting reversed worlds. My Danish dictionary suggests that the reason linden trees have this capacity is their strange, supple, hanging, moving, snakelike branches. This fits well with the concept of the *Lindorm*, "Linden-snake," a snakelike monster that makes its slimy path right through the *trylleviser*. Bengt Holbek (personal communication) suggests that the word *lind* itself at one time meant "snake." This would make *lindorm* redundant.

29. These stories suggest the notion of the *følgje* or *fylgje*, a type of soul or companion who follows, as the name suggests, the individual. Faye gives an account of these (1948: 69–70) in which he stresses the role of the *følgje* as a protector against attacks from supernaturals. People who are changed into animals and the like have been let down by the *følgje*. The reason that the changed individual can speak and ask for help may be that the *følgje* is present as a soul without a body, or perhaps the *følgje* can take the shapes of animals: the human body has been removed, and all that is left is the *følgje* in the shape of an animal.

The whole pattern is similar to the notion of the "shadow," as in Andersen's story of the same name. Qvigstad (1927) has a story (#36, 2: 97–125) called "Følgesvennen" that is similar to Andersen's story and that suggests the *følgje*.

30. Barthes 1970: 13.
31. De Lauretis 1984: 33–34.
32. For an excellent discussion of this, see White 1972.

33. Foucault 1985.

34. Freud has made a similar "evolutionary" argument in *Totem and Taboo*. I am grateful to Daniel Burston for having brought this to my attention.

35. This interpretation of the ballad has to be seen as an exemplification of the ballads as "sliding maps" of meaning. The symbol of the trolls demanding the woman means both that nature demands a human sacrifice from people in return for the land the farmer is taking (perhaps its original meaning) and that the real desire is the woman's for the troll, as an antidote to her fate as the "captive" of human patriarchy. It means also, to another audience at another time, that trolls really are the victims of witches and can only be released, rehumanized, by the kiss (i.e., love) of a human. I am sure there are other layers of meaning that I have missed here.

36. Actually, there is a possible fifth stage where the monster becomes the vicious capitalist, out to amuse himself with the daughters of the poor. He goes to the ball, meets a young, beautiful girl, "her parents' pride and joy," uses her, and abandons her to a life of destitution and prostitution. Her parents die of grief and shame and her life is destroyed, while he is back at the ball the next Saturday, dangling the keys to his Mercedes coupe in front of his next victim. The song referred to here is by the Danish folksinger-*cum*-politician Per Dich and is called "Sådan er kapitalismen" ("Those Are the Ways of Capitalism").

A sixth stage might be the reappearance of the demons as the supernaturals of the technological age of space travel and robots: the aliens that populate scores of movies every year. They can be friendly and loving like Spielberg's E.T., or cunning monsters like the creatures of *Aliens*. The interesting thing about extraterrestrials is that, like demons of yore, they inhabit the areas outside the human sphere (albeit areas, in both cases, that humans want to conquer and make theirs; perhaps the reason we speculate so much about the creatures inhabiting those areas is precisely that we want to populate them with someone we can hate and conquer). The modern demons have been informed by modern technology so that they are more mechanical and robotlike than those populating the Scandinavian forests and streams in the fifteenth century. The modern demons also have been updated on their abilities. The trolls, demons, and so on, of the ballads and folklore had supernatural abilities—they could change shape, were immensely strong, could fly, and so on—but they could do this because they were supernatural: The content of their super powers was expressed in religious terms. The modern supernaturals, the aliens, have radar vision and super brains, they can change themselves to any human shape or speak any human language; in short, they are often remarkably like computers: The content of their super powers is expressed in scientific-mechanic and biological-genetic terms. Their shapes reflect our knowledge that living creatures on other planets, even intelligent creatures, need not look like humans, since they represent separate creation. The comparison between demons of yore and aliens is brought out in a curious book by Whitley Strieber, *Communion,* in which the author of the *The Wolfen, The Hunger,* and other works of "horror fiction" recounts his personal encounters with aliens who look just like gnomes or fairies. And, nota bene, Strieber's book is not billed as fiction. He wants to be believed and taken seriously.

CHAPTER 3

Marginal Maidens: The Image of Women in the Ballads

The Story

Since the ballads we are dealing with share many features, it is most reasonable to outline briefly the story told in each with the purpose of extracting a shared pattern and set of symbols. Then the ballads can be analyzed as what they essentially are: one core story in slightly different guises.

DgF 37: *"Jomfruen og Dværgekongen"*

The Danish ballad scholar Iørn Piø classifies this ballad as old. It is one of the ballads he authenticates as being of an oral folk tradition.[1]

The title translates as "The Maiden and the Dwarf King." *DgF* gives seven versions of this ballad: A, B, C, D, E, F, G. The parenthetical capital letters in the story outline tell what parts of the story each version has.

1. (A, B [abbrev.], D [abbrev.]) A knight sits in the woods, he begins to dream and wish he could have the king's daughter. A dwarf is listening and he too begins to desire the girl. He accosts the knight and promises to procure the girl by the use of runes.

2. (A) The dwarf goes home to his mother and tells of the knight who loves the girl and his own desire to deceive the knight. He asks her advice about actually getting the girl. She says do not forget tonight she will go to evensong.

3. (A) The dwarf writes runes on a *spange,* an old Danish word for a single plank across a brook or ditch, and a path the maid has to pass.

4. (A, B [abbrev.], D [see below], E [expand.], F [abbrev.]) In the evening, the maid gets dressed and goes off to church. She follows the

54

path that runs along the mountain and rides right into the mountain. In D we meet the maid as she knocks on the dwarf's door. He refuses to let anyone in until she says she is the one he loves. Then he lets her in. In E she obtains permission from her father to go to evensong. The father warns her about the *Bjærgmand* ("mountainman"). She dresses in her best clothes and takes "the little green path" while the *Bjærgmand* follows on the wider road. He takes her into the mountain.

5. (A, E [expand.], F [expand.]) In A the maid is welcomed into the mountain by the dwarf who says her beloved, the knight, has deceived her but she is to be his guest. The next morning he accompanies her back to her mother's. In E and F the girl from this point on lives with the dwarf for eight and nine years having matching numbers of children, all boys in E, in F the youngest is a girl who "makes her cheeks so pale." The heroine asks the dwarf's permission to go to her father's (E), mother's (F); E: "Yes, surely you may / do not talk of your fate"; F: "Yes surely you may go to your mother's / as long as you will return to your young children."

6. (A) She is living with her mother and suitors come en masse, five kings and nine counts, but she will have none.

7. (A, B, C [expand.], E [abbrev.], F [abbrev.], G [expand.]) The maid returns to her home and is asked questions by her mother (except for E, where the father does the asking) about why no one can have her (A); her appearance, which suggests that she is pregnant (B, G); where she has been all those years (E, F). She admits that she has been seduced by the dwarf and that she has children by him. In two versions she is rejected by the mother. In G, which begins with the conversation between mother and daughter, this is the main part of the ballad. This version resembles A since it is clear that the girl is still living at home while secretly visiting with the dwarf. The mother asks her where she gives birth to the children. The answer is that she gives birth in various places. The mother also asks what the dwarf gave her for her honor. A silk slip, a pair of shoes with silver clasps, and a gold harp to play when she is sad, she replies.

8. (A, B, C, D, G) The dwarf has been listening to or has been summoned by her playing and comes to confront her about her having complained to her mother. In one version (C) he says that if the maid had not told her mother, she would have kept her longer (the mother has rejected her). He is angry and beats her. He either takes her home with him or orders her to follow him to the mountain.

9. (A, G) Amid tears and sorrow the maid bids her mother and father and family and friends adieu: she shall never see them again.

10. She arrives into the mountain where she is greeted by her children. They bring her a chair, something to drink, and so on. In some versions the children are sympathetic to her, but in most they are hostile, asking her why she deceived their father. In a couple of versions the children give her poison. In one she asks the maid to bring poison. In most versions it is said that she dies, in the other versions it is implied. Sometimes he buries her "like other decent girls." In one version the dwarf Christianizes his kingdom.

DgF 38: "Agnete og Havmanden"

Piø claims that this is a ballad written in the eighteenth century: "The two oldest versions of this ballad about Agnete and the merman exist as a broadsheet from the end of the 18th century. . . . All the versions that are known from the popular tradition in the nineteenth and twentieth centuries can be traced back to these prints."² So, this, perhaps most popular of the ballads, is a literary product from the 1780s.

"Agnete and the Merman" is quite similar to the previous ballad. It exists in four versions in Danish: A, B, C, D. We can apply the same schematization as used for "The Maid and the Dwarf King," except that the beginning differs. The Agnete ballad begins with the maid on a bridge or a field where she is accosted by the merman or mountainman (as he is in C).

1. (A, C, D) Agnete is walking on Højelands bridge (C: in the fields) when a merman comes up from the bottom of the sea and asks her whether she will be his sweetheart (A), whether she will follow him to the bottom of the sea (D), or else (C) he beckons her into the mountain, promising her "the reddest gold." She accepts in A "if you'll take me to the bottom of the sea" (which is where he just came from), in D "if my parents won't know"; in C she walks around the mountain a while and then right into it.

2. (A, B [abbrev.], C, D) She lives with the merman/mountainman for a number of years, having a matching number of children. Singing a lullaby by the cradle she hears churchbells ("the churchbells of England") and longs for home. She asks the merman's permission to go to church. He allows this on condition that she will return to her children. In two versions she also has to promise not to wear her gold, not to let

her hair down, not sit in her mother's chair in church, and not to bend her knees when the priest mentions God's name.

3. (A, B, C, D) Agnete arrives in the church, where she meets her mother. In the versions where she was forbidden to do various things she does them, she wears all her gold, sits in her mother's chair, and so on. The mother asks her where she has been all those years. She says she has been in the sea and has had children by the merman. In some versions the mother goes on to ask what the merman gave her for her honor (virtue) "when he made you his wife." "He gave me a handsome gold bracelet / no better is tied around the queen's hand" (A). In D she got, besides the bracelet, a gold knife and fork, gold clasps for her shoes, and a harp of gold to play when she was sad. In the D version the mother leaves at the end of this section, leaving a saddened Agnete behind.

4. (A, C, D) The merman now arrives in the church, "and all the little pictures they turned themselves around"; he is described as having hair "like the purest gold" and having eyes "so full of joy." He walks right up to the altar and says to Agnete that her little ones long for her. She rejects him, refuses to think of the children and to come back to them. He preses her but she is adamant, she is not going back to the sea. In one version he then tries to get her to come back by promising her gold. Nothing works. In A this is where the ballad ends: she refuses to think of the children she has left. B ends where she admits to her mother that she has eight children by the merman. In C he "gave her a disease so harsh / Agnete she died right then." The D version has a more complex ending (probably this is the one that gave Ibsen his idea of the humanized merman): "The merman he left in a sorrowful mood / Agnete she stood on the beach and heartily she laughed. / Ho, ho, ho! / Agnete she stood on the beach and heartily she laughed."[3]

DgF 39: "Nøkkens Svig"

Piø categorizes this ballad as belonging to the "aristocratic tradition." He pinpoints three different traditions and states, "variations between the three versions can not in any obvious way be explained as oral tradition. They are, rather, three ballads composed with pen in hand, probably by three foresingers to be used at evenings of dance for the nobility in the sixteenth and seventeenth centuries."[4]

"The Deceit of the Nix"[5] is found in three versions in Grundtvig: A,

B, C. This story is different from the two we have just covered in a number of ways but shares a core with them.

1. (A, B) The ballad first gives a bird's-eye view of a dance at the king's court. Then we move a little closer and see maidens dancing with their hair down, knights with their swords drawn. Finally the focus is on one of the two protagonists: the king's daughter who is singing. We are at a social gathering where folk ballads are being sung and people dance a round dance. Next we are introduced to the other protagonist, the nix: he hears the proud girl sing from his home under the ice. He decides to see if the girl will "have him."[6] The setting in the B version is different, the dance takes place in the cemetery. The maid is named; she is "Marstigs datter." The nix is called "Øgler." Otherwise the technique and the story is the same.

2. (A, B, C) The nix now makes clothes for himself and calls himself Mr. Alfast, son of the king. He makes a horse and rides to the dance in a gold saddle. He arrives at the castle. In B he goes to town and has clothes made, in C he asks his mother how he can get Marstig's daughter. The mother is in this version the one who makes him a horse and bit from water and sand and changes him into a "knight so fair."

3. (A, B, C) He enters the dance. The maid asks him to dance (in A, the scenario in B and C is different). He says "I will not dance with you / except if you will follow me." He goes on to promise her a gold crown and a gold bracelet, both worthy of a queen.

In B the setting has changed to the inside of the church. The handsome young knight (Øgler) enters—all the little pictures turn around— the priest asks who he might be. He is an envoy from the king of Norway. The maid says "ved sig enne" ("to herself"), "Christ give, knight, you were mine." He knows this even before she says it and walks right up to her. From that point the story is as in A.

In C the setting is as in B including the priest who asks who the knight might be. Her reaction to him is worth citing, "Marstig's daughter smiles under skin: God give that knight were mine." He again walks right over to her—across church benches, and so on—and asks if she will be his and follow him home. She gives him her hand and says yes, she will. They leave the church with a whole wedding party, dancing along until they come to the beach. There they are alone, the others have all left.

4. (A, B) She asks how she can follow him with all the people who are

watching over her, her father, mother, siblings, and eight good knights? He says that even if her entire family were watching over her, she has to follow him. He makes the two of them invisible, puts her on his horse, and rides off over the heather. They ride through woods and opens and get to the sea.

In B the fiancé is added to the group of people who make escape difficult. But Øgler makes them invisible and they ride off. When they get to the meadow thirty royal knights meet them, when they get to the heather they all become "throlle saa lede," "trolls so vile." He, Øgler, the troll, becomes "saa sort som iordt," "as black as earth," and she is scared. They reach a sound and Øgler asks them all to stop a while.

5. (A, B, C) In A she asks "Hear thou, Sir Alfast, my fiancé, / what willst thou by this wild water?" The answer is blunt, "I am not Sir Alfast, your fiancé, / my home it is in this water." She sinks into the water: "you could hear it far away, / how the maid in the water did scream."

In B he goes to get a boat. She prays for her parents and fiancé. The voice of the ballad singer is heard warning all young maidens about dancing too proud. Øgler takes the girl aboard the boat—made half of blood and half of water—and they sail to the middle of the sound where they sink. The end is like A. C follows B, but is somewhat abbreviated.

DgF 40: "Harpens Kraft"

Piø does not categorize this ballad. But it may be old. There are six versions in DgF: A, B, C, D, E, F.

1. (A, B, C, D, E, F) "The Power of the Harp" tells of a young couple who are engaged to be married. They play a board game (like checkers). But she is distracted and cries. He asks why she is crying, is it because she is to marry him or because he is not rich? No, she is happy to be his and he *is* rich. She is crying because of "Blyde, / that I have to ride across." He promises to send a contingent of knights with her and to repair the bridge. A hundred men shall ride beside her, twelve in front, and so on. The only variations are that some versions do not have the initial board game.

2. She rides to the bridge on a gold-shod horse with her huge retinue. In two versions the retinue is distracted by deer, in the others her horse simply falls on the bridge and she ends up in the river, despite the

massive guard. Her fiancé procures a harp (sends a boy, has it made in town).

3. He plays the harp (in one version a friend of his does) to stunning effect: the fish jump out of the water, the birds fall out of the sky, the bark cracks on oaks and birches and lindens, the horns fall off the cattle, the spire falls off the church. In one version "He played more than he should have / he played the dead out of the ground." He also plays the girl right out of the troll's arm.

4. The troll comes up from the bottom (A) with the maid in his mouth. He promises to give both her and her sisters back if only he will stop playing. He will not and cuts the troll in two with his sword. In some versions he simply plays until the troll lies dead in the water. In the D version his playing is equated with runes. In a couple of versions the troll does not die, he just gives back his prey.

5. In two versions (E, F) there is an ending added on. After this grueling experience the knight rides home with his bride. He keeps on playing "so lustily" for his bride. He plays with great desire, plays until the quint did burst, "then his harp changed its sound,"

> For the bride who once had been stolen,
> one year later gave birth to Sir Peder's son.

> What young man plays the harp well,
> will not let his beloved be taken away.

This ending is a rare and delightful example of a narrator's willingness to be sexually playful.

DgF 41: "Rosmer"

Piø does not mention this ballad. Grundtvig gives five versions: A, Ab, B, Bb, C.

1. (A, Ab, B, Bb, C) Fru Hille-lille, "Lady Hille-lille," builds a castle that "Shines over all of Denmark." Her daughter is stolen. Her sons take off on ships to find her. They sail eight years until they come to a high mountain where they go ashore. A maid—Iomfru Suannelille, "Miss Suannelille"[7]—sees them and asks who the foreign men may be. The youngest brother answers: they are three sons of a widow looking for their sister who was stolen long ago. When he says where they come

from and the mother's name she immediately recognizes that they are her brothers. She warns them about Rosmer and hides them.

In the B and Bb versions the king of Iceland builds and mans a ship to go out and rid him of Rosmer. Rosmer sinks the ship and all die except for Aluar, the son of the king, who finds a little house. The house is Rosmer's and his sister greets him.

In C some men build a boat to go to Iceland. They set the ship to sea and it sinks, a feat caused by the vile troll. Young Roland finds a path to Eline's house.

2. (A, Ab, B, Bb, C) Rosmer comes home and smells Christians. The maid says a bird flew over the house and dropped a bone. Later she fusses over Rosmer and says her relative-countryman has come and will he please not hurt him. Rosmer swears her relative shall be safe. In some versions he puts the brother on his knee and plays so rough with him that she has to remind him that his big hands will hurt such a fragile young thing. In the B, Bb, and C versions "He was there eight years / and longer than he wanted / he could not control his male nature[8] / he made proud Hellelilde pregnant." In other words, we have incest, since the lovers are brother and sister.

3. (A, Ab, B, Bb, C) They begin to long for home and she goes before Rosmer to ask his permission for the brother to leave. Rosmer is both willing to let him go and very generous: he is going to give him a chest full of gold. She substitutes herself for the gold. Rosmer carries the man on his back and the chest in his mouth back to the ship–terra firma.[9]

In the incest versions, the brother now tells Rosmer that the maid is pregnant. Rosmer wants to kill him but is curtailed by having sworn to let him live. When he comes home the girl is gone. He becomes a granite rock (C) or he "springer i flint," "explodes like flintstone." In all of Grundtvig's versions the siblings make it home, and all are happy to have them back. In other words, the incest has no repercussions. We do find, however, that in an extremely elaborate Faroese version "Gongu-Rolvs Kvædi," Rolv comes back to Norway and tells that he has slept with his sister. The king is willing to forgive him, but Rolv is so weighed down by his sin that he lets himself be baptized and dies.[10]

DgF 183: "Kvindemorderen"

Piø says this ballad was written by a man called Winding around 1800.[11] Since this is not a *tryllevise*, I will later give a story outline based on a version edited together from all the various versions at the point in my analysis where I need it.

The Pattern

It should be obvious that these ballads share a number of features.

1. First of all, they share a cast of *characters*. These ballads always feature

- an unmarried maiden (for reasons that will become clear I will call her "marginal"), and

- a troll or demon.

They all have at least one of the following:

- a mother (sometimes both the troll's mother and the girl's),

- a father (only the maiden can have one),

- siblings (this is a marked category; siblings only occur if parents do);[12]

- a fiancé;

- a priest;

- children of the maid and the troll or of the maid and her husband.

2. We also always find three types of space represented: cultural space, marginal space and natural space:

- *Cultural space:* Farm, rooms, church, court.

- *Marginal space:* Bridge, "little green path," cemetery, field, meadow, ships. I call these spaces marginal because they span nature (bridge, "little green path") or share boundaries with both culture and nature (field, cemetery, meadow), or they are cultural spaces in the midst of nature and subject to nature's whims (ships, to a certain extent "little green paths"). In all of the ballads these types of spaces are dangerous, people encountered in them are easy victims of demons.

* *Natural space:* Brooks, rivers, the sea, the woods, mountains, heather (the knights in "Deceit of the Nix" who meet Øgler and the girl on the meadow—which is as far as they have dared venture—become trolls once they are on the heather), beaches.

These spaces are important because of the kinds of action that can take place in them. Maidens are never accosted by demons at home, unless they are already involved with one as in "Agnete" and "Dwarf." In one case a girl is approached in church but only after having shown herself as marginal in a way that penetrates the culture-nature boundary (the proud girl in "Nix"). In all other cases interaction between maidens and demons takes place in marginal spaces.

3. In each of our ballads there is a travel or journey through or across nature. The maid always has to move from one cultural compound or space to another, either from her father's home to her husband's home, or from home to church. This journey is always when she is approachable.[13] This proves important in the analysis.

The girl is taken by the troll when she is en route from her father's farm to another cultural space. She is taken while she is in marginal space and she is taken into natural space: under the water, into the mountain. This is the core of the story, we find it in every single one of the ballads.

The Analysis: The Core

"Harp" has only the core: the maid who has to move from her father's home to her future husband's. The intrigue is the crossing of the bridge. The other tales add on to the periphery of this core story. These ballads are like a stone thrown into the water. The original ring caused by the stone is the innermost of a number of concentric circles all caused by the same event: the stone thrown into the water. The outer circles do not tell a different story from the inner ones; they are all witnesses to the same event, just further removed from it.

When I say that the "outer rings" point toward the core event in the ballads, I mean this in two ways: (1) the optional introductions lead into the core event, (2) the optional introductions are full of symbols that suggest the core event, symbols of nature-culture and of female sexuality. As a matter of fact, there are no "neutral" symbols in these ballads: they all build toward the same conceptual edifice.

Out of scores of analyses of the folk ballads, two are especially interesting and important. Villy Sørensen argues, as I have above, that the ballads are like constantly changing organisms that manage to survive as a viable art form only as long as they reflect or derive their symbols from the reigning cosmological order. This point of view underlies the entire essay, but is perhaps best expressed in his conclusion,

> The present account . . . has possibly from time to time given the impression that the ballads have emerged as conscious "reflexions" of each other. Especially in the case of the folk ballads—which have lived in the mouths of "the people" and of the poets too—such literary inbreeding might seem possible: a singer might be tempted to rewrite a poem that time had rendered obscure, be it in a more realistic or a more agreeable fairy tale form.[14]

Sørensen's main point is that the demonic, as it emerges in the ballads, has a psychological function. The ballads are about love, "romantic" love. The, as he calls it, demon is the fear the individual has inside at the time when he or she has to leave the parental home to move into a new environment. In his discussion of "Harp," he states,

> But the troll is apparently especially interested in girls of marriageable age, and the mysterious bridge he is hiding under can best be described as the *transition* from one state to another, from the state of being single to being married.[15] (emphasis mine)

The reason this transition is so fearful is that, "In the engagement situation we humans want to give ourselves and yet we fear—losing ourselves."[16] The demon is thus a projection of one's own fears onto the future spouse; the spouse-to-be is the demon: "the protagonists . . . in the engagement situation at the same time relate to a person they love and wish to give themselves to and a demon they fear and give in to. . . ."[17]

Sørensen's reading of the magic ballads is a major step in the right direction—interpretation. One might, however, note that he seems to forget that the ballads are produced in a socioeconomic context. Sørensen's ballads float freely in the superstructural layers without moorings in the infrastructure. This is not the case in Steffen Mossin's "Folkeviser: Et led i en historisk rekonstruktion af en kulturarv" ("Folk Ballads: A Link in a Historical Reconstruction of a Cultural Heritage").[18]

Mossin takes the point of view that the ballads express social concerns located in the socioeconomic reality of the people who created them. For him the central element is the family. The ballads focus on an important social aspect of the life of any society, the reproduction of the family: weddings.

Mossin finds that the major conflict in the ballads is a conflict vis-à-vis *nature*, which in a technologically simple society is dangerous.[19] But nature is not only dangerous, it is also that which allows culture to reproduce itself, it ensures the "manpower" needed to fill in social roles and functions as incumbents die. Nature is thus a necessary evil, it is an obstacle the individual has to face and defeat in order to secure the continued existence of the family. Discussing the ballad "Elveskud" (to which "Olaf Liljekrans," is the Norwegian equivalent), he says, "It says that Oluf, and with him his family perish *because* Oluf rejects nature."[20] Mossin goes on to make the same equation that Sørensen made above. In the ballad "Elveskud," the demon is an elf maid who represents one aspect of the maid Oluf is engaged to. She is nature in the sense of sexuality.[21] In failing to face up to the elf maid/nature, Oluf also is doomed to be incapable of facing up to his own sexuality in his relationship with his fiancée. In his brief outline of an analysis of "Harp" Mossin says, "The most important point of this ballad is its underscoring of the fact that nature has to be processed in the wedding situation and that until it has been processed it is demonic."[22]

Mossin clearly distinguishes between two types of space, natural space and cultural space. He points out that the natural space is, as already mentioned, inherently dangerous and that people, beings of culture, are in danger only when they pass through natural space.

Together these two analyses provide some of the elements needed to begin to understand the magic ballads: the bridge as a core symbol (although Sørensen does not seem to realize that it is a feature of ballads other than "Harp"), the nature-culture schism, the importance of the transition from single to married, to mention a few. Excellent though these analyses are, there is more to be said.

I will argue that the subject matter of the ballads is the control of *female sexuality*—in a patriarchal society it is not the lover who is the demon, but something in the girl. To argue this point it is necessary to draw also upon other magic ballads, notably the group corresponding to those here treated, the ones that deal with male sexuality.

The core event, the core symbol in the basic story is the maid who has to make a passage over a stream via a bridge. She has in all cases to span the distance between two cultural spaces—father's home/husband's home, home/church. She has to make this trip or journey without falling into the water, into the abyss where the troll is lurking.

The journey symbolizes the transition from childhood to adulthood, in other words, puberty. A change is taking place inside the girl, from being a child who is located in the cultural sphere, to use a popular metaphor "on her father's ticket," she has to become a sexually repro-ductive woman who, once she is married, will "travel on her husband's ticket." The critical point is the period when she is no longer a nonsexual child nor yet a married woman. This part of the trip she has to make "without a ticket." She is, in other words, *marginal*, she is, for a short period, both inside and outside culture. Her enculturation and mem-bership in her family of procreation, her father's family makes her part of culture, but the natural processes inside her, the onset of sexuality and menstruation place her outside culture, in nature. Why? Because female sexuality is like nature in some very important aspects: a woman is, like nature able to produce offspring, renewal. A woman is like nature subject to mensual, recurrent processes.

Because women are closer to nature than are men,[23] for a woman to be put safely and squarely back into culture, her sexuality has to be put under social (read: male) control, she has to marry. The offspring pro-duced within a legal, religiously sanctioned marriage is located inside culture, since the children legally "belong" to the woman's husband, the pater, whoever the genitor might be. If, on the other hand, a young woman starts having children—that is, gives in to her nature—before she is married, those children have no legal access to culture. They are social outcasts who do not belong in any patriline or kin group.

The journey itself is a metaphor for puberty. Structurally the journey is the equivalent of a rite de passage given artistic and symbolic form in

66

the ballads. The rite de passage, as originally described by Arnold van Gennep and as elaborated upon by Victor Turner,[24] is a metaphorical telescoping of puberty into a ritual. The point of the ritual is to transform the individual from one social identity to another. The child is transformed, as a result of biological processes, symbolized by the ritual, into an adult who is able to start a family and take on adult responsibilities. The ritual itself can vary, lasting anywhere from a few hours to several months, but it always contains the elements of (1) previous state, (2) liminal state, (3) new state. The important state here is the second one, the liminal, which is a state where the individual is suspended in midair: he or she is temporarily placed outside normal time and space in a mythic space and time.[25] Once the liminal state is traversed the individual can take on the new social status. One might say, and it is indeed often expressed this way in rites of passage, that the entire ritual is a drama in which the child dies only to be reborn as a grownup.

The actual ritual itself often involves removal from the normal environment. The child is taken off into the wilderness and normal reality is stood on its head, taboos are temporarily lifted, ordinary rules of interaction are absent. The celebrant is often tortured—sometimes ritually "killed"—by adult members of the society masquerading as spirits or animals or mythic beings. The celebrant herself is disrobed or clad in unusual clothing and subjected to treatment that is both scary and, possibly, physically painful.

An example of a ritual that resembles the story of the ballads is the female puberty ritual of the Bakweri of coastal Cameroon.[26] The ritual is called the *liengo la mongbango*. The young girl or woman "signals" that she is ready to make the transition into adulthood by displaying certain symptoms. The crucial symptom is that she disappears into the bush "as if attracted by spirits."[27] This is interesting when we remember the girls in the ballads who walk the fields or ride through the forest, when approached by the demon. After a series of ritual acts which it would lead too far to get into here, the girl lives for a while in the wild with her *liengu*, or mermaid, sponsor. Ardener continues:

She is now dressed in fern-fronds . . . rubbed with camwood, and led through the village tied to the middle of a long rope held by her companions in front and behind. Outside her house, both sets of people pull the rope, as in a tug of war, until the rope comes apart, when the girl falls down, as if dead. She is revived by being called nine times in the *liengu* language, after which she gets up, and is dressed in new clothing.[28]

In this, as well as other versions of the ritual, the girl is at some point washed in the sea or a stream or she is pushed into the water. I need hardly point out how much this shares with our pattern, and how transparent it makes the symbolism. The girl, because of her gender, is attracted to nature, she goes through a ritual that cures her of the attraction and that makes her—at least partially—belong inside culture. As part of the ritual she is literally made the object of a tug of war: nature and culture are both pulling at her; this is the story of "Harp," with the merman and the fiancé both trying to secure the girl for themselves. Next, she falls down, "as if dead," that is, she is ritually dead and is awakened as a member of the adult women's group by *liengu* songs, songs that are the property of women solely. In her new incarnation as a woman, she puts on new clothes—again a symbol of her being a new, reborn, person. Although I am aware that the comparisons can be taken too far, I cannot but mention that in the ballads, new clothes given or offered to the girl are a staple. The meaning of this could be that the demon is suggesting that she skip the ritual and the social stamp of approval and become a woman—wearing a new dress/identity—here and now.

With this ritual in mind it can be seen that the journey described in the ballads, most clearly in "Nix," follows closely the rite de passage pattern. The maid has to make a journey through the wilderness in order to take on her new social role as wife. The journey goes through a wilderness—in actual case it passes over—an abyss where a mythic being is lurking. This corresponds to the Bakweri girl disappearing in the bush as a result of an attack by spirits. She is dragged under the water ("dies") and is only released when the monster is killed or rendered impotent (also a common ritual feature, the killing of the monsters by the celebrant's kin). Once she is "on the other side," as it were, she can go on with her life as a wife and mother.

Now it is possible to understand the meaning of the symbols in the core segment. The maid has to go through a transition. It is worth noting that when the maid is returned the nix has her in his mouth. The mouth, according to Freud is a symbol for the womb: another suggestion that the girl after her ritual "death" is reborn.[29]

The above describes the original ("pagan") signification of the core segment: female sexuality is at issue, but the focus is on the rite of passage, on the transition from one social role to another. With Christianity the sole focus is the control of sexuality, and especially female sexuality. As Foucault, discussed above, says, Christianity equates sex with sin.

When Christianity was originally introduced into Scandinavia, a process that lasted several centuries from circa A.D. 800 onward, a previously homogenous population was suddenly split into two religious communities. It can be assumed that each community was religion-endogamous, that is, that Christians were supposed to marry Christians and pagans, pagans. In this situation it can also be assumed that the Christians, in their attempt to discredit the Norse religion, equated paganism—and thus pagans—with the types of demons and spirits that populated the pagan cosmology.[30] Christians did not, at least not initially, deny outright the existence of demons and spirits: they condemned them and equated them with the devil, with evil. Paganism, then, populated even the Christian cosmos with trolls and mermen, but Christianity equipped its believers with a "magic" stronger than that of any nix or mountainman, a magic that could make trolls into rock, and that could save young men from the sexual allure of even the most beautiful elfin girl.[31]

As the pagan supernaturals are part and parcel of the cosmos of Christians, so pagans themselves are part of the cultural environment. Ibsen plays, as we shall see, with the Christian-pagan opposition in both his essay on "Kjæmpevisen" and in, for example, *Hærmændene på Helgeland*, and *Kjæmpehøien*. Pagans are there, live and in the flesh, and they constitute a real threat to the hegemony and final victory of Christianity insofar as they refuse conversion or, worse still, marry Christian women and produce new generations of little heathens. It becomes incumbent on parents to impress, with all possible vehemence, on their children, but especially the daughters, that pagans are not eligible as marriage partners.

The Christian versus pagan dichotomy is a feature of many ballads. Among the *trylleviser*, the most obvious example is *DgF* 71, "Brudefærden til Hedenland" ("The Bride from Heathenland"). In the "Ag-

69

nete" ballad the opposition can be demonstrated by referring to internal evidence, such as the rejection of Christianity by both the merman and Agnete herself.[32] In the English version of this ballad, Child's number 41, it is obvious: Hind Etin has stolen the king's daughter Margaret and she lives with him and has his children. She is always sad and crying and one day when the oldest son is accompanying his father on the hunt he asks why his mother never is happy. The answer is,

> "For your mother was an earl's dochter,
> Of nobel birth and fame,
> And now she's the wife of Hinde Etin,
> Wha neer got christendame."[33]

With two religious groups at loggerheads, fighting for control, women became extremely important because of their procreative powers[34] and marrying a pagan became equated with marrying his religion and the death of the girl and the loss of her offspring for Christianity. In the ballads this is always the scenario: the girl dies or is condemned to forever be excluded from her own group and religion and her children by the demon are always with him in the end.

The above refers back to my argument from Chapter 2 that the entire symbol complex of the ballads underwent subtle—or not so subtle— changes in meaning as society changed. What had been primarily a telescoped rite of passage, became a lesson in the consequences of marrying outside one's religious group.

Only if we read these ballads as a group of texts can we come to a real understanding of the constituent symbols in the individual ballad. The ballads in our group are complementary, no one gives the pattern in its entirety, but read together they illuminate each other. So, for instance, it is a weakness, or, more to the point, a lack, in the analyses of Sørensen and Mossin, discussed above, that they see the magic ballads as primarily concerned with what happens to young men in "the marriage situation."[35] I hope to have established by now, that the ballads deal both with men and women (the group of ballads that correspond to the group we are discussing here, those focusing on males, will be discussed below). When they are read as a group as variations on a theme it becomes clear that the primary situation dealt with is not the engagement, but sexuality, puberty. In most of our ballads the fiancé is not even in the cast of characters; in those where he is, he seems but an addendum (e.g., in the "Nix" ballad, some versions mention a fiancé, but he is of no consequence, used only to reinforce the image of all the girl has lost in choosing the freedom-*cum*-pleasure principle, the nix). The things that are always there are the girl, some kind of symbolic rendering of society (mother, church, priest, father, fiancé), the "journey," and the demon. Thus we must make these symbols the center of analysis.

The Journey and the Bridge

Since it still may not be obvious that all of the ballads deal with maidens in marginal places and, indeed, with "journeys," I am going to show how these images are represented in the various ballads. But let me first mention that Feilberg discusses the ubiquitous bridges in folklore which are dangerous because brides get stolen on them and speculates about the meaning of the dangerous point being a bridge.[36] He first suggests that the bridge may have been built by the troll and that the troll simply is extracting a toll, but rejects this explanation in favor of one that says the bridge is only an elaboration of an earlier ford in the same place. The ford, of course, meant that people and horses had to wade through the actual stream—albeit where the water was shallow. The bridge is but an extension of the ford that was "created" by the troll and thus he is indeed extracting a toll. This fits neatly with the stories from all parts of Scandinavia that tell of streams and rivers and brooks that demand an annual sacrificial victim (see note 7 to this chapter).

In the "Harp" ballad the central aspect of the story is always the actual crossing of the "Blide" bridge, so this ballad is clear cut with regard to my claim. The bridge is a dangerous place, fear-provoking— the girl is crying when she thinks about it—and it has proved that it is dangerous by destroying her older sister: this is a "bridge" every young girl has to pass over.

In some versions of the Agnete ballad it is also quite clear, namely those where Agnete is standing on a bridge or walking across it. Where the bridge is absent other types of marginal space are introduced. In one version she is in the fields crying. But fields are also marginal with regard to the nature-culture schism. It is not quite clear if by the "fields" some kind of semiwilderness is meant, such as a meadow or grazing area for cattle or fields in the sense of agricultural land. In the former case the marginality is obvious, but even domesticated fields are marginal: they are the very buffer area between the core of the human sphere, the farm buildings, and nature just beyond. So, Agnete is walking away from the farm, from the human environment, and she is crying. She is full of fear or sorrow. This is a marginal girl, just the kind a mountain-man would notice and choose as his victim. The Danish philosopher Søren Kierkegaard, in his reading of this ballad, says of Agnete that she is "a woman who demands the interesting and any such can always be sure that there is a merman around. For mermen notice these things without half trying and steer towards them like a shark towards its prey."[37]

In the "Dwarf" ballad the image of the bridge recurs as the *spange*. The places where the Dwarf can "get at" the maid are the little bridge she has to pass on her way to church and "the little green path," leading through the forest, that is, wilderness. The path is like the bridge, it is a man-made route through enemy territory and it is dangerous, as the father points out in the E version where he warns her against the moun-tainman.[38] All this is to say that the "little green path" through the forest is the structural and symbolic equivalent of the bridge in "Harp" and "Agnete."

In the "Nix" ballad we find neither the bridge nor the "little green path," but we do find the "Journey," on which the maid, Marstig's daughter, is taken by her lover/husband, the nix. With regard to the marginal space this ballad seems to break the pattern. But examined closely this turns out not to be the case. When we first meet the maid she is the foresinger at a social gathering (a wonderfully self-referential image for the ballads). She is, in other words, serving a social function possibly as the one who is supposed to convey the moral message to young girls about the effects of making themselves available to disaster by straying from the group. But she herself is straying from the group, she is "proud," she feels superior, feels she does not belong amongst her own, she feels no one is good enough for her. Her song penetrates the nature-culture boundary and becomes the sign the troll needs, the sign that tells him she is a girl who wants "the interesting." Her song, which the nix hears, is structurally equivalent to "the little green path," the bridge or the field. She is marginalized by her behavior and something in her personality. She is "physically" in the group, but she marginalizes herself by her pride and by her singing which reaches the nix "who lay under the ice." The nix hears her song and thinks to himself, "I wonder if she'll have me." He has noticed her because she is, as all the other maidens we are dealing with, marginal.

It is worth mentioning, incidentally, that the social gathering that begins the ballad usually is described in sexually suggestive terms: "there danced maidens with their hair untied / there danced knights with their swords drawn"—clearly sexual symbolism. The stage is set for the sexual transgression of the maid which is exactly what the ballads, as I argue, deal with.

The important difference between the "Nix" ballad and the others is that this girl is described more forthrightly as marginal not because of a projected, spatialized danger lurking in certain types of space, but because of something inside herself, something that causes the nix to think, "I wonder if she will have me." She shares with her sisters in the other ballads the feature of being of marriageable age and of being marginal. We can now see a pattern, a continuum of marginality: the girl in "Harp" is marginal because she is at a vulnerable stage of her life, but she is otherwise innocent: she is not wanton, proud or rebellious—and she is also the only one who always is saved by the male principle, her fiancé, to live a life of happy procreation.

The girl in "Nix," on the other hand, is at the opposite end of the continuum. Not only is she marginal because of the biological stage she is going through, she is guilty of a social sin, pride, refusal to live on society's terms—and she is sexually wanton. She sees the knight and wishes (sometimes right in the church—sin upon awful sin: sexual lust in the house of God) that he were hers. She is punished by death—the scream can be heard miles away. In other words, the message to girls listening to this song is: if you set yourself apart you will be destroyed, but if, on the other hand, you do as you are told, you may have a fearful and scaring experience but you will be saved in the end. Patriarchy will save you from the dangers inside yourself.

The other ballads fall between these two extremes: "Agnete" is both placed in a marginal space (bridge, field) and psychic marginality is hinted at: in the C version she is crying, in the others she is formally jumping at the opportunity to leave her cultural environment. When in

A the merman asks her if she will be his sweetheart, her answer is immediate and to the point,

> "Oh yes, certainly I will,
> if you'll take me to the bottom of the sea."

In the D version, when asked if she will go to the sea with him, her answer is equally direct and complementary to her answer in A,

> "Yes, I would like to go to the sea with him,
> if my parents won't know."

She is not only marginal because of biology, she is marginal because she is one of civilization's malcontents. She is wandering, hovering on the outskirts of culture, apparently waiting for something "interesting" to happen. She has thus marked herself off as the perfect victim for the demon who needs some kind of sign to be alerted to a girl. He will never attack or approach, not even discover, the girl who does not give off vibrations that attract his attention.

Agnete is marginal because she apparently does not want to take on her role as culture demands it of her. She is rebellious, the merman and the sea—to her—signify escape from culture and its demands and constraints. This suggests that the ballads—over and beyond their function, to be spelled out below, as teaching tools, as cultural reinforcers—may have had the function of being "escape valves": descriptions of female fantasies of escape from cultural and male control. In other cultures at other times we have found dreams of fantasy escape taking the forms of social institutions or semisecret societies. A Danish student of witchcraft, Gustav Henningsen, has found evidence among the papers of the Inquisition dealing with rural Sicily that at the time of the Inquisition there existed fairly openly a witch cult in which many women, and some men, participated. The cult involved nightly outings into the woods to enjoy sexual encounters with demons. That this cult had the function of escape valve for women seems obvious from the data presented by Henningsen.[39]

On first look, "Dwarf" belongs in our typology here with "Harp," in that the girl is not in any obvious way described as either rebellious or proud. She is simply a girl who is not yet married, but she turns out to have been the author of her own disaster, admitting when she meets her mother after years of living with the mountainman that she has been seduced by him. She was not the prudent, obedient girl she should have been, and she has thus deserved the punishment she finally gets: rejection by her family and/or death.

As already mentioned, the Agnete ballad was written by a "man of letters" around 1780.[40] The ballad was first published as a broadsheet and subsequently spread all over Denmark and Norway. Later this literary product was absorbed by the living oral tradition. The ballad, although written in the late eighteenth century, is based on already existing material such as the German ballads "Wassermans Braut" and "Die schöne Agnete" and the "Harp," "Nix," and, especially, "Dwarf" ballads. It is a reinterpretation of "Dwarf," infused with psychological and social sensibilities that might have the ring of truth to the author's contemporaries. Agnete is a rebellious girl who does not want to submit to patriarchal rule and the late eighteenth and early nineteenth centuries were when the ideas of romantic love and choosing one's own spouse began to be spread abroad. The ballad tells of the results of such rebelliousness.

I interpret the actions of the girl in "Dwarf" in the same way: she asks her father's permission to ride to evensong, is warned about the mountainman, but apparently disregards the warning. She takes the "little green path" and rides straight to the mountain (we are told of course that the reason she does this is that she is bewitched, but I interpret the runes cast by the dwarf as nothing other than his ability to awaken her sexual desire).

That the runes indeed have this effect on women (when accompanied by the right formulas) is suggested by the places where they typically are placed: on things the girl has to pass over, that is, the runes have access to that part of the woman's anatomy that is the site of sexual feeling. One might say that this is too literal a reading, but the point is brought home with some force in a ballad called "Sir Stig's Wedding" (DgF 76). The Stig of this ballad wants to arouse the interest of a young woman by the name of Liden Kierstin, and decides to see if the runes he has "learned" can do the job. During a dinner party—he serves at the king's court—he throws the runes at her, but misses, and the runes end up under the wrong skirt,

75

He intended to throw runes to Liden Kierstin:
and they drifted under Miss Regisse's skirt.

Riddersti he blackens like earth:
Miss Regisse she is as red as blood.

That very night the maid Regisse comes to his bedchamber and wants to sleep with him. He ends up marrying her, which is bad since she is the wrong girl, but good since she is the king's sister. The point, however, is that the runes have a very direct and "physical" effect on the victims. What happens in "Dwarf" is that the girl is seduced by the dwarf. Notice that nobody ever blames the dwarf. This is what one would expect from him, he is only fulfilling his natural function in seducing young maidens. The one invariably blamed and punished by the representatives of culture is the girl.

The girl in "Dwarf" is closer to Agnete than to the absolute innocence of the girl in "Harp" and the reason she is punished is that she is seen as guilty by the representatives of the social order. Similarly, the girl in "Kvindemorderen" (which will be discussed in more detail below) is, as far as can be ascertained, either wanton or rebellious: she is willing to steal all her father's gold and riches for her lover. But she gives the story a new twist: she kills the seducer, that is, she kills the desire to sin in herself.

At this point, having established the meaning of the core sequence of the ballads, and before interpreting the symbols beyond the core, it will be useful to examine the function of the ballads.

The Function of the Ballads

I make a double claim: (1) The ballads are—over and beyond their function as entertainment—teaching tools. In the case of the ballads under discussion here, they are supposed to teach young (pubescent) women that their only chance of coming through that stage of their lives unscathed is to submit to the rules of patriarchy represented first by the father and then by the husband. (2) The ballads assume that women are more easily led astray than are men. I shall look into the validity of these two claims before I finish my interpretation of the ballads themselves.

The anthropologist and folklorist William A. Bascomb puts it thus,

> Finally, anthropologists are becoming increasingly concerned with the functions of folklore—what it does for the people who tell it. In addition to the obvious function of entertainment or amusement, folklore serves to sanction the established beliefs, attitudes, and institutions, both sacred and secular, and *it plays a vital role in education in nonliterate societies* . . . . In addition to its role in transmitting culture from one generation to another, and to providing ready rationalizations when beliefs or attitudes are called into question, *folklore is used in some societies to apply pressure to those who would deviate from the accepted norms.* Moreover, even the function of amusement cannot be accepted today as a complete answer, for it is apparent that . . . folklore serves as a psychological escape from many repressions, not only sexual, which society imposes on the individual.[41] (emphases mine)

The ballads served a didactic purpose. They were supposed to teach young women of the dangers lurking in their own nature and to alleviate their fears of growing up and becoming women.

In this regard it is worth remembering that the ballads also served as entertainment. We can assume they were performed at dances with a foresinger and everybody else joining in on the chorus. The entertainment value must have been considerable when we take the social, kinetic, and musical-rhythmic aspects into account. The individual young woman could experience while safely situated in a group of her peers, the scary story of someone just like herself going through something terrifying. The psychological effect of experiencing this fear in the absolute safety of a large group cannot be overestimated. The ballad and its content tells her of the dangers lurking within and without, and the group reminds her that as long as she does not stray, give in to her own asocial tendencies, she is safe. The experience can in many ways be compared to the experience many children have today when they go— in droves armed with sweets and popcorn—to a scary movie. They sit in the darkness with their friends and watch something intensely fearful. The danger on the screen is a projection of their own nameless, unconscious fears, and the shared social experience, the proximity, the giggling, the holding on to each other, the screaming, and so on help remind them that they are safe within the boundaries of social living, of a group, of a society.

So, the ballads are projections of common fears growing up—biology—have created in young people. In the *trylleviser* the worst scenario is played out. The powers of darkness are victorious and the marginal girl (and what woman, as I have said, who is caught in the vacuum between child and woman is not?) is lured, stolen, charmed to leave her group and join a stranger. Seen this way, the ballads show remarkable psychological insight. There is a store of knowledge of female adolescence embodied in the portraits of young women. There is also a store of knowledge of how to impress on young women what their priorities and duties are.

Second, the ballads were the products of a patriarchal ideology that sees the control of women, that is, of female sexuality and procreative powers, as one of its most intricate and momentous duties. I am not saying that the ballads were necessarily written by men—their very nature as fantasy escape valves would suggest that women often were the authors—but I am saying that whoever wrote these ballads shared in the goals of patriarchy. The ballads are designed to point out to women the dangers in nonconformity. The ballads point out, reinforced by the social setting for their dissemination, that women are only safe as long as they do what they are told and marry the one their parents have chosen for them. Women have to walk across that bridge, past the abysses below, and settle among their own kind.

The question that suggests itself with regard to the ballads and to the male claim to have a right to control female sexuality is the one formulated by the anthropologist Sherry Ortner, in her article by the same name, "Is Female to Male as Nature Is to Culture?" In other words, is there something about women that ties them to nature and makes them strangers in culture? Most societies, claims Ortner, see women as closer to nature than men because "woman's *body and its functions,* more involved more of the time with 'species life,' seem to place her closer to nature, in contrast to man's physiology, which frees him more completely to take up the projects of culture."[42]

In her article, which deals with the universality of male dominance, Ortner goes on to say that the vast majority of societies in the world neatly divide the world between a natural sphere and a cultural one. Men appropriate the cultural sphere as their own, their "creation." Culture is the counterpoint to nature, its opposite, it is distinctly human, and distinctly male. Men had to create this fiction of culture as a male domain to be able to wrest the power away from women who originally, because of their natural creative powers had the upper hand (essentially, but not quite, the argument of Bachofen that a stage of matriarchy preceded the present patriarchal stage).[43] With the sharp distinction between nature and culture and with the values assigned to the two realms, culture being good and nature being at worst evil—and at best dangerous when not under cultural control—women were put at a disadvantage relative to men exactly because of their natural creativity that in the earliest human societies gave them a high status. For women to gain access to culture, the male domain, the entrance price was that they had to submit to male rule and male control, most importantly, of their very natural functions: their sexuality and procreative abilities.

There are ethnographic examples from all over the world that deal with the marginality of women in patriarchal cultures and even if exceptions can be found, Ortner's analysis seems to work for the Danish ballads and their subject matter, which is why the Bakweri mermaid ritual offers such a striking analogy. The Bakweri are an agricultural society living in the coastal areas of Cameroon. Both men and women are active in the agricultural pursuit, each gender being responsible for different crops. The Bakweri tell a story—it seems to be a myth of the origins of Bakweri society—according to which man, *moto* (the equivalent of German *Mensch*, human being of either gender), won a contest to live in villages by building a lasting fire. All other beings were relegated to nature. One being, *Mojili*, was chased into the water. "Mojili is responsible for young girls becoming mermaids."[44] Women and children are attracted to the wilds, to the water and the forest, and rites are performed to "control these manifestations."[45] Ardener goes on to say,

> The possible marginality of women when men are defining "the wild" is evident. Thus the idea of the denizens of the wild, outside Moto's village, being a danger or attraction to women and their offspring is comprehensible in a male model of the universe, in which female reproductive powers do not fall under male control.[46]

In Bakweri society, however, men are not alone in defining cosmos and the role of females in it. Women have their own model, according to which they, indeed, belong in a sphere that incorporates both the wild and the village. In other words, women define themselves as belonging both in nature and in culture. They do not attach a negative value to belonging in nature, as do men, who are aware that the part that is outside of the male domain, culture, also is outside of male domination. Bakweri women thus have an economic sphere of their own and they have some control of their own sexuality—much to the dissatisfaction of men. But the women also go through rites, usually around puberty, that are supposed to render them "immune from any attack by the water spirits."[47] The rite is enacted after a girl has had a fit or seizure which suggests that a water spirit has entered her. The ensuing ritual[48] "cures" the woman in that the spirit is rendered harmless, but it also has the effect that "the girl is regarded as being a familiar of the water spirits and one of the *liengu* women."[49] The rites, then, conform to male demands that women reject the "call of nature," but this is done in such a way that women through familiarizing themselves with the wild, that is, through reaffirming their belonging in the wild, carve a space in cosmos for themselves that overlaps with both the cultural and the natural but is under their own control.

Moving much closer to the society described in the ballads both in time and in space, my next "ethnographic" example is southwestern Germany in the sixteenth century. H. C. Erik Middelfort describes in his paper "The Social Position of the Witch in Southwestern Germany,"[50] the misogyny growing out of a changing social structure that gave rise to an increase in witchcraft accusations. He points out that women who were outside of patriarchal control, spinsters and widows, were disproportionally represented amongst those accused of being witches. He goes on to say,

Two attributes of women did obviously increase the likelihood that they would be suspected of witchcraft. One was melancholy, a depressed state characterized occasionally by obscure or threatening statements and odd behaviour. *Many women in their confessions emphasized the fact that they were seduced into witchcraft at a time when they were sad, dejected, or even desperate.* . . . The other dangerous attribute, as already suggested was isolation. *Women belonged under the protection and legal power of their father until they married. When they married, their husbands took over this power intact.* . . . *The struc-*

ture of society was so completely geared to the family that persons without families were automatically peculiar, unprotected and suspect.[51] (emphases mine)

This example shows the importance of being married, especially for women. Women do not have a separate social identity in a patriarchal society, they are the wards and responsibilities of men. Single women are a liability because they are likely targets for seduction by spirits. In the ballads the maidens are, as I have pointed out, marginal, suspended in thin air, because of the transition from being under father's control to being under husband's control: they, like Middelfort's spinsters and widows, are, for however short a time, outside the patriarchal—that is, cultural—sphere. The women seduced to become witches share another feature with our maidens: they are often, like Agnete, sad and depressed—perhaps because of male control.

The last example is drawn from myth, from the star husband myth cycle as discussed by Leavy, in her book on the swan maiden motif in folklore and literature. After having established that woman's role is what the star husband tales are about, Leavy says,

The Caddo Indians begin their version of the star husband tale with a description of a family and the deviance of a young girl that threatens its stability: "Long ago there lived a large family—father, mother, and eight children, four girls and four boys. They were all beautiful children, especially one of the girls, who was exceptionally beautiful. The time came when three of the girls were married, but the youngest and most beautiful would not receive the attention of any one. The girl was peculiar in her tastes and *roamed around alone. She wished to go away somewhere, for she was tired of her home.*"[52] (emphasis mine)

The girl described in the Indian tale shares features with the maids in the ballads, she roams alone and is tired of her home, this description fits Agnete and the maids in "Dwarf" and in "Nix." The girl, as in all the tales, marries a star and moves to the heavens to live with him and have his children. She often returns to human society and lives a normal life. Leavy makes the point that the star husband tales are especially interesting because the protagonists are women, and goes on,

81

It is perhaps because woman's role is featured in the star husband tales that many of them reflect a veritable female rite de passage, although negatively portrayed. The young women's deviant behavior is often associated with puberty and thus the onset of female sexuality.[53]

Some of the tales, states Leavy, explain "the apartness of women with reference to their menstruation," a feature also stressed in my discussion of the ballads as rites of passage.[54]

In the Indian tales, the pubescent girls are too old to be children but not yet ready to take on the responsibilities of adult women. They are at this stage of their lives particularly vulnerable to fantasies about demon lovers and to taking demon lovers. Part of this is also a rebelliousness and "a lack of respect for adult authority, indicating an inadequate internalization of the tribe's values."[55]

In all three examples and in the ballads themselves it is clear that there is something innately different about women that makes them fall prey to seduction, to forces outside the realm of culture and thus inimical to it.

Since the male argument is that women are somehow embodiments of nature, it follows that men must be the signifiers of culture. This is of course what Lacan says, when he says that "the phallic signifier" is the agent that pulls children into the sphere of culture and symbolization. But why are men the signifiers of culture, why is culture the male "realm" par excellence? Since men do not have an inherent, nature-given creativity they have construed a realm that would be exclusively theirs, their creation. Culture is men's excuse for claiming the right to be in charge, to rule the world, because culture universally is claimed by men as the distinctively male creation.[56]

It is interesting to note, in this context, that almost all cultures have made a more concerted effort to "shape" women than men. Women are usually the ones who are subject to deforming operations such as bound feet, clitoridectomy, infibulation, deformed skulls, and so on. Women are most often required to change their appearance by overeating, starving themselves, painting themselves, adorning themselves with constraining and uncomfortable clothes, walking in an unnatural way, speaking with unnaturally high-pitched voices, and behaving in a submissive, dominated way. Women are inherently ambiguous in terms of the nature-culture schism, they thus need to stress much more so than men their submission to culture and to men. They have to cover up their bodies and bodily odors that reveal their nature as "procreative machines."

When one knows that the core is a telescoped and poetic rite de passage and that the function of the ballads is the teaching of socially defined morality, it becomes easier to understand the symbols beyond the core: the events leading up to and following the journey.

Symbols Beyond the Core

Back to the interpretation of the ballads. I have analyzed the nature of the core elements, the journey across the abyss or through the wild. What is left for me to do is to see how the "outer rings," the elements of the ballads beyond the core fit in and highlight the core theme.

My claim is that the events before the journey are exemplifications of various (psychological) attitudes a young woman can display in the transitional situation; the events after the journey show the consequences of these attitudes.

Since the ballads are very different when we get beyond the core it makes most sense to look at them separately. In "Harp," as in the Bakweri ritual, it is shown that all young women must, at least briefly, fall into the demon's trap, but the severity of the consequences depend on herself. If she has been wanton or rebellious, she will suffer or be destroyed; if not, she will be saved by the heroic representative of the patriarchal order. The maid in "Harp" is innocent, she fears the journey and has no sexual desires or rebellious leanings, and she is saved. In this ballad, which is a Scandinavian version of the Orpheus myth, we are introduced to the young lovers as they play *tavlebord*, a board game, often used in the ballads in general as a symbol for sexual play. In this case it can be assumed that the board game is one of (innocent) sexual play between spouses-to-be. But something is amiss, she is crying. It is quickly established that the reason is neither social nor personal: she is not crying because he is not good enough for her, nor because she does not want him. She cries because of *Blide*, the bridge she has to cross on her way to his house: she is afraid, as I have said, of the forces inside herself that may destroy her. He tells her not to worry, he will take care of it, he will guard her heavily.

Of course she has to go through puberty, and of course she is almost destroyed by it, but her fiancé—in a tug of war with the demon—extracts her unscathed from his scaly embrace and gets her safely to the other side, to adulthood.

The journey ends in disaster: she falls into the abyss despite all safeguards. But the "Harp" ballad, unlike all the other ballads, describes—as part of the core—the struggle between the fiancé and the demon over the maid. The ballad uses music and the harp—a cultural product[57]—to symbolize the power of culture over nature. In all versions the harp has to be sent for, it is brought from the cultural compound, in one version the fiancé sends his servant to the town to have the harp made: it is a symbol of what man-made culture is all about: tools created in the cultural domain—the town—to be used to extract from nature what man wants. The playing of music renders nature helpless and it has to give up its prey. In order to strengthen the image of the power of culture over nature, his playing affects all of nature: the fish come out of the water, the bark comes off the trees, the birds fall to the ground, and so on; the demon's having to give up the girl and her sisters and beg the knight to stop playing is but part of the totality of the picture. The wonders worked by the playing of the harp are an artistic rendering of the "magical" power of technology: human technological inventions can help people do all the things listed in the ballad: pull fish out of the sea, peel bark off the trees, make birds fall from the sky. The whole harp image is a metaphor for my contention in the previous chapter that technology, along with religion, is a buffer humans put between themselves and the (super)natural powers. If humans can make birds fall out of the sky, they can also control the powers lodged in nature, such as the nix.

In "Nix," the maid, Marstig's daughter, goes on her journey, with a man she has chosen in rebellion and pride against all rules and social decency. Leading up to the journey, the maid participates in a social gathering in the church. The focus is on her wantonness. The nix, having transformed himself into a handsome young man, abducts her from the church in the midst of all her friends and relatives.[58] The church is symbolic of her belonging in culture and of the depth of her sin: she has sexual desires in the house of God. Her pride and wantonness are projected onto the nix who leads her to her destruction. This projection calls to mind the fantasy of the Indian girl gazing at the stars: she wants to get away from culture, from male control. But there is no happiness in giving in to the cravings of animal nature, as soon as the "wedding party" of the girl, the nix and his attending trolls, get beyond cultural space, he shows his real face: the dark and disgusting disfiguration of the loathsome troll. She has to follow him to the beach and further into the water. This girl literally drowns in the sea of her own asocial passions. One version of the ballad (B) has the initial dance set in a graveyard, this eerie image shows the death-and-destruction-bound nature of this dance with pride, rebellion, and uncontrolled sexuality: the girl is dancing a dance of death, she is dancing on her own grave.

The "Agnete" ballad begins with the disaffected girl in the marginal area and rushes past the introductory material: her marginality and willingness to escape parental/patriarchal control. This ballad, like the "Nix" ballad, is essentially about the wages of sin, the outcome of trying to extricate yourself from social constraints. The bulk of the ballad deals with her fate *after* the initial act of rebellion. She is not, like Marstig's daughter, unceremoniously destroyed, leaving only a scream that could be heard over several counties behind. She is married to her demon and has his children. The ballad is, at least on one level, a ballad about the consequences of marrying "for love" against the will of parents.

Both the "Agnete" and the "Dwarf" ballad describe in painful detail the fate of the rebellious or unprudent girl. She does not escape male control. On the contrary, and ironically, she has children by the merman just as she would by a human/Christian husband. She is the one who takes care of the children. When the church bells toll[59] she is sitting by the cradle singing a lullaby, certainly a recognizable picture of the traditional female role, and she has to ask her husband's permission to go to church just as she had to ask her father's to go to evensong in one version of "Dwarf." So, on the one hand, she has not escaped cultural control and the traditional female role, if that was what her rebellion was aimed at (we shall see in the next chapter that this point became a focus for the romantic writers who became fascinated with this particular ballad). On the other, she is, as the lover of a pagan/demon cut off from her family and friends and from Christianity.

In the versions of the "Agnete" ballad where she manages to return to Christian society, she has to give up her children. In the other versions and in "Dwarf" she is either killed by the merman or by her children or she commits suicide. In the Norwegian version of the ballad (Landstad #33), she is given a drink that makes her forget her social and religious provenance—that is, she "dies" as a member of Christian society. Whatever her fate is, it is never a happy one, she invariably has to give something up, she is invariably the loser (in the "Agnete" ballad, the merman, of course, loses too). This becomes clearer if we reverse the story: had she married someone acceptable to and chosen by her parents she would not have to give up anything, she could visit her parents as much as she would like, she could go to church and she would be able to live a happy productive life as a woman loved by husband and children. Notice that when she marries the merman/pagan, the love of the children is not an automatic thing. In some versions of both ballads the children are the ones that punish her for her betrayal of their father by beating her or killing her. Women, in a patrilineal society, are strangers in their husband's group. If they cut themselves off from their parents—by disobediently marrying someone not approved—they cut themselves off from the only group in which they have a birthright, they cut themselves off from themselves.

The "Dwarf" ballad, in some versions, has one last layer, namely the initial story of the knight and the dwarf who meet in the forest and strike a deal about the girl. This section, like all the other "feed-ins," is meant to introduce the basic themes of the ballad symbolically. The first theme introduced is the usual one of males wishing to seduce women: both the knight and the dwarf have designs on the girl before we are even introduced to her. There is a warning to girls in this: watch out for men for they will seduce you if they can. The setting is the forest, which has two meanings: it is nature and a place where uncontrolled sexuality has free play. The forest symbolizes both the wild and the part of female nature that is open to seduction.

I argue, based on the above, that this first part is set in the girl's unconscious, where the pleasure and reality principles are fighting for control—to put it in Freudian terms. The dwarf or elf king is victorious. (The desires of the knight need not, indeed, seem not to be inherently bad, he wants to win the girl's love and then, presumably he wants to marry her. There is a further suggestion of this in the ballad when the dwarf tells the girl after having lured her into the mountain, that her

86

fiancé has betrayed her.) So, the forest is the dark, unconscious areas of the girl's mind where the dwarf, uncontrolled sexuality, lives and the conversation between the knight and the troll is the fight inside the girl between propriety and desire.

The runes that the dwarf plans to use externalize the lust; they are put on the path the girl has to travel to get to church, where she, presumably, would be safe, and they cause her to stray, to give in to her sexuality and start a relationship.

Before closing this chapter I need to address briefly the two ballads in our group that have not so far been discussed. The reason they have been left out of the discussion until now is that they do not really belong with the group of ballads targeted here. *DgF* 183, "Kvindenmorderen," in Child "Lady Isabel and the Elf Knight," is in Danish not a magic ballad. "Kvindemorderen"[60] deals with a man who, without the use of magic, seduces young women and then kills them. The main reason for including the ballad here is that we think it is one of the ballads that exerted an influence on Ibsen (it is even possible that Ibsen knew the English version, which was available in Danish translated by Svend Grundtvig in his *Engelske og Skotske Folkeviser* as "Stolt Isabel og Elve-Ridderen."[61]

The Danish ballad tells of Ulver and Vænelil. Ulver wooes Vænelil with promises of wealth and eternal happiness if she will elope with him. This is like the ballads already discussed where the demon also promises gold and riches. She points out that getting away from all the people who are guarding her is going to be difficult (à la "Nix"). The escape is, as in "Nix," effected by making her "invisible": she is dressed, with a helmet and sword, like a knight. When they get into the meadow (i.e., the wild), he wants to rest. He begins to dig a grave. She asks who it is for and he says he has already seduced and killed eight maidens and she is going to be the ninth, the grave is for her. She proposes to delouse his hair, a symbolic way of stating an intimate relationship between them. He puts his head in her lap and lets her do it. With his head in her lap he falls asleep. In his sleep she ties him and when he awakens—she has promised not to kill him in his sleep—she kills him and thus saves her life and her virtue and can return, on his horse, to her mother, "so fair a maiden."

The English ballad is similar to the Danish in all the essentials and it tells how the fateful pair are brought together. The elf knight, being located in nature since he is a part of it, plays his horn and arouses amorous (read: sexual) desires in Lady Isabel,

> If I had yon horn that I hear blawing,
> and yon elf-knight to sleep in my bosom.[62]

As in "Nix," the elf at once knows and materializes by her side. The story told above ensues.

This is similar to the "Nix" ballad: The demon notices the girl as "marginal" because of her "illegal" sexual desires. In "Nix" he hears her sing and recognizes her as a possible target, in "Isabel" she hears him and responds in a way that marks her off as a possible target, in "Isabel" she hears him and responds in a way that marks her off as a possible victim. If he symbolizes uncontrolled sexuality it is quite obvious that he represents the "natural" in her, which longs to escape from social constraints to act out secret desires. His horn is her nature "calling," this is also why he can hear it, he is part of her. Where "Isabel" differs from "Nix" and from all of the other ballads is where Vænelil, when she discovers Ulver's designs not only on her virtue but also on her life, saves herself. Thus the story we have been telling so far is turned on its head and the girl goes from being victim to being heroine. It can be argued that she kills the desire in herself to stray from the path of propriety and is able to return to mother and culture intact and marriageable. Isabel is a heroine—as she proudly proclaims in one Flemish version of the ballad—and she saves herself. But note that she does not free herself from the social constraints put on women, she saves herself so she can perform her designated role as a woman which includes entering into marriage with her virtue intact. I would be wary to construe Isabel—or for that matter any other of our ballad maidens—as an example of true feminist rebellion. They all carry within them the seed of such rebellion, to be sure, but those who go through with the act of protest are destroyed or languish in eternal unhappiness, and those whose fall from the straight and narrow is aborted end up submitting to society's demands.

Even in these dreams of escape from patriarchy the social order is victorious since freedom is equated with death and destruction. The dream is dreamt within a patriarchal framework, it is steeped in patri-

archal ideology: women are seen as sexually wanton, life outside patriarchy is not one, and so forth. Probably the ballads are realistic in their
depiction of both gender relationships and of the chances for women to
free themselves from "captivity."

The "Rosmer" ballad differs even more from the already known pattern in that this ballad is not really a ballad about the girl, Svanelille,
but about her brother who comes to save her. We are not told about the
circumstances around Rosmer's abduction of the girl, nor are we told
that she is particularly proud, wanton, or otherwise marginal. Her being
in the possession of the merman Rosmer is just the trigger that starts
the real story, namely, the brothers who search for her.

The ballad does, however, throw some light on our thesis here. Rosmer, it seems, has stollen Svanelille to woo her, not to rape or kill her
unceremoniously. It is not spelled out in this way in all versions of the
ballad, but it seems clear that her relationship to the brother is her first
sexual relationship (she has no children by the demon but immediately
becomes pregnant when she starts sleeping with her younger brother;
in the ballads sexual relations always result in children). The focus is
on how she and the brother manage to get away from the demon unscathed and this is where her special talents are more effective than his.
She has clearly learned to deal with Rosmer and seems quite at home in
the new environment, whereas the brother is ill-suited to survive in this
world where the things that are symbols of power in his world have no
effect. His sword is useless; his manly directness and aggressiveness
would, as his sister points out, be deadly, for his strength is nothing
against that of Rosmer. The only reason they manage to escape is that
they rely on her feminine talents. She uses cunning, offers promises of
love and, in the end, deceives the demon by putting herself in the chest
(coffin) with gold he was going to give the brother as a departing gift.
In my reading of the ballads this makes perfect sense; she can deal with
Rosmer—nature—more easily because she herself, being a woman, is
closer to nature. Male virtues, on the other hand, are doomed to fail in
nature where a different set of rules for behavior reign.

That Svanelille is saved is of course due not only to her special talents
but also to her brother's bravery and loyalty: he goes out to find her
braving all manner of dangers and obstacles and persists until he finds
her when everyone else has given up or is dead. Thus the ballad might
be interpreted to say that male and female are complementary, which I

am sure was a genuine belief of the society that created the ballad. The incest can be interpreted along pagan-Christian lines; in a situation where marrying out (exogamy) posed a danger to the entire religious community, incest might be a symbolic representation of marrying within the group (endogamy). Significantly, the incest theme is found in several Ibsen plays: for example, *Rosmersholm* and *Lille Eyolf*.

However the incest is interpreted, the "Rosmer" ballad is especially interesting because it exemplifies both the nature-culture schism (Rosmer vs. Svanelille and the brother), the male-female schism (Svanelille vs. her brother), and the pagan-Christian schism (Rosmer vs. Svanenille and her brother). One reason that Ibsen focused attention on this ballad may be that he was interested in all of those oppositions.

Briefly recapitulated: the ballads that have been the objects of analysis all share the features of being telescoped rites of passage and being about (male) control of female sexuality.[63]

The Corresponding Male Ballads

There is a group of ballads that deal with *males* who are lured by demons. This group contains the following ballads: *DgF* 43, "Hr. Luno og Havfruen" ("Sir Luno and the Mermaid"); *DgF* 44, "Hr. Hylleland henter sin Jomfru" ("Sir Hylleland Gets His Maiden"); *DgF* 45, "Hr. Bøsmer i Elvehjem" ("Sir Bøsmer in Elf Home"); *DgF* 46 "Elvehøj" ("Elf Hill"); *DgF* 47, "Elveskud" ("Elfshot"); *DgF* 48, "Hr. Magnus og Bjærgtrolden" ("Sir Magnus and the Mountain Troll"). In all of these we are told of a young man who comes in contact with a female demon, be it a mermaid, an elf, or a troll. In all but one ballad the young man successfully or fatally counters the demon.

Briefly, the stories of the ballads are as follows: In "Sir Luno" the mermaid is tied to a stone by the use of runes; in "Sir Hylleland" the troll, who is a girl who has been changed into a virtual vagina dentata, is saved and released by her fiancé.[64] In "Sir Bøsmer," we are dealing with the sole example of a male who is effectively lured by elves. This young man dreams of beautiful elf girls and goes, against warnings, to meet them. He drinks a "spiked" glass of wine and forgets his human identity. I shall return to this ballad below. In "Elvehøj," a young man on the way to his wedding falls asleep on a hill in the woods. He wakes up to find himself surrounded by beautiful elf maidens who invite him to join in. He refuses, they offer him drink and gifts.[65] Again he refuses. He is finally saved by invoking the name of Jesus or by the first rays of morning sun. The young man in "Elveskud" is similarly enticed but flatly refuses to give in to the elf maidens stating that he is faithful to his fiancée. The elves give him a deadly disease, and he barely manages to ride home, where he dies. "Sir Magnus and the Mountain Troll" is an ironic ballad. A female is wooing a young, handsome knight, promising him all kinds of wonderful things. Finally he answers,

> if you were like other women:
> but you are so vile a Mountain Troll,
> as one might in the mountain find.

She hangs on to his horse as he wants to ride on, and he chops her to mincemeat with his sword. Then he rides off.

Without getting into a major analysis I want to point to the fact that these ballads are virtual opposites of the corresponding ballads involving women. The men, with one exception, either control the demon or are of so strong faith—that is, are so securely part of Christian culture—that they can escape the clutches of demonic nature. When the man does not escape, as in "Elveskud," he at least rejects the advances of the elves by referring to his fiancée, a pattern we never find in the "female" ballads, where the fiancé is but one of a number of obstacles on her way to freedom. Again, only one of the "male" ballads tells the story of a young man who gives in to the demons. Hr. Bøsmer dreams of the elf girls and rides out to find them. When he does he accepts a drink from them and forgets his identity as a human man, he identifies himself, upon being asked by the elves, as an elf and one of the elf maidens as his fiancée. In other words, Hr. Bøsmer is the equivalent of the female victims of demons. The difference, of course, is that he is actively going out to find the beautiful woman he has dreamt of. His actions are deliberate and focused; he is not just standing around waiting for something to happen. He is looking for sexual gratification even if he knows it may destroy him. The ballad about Sir Bøsmer brings out the point that the crucial aspect of contacts with the *huldrer* or elves is not to eat, drink or participate in their dance. If you do any of those things you are lost, you become "what you eat."[66]

Male sexuality is what makes men seek women (representatives of nature with all its attendant evils and dangers). For this reason women, as representatives of nature, have to be enculturated; they have to submit to culture and to male control of their sexuality and procreative powers. The goal is, of course, to give men a sexual outlet inside culture: marriage solves the problem in that it locks women into culture and submits them to Christian (i.e., patriarchal) rule.

An attendant aspect of this is that men, if they have sex with women who are not "in culture," are entering the realm of nature and become subject to its rules. They can lose themselves. So, the male ballads are a warning to young men not to stray from the flock: everything they need is in their own sphere; they do not have to venture onto nature's turf. It is interesting to note that also the female ballads are about male sexuality: women are told that they are best off submitting to the rules of patriarchy and to male desire, since they at least have their religion, their children, and their family if they marry the man their father has chosen for them. When we look at Norwegian *huldre* stories, which we shall in some detail below, it becomes even more obvious how different the patterns for men and women are: women who get involved with *huldre* men become *huldrer* and are lost to human society, but *huldre* women who are attracted to human men can go through the marriage ceremony in church and become like other human women. They even lose their tail when they become Christians.

Men are never rescued in the Danish ballads, nor in stories or myths: they are either lost forever or free themselves through their willpower and strength, whereas women in some cases are rescued by males ("Rosmer," "Harp"). That men cannot be rescued suggests that a man's choice is his own and, unlike a woman's, irreversible. That males can free themselves suggests both greater resistance and the fact that men are naturally closer to culture (pun intended); they do, after all, carry the "phallic signifier."

Notes

1. Piø 1985: 149.
2. Ibid.: 140–41.

Marginal Maidens: The Image of Women in the Ballads

3. The story of Agnete and her sad merman is recorded also in a Jutlandish—from Frisenborg Gods, near Aarhus—popular legend (*folkesagn*). Thiele (1843–60: 259–61) has a story called "Havmandens Klage" ("The Merman's Lament"). The girl's name is Grethe. One day as she is at the beach collecting sand in her apron, a merman gets out of the water. He has a green beard and a handsome figure. He promises the poor girl as much silver as she can ever desire. She accepts, and he takes her by the hand and leads her to the bottom of the sea. They have five children. She hears the church bells and wants to visit family and church. He lets her. When she does not return he calls her name and reminds her of the children who long for her, three times,

and since she still didn't come he began to cry and returned to the bottom of the sea. But Grethe stayed from that time on with her parents and let the merman look after the miserable little children himself, and often his weeping and his cries of woe can be heard from the depths. (260–61)

4. Piø 1985: 221.

5. In Scandinavian folk belief, a *nøkke*, or *nix*, is a water spirit living in rivers and brooks. Faye describes the *nøkke*:

This water troll lives mostly in rivers and lakes, sometimes also in fjords. Annually he wants a human sacrifice which is why you also hear that in any river or water where a Nøk lives, annually at least one human disappears. When one is to drown the nøkke can be heard to yell in a hollow and frightful voice, "cross." . . . he can change himself to all kinds of things, now to a half a boat in the water or a half a horse on the beach, now to gold and precious stones. If you touch these the nøkke gets power over you. (Faye 1948: 49)

Since we have instances of women being freed by the "magic of harps," I quote also what Faye says about the *grim* or *fossegrim*,

Related to Nøkken is the musical Grim or Fossegrim, a being that lives around runs and rivulets. He plays, especially on quiet and dark evenings, to lure people to come to him and he teaches those to play the violin and other stringed instruments who on a Thursday evening with their heads turned away offer him a white kid which is thrown into a run going north. If the victim is meagre the student cannot bring it further than to tune his violin, but if it is fat the Fossegrim takes the right hand of the musician and leads it back and forth until the blood flows from each fingertip. Now the apprentice is an expert and can play so uniquely well that the trees dance and the runs stop running. (1948:54–55)

Two points emerge: (1) the *nøkke* is accustomed to an annual victim (shades of "Harp" and the sisters who have been taken); apparently the *nøkke* is extracting a toll, as mentioned above, for letting people cross; (2) the ability to play magically is derived from the troll himself. I remind the reader of my discussion of the runes in connection with "Hr. Luno og Havruen." Note also the similarity of the effects of playing to what the fiancé effects with his playing in "Harp."

6. Again that strange expression, noted above in my discussion of "Trolden og Bondens Hustru."

7. *Suan* means "woman": she is woman in general. She has, incidentally, different names in different versions.

8. The Danish word is *manddom*, which means "masculinity," "male nature," but also "penis." If penis is meant, we are reminded of Saint Augustine's version—as discussed by Michel Foucault—of the punishment for Adam's transgression: loss of control of the male limb.

9. To the ship in A, to terra firma in the other versions, which are set under the sea.

10. This may be an indication that Christians believed or imagined, as a sexual fantasy perhaps, that pagans were given to all manner of "polymorphous perversity."

11. Piø 1985: 45.

12. That is, they occur as an *active* category: they do things to save the maid. Sometimes they are just part of the list of all the things the maid is losing in going with the demon. In "Harp" there are from two to five sisters, but they simply duplicate the maid herself: they are just "statistics."

13. This is actually not true of "Rosmer," but I shall argue below that "Rosmer" is not really one of "my" ballads. It is not a ballad about the maid—the protagonist is her brother.

14. Sørensen 1959: 201.

15. Ibid.: 165.

16. Ibid.: 168.

17. Ibid.: 170.

18. Mossin 1974.

19. He touches on this point in passing. He does not spell out the projection of nature onto the demonic as I do above.

20. Mossin 1974: 36.

21. Actually Mossin does not spell this out, but one must infer it, otherwise the analysis makes no sense.

22. Mossin 1974: 44.

23. Sherry Ortner discusses this in her paper "Is Female to Male as Nature Is to Culture?" (1972).

24. See Victor Turner 1969, esp. ch. 3, "Liminality and Communitas."

25. The notion of "dreamtime," widespread in Australian aboriginal religions, is similar to this. See Duerr 1985.

26. I go into this society, as discussed by the anthropologist Edwin Ardener, in greater detail below.

27. Ardener 1975: 9.

28. Ibid.: 9–10.

29. There is also a strong similarity between this process and exorcism: a spirit is driven out of the individual after a degree of familiarization has taken place.

30. As I have demonstrated in Chapter 2; see note 27 to that chapter.

31. "Hellig Olav" ("Holy Olav"), mentioned above. Olav turns the troll into rock. In the Danish ballad "Elverhøj," the young man escapes the elfin maidens only by mentioning the name of God.

32. It does not matter much if there actually was a historical period when Christianity and paganism were "at loggerheads," although I cannot imagine that conversion was instant and without animosity. The point is that the folklore abounds with examples that suggest such a stage. In other words, whoever wrote the tales and ballads was convinced thare had been a period of religious competition.

33. Child 1965: 373.

34. In the ballads this is often symbolized by equating young women with wealth. They are weighed down with gold and silver; they have lush, golden hair; when they are asked what they got in return for their virtue, the answer is always that they got gold, silver, and silk: the kinds of items a young girl would receive in connection with marriage.

35. I have already established that the majority of instances of people who were abducted or stolen or lured were women, thus the central arguments of both Sørensen and Mossin are, at best, tenuous. See page oo in Chapter 1 and note 21 to that chapter.

36. 1910: 52.

37. Kierkegaard 1982: 87.

38. The importance of the forest as marginal and dangerous space for humans is pointed out also by Hayden White (1972).

39. Henningsen 1980.

40. Piø 1985: 140–41.

41. Bascomb 1980.

42. Ortner 1972: 73. Ortner's question is of course polemical. Several works that have been published since take issue with her equations. Among the most notable are the volume edited by MacCormack and Strathern (1980), in which a number of ethnographic counterexamples are described and discussed, and Kapferer (1983), esp. ch. 5, "Exorcisms and the Symbolic Identity of Women," where the complexity of the issue is demonstrated (92–111).

43. A more interesting and intelligent theory of a prehierarchical stage is hypothesized by the anthropologist Cucchiari (1981), who tries to come to grips with the emergence of hierarchy and universal male dominance. His point is that for a hierarchy to emerge there has to be a previous nonhierarchical stage. This stage, he speculates, must have been pregender, genitofugal, and even prekinship in terms of principles of social organization. The paper is highly speculative but also both thought-provoking and well-argued.

44. Ardener 1975: 6.

45. Ibid.: 6.

46. Ibid.: 5–7.

47. Ibid.: 9.

48. There is actually a whole group of rituals that differ slightly in form but are similar in content.

49. *Liengu* is the Bakweri word for "water spirit" and for "mermaid." Women have a *"liengu* society," with a secret language.

50. 1970: 174–90.

51. Ibid.: 181–82. Two excellent works that unfortunately came to my attention too late to be incorporated into my argument make much the same point with regard to women in patriarchal society. Burmeister et al. (1987) is a good account of the lives of peasant women in the nineteenth century, and the first few chapters of volume 1 of Berg, Frost, and Olsen, eds. (1984), reinforce this. Both books are highly recommended as attempts at writing history where the focus is on women.

52. Leavy, unpublished manuscript.

53. Ibid.

54. Ibid. Leavy and I reached our conclusions concerning the ballads and the star husband tales independently. Leavy suggested that I read her material on the Indian tales after reading an early draft of the present chapter.

55. Especially in societies where the entire cosmos revolves around the opposed but complementary principles of male and female, adherence to gender roles and the concomitant social obligations and expectations are of crucial importance, because a break would mean an act of rebellion against the cosmological order. Ibsen uses this theme quite often, but most clearly in *De unges forbund*. I refer to a relevant passage from this play in my analysis of *Rosmersholm* below.

In traditional societies it is incumbent on parents, as part of the enculturation process, to impress on the young their expected roles. Almost the only time an individual is seriously outside the cosmological order is the period of adolescence. This period is also traditionally the time when revolt against a perceived rigid order is expressed. The revolt can be expected to be both more vehement and more dangerous among those who give up most by submitting to the gender pattern and the (patriarchal) order—namely, women. The revolt of women is dangerous because they are the ones upon whom the continuation of society depends. They are the ones who "create" new individuals to step into social roles.

The whole idea of sexual complementarity is discussed in an interesting and provocative way by the German sociologist Ivan Illich (1982). His point is that with complementarity comes also a strong gender identity, a strong social identity. Because we have been obliterating the gender boundaries in our modern industrialized societies, we have done away with *gender* and are left only with *sexes*. The result is that we today find many people who have problems with their (gender) identities.

56. This is, of course, a male myth: culture, such as it is, is a joint creation.

57. I made this point in Chapter 2; see note 24 to that chapter and the surrounding text. This is, incidentally, a symbol that Ibsen, interested as he was

in the artist and the role of the artist, did not miss. Harps are ubiquitous symbols of art and artists in his plays—for example, in *Gildet på Solhaug*.

58. Kristensen (1931, vol. 2: 179) tells a similar story of a woman who was stolen while attending service in the church. Her husband rides out to get her back. He finds her at the elf hill dancing among the elves with her hair loose. He rides right into the throng of elves and gets her on his horse. The elves pursue, but the humans manage to escape by riding along cultivated fields.

59. Ringing the church bells could bring back people stolen by *huldrer* and *vætter*, types of supernaturals that are similar to elves and *huldrer*. This happens in many stories in the collections of Faye (1948). Feilberg makes the point quite clearly: "What people did immediately when the accident [a person being stolen by trolls] had happened was to ring the church bells" (1910: 58). This was most effective if the church bell was taken to the place where the person had disappeared and the bell then rung for three Thursdays in a row. A number of stories emphasize that it is crucial to ring the bells for a long, long time.

60. There are several other Danish versions of this ballad, such as "Rigmor and Guldborg" and "Den Kloge Pige." A full listing of versions in other languages can be found in Nygard, 1958.

61. Grundtvig 1846: 201.

62. Child 1915: 55.

63. The question of how the audience came to understand the symbolism in the ballads cannot be addressed here, but recent work in psychology concerning the collective social unconscious might give a clue in this regard. For the interested reader, I refer to an excellent article by Daniel Burston (1984).

64. The story is very similar to the Zuñi story of the virgin with the toothed vagina, who is also released from her predicament. We can assume that the Danish ballad serves the same purpose as the Indian: overcoming male fears of female sexuality. It is known from the work of Wendy Doniger O'Flaherty that toothed vaginas are symbolic of the clitoris, the "dangerous" part of female sexual anatomy, which makes demands on men and puts male virility and sexual performance in question. See O'Flaherty 1980.

65. How and when you meet the elves or *huldre* is an interesting issue. Feilberg (1910: 37) mentions that you are especially open to attack when you take a nap at noon in the woods, "especially sleeping in the midday hours is dangerous that is when the elf people appear." It is interesting that sleeping should be so dangerous, especially sleeping in the woods. The reason may be that there was an attendant belief that the soul leaves the body during sleep. (See Qvigstad 1927, vol. 2: #85, "The Human Soul Has the Shape of a Bumblebee"; the story tells of two men who sleep in the woods. One's soul, in the shape of a bumblebee goes on a little excursion in the woods.) The soul is like the demons (indeed, it becomes a demon after death; see Qvigstad's stories about *Dauinger*, "ghosts," in the volume already cited), and thus it can easily consort with them. Feilberg makes this point in connection with a discussion of some Icelandic stories: while the body is asleep, "its ghost is spending the time in elf-home." This has a

97

Freudian ring: in sleep the unconscious percolates up into consciousness in the form of dreams. Dreams have a culturally determined content, that is, the types of creatures that populate your dreams are culturally and socially determined. Woods are places where *huldre* and other demons live, so if you are sleeping in the woods, the chances are that you will dream of them. If we think of my analysis of the dwarf and the knight who meet in the woods in "Dwarf," it becomes obvious that sleeping and dreaming in the woods add up to a freedom from culturally determined constraints: you can dream dreams where you are free, sexually free and free from social expectations and duties. Sure enough, what men typically see in the woods, as they are taking a nap and opening the doors to the unconscious, is described by Feilberg: "In a group of these myths . . . it is the wonderful singing and their seductive dance that attract" (1910: 29). Feilberg adds that the elf women often dance their victims to death. If we read this with our Freudian glasses on, we can say that the man dreams of having sexual intercourse with elves (who are not subject to the kinds of constraints human women have, who are like women in pornography, always willing and always seductive). Freud (1966: 157) equates dreaming of dancing and other rythmic activities with dreaming of sexual intercourse; the superego, meanwhile, impresses on the man that he will "die" if he does what his libido would like. This death would be a social death: he would have no place in society, would become invisible, as the one man who gives in to the elves does: he drinks of their cup and loses his memory of who he is, becoming crazy or persona non grata.

66. Langset (1948, #24: 67) tells a story of a woman who is washing cups in the river. A silver spoon comes floating along; she takes it. Then other silver items, including a wedding crown, come floating; she takes them too. A demon (*nøkke?*) comes and says that since she has taken the silver, she now belongs to him. Only by using cunning does she—barely—escape him. Feilberg states, "If you take gifts from an unmarried *huldre* you will never escape her again" (1910: 33). Eating *huldre* food also binds you. Solheim (1952: 476) tells the story of a young girl who was taken by the *huldrer* and kept among them for five days. Among the things they did to tie her to them forever was to entice her to eat, which she refused, leading to her eventual escape.

CHAPTER 4

Ibsen and the Ballads

The Danish Romantics

Born in 1828, Henrik Ibsen was a child of the romantic period and his work—even of his later, realistic plays—gives evidence to this fact. As Leavy points out, Ibsen kept reiterating the same basic themes, redistributing light and shade and focus. An important influence on Ibsen when he was a young man was the Danish romantic movement, especially the influential Johan Ludvig Heiberg, on whom I have written elsewhere.[1] The Danish romantics, with Heiberg as their theorist and most eloquent spokesperson, held that it was incumbent on writers to create a truly national literature. To accomplish this they had to find ways in which the national soul had expressed itself that could be transformed into literature.

For the Scandinavian countries this was relatively easy: there was a store of ancient myths and ballads that were "the soul of the people"— neatly laid out in rhymed stanzas and populated with ready-made colorful and mysterious beings—at least, that is what the romantics believed. For a while there was some disagreement as to whether the sagas and the stories from Nordic mythology or the ballads were better fitted as material upon which to draw. Heiberg made the final judgment: the ballads, because they were inherently poetic and not as dry and terse as the sagas, constituted a better foundation upon which to build the house of a national drama.[2]

Ibsen's earliest dramatic attempts were heavily influenced by Heiberg and by other Danish romantic writers; thus Ibsen's early—and not very successful—play *Kjæmpehøien*[3] was modeled after Heiberg's equally bad *Elverhøj*, which, however, has stayed in the repertory of the Danish

Royal Theatre. Halvdan Koht says in his introduction to *Brand*[4] that among the models for this play was the Danish poet Paludan-Müller's epic poem *Adam Homo*. *Peer Gynt* has among its literary models other poems by the same Danish writer, and the novel *Phantasterne* by Hans Egede-Schack[5] and Heiberg's epic pome—and best literary effort—*En Sjæl efter Døden*, ("A Soul After Death"). And the list goes on. It may have been to Ibsen's advantage that he, after a negative review from Heiberg, moved somewhat away from this Danish arbiter of taste and started forging his own literary style. Despite this, he remained interested in the thematic material that had inspired him in his earliest plays.

Before moving into an analysis of Ibsen's use of folklore let us look at how the Danish romantics used it. Almost every Danish writer in the nineteenth century wrote material based on the ballads. Interestingly, the group of ballads that inspired Ibsen, the *trylleviser*, were also the primary source for the Danish romantics. This may seem curious, but on closer examination it becomes intelligible.

The romantic writer was distinguished from writers of earlier ages by being conscious of himself as an artist. He was not reduced to a public servant teaching received wisdom and manners to the young, nor was he any longer the public relations man of the monarchy. He was something unto himself with an agenda of his own to be created—and he was different. He was visible as an outsider both to himself and to society. His major concern became defining his own role vis-à-vis the society out of which he came, to which he addressed his literary products, but from which he also felt estranged. He too was both of bourgeois society and a stranger in it. He was, in other words, marginal.

All of the *trylleviser* analyzed in the previous chapter deal with individuals who are marginal. They are caught between the social sphere (patriarchal Christian society) and the natural sphere (the demons and abysses beyond society). Their situation is a good metaphor for that of the romantic artist, caught between culture, embodied as bourgeois society, and the creative and antisocial urge within. The artist is Agnete, Liten Kjersti, Hillelille, or whatever her name may be: the artist wanders in solitude in society's marginal outskirts. If he gives in to society's demands he becomes himself a bourgeois and his creativity is gone: he is condemned to live a life of boredom, constrained and captured in an ordinary job and an ordinary marriage. If he gives in to his creative urge he may be destroyed by his own creative demons. He will be forever an outsider both in the cultural sphere and in his own demonic sphere. The only thing that will survive is the offspring produced by the marriage of the human soul to the demonic: his artistic output. In this he is again like Agnete: she too perishes in the interface between the cultural and the demonic, leaving behind only her children, half human, half demonic.

One of the best literary expressions of the romantic dilemma is Ibsen's *På viddene*. In this long poem is chronicled a romance between a young man and woman living in a Norwegian valley. He embarks on a quest for "vision" and for manhood, metaphorically described as a hunting trip to the mountains. He meets a mysterious stranger—who can be interpreted as death—who helps him quell his longing for home and hearth. He yearns for his mother and his beloved and for the warmth and coziness of the fireplace. But he must fight these longings in himself, he must become steeled to the loneliness and the dangers of life alone in the mountains. In the last three stanzas he has achieved his goal. (I quote the original Norwegian here because the energy and power of the poem are hard to capture in English. I provide a literal translation in the note with the reference.)

> Den siste styrkende saft jeg drakk;
> ei lenger på vidden jeg fryser;
> mitt seil gikk under, mit livstre knakk,
> men se hvor smukt hennes røde stakk
> mellem birkestammerne lyser.
>
> Det går i galopp, men se, der blev
> de borte i kirkesvingen.
> Mitt veneste minne, i lykke lev!
> Nu bytter jeg bort mitt siste stev
> for et høyere syn på tingen.
>
> Nu er jeg stålsatt, og jeg føler det bud
> der byder i høyden å vandre!
> Mitt lavlandsliv har jeg levet ud;
> her oppe på vidden er frihet og Gud,
> der nede famler de andre.[6]

The similarity of this poem to the pattern described above is obvious. It is about the role and fate of the artist. The theme repeated over and over in Ibsen, in *Love's Comedy*, in *Olaf Liljekrans*, and in his last five plays, most strikingly and starkly, perhaps, in *When We Dead Awaken*.

The Danish literary output inspired by the *trylleviser* displays varying degrees of originality and talent. To give an idea of how pervasive the influence of the folklore was, I list some *tryllevise*-inspired works by Danish romantic writers: Adam Oehlenschläger's *Agnete, Bjergtrolden* (*The Mountain Troll*), and *Rosmer Havmand* (*Rosmer Merman*); Jens Baggesen's play *Trylleharpen* (*The Magic Harp*) and his poem "Agnete fra Holmegaard"; Emil Aarestrup's "Flodpigens Sang ("Song of the River Maid"); Christian Hauch's "Den Bjergtagne" ("The Girl in the Mountain") and "Bjergpigen" ("The Mountain Girl"). And there is Hans Christian Andersen's famous story of "The Little Mermaid" who longs to be united with her beloved, a human man, and to achieve a soul. It is, perhaps, less well known that Andersen also wrote a play entitled *Agnete og Havmanden*.[7] The title is, as will be recognized, that of one of the *trylleviser*. I shall discuss this particular play later on in this chapter in connection with Ibsen's *Lady from the Sea*. The list can be extended ad infinitum.[8]

To see how similar, thematically, the Danish works were to Ibsen, let us look a little closer at two of the works mentioned above. Baggesen's "Agnete fra Holmegaard" ("Agnete from Holmegaard") is, of course, a version of the "Agnete" ballad. This Agnete is, when we and the merman meet her, already married and has two young daughters, but she is always alone, "she had no peace—no peace / she made others happy / but she was never happy." She is staring into the waves when the merman emerges. He promises her gold and riches. She accepts but not because she is attracted to the gold and glitter, nor because she per se is attracted to him,

She is attracted to the reflection of the sky, the heavens that she sees in the sea. This Agnete is the romantic artist, forever a stranger in bourgeois society, doomed to feel outside, *verfremdet*, alone. The artist sees and yearns towards an ideal—a platonic ideal—a world of beauty and perfection. In the ballad this is symbolized by the heavens reflecting in the sea. Agnete diving with the merman to the bottom of the sea is the artist giving in to his own nature that demands of him that he abandon materialism and social constraints to free his creativity.[9]

This Agnete lives happily with her husband-merman on the bottom of the sea and has two sons by him. But like the Agnete of the ballad she wants, after some years have passed, to go back to see her family and go to church. She meets her mother. The mother begs her to come back to stay, but no, Agnete loves her merman and her two little sons more than anything else. She loves her sons by the merman more than her daughters by the human. "The sons are the product of the 'artist's' descent into the realm of the demonic and thus closer to her heart and more innately valuable than the products of a merely human union."[10] In the end she is destroyed, of course; as she stands by her mother's grave her blood freezes. She staggers and she dies as the artist must, forever torn between two realms. "Now they long for her both here and there."

In Emil Aarestrup's very original "Flodpigens Vise" ("The Song of the River Maid"), a mermaid tells her own story, "of sitting quietly at home when she heard distant sweet tones of a cither. The music beckoned her. She ran through the bowels of the earth to get to the river grotto where a youth was singing and playing. He seduced her and left her, 'I sat alone and left behind again.'" Aarestrup turns the usual story on its head: the human seduces the child of nature, the mermaid. "She becomes the beauty of nature infused with soulful love and then deserted— to become the beautiful but sad poem the reader has before him or her. She has been lured out of her natural element and is stranded in liminal space—the river grotto—to be seen and admired but forever alone."[11]

The Danish *trylleviser*, incidentally, served as an inspiration not only for Scandinavian writers; Matthew Arnold drew upon them too for his "The Forsaken Merman"—our own book, of course, owes its title to that poem—and for "The Neckan."[12] The extent to which these ballads served as a ubiquitous inspiration to the romantics shows how powerful their imagery was to this period and helps us understand Ibsen's ongoing infatuation with and use of them as a storechamber of themes and characters.

An interesting and very different treatment of the ballad material is Kierkegaard's. In his *Frygt og Bæven*,[13] (*Fear and Trembling*), Kierkegaard discusses the "Agnete and the Merman" theme to reach an understanding of what he 'calls the "demonic." In general, Kierkegaard struggles to gain an understanding of the biblical myth of Abraham and Isaac. He is concerned with understanding the core of the sacrifice of Isaac on the mountain. The core is of course that Abraham's behavior is inexplicable—logically inexplicable. What makes Abraham special is his deep belief in "the absurd": his uncompromising and unfaltering belief in God. Kierkegaard grapples with the problem of how to apply Abraham's understanding to himself—he endeavors to understand so he too can believe in "the absurd." As a help toward understanding the nature of innocence, of guilt, and of "the demonic"—for Kierkegaard a state of "hiding" from having to face reality and its choices—he enters into a discussion of the Agnete ballad. Kierkegaard's reading will be a major interpretive tool in my reading of *Rosmersholm,* and I therefore defer further discussion for now.

The Early Ibsen Plays

Ibsen's early plays are very consciously and demonstratively inspired by Nordic folklore. This is both uncontroversial and often commented upon. In the introduction to *Olaf Liljekrans,* Francis Bull says,

> When, in actuality, Ibsen has given his play the name of the ballad of Olaf Liljekrans, it probably has to do with the fact that some of its central themes reverberate in Olaf's dream and in the imaginings of Alfhild and with the fact that many stanzas and verse lines from the ballad show up almost verbatim in the play. Also several other ballads that Ibsen knew from Landstad's collection have made an imprint on "Olaf Liljekrans."[14]

The passage is clear enough in its acknowledgment of Ibsen's interest in and use of folklore, but begs further comments as to how deeply the earliest plays are indebted to folklore and as to what Ibsen's major sources of folklore were: First, there are many more and more important features of the ballad in *Olaf Liljekrans* than Bull lists. I sometimes have the impression that he did not know the ballads well or that he missed themes because he assumed Ibsen knew only the Norwegian ballads. For instance, the entire start of the play is the story the *tryllevise* "Elveskud": Olaf's mother and the men from her farm are searching in the mountains for Olaf who has disappeared on his way home from a visit to his bride-to-be in the adjacent valley. As a result he is late for his wedding. When the mother meets the wedding party of the bride, she answers to the question about Olaf's whereabouts that he is out hunting. This is exactly the story of the ballad. As in the ballad he has been wayled by elves—or at least he thinks Alfhild is an elf. He believes this so strongly that he claims to have lost memory of anything that happened before—again, exactly the story of the ballad.[15]

Second, I agree with Maurice Gravier when he says that Ibsen was influenced by the Danish ballads more than the Norwegian ones.

An excellent collection of ballads had been published in 1853, those by Landstad (*Norske Folkeviser*). In the preface to the second edition of the plays, Ibsen notes he has very closely read the ballads in this book. What he did not say, but what seems highly likely to whoever has read *Festin de Solhaug* and the following drama, *Olaf Liljekrans;* he had also assiduously studied the collection of Danish ballads. Through the linguistic style, citations, and style of the ballads that one can uncover in these two plays, it is clear that they were closer to the Danish model than the Norwegian. The latter seems much more the *gammelnorsk* than the dialect of Telemark. They would not have been so easily accepted by the urban Norwegians at this time.[16]

It is, in fact, more than likely that Ibsen knew and drew upon the Danish ballads: he must have known them. He uses expressions and story bits that simply are not found in the volumes published by Landstad but that are available in the Danish collection by Grundtvig (and in collections Grundtvig used that Ibsen may have known). Further, as I have already pointed out in the previous chapter, the Norwegian ballads are more often than not derived from the corresponding Danish ones.

For Ibsen, as for the Danish romantics, the value of the ballads was that they provided material that could be used to bring out the inherent conflict between a stifling bourgeois order and a dynamic, natural, and demonic creative urge. This relationship between the artistic and demonic takes different shapes in the oeuvre of Ibsen. Below are the two main guises of the demon vis-à-vis creativity.

1. The artist is the demon who has a pent-up natural force inside him. The woman who loves him provides him with a soul. She also, somehow, embodies a secret of "creation." Often she has to sacrifice her

own ability to create (have children) for his. She transfers her creative ability to him. It is almost a reverse copulation image: she "injects" soul into him, and he carries "the child."

The artist—sometimes the woman—is a praying mantis who, after copulation, after the creative act, eats his mate. It is not always quite clear who is the seducer and who the seduced: *Olaf Liljekrans, Gildet på Solhaug, Rosmersholm.*

2. The artist is "Agnete" who needs the infusion of the demonic to become creative. The artist, like Agnete has to let go of the social moorings and live outside bourgeois society. The demonic seems sometimes to be both inside and outside the individual as in the "Dwarf" ballad, where the maid's moral conflict is projected onto the dwarf and the knight vying for her "soul" in the dark woods of her subconscious.

Ibsen and the *Huldre*

No discussion of Ibsen and folklore would be complete without dealing with this, the most Norwegian of demons, with whom he had a lifelong— at times strained—relationship.

The reason I give more space to the ballads than to the *huldre* lore in this book is that the former provide a story pattern and a gallery of characters, whereas the *huldre* comes to Ibsen alone, a psychological configuration, at once beautiful and disgusting (the tail), seductive and dangerous, an aboriginal creature who holds the promise of being humanized. Ibsen's *huldre* is animal nature, a projection of the artist's soul whose beauty he likes to show off while desperately trying to keep her hairy tail hidden under her dress. The object of this short section is to introduce the *huldre* as she emerges from the folklore and to follow her trail through Ibsen's plays.

An old fairy tale tells that this is how the huldre-people came to be: once Our Lord was out for a walk and he went into Eve's house to rest up a bit. When Eve saw him, she was just washing her kids. Some were clean and neat but others were still dirty and unkempt. These latter Eve took into the woods and hid them. So, when Our Lord entered, the children ran up to him and he took them on his lap and played with them and they were very happy. But then he asked Eve if she didn't have more children. She denied this. Then Our Lord became angry and said:

"Alle som er dulde
skal verte hulde,"

["all who are hidden / shall be huldrer,"] and then he left. When Eve looked for the children in the woods they had become so strangely different and troll-like with long tails and ugly snouts and so bad that she did not know what to do with them and she had to chase them out into the woods. From these all huldre-people descend.[17]

Huldrer are often described as beautiful but that is a false appearance. Mostly it is the young huldre girl who is so lovely with brown, shiny hair, blue eyes and as rosy-red a tiny mouth as you could wish. She is dressed in blue with silver threads, rings and adornments like a princess and she is pleasant and refined in all her manner. And many are the young guys she has lured into her snare so that their minds were entrapped by her kindness. But just as soon did they find her disgusting as they discovered the long, hanging tail that she for the longest time had endeavored to keep hidden.[18]

The above description of the *huldre* is typical and brings out some of her basic characteristcs. Faye describes her in the following way, adding some further *huldre* traits,

In the various parts of the country are found myths about a supernatural being who lives in the woods and mountains and is called "Huldra." This creature looks like a beautiful woman. Ordinarily she is dressed in a white dress and a white shawl but she also has a long cow- or fox-tail, which she, however, can let hang down or pull up as she pleases. When she is amongst humans, whose company she seeks, she hides her long tail carefully. She is especially fond of young and handsome men with whom she likes to dance.[19]

Huldrer are part animal with their long tails, but they were once humans and are forever attracted to the human sphere. To this can be added that it is said that *huldrer* always are sad because they have no God.[20] Having no God is the same as having no immortal soul. Perhaps the *huldrer*, like the demons of the ballads, are attracted to humans, in part because they want to become human again and get a soul, literally or symbolically. Often *huldrer* marry human men,

> Marriage between Christian men and *huldrer* are recorded in many fairy tales and myths; but then the huldre always loses her tail when she stands before the altar. It is worse for a Christian girl who marries a huldre man—she becomes a huldre and has to live in the mountain and never see God's lovely sun or day again.[21]

The marriage between a *huldre* and a human man is not vastly different from any other marriage, except for two things: the *huldre* woman often retains certain quirks, such as, for instance, sudden desires to cook and eat her own children, and she is enormously strong, as is demonstrated when the husband mistreats her: suddenly the wife will bend an iron bar or straighten out a horseshoe when she has had abuse enough. After this incident peace and quiet—plus mutual respect—is restored. The woman will only show her strength when pushed to the limits, her basic attitude being that she, as a woman, has to be obedient and subservient to her husband.[22] Leavy explores these themes in her analysis of *Hedda Gabler*.

The *huldre* in folklore, then, is beautiful, seductive, fond of dancing, and attracted to human men. She desires a soul and is willing to marry a man and be a subservient wife as long as she is not mistreated too badly. But she has the power and strength and passion of nature in her even after her tail is gone. In a word, she is both desirable and dangerous.

Ibsen who, like so many of his contemporaries, was searching for the eminently national to inscribe in his works, used the *huldre* as a positive symbol in the early plays. In *Gildet på Solhaug*, Gudmund Alfsøn says to Signe,

> I must laugh when I remember how often I have
> thought of you as I then carried
> you on my arm. Then you were a child
> now you are a *huldre* who bewitches and plays games.
> *Signe:* Yes, beware! If you make the huldre angry,—
> watch out,—she'll catch you and entrap you!
> *Gudmund:* I feel as if that already has happened.[23]

Despite her threats this *huldre* has no tail; she is only desirable, not dangerous. She is a symbol of the national, the pure, and the strong and beautiful soul of Norway.

In *Olaf Liljekrans*, Olaf tells of meeting Alfhild, in terms that suggest the huldre:

> My head was heavy, my soul tired,
> I longed to sleep awhile.
> I lay me down by the linden's root
> in the lovely, whispering groves
>
> • • • • • • •
>
> Then I was in the dance of the elfin women
> the most beautiful of them offered me a wreath
> of blue bells and waterlillies white,
> she looked into my soul with gentle eyes . . .[24]

Alfhild is here described as an elf, but elves and *huldrer* are interchangeable. This "elf" is dangerous only to Olaf's peace of mind, there is no hidden animal with sex and destruction on her mind. Alfhild is just a nice and normal Norwegian girl who has had an overdose of folklore as a child. In the early Ibsen plays *huldrer* are only desirable, not dangerous.

The plays in which the *huldre* is a positive and innocuous symbol of the pure and national are also the ones written while Ibsen was still unambiguously proud to be a Norwegian. Later on he began to have doubts about Norway that were reflected in his use of the *huldre*. He looked upon the artist who tries to find his (national) soul in folklore with contempt. In *Sancthansnatten* Ibsen used the *huldre* to playful and bitingly satiric effect. Julian Poulsen is an early and wild parody of the idealists of the later plays (Young Ekdal in *Vildanden*, to mention one). He characterizes himself as "dark and wild" and is a budding poet who is looking for his origins. He finds those origins expressed in the demonic creatures of yore,

> *Poulsen:* I, for my part, see pixies, little people and such
> as symbolic conceptions with which the good brains in the
> old times expressed those ideas which could not be given

the right scientific names. You see, that's how nature becomes so interesting—so philosophically profound.[25]

Poulsen, seeking the national, fell in love, as he says, with the *huldre.* "I loved her, I was happy in my love; I read our poets and found in them constantly new nourishment for my national passion."[26] He discovers, however, to his horror a feature in his love that abruptly puts an end to the "affair":

I discovered that the huldre had—had—a tail! . . . I can't describe my suffering; estheticism and nationalism fought a battle of life and death in my bosom—but I might as well admit it, this time upbringing had it over nature,—I had to give up my love. . . . What more to say, my originality,—my primitivism—I mean—was lost.[27]

Culture conquered nature—in Poulsen's bosom. In other words, Poulsen cannot deal with whatever is primitive and original in the people's soul. He tries to make and cover up by carrying a hunting knife and writing "orthophonically" (phonetically—as opposed to Danish spelling).

Where "*huldre*-ness" was an adornment a girl could wear as a national dress in the early plays, the *huldre* Poulsen thought he loved showed her tail, that is, the real, raw unpolished *volksseele.* He had to realize that he had not bargained for something that was not amenable to being hooked onto nice rhymes and a happy end. The mature Ibsen became disenchanted with the naiveté of the romantic movement and its search for folksy origins.

Much has been written about Ibsen's disenchantment with his countrymen around the Dano-German war in 1864. He wanted Norway to enter the war on Denmark's side and not just sit on the fence. In the play that, at least in part, grew out of his anger at Norwegian callousness, *Brand,* he painted the Norwegians as wishy-washy and unwilling to make any commitments. The strong and passionate—to the point of absurdity (in both senses of the word)—protagonist of the play, Brand, is a *huldre* or demon who has read Kierkegaard's *Either-Or* and confronts his latter-day descendants with the fire and vehemence of their viking ancestors. That play has another character who is reminiscent of the *huldre* and demon tales—the girl Gerd. Gerd is an idiot. In the folklore, individuals who have been with the *huldrer* and who come back are often depicted as strange or feeble minded. If we assume, as indeed is suggested in *Brand*, that Gerd has been with the trolls, we could speculate that she is Ibsen's satirical answer to a hypothetical question of what would happen to modern Norwegians if they were to live among the mythic ancestors they so declare they want to emulate. Anyway, the *huldre*—if Brand is one—in *Brand* is no dance on the *sæter;* he is a passionate and dangerous madman.

In *Peer Gynt*, Peer has sexual relations with both *sæterjenter* and *den grønkledde*, "the woman in green," who may be a *huldre*, after leaving the village.[28] These *sæterjenter/huldrer* are not good little innocent girls just waiting for a man to come along and marry them, they are dangerous, threatening even, and have a raw and violent sexuality.

In the realistic plays, the *huldrer* and other demons go underground— just like the demons of yore did when Christianity took over—although they are still very much there. The demons and *huldrer* of the late plays are restored to their folklore stature—both seductive and alluring and dangerous. Hilde Wangel, Hedda Gabler, and Rebekka West, who all have demon natures, are beautiful and tantalizing, and they can destroy a man unless he is as strong and as passionate as they are. The men, of course, as we shall see, never are. But this is the story we are to tell in the rest of this chapter and the following ones by Leavy. For a specific image of the *huldre* in the late plays I refer especially to Leavy's analysis of *Hedda Gabler* below.

Folklore Themes in the Early Plays

Certain folklore-derived themes, ubiquitous in the early plays, show up—albeit in changed form—in the later plays. I have pinpointed five specific such themes, to be discussed individually below: (1) formal devices; (2) folklore as personality trait; (3) seduction; (4) male/female; (5) pagan/Christian.

1. Formal Devices
Certain formal devices are taken over by Ibsen from the ballads. He utilizes the same basic cast of characters, especially in the early plays, that are the stock characters of the ballads. He always has (1) a young

man or woman who is of marriageable age (indeed, as in *Olaf Liljekrans* and *Brand*, the young man or woman may be in the process of getting married when they meet the demon who abducts them), (2) a demon (both the young person and the demon may be multiplied), and (3) the representatives of society, usually parents or priests/teachers. In some plays, such as *Hærmændene på Helgeland*, we meet the young people many years after they married the wrong partner, and we are shown how terrible the outcome of a mismatch is.

Another formal trait Ibsen takes from the ballads is the use of various types of space. He clearly deals in two—sometimes three—types of space:[29]

(1) natural space: the sea, the fjord, the mountains.

(2) marginal space: *sæter* (mountain pastures), gardens. Sometimes the cultural space is marginalized by the invasion of "nature": the sets of the plays, for example, are often described as being full of live plants.

(3) cultural space: houses, churches, towns.

Set descriptions in Ibsen are important: often the set is described in such a way as to suggest the two realms of nature and culture simultaneously, preparing the reader or audience for some kind of interaction between the two spheres.

One last formal feature, which is found only in the early plays, is the use of folk-ballad metric devices[30] and of language typical of the ballads. The following passage quoted from *Gildet på Solhaug* exemplifies this use of "ballad language" and ballad meter and leads into my second point. (I quote again in the Norwegian since the metric and linguistic devices are inextricably connected with the original text. Again a translation is found in the notes.)

> *Det var seg* årle, da klokkene klang
> *meg lystet* å ride til kirke;
> *de vildene fugle* kvidret og sang
> *alt mellem* siljer og birke.
> *Der var en gammen* i luft og li;
> kirketiden *fast* var omme;
> ti alt som jeg red ad *den skyggefulde sti*
> meg vinket hver *rosenblomme*.
> Jeg trådte så tyst på kirkegulvet inn;
> presten sto høyt i koret;

han sang og leste; med andakt i sinn
lyttet menn og kvinner til ordet.
Da hørtes en røst over fjorden blå;
meg tyktes alle de billeder små
vendte seg om for å lytte derpå.

• • • • • • •

Det var som et dypt, et ufattelig bud
manet meg utenfor kirkens mur
over hei og dal, gjennem li og ur.[31]

This passage has the image of the maid who rides to church along the "little green path," who enters to hear the priest and is "magically" called by a voice from outside the church, from the fjord, to leave the church and join the source of the song.[32] The language is very consciously balladesque. The expression "det var seg" ("It was it") is a standard first phrase of the ballads. The "pictures that turn" are obviously from the "Agnete" or "Harp" ballads. The passage shows how the folkloric material is used in the early Ibsen plays.

2. *Folklore as a Personality Trait*

In all of the early Ibsen plays we find a character—or several—who has "drunk" folklore with the mother milk. In *Gildet på Solhaug*, Margit and Signe grew up to the accompaniment of Gudmund's harp and folk ballads. In *Fru Inger til Østråt*, Eline—who, incidentally, is self-confessedly *stolt*, "proud," and *hovmodig*, "haughty" (à la the maid in "Nix" who is *stolt* and *Hoffærdig*)—grew up with stories told by Bjørn, an old and beloved servant of her mother's. Eline is Agnete to Niels Lykke's Merman (he is described in similar terms as the merman: beautiful and blond), or she is Isabel to his elf knight, or maid to his nix, and so on. In *Kjæmpehøien*, Blanka has listened to Roderik's stories about the Viking heroes; in *Olaf Liljekrans*, Alfhild (an elf of name too) has lived secluded from other humans with her father—the impecunious bard who seduced and eloped with a rich farmer's daughter—in the mountains her entire life. Anne in *Sancthansnatten* has listened to her grandfather sing ballads and tell stories since she was very young. Peer Gynt has become one of the mythical creatures his mother used to tell him about. Selma Bratsberg of *De Unges Forbund* is a self-declared "fairy-tale princess," complete with an evil stepmother who changed her so she had to wait for the kiss of a prince to be released.[33] We can almost say that "folklore" is "a personality trait" in some of the early Ibsen characters. The person who has this trait is always a hero or heroine, a sympathetic person, whether destined for happiness or tragedy.

In some cases a character is given, instead of the folklore trait, a name saturated with folkloric connotations—for example, Svanhild in *Kærlighedens komedie*. The name serves the same purpose as the character trait: it gives expectations of a certain type of "mythic" personality. As we shall see below, one of the other characters of *Kærlighedens komedie*, Falk, has exactly those kinds of expectations with regard to Svanhild.

The symbolic function of the folklore character trait is almost painfully simple: I take *Gildet på Solhaug* as an example: Margit and Signe have been brought up on old Nordic ballads as sung by the then poor but handsome Gudmund. They are steeped in the national lore which means they are natural, Norwegian—or, since Ibsen was more of a Scandinavian than a Norwegian nationalist, Scandinavian—women. They must marry for love, since marrying for economic or dynastic convenience is unnatural and the route to unhappiness. Margit marries the old and wealthy Bengt and is lost, trapped forever in the mountain. She expects that Gudmund will come and free her. But Gudmund, having seduced Signe with his song, chooses the younger, unmarried, and thus uncontaminated sister.

The phenomenon is found in much of the Scandinavian romantic literature. The young and eminently national—symbolized by naming or, as in *Gildet på Solhaug* by having "ingested" national folklore—represent the vitality of nature and beauty. Older people who try to arrange marriages represent an unnatural order: bourgeois, patriarchal culture. We find this expressed most clearly, perhaps, in Heiberg's plays: the older generation are always trying to keep young lovers apart—usually because the young man is poor—and to marry the girl off to some rich but old and ugly man. The young couple—with the help of archetypical national (Danish) characters—outwit the parents or guardians and get each other in the end. Usually the young and their helpers have simple Danish names and folksy happy dispositions, whereas the enemy, the guardians and parents and their accomplices, have disgruntled dispositions and foppish foreign names and professions.[34]

3. Seduction

Ibsen also plays with Kierkegaard's major theme: seduction. For Ibsen seduction is the interface between two realms. Two beings, a male and a female, rocket towards each other along different paths—coming from different spheres. The encounter between the two bodies usually leads to their destruction. Or they meet and part after a while (as in *Kærlighedens komedie*). The two beings are construed as a mythic (meaning national, innocent, forceful, dynamic, *natural*) being, and a human (meaning foreign, weak, unable to act, *cultural*). The two are complementary opposites: only through their union can the miracle happen, the creation of an artist or "great man." Because of the "law of complementarity" the two must meet, their paths have been laid out by destiny. The encounter always takes the form of a seduction: the demon seduces the human and the human is destroyed: Margit in *Gildet på Solhaug* has her life destroyed because she fell for the mountainman's gold and married him.

In most of the early Ibsen plays we find the above basic story pattern or a variation upon it. In other words, the nature-culture schism is played out as Norwegian (traditional, young, Northern, *sæter*) versus imported, foreign-derived culture. The point of using the ballads is to suggest the national, the true and real tradition, which is as true and real as the people themselves. This has the outcome that imagery from the ballads may be stood on its head: where the image of the pictures turning their backs in "Harp" is frightening and hostile, it is in *Solhaug* "cutesy" and positive.[35] The teeth of the ballad have been pulled and the nix is paraded as a domesticated (Gudmund) Alfsøn.

In *Fru Inger til Østråt* we find two consecutive versions of the story: Fru Inger herself had, when she was young, an illicit affair with her "elf knight," and she is doomed forever after to live for the fruit of that union, a son whom she has never seen. The more elaborate story is that of Eline and Niels Lykke. He too is an elf knight, who has seduced and destroyed hundreds of women including Eline's sister. She knows of his reputation but falls for him despite all. He recognizes in her the woman who could have turned his potential, which has been used for evil, into greatness. But they meet too late. He, the elf knight, almost against his will, destroys her too. This is evocative of Kierkegaard's treatment of the "Agnete" story. One of Kierkegaard's scenarios has the merman recognize in Agnete a woman who can save him and make him human.

The merman does not want to seduce Agnete although he has seduced many others. He is no merman any more. . . . Yet he knows . . . that he can be saved by the love of an innocent maiden. But he has a bad conscience vis a vis the girls and does not dare approach them. Then he sees Agnete. Often he has already, hidden in the rushes, seen her wander by the sea . . . he approaches Agnete, wins her love, he hopes for salvation. But Agnete was not a quiet girl, she was fond of the roar of the sea. . . . She wants to take off, off, charge wildly towards eternity with the merman, whom she loves—then she entices the merman. She turned down his humility, now his pride is awakened. And the sea roars, the wave is frothy and the merman embraces Agnete and hurtles himself into the abyss with her. . . . Soon he was tired of Agnete, yet her body was never found. . . .[36]

To anyone who knows the story of *Fru Inger til Østråt* this is almost a perfect rendition of the story of the proud, wild, stubborn Eline and the handsome, sly Niels Lykke.[37] Ibsen clearly sees the Danes, who ruled Norway at the time of the play, as more polished and culturally sophisticated than the honest, innocent, natural, or "raw" Norwegians. The complexity derives from the fact that Lykke is symbolic of both culture and the demonic and Eline of both nature and the human sphere. Ibsen constantly does this, mixes things together: often a character embodies both nature and culture, both seducer and seduced. This is clearest—except for the late plays—in *Gildet på Solhaug*, where everybody claims to be both elf/*huldre* and seduced by an elf/*huldre*.

The story of Eline and Niels Lykke in *Fru Inger til Østråt,* the mutual accusations and confessions of being demons in *Gildet på Solhaug,* and the confusion in *Olaf Liljekrans* as to who is the demon, bring out the dramatic and conceptual weakness of Ibsen's use in the early plays of the folklore trait:

- The folklore is not integrated into the play, it is a "crutch" (exactly as in Heiberg). Characters compare themselves and others to demons and folklore figures, but they never are demons. They are just ordinary humans who like to quote folklore.

- The folklore is a literary and linguistic device: it is not internal to the plays. The use of folklore sounds hollow because form and content do not work together well.

- The reason so many early plays can have "happy endings" is that there are no real demons in them, just people who pretend.

- The reason the "saga plays" (e.g., *Hærmændene på Helgeland*), are stronger and more believable and exciting is that the characters embody the same types of personalities that can be found in the real sagas.

4. Male/Female

Ibsen's plays, like the ballads, express the theme of beings from different realms colliding as a male versus female theme. Ibsen saw that the ballads place men and women on opposite sides of the nature-culture schism. From the image of seduction, from the male-female schism (but also the complementarity—on the order of yin and yang) and from the meeting of nature and culture is derived one of Ibsen's central themes: the nature of greatness, of creativity, of ability to act and realize great ideas. All of Ibsen's plays from the first to the last are about the ability to be the most one can be, about the great act, work of art or idea. His focus is always on a character—usually, but not always, a man—who has the potential for greatness. He may, as in *Kongsemnerne* have the potential for being a great king,[38] or he may, like Falk in *Kjærlighedens komedie* have the potential for becoming a great poet. Whatever the potential is, the protagonist has to solve the problems of dealing with life and love before it can come to fruition. In the cases where the person who has a gift is a man, he has to secure the support of the right woman. In *Fru Inger til Østråt* the "elf knight," Niels Lykke, having met the proud and poised Eline Gyldenløve, complains that the source of his moral downfall was that, until now, he has met only "easy women":

> It is said of me that I'm as false as the froth on the waves. That may be true, but if I am, the women taught me to be that way. If I had found what I sought earlier,—had I found a woman, proud, noble and poised like you—then, certainly my course had been different. . . . For that I believe; a woman is the mightiest in the world and it is in her power to shape a man so that he goes in the direction God, the Lord, wants him to go.[39]

In almost every single Ibsen play the conflict revolves around con-

117

necting the right man to the right woman. And in almost every single one the connections are not successfully made. The problem most often is that one partner has married for career or pecuniary reasons (Skule in *Kongsemnerne*, Margit in *Gildet på Solhaug*, John Gabriel Borkman) or that one partner is somehow tainted (Peer Gynt when he at last returns to his Solveig, Niels Lykke who has caused Eline's sister's death in *Fru Inger*, Rebekka West in *Rosmersholm*). The subject matter, the intrigue of the play then is to let the readers/audience slowly discover for themselves why the union that seems perfect and made in heaven cannot be.

Women, in Ibsen, are not in and of themselves creative; they can only serve as helpers or inspirations for men. Men invariably need women's help. They need "soul."

The perfect unions almost never happen in Ibsen because the dangers lurking around them are so formidable. If one partner is tainted by having somehow destroyed his or her own purity (sexual wantonness in women, greed or immorality in men), the union cannot be and even if it briefly is, the result is going to be negative: a changeling is the inevitable product (*Brand, Vildanden, Lille Eyolf, Fruen fra havet*), a sickly and/or strange individual that is not the new superhuman that should be the issue of the perfect union. In other plays (*Rosmersholm, Hedda Gabler, John Gabriel Borkman*, and *Når vi døde vågner*), the issue is not a child but a work of art or an idea/cause, but the result is the same: the issue is tainted, bound for destruction or where it should be is emptiness (this last is, as I argue below, the case in *Rosmersholm*).

One more thing should be noted on the subject of male and female in Ibsen: Ibsen's men are often weak and lacking in virility, whereas the women are strong, willful, and dominating. This is another cause of disaster in gender relations. Strong women are inherently destructive: both self-destructive and prone to destroy the men they encounter. The classic example, of course, is Hedda Gabler, but they are there in the early plays too. Margit in *Gildet på Solhaug* destroys both herself and her husband Bengt Gautesøn; Eline carries the seed of her own destruction within her—she is self-described as having "det ville sind" ("the wild spirit");[40] Hjørdis in *Hærmændene på Helgeland* is almost certainly an early study for Hedda Gabler (this will be discussed below). The weak men who are attracted to these wild women are unceremoniously destroyed.

Since the encounter between the strong women and the weak men always leads to disaster, we can assume that Ibsen does not approve of this "reversed gender pattern." In his late plays he manages, however, to keep his distance, to refrain from inserting editorial comment. The evaluation is hidden in the plot and the audience has to make its own observations. Also the late plays are more concerned with psychological shadings and interplay than the more cartoonlike early plays. Perhaps this quotation from *De Unges Forbund* indicates Ibsen's own opinion in the matter,

> *Fjeldbo* [Speaking of Stensgård—an early Mortensgård]: I have known him since we were children. His father was a withered good-for-nothing, a dullard, a nobody; he ran a little store with pawnbroking on the side, or, rather, it was the wife who ran it. She was a crude woman, the most unfeminine I've known. She had her husband declared incapable of managing his own affairs, not a heartfelt thought was there in her. And in that home Stensgård grew up. And then he went to preparatory school too. "He shall study," the mother said, "he will become a good debt collector." Ugliness at home; elevation at school; the spirit, the character, the abilities,—all headed in different directions. What other than a split personality could it lead to?[41]

Ibsen is, however, not per se, against strong or willful women. They just have to have a male match: someone who is even stronger, even more willful, someone who is capable of controlling them. A forceful woman has to have a man she can sacrifice herself for, a man she can act as a support for, as seen in the following passage from *Hærmændene på Helgeland*. Hjørdis is addressing Sigurd hin sterke ("the Strong")

> *Hjørdis* (with poise): I became homeless in the world from the day you took another wife. You did wrong then! All good gifts a man can give to his true friend,—everything, just not the woman he loves. For if he does that he breaks the secret thread of the norns [Nordic goddesses of fate] and two lives are wasted. There is an unerring voice in me which says that I was created so that my strong will could

lift you and carry you in hard times and that you were born so that I in one man could find all that I find great and excellent. For that I know, Sigurd,—if we two had stuck together you would have been famous and I happier than all others![42]

Sigurd is a great Viking hero, married to a weak, domesticated woman, Dagny. Hjørdis is married to Sigurd's foster brother, Gunnar. Both Sigurd and Gunnar were originally in love with Hjørdis—although Sigurd kept his infatuation a secret. Hjørdis let it be known that only he could win her who dared kill a ferocious white bear. Gunnar convinced Sigurd to do the deed and then let all the world—and Hjørdis—believe he was the man of superior courage. What Hjørdis—and, I assume, Ibsen—is saying is that she and Sigurd were meant for each other. If they had been married he could have fulfilled his potential for greatness. Earlier in the play the point has been made that he wanted to marry only a woman as fierce as himself because only such a woman could bring out his potential.[43]

5. Pagan/Christian

The last major carryover from the ballads is that Ibsen uses the pagan-Christian dichotomy extensively. In the early plays it is used quite literally; for example, in *Hærmændene på Helgeland*, Sigurd toward the end tells Hjørdis that they will not even be united in Valhalla because he has converted to Christianity. It is also the sole point of *Kjæmpehøjen*, where the southern (i.e., Christian) and the northern (i.e., pagan) Vikings are juxtaposed. The result in this very sketchy and weak work is that the two are joined, combining southern spirituality with Nordic raw power. In *Kjæmpehøjen* it is, incidentally, laid out quite clearly that the preeminently feminine is the spiritual, whereas men represent raw strength, which has to be guided and softened by the complementary feminine. Blanka, the Christian "swan maiden" stranded somewhere in Greece, dreams of a blond and Nordic Viking. When he comes he is a pagan wild man who is converted by her spirituality and love. After they have become a couple and are about to set out for Norway, Blanka says,

Blanka (enthusiastic, tearing the banner from Jostein's
hand): Yes, now on our way. Toward the north our voyage
goes
through storm and froth on the blue waves.
Soon the day will break over the pinnacle of the Jøkel,
Soon the Viking raids will be but a memory!
Already the Nordic Viking sits on his grave;
Gone is the day when he flew mightily
from coast to coast with thunder of weapons and flames!
Into the dust sinks the hammer of the god of thunder,
and the North becomes itself a grave for Vikings.
But forget not a promise that Odin gave;
When moss and flowers shall cover the sides of the grave-
hill,
The spirit of the hero shall fight on Idavold!—
Then also the North will emerge from its grave
To purified accomplishment of the spirit on the sea of
thought![44]

This is obviously bombastic word soup, but the meaning is quite clear:
the spirituality of the south (represented by Blanka and Christianity)
shall combine with Nordic power and ferocity to create a new and forceful spirituality. A new, uniquely Scandinavian art and a new Scandinavian race of men and women will emerge. This new art and race are still
being sought—albeit in a superior artistic form—in the late Ibsen plays,
notably *Rosmersholm.*

The Late Plays: *Rosmersholm*

The image of the north as the home of the uniquely Nordic and of a
forceful *volksseele* is ubiquitous in Ibsen: Eline in *Fru Inger til Østråt*
perceives herself as wild and unkempt as opposed to the slick and mundane Niels Lynge, who is from the south, Denmark. In play after play
we find the same pattern. In *Hærmændene på Helgeland* the real Vikings
are Icelanders, whereas Gunnar, the representative of farming culture
and peacefulness is living in Norway (which, relative to Iceland, is to

the south). In *Rosmersholm*, Rebekka West is from the northernmost part of Norway, from "Finnmarken." This is interesting in light of the fact that Ibsen, in his essay on *Kjæmpevisen*, says that to the early Scandinavians the Finns were the epitome of demonic beings who had mysterious powers. They were, Ibsen surmises—by comparison to the Aryan Scandinavians—small and dark and they had learned to wrest the iron and the gold from the mountains. When they were driven north by the victorious Vikings they became creatures of the night: mountainmen, nixes, and trolls.[45]

The far northern parts of Norway were also where Ibsen went to collect folk ballads—an indication that he thought the most typically Norwegian ballads would be found in this area. So we can assume that Rebekka West is conceptualized as representing all the north means to Ibsen. Add to this that her name is West, not a name native to Norway—she is "foreign," strange. To the west of Norway is the sea. The man who, as it turns out in her third-act conversation with Rektor Kroll, was her father—and with whom she (as Freud, among others, has pointed out) had an incestuous relationship—was a ship's doctor. This web of features makes Rebekka a creature of the sea and of the far north. Her father was an "elf knight" of a sort.[46] Born as the result of an illicit union, adopted by her biological father/lover, Rebekka is a reversal of culture and social propriety. She is nature: violent, cunning; the storm of the sea is in her. In Kierkegaard's term, her strength is "the passion of nature."[47]

A major difference between the use of folklore in the early and the late plays is that in the late plays the folklore is not just a stylistic device. The characters of the modern, "realistic" plays do not constantly compare themselves to ballads or break into recitation of ballads to sum up their feelings. Characters like Rebekka West do not have folklore as a mere "character trait." Rebekka is a demon, a mermaid, a representative or the raw *volksseele* without cultural varnish. She does not declare herself, as do heroines of the early plays, with "cutesy" affection, a *huldre*—only to be shown to be an ordinary but sweet young girl. She is raw and dangerous: the spirit of a demon or pagan Viking. Ibsen strands her, like an E.T., on a foreign planet and in a culture that has no defenses against her.

In *Rosmersholm* Ibsen plays with the idea suggested in the passage from *Kjæmpehøjen* quoted above: the merger of a refined "southern" culture with a wild and unkempt Nordic wild woman. Ibsen inserts a character who embodies all the ferocity and power of a nix into a tame and domesticated modern setting and sits back to watch what happens. He wants to see how modern Norwegians would react to a representative of the national "soul" they all claim to want to recover. In *Rosmersholm* the meeting between Christian culture and "aboriginal" nature leads to tragedy and destruction.

The image of the idiotic Poulsen in *Sancthansnatten,* who stops being in love with the *huldre* when he discovers she has a tail,[48] is akin to what in a serious way happens in *Rosmersholm.* A real live folklore demon is confronted with modern inhabitants of Norway. She does not have a tail, but she has something that is almost as exotic: she is passionate and has "a courageous free will." Ibsen's dark vision of this encounter is that the two cannot coexist peacefully, nor can they merge to form a higher unity. Rebekka becomes a convert to modern, soft culture and loses her strength and ability to act. In the end she and Rosmer destroy each other. On the other side, Johannes Rosmer embodies modern Norwegians in *Rosmersholm.* As his name suggests, he is of old Nordic stock. He too has merman blood in his veins. But the Rosmers went ashore many generations ago like the first sea creatures that crawled out of the primeval sea.[49] The Rosmers have been on "Rosmersholm, the family estate, for centuries. The walls in the Rosmer living room are covered with portraits of ministers, officers and government functionaries in their uniforms."[50] The Rosmers are culture. Ibsen's experiment is to have the converted merman be confronted by one of his own "ancestors." Is the culture just a veneer that can be removed when Rosmer needs to dig into his aboriginal nature, or has the merman nature withered away over the centuries? In other words, is Johannes Rosmer a merman only in name? Is he all soft culture or is there an ore of natural strength underneath?

Ibsen had used the theme of a character who has a mythic name but has trouble living up to it before. In *Kjærlighedens komedie,* the young poet-to-be, Falk, comments on the name of the young woman he is in love with, Svanhild. He says to her that her name is ridiculous and goes on,

Falk (laughs): Hm, "Svanhild"— "Svanhild"—(suddenly serious) How come you got such a memento mori from the time when you were young?
Svanhild: Is it ugly?
Falk: No, it is lovely as a poem, but much too big and severe for our times. How can a modern maiden fill out the thought that "Svanhild" holds? No, cast it away as an obsolete attire.[51]

As it turns out, Svanhild cannot fill out the name. She is a typical Ibsen heroine, strong-willed, independent, and spirited, but she is no Svanhild. She is a modern girl who cannot live for an idea, for "daring the deadly leap" unless there is a pot of gold on the other side. Falk demands the ideal. Being himself a typical Ibsen hero, he demands that she should be willing to go for the sake of going, "Such going *for the sake of going* belongs to nobility, and the noble venture is in our times called nonsense; is that what you meant?"[52] And it is, of course. Svanhild is a sensible girl with a strong sense of purpose. She ends up marrying the rich "troll" Guldstad (Goldtown), who can support her. She is still another early Ibsen character who is billed as a folkloric personage but who is just a modern woman with an ill-fitting label. Rosmer is, by way of labeling, similar to Svanhild, but unlike Svanhild he meets a real mermaid who may bring out his true nature.

The interaction between Rosmer and Rebekka West is the focal point of *Rosmersholm*. The supporting cast of characters sets these two in relief and help bring the relationship between them to a head. The supporting characters embody characteristics of the supporting characters of the ballads. Rektor Kroll, for example, is the representative of the old order, the structural equivalent of the parent or priest in the ballads. The first time he shows up at Rosmersholm, he sets out clearly who he is and what he represents: an old autocratic and patriarchal order.[53]

Kroll retains several of the functions of the parent figure in the ballads. Thus, he is the one who, when Rosmer tells him that he has been "seduced," first tries to convince him to return to the straight and narrow, and who, when Rosmer persists, rejects him, "not your foot in my house!"[54] As may be recalled this is the story of both "Dwarf" and "Agnete," where the maid is interrogated by the parent and subsequently rejected.

Rosmer's first wife, Beate, represents a maid who is seduced. She is never actually seen in the play, but her shadow looms large: the play opens with this set description,

(The sitting room at Rosmersholm, spacious, old fashioned and cozy. Downstage to the right a stove adorned with *fresh birch branches and field flowers*. In the wall a window and in front of it a table *with flowers and plants. . . . The window is open, also the door to the foyer and the door to the outside*. Outside big old trees are seen. . . .) (emphases mine)[55]

The significance of all the flowers and of the open doors and windows is that Beate could not stand the smell and the mix of colors of flowers. Beate was a sickly, domesticated woman. Now that she is gone it is almost as if the boundary between the inside and the outside, between natural and cultural space has been broken down. Rebekka has surrounded herself with flowers and plants. The set is a symbolic representation of both Rebekka and Beate. Rebekka is a breath of fresh air. She, like the flowers and plants, is a being from the outside which has moved into the house. In the end, she, like them, will wither and perish, uprooted as she is from her natural element.

Beate is also present in another feature introduced on the very first page of the very first scene: the *Mølleklop*, the bridge across the river, which Rosmer does not dare pass over. Beate threw herself into the water from that *Mølleklop* and ever since Rosmer has avoided it. This is reminiscent of the bridge motif in the ballads. We learn late in the play that Rebekka, the mermaid, was the one who "seduced" Beate and made her jump into the river. With the domesticated woman gone, we are ready for the battle between nature and culture, between female and male: the battle between Rebekka and Rosmer.

An interesting question suggests itself: Why is Rebekka interested in Johannes Rosmer? He is a typical late Ibsen male: dull, almost frightened of sex, and, on the whole, uninteresting. From some of the things Rebekka says, it seems that her original attraction was to his position: he is influential and well off. Ibsen's mermaid, like the merfolk of the ballads, is attracted to the otherworld, the cultural realm, of which he is a prominent representative. She wants, perhaps, a soul. Kroll says to her that she "carries a cold heart."[56] What she does not understand, if a soul is what she wants, is that the price she must pay is her ability to act, her will, her very passion. Like the troll of "Trolden og bondens hustru," she will be changed by the love of a human into a human: the troll became a handsome prince, Rebekka becomes a frail and dependent woman like Beate—acquiring culture, becoming human, means giving up freedom.

At one point Rosmer accuses Rebekka of the ultimate female crime in an Ibsen play: he accuses her of never having believed in him and his ability to "do something great in life." She thought, he says, "That you could use me to get what you wanted. That I could serve your ends."[57] Actually she has committed a double crime: first, she has not believed in him: in Ibsen, a man can only achieve greatness, as Falk says in *Kjærlighedens komedie*, through the love of a pure and unselfish woman (the quotation is given below in my discussion of *Når vi døde vågner*). Rosmer is a failure because Rebekka did not believe in him. Second, and worse still, Rebekka has wanted to reverse the pattern: she has wanted to become a man, she has wanted to use him to obtain her goals. The great ideal, the dream of making everybody equal—equal in nobility—is not Rosmer's, it is Rebekka's. She wanted his *skyldfrihet* ("innocence," "absence of guilt") and purity to support her attempt at greatness. That is the ultimate sin: the woman who acts like a man and makes the man her tool.[58]

The outcome of the encounter between the mermaid and the descendant of Rosmer Merman is disaster for both of them. When Rosmer is about to go out to spread his message of universal nobility he suddenly discovers what his satiric reflection Brendel discovered on *his* eve of truth: "For twenty-five years I've been sitting like the miser on his chest of money. And then yesterday—when I open and want to take my fortune out—it isn't there. The teeth of time had crunched it to dust. There was nichts and nothing in the whole to do."[59] And Brendel is Rosmer's reflection: he is, when he sets out to give his speech in town, wearing Rosmer's clothes. His ideas, like reflections in water, are even more blurred and amorphous than Rosmer's. As far as will and ability to act is concerned, Rosmer is only a merman of name: there is no hidden ore, no aboriginal nature he can produce when he needs it. He is an empty shell.

The "humanized" Rebekka decides to go away when she discovers that her past makes her unsuited to be a companion and support for

Johannes Rosmer and his great idea. But she does this only after she has been symbolically seduced by him and has lost her "mermaid" nature. She has been rendered powerless by Rosmer's magic "runes" as was the mermaid in "Mr. Luno's and the Mermaid." Rosmer, and what he stands for, is, like the runes, the epitome of culture. He has tied Rebekka with his particular brand of runes: "the Rosmer outlook on life." In the last scene between Rosmer and Rebekka, she complains that she has lost her will, her ability to act, "Rosmersholm has broken me . . . now I'm bent under a foreign law."[60] A little further on she says, "Rosmersholm has stolen me . . . I've lost the ability to act."[61] And still further on in the same scene, "It is the outlook on life of the Rosmer family—or your outlook on life, at least,—which has infected my will . . . and made it sick. Slave-tied it under laws that did not exist for me before."[62] In the end the seducer is seduced—Rebekka, who seduced Beate, is seduced by Rosmer, who has only that in common with his merman ancestor that he is a (would-be) seducer and destroyer of women.

The whole question of seduction is complicated in *Rosmersholm*. Rebekka is a seducer. She admits to Rektor Kroll that she seduced Beate to jump in the Møllefoss. At some point prior to her arrival at Rosmersholm she had that rock of upstanding citizenship—Kroll—charmed, as he says to her, "Who could you not bewitch, if you wanted to?"[63] and Brendel calls her, "My attractive mermaid."[64] But also Rosmer is a seducer. He has "seduced" Rebekka, as he seduced Beate: Beate would never have done what she did if it were not for the fact that she loved Rosmer more than her own life. When he demands proof that Rebekka really loves him, he "seduces" her to take her own life. When Rebekka has said she will bring him the ultimate proof, that she will "carry the hot iron" (as Håkon Håkonsson's mother does in *Kongsemnerne*)[65] he exclaims, "There is a seductive horror in this."[66] His merman nature shines through at last. At the very end when Rosmer and Rebekka are on their way out to Møllekloppen to commit double suicide they try to ferret out who has seduced whom:

> *Rosmer:* The man shall follow his wife, just as the wife her husband.
> *Rebekka:* Yes, tell me *this* first. Are you the one following me? Or am I the one who is following you?
> *Rosmer:* That we will never get to the bottom of.

Rebekka: But yet, I'd like to know.
Rosmer: We follow each other, Rebekka, I you and you me.
Rebekka: I believe that is true.
Rosmer: For now we two are *one.*[67]

Ibsen is clearly playing with the problem of which one is the demon? Who is abducting whom to the otherworld of the sea. In a brilliant essay Erik Østerud examines the seduction theme in *Rosmersholm* in the light of Søren Kierkegaard's discussion of "Agnete og Havmanden."[68] For Østerud the focus is on the psychological. He gives (Freudian) psychological profiles of the two protagonists. He finds both Rebekka and Rosmer to be necessary products of their upbringing. He discusses with great insight the sexual tensions and repressions between them. And he sees clearly that they change roles as the play progresses. Initially, she is the seducer, but in the end, "it is Rosmer who seduces and Rebekka is the victim of the seduction."[69] The only thing lacking here is a recognition from Østerud of the tangled web of mutual seduction at the end. In Kierkegaard it is there: he sees both Agnete and the merman as seducers who get caught in an evil spiral where a lack of understanding of the other's motives leads to the final disaster: the merman does not obtain the soul he had hoped the—as he thought innocent girl—would help him get, and the girl who wanted adventure and excitement gets death and destruction instead. There is no doubt in my mind that Ibsen must have read *Fear and Trembling* and that he read the treatment of the "Agnete" theme with special interest, for, as Østerud points out, Kierkegaard's discussion is almost a synopsis of *Rosmersholm.*[70]

Kierkegaard sets up two different scenarios for the "Agnete" ballad. In the first, the merman sees Agnete walking on the beach, pensive and always alone. He decides to seduce her like so many girls before. He approaches her, wins her confidence, takes her in his arms and is just about to take off with her to seduce and destroy her, when he looks into her eyes. Then he is immobilized by her gaze which is full of trust and humility. He cannot go on with his seduction. He sets her down with an excuse and leaves her behind. "And Lo, the sea does not roar any more, its wild voice is silent. Nature's passion, which is the strength of the merman, abandons him, everything becomes quiet."[71] This is how Kierkegaard describes the reaction of the merman to Agnete's trust and innocence and it is too similar to be coincidental to the way in which

Rebekka describes her own initial infatuation with Rosmer, "It was upon me like a weather by the sea. It was like one of those kinds of weather that we can have in wintertime up north, it takes you,—and carries you with it,—as far as can be. No thought of resisting."[72] But like Kierkegaard's merman, Rebekka was immobilized by her victim's very trust and innocence, and before she knew it he had seduced her and she could not go through with her own seduction.

Kierkegaard's second scenario has the merman shy and afraid of approaching the beautiful girl who keeps coming to the beach. At last he does, encouraged by something in her, and she is willing, for she is no quiet girl—she wants adventure and loves the roar of the sea. He had hoped that she—fairy tale style—would help release him from his soulless state by giving him a kiss. But she is no innocent girl, and he ends up destroying her once she has reawakened the merman nature in him that demands passion and destruction.[73] This is a description of Rosmer's seduction of Rebekka: he had thought that he, with her help, could become a great savior to the people, that he, supported by her innocence and belief in him could ennoble—give a soul to—the common people. He and she would do this as "bosom friends" or platonic lovers at the most. But when she tells him that she is no innocent girl—she is a girl who had a passionate and sexual desire for him—he is, at first, shocked, but then his merman nature is awakened and he wants to do as he has done to "other girls" (Beate), drag her into the sea to her destruction. The tragic irony, says Ibsen, is that in the end they must perish together, go to the otherworld together, because they never understood each other well. They have both lived in fantasy worlds where the other was not what she or he really was but where they were embodiments of a fantasy.

Once they finally know each other as they are, once they together inhabit the same real world, it is too late. She has accepted his, cultural, reality, which they both wanted to do away with—he has never left it. But with her acceptance of his "world" comes also a recognition that she does not fit in it or deserve a place in it. He has to realize that his platonic love was not so platonic, and that his beliefs in freedom and personal responsibility did not permeate his being. He is what he must be as the last of the Rosmers: a representative of a particular ideology and social order. He and she do not belong together in that social order, but they belong together in the sharing of guilt and in their love for each other. Their demise together is the logical outcome of the play. It is equally logical that it is not clear, nor will it ever be, who in the end seduces whom. There is almost an image of fate here. Rebekka—like the norns, referred to by Hjørdis in *Hærmændene på Helgeland*—is from the very beginning knitting the web of fate's threads together. She is knitting the white shawl. This is tied in with the symbolism of the white horses. The shawl is finished when the play is, and the fates and lives of Rebekka West and Johannes Rosmer are laid bare: the white horses come and get them.

The Rosmer of Ibsen's play has stood since mythical times as but a stone replica of a merman, a petrified image of strength and will and ruthlessness. He lost his ability to act centuries ago, and when he is confronted with a Rebekka who still has the capacity of passion and the spark that could get him started he embalms her in his own affliction and renders her powerless and unable to act.

So the outcome of the meeting between the aboriginal Nordic mermaid and the descendant of mermen, says Ibsen, is bound to be a failure because there is nothing left of the original timber in the Norwegian nobility. Ironically, the ability to act and to change things—not in direction of highfalutin nobility for everyman—but in the direction of a new class taking over, is lodged in Mortensgaard. He is, as Brendel points out when he hears his name, a man of the common people, a pragmatist. His ability to act is not weighed down by any cumbersome idealism. He is cunning, stubborn, ruthless, a man of action rather than ideas.

There is bitterness in Ibsen's image of his own time and his own people. He sees that the needed reforms will not be carried through by those who have the education and the ideals. They will be carried through by those who need them, and they are not idealists, but power brokers. The old order is represented by the almost fossilized Kroll and by the unrealistic idealist Rosmer, whom no amount of infusion of energy and raw power can make into a man of action. The reforms will be made, but the world they will usher in will not be one of a new national pride and universal nobility. It will not soar toward the heights but will plod along in the petty and the mundane.

Fruen fra havet

In *The Lady from the Sea*, Rebekka has married Rosmer. Or, at least, Ibsen is still playing with the relationship between a mermaid—a mythic aboriginal Norwegian creature—and a modern man. But the parameters and values have been changed. First of all, Doktor Wangel is no descendant of mermen, and with his German-sounding name, he has no great cause: he does not want to lead his national flock back to a pristine state of freedom and nobility. It has been suggested that Dr. Wangel is modeled after Freud;[74] whether true or not, it suggests what he is: a man who cures the individual, not mankind. And Ellida is no treasure-hunter like Rebekka. She is more akin, as Gravier has pointed out, to Margit Gautesøn of *Gildet på Solhaug*, who married the wealthy Bengt as life insurance while the man who had "enchanted" her was abroad seeking his fortune. Ellida is also a "swan maiden," as Leavy argues below: she is a poor stranded sea creature who has been "tied" to Dr. Wangel by his money. What Ibsen is interested in this time is exactly the obverse of what was the focus of *Rosmersholm*. In that play he wanted to find out what happens to a modern man when he is confronted with a mermaid. In *Lady from the Sea*, the spotlight is on Ellida, the mermaid: how will she deal with being stranded in a human family and married to a human man?

Ellida is a mermaid, she embodies characteristics that one would expect in a sea creature,

> *Wangel:* And then she is so changeable,—so unpredictable, so suddenly changing. . . . In its deepest ground it is something inborn in her. Ellida belongs to the merpeople. That's the heart of the matter.[75]

This confirms, once again, my argument that the major difference between the early and the late plays is to be found in the way in which the folklore is utilized. In the early plays the folklore was projected out: characters were talked about as specific mythic characters, or they compared themselves to ballad characters. Ellida does not quote folklore, she does not speak in beautiful ballad meter; she is a mermaid trapped outside her element. The folkloric material is projected inward. Characters are folklore demons and struggle with their nature vis-à-vis the human world.[76]

Having pronounced Ellida a mermaid, I want to suggest a slightly different scenario: It is quite possible that Ellida is not, after all, a mermaid—although she thinks she is. She is rather a bewitched "maiden," trapped in a mermaid's body or, rather, mind. In this scenario, to be discussed further below, the real mercreature is Alfred Johnston alias Friman. There are some compelling reasons for this. Johnston shares with Rebekka West, whose mermaid nature has been established, a number of significant traits:

Rebekka	Johnston
Born in Finnmarken	From Finnmarken (born Finland)
Father sailed all his life	Sailed since he was young
English-sounding name	English-sounding name
Marginal (child of illicit union)	Father came over from Finland with the boy. He is a *kven*, a marginal person in Norway. Neither Norwegian nor Finnish (actually a *kven* is Swedish; the term has strong negative connotations)

The point here is that the character who most likely is a merman is Johnston. Ellida is in his power, but she is ultimately human.[77]

The nature-culture opposition is central to *The Lady from the Sea*. Erik Østerud gives an admirable rendition of this theme in the play,

The partners in the marriage held each other trapped in alienating myths, which made it impossible to realize a full and total love relationship: a *culture-* or *civilization-myth* . . . and a *nature-myth* which took its material from the folk ballad (the mermaid motif). . . . The myths had kept the married couple away from each other in terms of understanding and of emotions. Dr. Wangel had blocked Ellida's integration into the home environment by revering her as a "mermaid": she came from merpeople and could not be "transplanted." In the same way, Ellida had put distance between herself and Wangel by maintaining the theory that the development of civilization had been a disaster for mankind. . . . But there were possible ways of being transplanted from sea to land, from nature to culture—not by giving up one for the other, but by letting the two aspects of the psyche cooperate in the totality of human life.[78]

Østerud then goes on to tie things up via Hegel, and this is where I part company with his, otherwise admirable, reading: he says that the two positive elements (nature, culture) synthesize in Hegelian fashion, a fact that is expressed in the ironic use of the term "acclimatization." I agree rather with Leavy when she says that the price for the restored order and happiness is paid by both partners. Ellida excises the "natural" in herself; she casts aside the mermaid costume and becomes the proper domesticated wife, ready to sacrifice herself for husband and children. But Wangel also loses his lady from the sea.

The expression of the nature-culture opposition in the play is, over and beyond the basic mermaid-human schism, expressed exactly as in the ballads. Ellida is from "natural" space, a place which is totally isolated and right on the sea. As a matter of fact, she grew up in a lighthouse, surrounded by water. Wangel makes the point that she was called the "heathen" (or "pagan") because she was called after a boat and not by a good Christian name.[79] In other words, the basic opposition is also expressed as a Christian-pagan opposition. Finally, once married to Wangel, Ellida keeps her distance from the rest of the household. She prefers a leaf-thatched hut she has had made for herself in the garden to the veranda of the house; she is always by the "wild" sea, whereas Wangel's two daughters, Bolette and Hilde, always are by the "domesticated" pond.

A favorite Ibsen theme, the "great cause" or "artist" theme, is in this play relegated to the second string of characters. Here it is, however, a repeat of the treatment it gets in *Kærlighedens Komedie*. The crucial trio of that early play, Falk/Svanhild/Guldstad are matched by Lyngstrand/Bolette/Arnholm. But the intrigue is the same, although expressed with more satirical bitterness. Young budding artist needs maid to inspire and "support" him. She must be willing to sacrifice all and to be discarded later on for someone younger (there are also similarities to the Gudmund Alfsøn/Margit/Bengt Gautesøn trio in *Gildet på Solhaug*). Bolette has the choice between the young artist who will—if he is indeed an artist—take her with him when he soars for the stars, and the well-to-do older gentleman who will give her all the material wealth she desires. As in the two earlier plays, Bolette chooses the older and more solid partner; she chooses the sensible, not the daring and exciting.

That the artist is the object of Ibsen's satire in this play is obvious, Lyngstrand, who aspires to become a sculptor, is a ridiculous fool, much like Julian Poulsen in *Sancthansnatten*, and Ballested who claims to be a painter is also a tourist guide and several other things. He does not take his art seriously and should not be taken seriously as an artist. But the works of art these two clowns paint or aspire to sculpt are central to the play. Ballested is painting a stranded mermaid on the verge of death, and Lyngstrand wants to create a "group" based on an experience he has had: the group is to include the young wife of a sailor, sleeping a restless and dream-ridden sleep, and the sailor husband she deceived hovering in the background, wet and ominous because he drowned. This provides two routes into the play. Ellida is both a stranded mermaid and an unfaithful "wife." What the two "artists" do not capture is the positive "synthesis" of these two negatives: Ellida's shedding her mermaid nature and liberation from the fateful marriage to the "drowned sailor."

I now return to the intertextual play between *Fruen fra havet* and the folklore. The significant folklore "other" is here the ballads about young men and women who are changed by trolls or witches into un-human shapes. I tie this in with my suggestion above that Alfred Johnston is the real demon in the play. He is the demon who has "bewitched" Ellida so she believes she is a mermaid. She is a human "trapped" inside the mind of a sea creature. She has been mesmerized by his eyes.[80]

The idea of Ellida as bewitched fits nicely with Lyngstrand's "sculpture," a sleeping woman, dreaming of the dead lover. This description suits Ellida perfectly: she is asleep even when she is awake; she is distant, constantly focusing on the image of the man who bewitched her.

Ellida's description of the Stranger is consistent with my labeling Johnston a witch: he has total power over her; she cannot say no to anything he demands. She is a zombie. Finally, the solution to Ellida's problem suggests the "trapped human": what releases her from the spell is the love of a human. In the ballads this is symbolized (as in, e.g., "The Troll and the Farmer's Wife") by a kiss. In *Lady from the Sea*, it is symbolized by the ultimate Ibsenian sacrifice: the willingness to give up the beloved so she can be happy.

Because Ellida is trapped in a mermaid's mind, she is unable to realize herself as a "natural"—that is, ironically, a domesticated—woman. This is exactly the story of the ballads, where the maid avoids wifely duties by eloping with the merman. And exactly as the maid who was trapped in a linden tree, Ellida is saved by the love of a human man.

I want to suggest that Ibsen may have incorporated into *Lady from the Sea* elements borrowed from Andersen's *Agnete and the Merman* (1833). The reason is that there are some striking similarities in both thematic treatment and in details. I mention a couple: Andersen's Agnete shares with Ellida a "natural" attachment to the sea. Agnete was born in the water during a storm, Ellida was born and brought up in a lighthouse, practically in the sea. The first scene of Andersen's play introduces a visitor who asks for Agnete and is told she is by the sea— as always. In *Lady from the Sea*, both Lyngstrand and Arnholm are told, when they ask, that Ellida is by the sea—as always.[81] Andersen's Agnete is, like Ellida, a young woman who refuses to be domestic(ated): she feels strangely drawn to the sea. Agnete's mother even gives an explanation of her daughter's affliction that is very similar to the one Wangel gives of Ellida's.[82]

Further, when Andersen's Agnete has married the merman, she sits in her under-the-sea home and sings a lullaby to her children by the merman. Her description in the song of the underwater world is very similar to Ellida's description of her conversations with Johnston about the sea.[83] The final point of similarity has to do with the refusal to be domestic and become a proper subordinate wife, mentioned above. For Andersen's Agnete, as for Ellida, the point behind marrying a sea creature is freedom. Agnete feels a strange attraction to the sea and simply cannot get herself to fulfill the role of wife and mother to a mortal man that is expected of her. Ellida both—as it turns out—in actuality and symbolically wants freedom (albeit freedom to choose). Symbolically this is expressed in her refusal to take on the "wife" role, her refusal to move into the human house: she refuses to give up the freedom offered by nature. Further, the stranger symbolizes—besides the sea—until the spell is broken, freedom from the "mountainman," Dr. Wangel, who has "seduced" her, if not with gold, then with a comfortable life.

The Stranger is first called "Friman" ("Freeman"), later he becomes "American." America is a symbol, and was then, of freedom from the constraints of the Old World. Lastly, on the model of *Rosmersholm*, it may be assumed that the merman symbolizes the aboriginal freedom and strength of the demonic creatures in the ballads that, to the romantics, signified the *Urseele*. The stranger is a freedom symbol until it becomes clear that he was the one who had "tied" her with his demonic powers. If we see in Dr. Wangel a Freudlike character, it would be tempting to say that he cures the "hysterical" woman who refuses to follow (nature's) oedipal call to submit to the "phallic signifier." Once the spell is broken—or the cure effected—Ellida can live out her love of Dr. Wangel and become the perfect mother for "their" children. She can move up on the veranda and take her baths—like everybody else— in the bathtub. When Wangel gives the ultimate proof of his love, Ellida is saved from the demons; she can shed her "mermaid" slough and revert to her original state of innocence and humanity.

There is no Hegelian synthesis of two positives—nature and culture— in the end, as Østerud claims. The "mermaid" is excised from Ellida, and she becomes a "normal," submissive, sacrificing housewife who sees mothering Hilde as her future calling.

Hedda Gabler

Many threads from earlier parts of Ibsen's production are brought together in *Lady from the Sea*. Thus, the "tainted relationship" is worked to a happy end, the aboriginal demon–modern man confrontation is given a new twist. One of the more interesting but sketchy details of the play that continues a thread from the past but that also points ahead is the image of the "rebellious amazon" girl or woman. The representative of that type of Ibsen character in *Fruen fra havet* is Hilde: the angry and mischievous stepdaughter of Ellida. Hilde is related to Margit in *Gildet på Solhaug*, to Hjørdis in *Hærmændene på Helgeland*, to Rebekka West, and she reappears in *Bygmester Solness*. These women all share having too many "male genes," as it were, which translates into such unfeminine character traits as sexual passion, personal ambition, fascination with war and weapons, and sometimes even a certain maliciousness. Hilde is malicious. She is fascinated with the fact that Lyngstrand, the would-be sculptor, is going to die. She enjoys making him talk about his great plans for the future while she knows, in the secrecy of her mind, that he will die without having achieved all the things he talks about. Hilde's fascination with death, her morbidity, and her enjoyment of playing mind games with men points to the next Ibsen play, *Hedda Gabler*. Hedda is an amazon, morbid and pervertedly playful, "masculine" yet seductive.

> *Miss Tesman:* Do you remember when she rode with her father along the road? In the long black dress? And with feathers in her hat?[84]

This is Hedda, the amazon, riding—all in black—with her father the general. The image is reminiscent of a description of Hjørdis in *Hærmændene på Helgeland:* "Hjørdis with a flock of servants. She is dressed in black, in a coat, cape and hood . . . [she] carries a light spear in her hand."[85] *Hedda Gabler* is—up to a point—a rewrite of *Hærmændene.* Hedda is a reincarnation of Hjørdis. There are a number of things that suggest this. Hjørdis thrives on blood and gore and on the fight. Hedda suddenly becomes alert when it is suggested that her husband Jørgen Tesman and Eilert Løvborg may have to compete for a professorship: "Imagine, Tesman, it will be almost like a kind of sports event."[86] But for the participants, as for Sigurd and Gunnar · in *Hærmændene* who have to duel, it is not a sports event—it is a fight for life and death. The image of Tesman and Løvborg as duelling vikings has already been suggested by Aunt Julle in the first scene, where all of the wonderful things that have clicked for Tesman are ticked off (his winning Hedda is among them). She speaks of Tesman's enemies as having "fallen," as in battle or in a match.[87] Still another clear similarity between Hedda and Hjørdis is that they both are mesmerized by weapons: those ultimately male (sexual) symbols. Hedda and Hjørdis both live in a dream world, a saga world, trapped in a violent and male-dominated society, but without recourse to participating on a par with the men. All they can do is twine the bow for their arrows or empty their guns aimlessly into the garden.

Ibsen is playing, once again with the idea of placing a mythic Nordic character in a modern setting. Hedda is a sister of the strong, violent, but beautiful women of the sagas. But if Hjørdis's position in *Hærmændene* was problematic, because she had married the wrong man, Hedda's is impossible. There is no "right" man for her. She has nothing but contempt for her husband, Tesman; Brack is a domesticated elf knight; and Løvborg—although the best candidate—is, in the final analysis, too weak. He has the passion and the lust for life that fascinates her, but he is too nervous and modern to be her match.

Hedda chooses instead to flee into a fantasy world, a fairy world. She becomes a *huldre,* a fairy-tale creature, obsessed with beauty and refusing to let the real world capture and swallow her. In his excellent Marxist reading of the play, Helge Rønning says, "Hedda Gabler's tragedy lies in the fact that freedom cannot be realized within the framework of the society she is part of."[88] For this reason she chooses to remain aloof, to live in a fantasy world. She refuses to be tainted with "reality": when Løvborg made a pass at her years ago she had to end the affair because "there was an imminent danger that reality would enter the relationship."[89]

The play presents with all possible clarity the options Hedda has as a woman in a male-dominated society. On the one hand she can be like Aunt Julle or Thea: self-effacing and sacrificing herself for others (principally men). Julle has to have another sick person in the house after her bedridden sister is dead; she has to have something to live for: sacrificing herself for someone, no matter whom. Thea finds her highest happiness in being able to *beånde,* "give soul to," Løvborg's great opus. She would never even think of trying to create something herself, being an inspiration, a supportive friend, a "greenhouse" for Løvborg's ideas is enough for her. On the other side is Diana, the night club singer and huntress (of men): a fallen and almost unmentionable woman. Hedda has, perhaps, most in common with this cheap facsimile of the Roman goddess of the hunt, but she could never be a social outcast. She has to remain in her paradoxical fairy land—a fact she is fully conscious of. When Tesman says to her (in connection with the possibility that he will have to compete with Løvborg for the professorship), "one should really never venture into the fairy land," she answers, with some consternation and amusement, "Do *you* do that?" She knows full well that he does not. The fairy land is her domain.[90]

Hedda Gabler can go on living, although bored and depressed at her social downfall, as long as she has her freedom. With Jørgen Tesman she has lost only a small part of that freedom: she can no longer be the proud and unapproachable "Marstigs daughter" waiting for her nix, but she is in control.[91] Tesman does not impinge on her separate reality: he is an inconvenience, but a minor one. But when reality presses itself upon her and wants to tie her down and steal her freedom, as Løvborg did when he made a sexual pass at her, and as Brack does when he suddenly has power over her: then she defends herself and her freedom. She threatens to shoot Løvborg and evicts him from her life and she dies a death of beauty—in her own fantasy world—before Brack can use his power over her. Hedda's protest and protection against the roles patriarchy will let her play is to remain outside society. When the wall to her fairy kingdom is about to fall down, forcing her into the role of mistress and sex object, she kills herself.

The folklore in *Hedda Gabler* is rich and varied. Hedda herself bears resemblance both to the saga women and to the proud girls of the ballads, only in her case the nix never came: she married a boring mortal out of despair. She was getting too old to play foresinger at the dance.

The nature-culture schism is interestingly expressed: Jørgen Tesman is not only the representative in a symbolic sense of "culture," he is *kulturstipendiat,* a scholar interested in culture. His interest is—ironically?—"domestic industry in the Middle Ages,"[92] the period when Hedda's alter ego, Hjørdis, was making the crafting of bows and arrows *her* domestic industry. He is oriented toward Europe, the south (almost anything is south vis-à-vis Norway). The south, Europe, is in Ibsen, as it will be remembered, always a symbol of culture. Hedda is not interested in his culture: she hated being abroad because it kept her away from "our circle," as she says to Brack.[93] There is a paradox here: Hedda hates "culture" in the sense of "high" culture and learning, but she is, despite her demon nature, so far "enculturated" that she is constantly attracted like a moth to the bright lights of human society. She is, in a sense, still a stranger to human culture; the attractions are those that would be perceived by someone watching from the outside.

Thea Rysing married the elf king, bailif Elvstad ("Elftown").[94] Not surprisingly, Thea was not happy with her dull old elf king who really just wanted a housekeeper. But she had taken his "gold" and was stuck in the mountain.[95] It is interesting, incidentally, how well the nineteenth-century marriage fits the model of the young woman locked up in a cave in the mountain. Especially if she married just to be supported. She had to sell her soul and her body to a troll/man in exchange for food and shelter. Once married, she was every bit as helplessly stuck as any girl in the mountain. Thea was lucky, however; the young knight with his magic harp came and "played" her out: Løvborg came and gave her the strength to escape: trust and love.

In *Hedda Gabler*, Ibsen uses a device that he is particularly fond of: he splits a character into two to get a more accurate closeup of both aspects of the character. Hedda and Thea represent two sides of Hjørdis, who wanted to sacrifice herself totally for the man she really loved and with whom she was destined to be. She also had a fierce and independent mind and a certain masculine aggressiveness and preoccupation with violence and death. Hjørdis also had courage and will to act. Thea represents the "feminine" side of Hjørdis, the side that wants to sacrifice and support. She also represents the courage and will to act. Hedda represents all the negative aspects: the masculinity, the independence and the obsession with violence, death and destruction. And Hedda is a coward; she cannot act, she cannot enter life. The only "real" act in her life is the one that shall secure that she will never have to enter reality: her suicide.

Hedda Gabler is, of course, also a play about the nature and provenance of art and the artist in a modern society. Løvborg is the artist, who, true to Ibsenian form, needs a woman to give "soul" to his art. He writes about culture history and—his most creative effort, his membership card to the rank of artists—about the future of culture. Løvborg and Thea work together like *kammerater*, "good friends," and manage to produce a masterpiece. But their relationship is tainted; it is built on treacherous soil. She is the wife of the elf king, she has sold herself to him, and worse still, he has loved, loves still, perhaps, another woman. They engender a spiritual child, but it is, as all Ibsen "children" born to tainted unions, doomed. When it becomes clear that their "friendship" was built on sandy soil, that she never really believed in him, the spell is gone and death and destruction is the only possible outcome. Løvborg, like all Ibsen artists, must have total trust to be able to create.

Løvborg has some of the demonic in him. He embodies will to live, even lust for life, and an unconventionality of spirit that puts him outside the ordinary human sphere. His appetites as well as his gifts are beyond the ordinary. As long as a loving woman is beside him, trusting him, tempering his wildness and giving his creative energies direction and soul, he is fine, but once she stops believing in him he is a victim of his own unruly nature.

This image of the artist is, of course, the one outlined at the beginning of this chapter: the artist is—as Ibsen and his contemporaries saw him—a man with boundless energies and gifts but without control. If he is left to his own devices he will self-destruct. If a woman loves and helps him he can create as long as she is there. But once she is gone, and she will have to go when her job is done, he falls prey, once again, to the wild animals inside himself.

The artist is in a no-win situation. He cannot create without the antisocial "nature" inside him, but it is equally true that he cannot create without a modifying influence from a representative of "culture," a creature with a soul to give. If the artist lets himself be tied too much to the woman who helps him, he will become domesticated, the butterfly dust will be mopped off his wings and he will be an ordinary man. The best he can hope for is to create one major work of beauty and that it will survive him. He is himself under all circumstances destined for destruction. The artist has, like the young man in the poem "På viddene," to know that someone loves him and trusts him and waits for him and sacrifices herself for him, but he has to "go it alone," he has to ascend the snow-clad and slippery *fjelle* alone, and watch the house of mother and fiancée from the heights—in the company of a stranger—death.

Bygmester Solness

In *Bygmester Solness* (*The Master Builder*) we find the metaphor of the artist who has to climb to the heights in the company of death transformed into reality: Halvard Solness has to climb to the top of high church steeples to realize himself as an artist. Solness has, however, an embarrassing problem: heights make him dizzy. In other words, Solness is not the great artist he would like to think he is.

In this play about the artist who is not, Ibsen can have his protagonist discuss the role of the artist in society with great openness. Solness does not have what it takes to be great, but he is convinced that he does, so convinced that he goes in constant fear that the powers that helped him reach, as it were, the pinnacle are going to cash in because of the sacrifices that were made on his behalf. Solness feels that the turning point in his life was one fateful night when his house—really his wife's house—

burned down. After this crucial and traumatic event followed other events: his twin sons died and his career as a builder took off. In his head he connects all these events, the mediating force being his secret and fervent wish that the house would burn. The fire did not start where he had imagined and wished it would, still he feels that his wishes, the trolls and devils inside him, made the fire happen. He gave the lives of his infant children—they were the sacrificial victims—for which the trolls gave him success. His great fear stems from his feeling that he did not pay the price, his wife Aline did. So although the trolls were paid off, he still feels he has an unsettled account. Indeed, Solness bears a resemblance to Goethe's Faust, who has an unsettled account with the devil.

The house and the lives of his children were the price he had to pay, just as the price the royal couple in "German Gladensvend" had to pay to make the troll let go of their ship was their unborn son. This ballad is a folklore source for the play, and we shall see below that another major theme in the play is derived from this ballad. The price Solness has paid for being a "master builder" of houses for happy families to live in, is his inability to have a family himself.

The image of Solness as a master builder hinges on his ability to build churches and steeples for churches. In this he is like that other master builder, Saint Olav, who Christianized Norway and built churches.[96] But Solness stopped building churches. He was a Saint Olav, he tapped into his Norwegian roots and created structures where Norwegians could gather, in other words, structures that helped symbolize national unity. He built a new steeple on an old church in the town Hilde Wangel comes from, and harp music sounded.[97] One might say that he was Olav reincarnate: he built a new tower on Olav's old church. The national symbolism is also brought out in Hilde's description of the event: "There was music in the cemetery. And many hundred people. We schoolgirls were dressed in white. And then we all had flags."[98] It is all there in this image: the church tower as an edifice that brings people together to celebrate their national unity (the flags), and Solness who is in the center, on top of the church steeple hanging a wreath on the vane. But then he stopped building churches and began building houses for ordinary people (just as Rubek in *Når vi døde vågner* stopped creating major art works to make busts of the rich instead).

From erecting buildings that united people, Solness went to constructing houses that isolated them. From being an idealist who wanted to unify the people, he became an entrepreneur and a capitalist who created a fortune by separating his countrymen. From being public property, the artist became the darling of the bourgeoisie. But when the artist abandons his ideals he stops—in Ibsen's opinion—being an artist. And, perhaps Solness never was an artist: he could never stand heights. It made him afraid to be alone on the pinnacle watching the people in the valley below, to use the image from "På viddene" again.

Perhaps Solness never was Saint Olav either: Hilde remembers all the grandeur surrounding the church tower. She remembers for him his role as troll and idealist. He remembers nothing. This may be a symbolic expression of his amnesia of his national roots in Saint Olav, the church builder. When Hilde forces him to remember what never was he begins to believe he can be the man her imagination has fostered, but when he ascends the tower and is at the pinnacle, he becomes dizzy and falls. He cannot recoup a greatness he never had.

While Solness may not be a real artist, his description of the artist's lot and the price he has to pay fit perfectly what emerges from other Ibsen plays on this subject. The artist has to be alone and not afraid of heights. He has to be prepared for being destroyed by his art. It is interesting to speculate on whether Ibsen saw in himself a Solness. Like Solness he began by creating idealistic structures that were supposed to hold a mirror up to the nation and show its soul. Like Solness—and Rubek—he became the darling of the bourgeoisie by creating structures they could live in, portraits of them. The simile is tempting and Ibsen may possibly have had—in his most depressed moments—a feeling that Solness was he. But we can, in hindsight, acquit Ibsen: his was a creative opus that extended far beyond his own time and class.

The price the artist has to pay is only part of the price that has to be paid. However, the woman who loves the artist has to pay an even more heart-rending price. She has to give herself totally, sacrificing her own happiness and her own hope of fulfillment. Aline Solness has to see her children die and her parental home burn down with everything she loved in it. She has to live a life of barrenness and devotion to her husband. This, of course, is Solness's rendition of it. He feels that Aline could not fulfill her potential for being a raiser of children because she had to be sacrificed for his success. And he feels guilty and lives in fear of a retribution he knows must come. More concretely, he lives in fear of the young. Like the old wolf who has reigned the flock for years, he is living in constant fear of younger males who might challenge him for the leadership of the flock or, worse still, who might leave the flock to start a competing flock.

Aline Solness interprets the events around the fire and the death of the children quite differently. She does not blame her husband but herself for the death of the children—and she has found peace in knowing they are in Heaven. Her big tragedy in life is that her house with all her memories has been destroyed. She can never find a home after that. She has lost her identity—but she has not, as Solness would like to believe, identified with him. She is a child lost forever in liminal space, just as Agnete, who left her parents' home to marry the merman, is lost forever in limbo between the human and the demonic spheres.

The reason Solness has to carry all the guilt around with him is exactly that he is not a real artist. As Hilde puts it, he has a "sickly conscience":[99] he lacks, perhaps, conviction in his own calling, he is not ruthless as the real artist must be. Where does Solness have the idea from that he is a great artist? He feels that he is one of the, as he puts it, "chosen, selected people who have been given the power to *yearn* for something, *desire* something, *want* something—so strongly and so—ruthlessly—that they *must* get it in the end."[100] He feels that it is not the person wishing who has the power to obtain what is wanted. It is the helpers who have that power. But only the chosen and stubborn individual can obtain their services. Solness feels that he has obtained the help of "devils," that the "troll" inside has served his purposes. He has, in other words, cast himself as a troll and is then both revolted and afraid of his own image.

Solness is a negative version of Oehlenschläger's Aladdin.[101] He sees himself as a "nature's happy son" who has obtained the magic lamp. The lamp gives him the power over the helpers and servants. The name of the kingdom Solness was going to buy for Hilde is also a witty allusion to Oehlenschläger's play: Appelsinia.[102] Aladdin, being lady luck's chosen, had the *appelsin* ("orange") fall right into his turban without doing anything. But Solness is, of course, no happy son of nature.

Solness is a wonderfully intricate and complex figure. He is an ordinary man who feels that he is chosen and thus has a debt to pay. But he is also a man with some gifts, notably power over women and the ability to build pleasing houses for ordinary people. I wonder whether Ibsen, through Solness, and through his "continuation," Professor Rubek (*Når vi døde vågner*), rebels against the romantic and Nietzschean image of the artist as chosen and special. Against this it can, of course, be argued that Solness is not a bona fide artist, but only a man who thinks he is an artist. I shall revert to this quandary in my discussion of Professor Rubek.

The women in *Bygmester Solness* are worth looking at separately because they are at the very core of the play. Kaja Fosli is a character taken from the folk-ballad toolkit. She is a "Harp" maid, engaged to be married, timid, and an instant victim for even an amateur troll like Halvard Solness. Having told her story before, Ibsen can afford to let it fizzle out. Miss Fosli is a dramaturgical device: she is a kind of dramatic tracer for Hilde Wangel. She introduces us to some crucial aspects of the Solness-Hilde relationship: she has been able to divine what Solness merely thought (reminiscent of the "Nix" ballad, where the nix "reads" the maid's thoughts). Solness is a Nix who can read his thoughts into someone else's mind. This theme comes up again with Hilde and her remembering his visit in her town. Perhaps Hilde only remembers what Solness, the dreamer, thought?[103] Kaja is also used as a backdrop for Hilde: she is weak and timid and sickly but in love with Solness. Hilde is the exact opposite on all counts, except that she too is in love with Solness. When Kaja has served her function, she is brusquely waved out of Solness's life and out of the play.

Aline Solness is a more interesting character, but also a shadowy one. In Solness's scenario, discussed above, she is the artist's wife who had to sacrifice all and to whom he owes all. To herself, she is simply a person without an identity. She is a typical Victorian wife: a woman who has lost all ties to the parental home, symbolized by the burned house. She has not managed to make the transition to a new identity as Mrs. Solness, possibly because he has never allowed her to. His guilt complexes—and possibly his contempt for her—have led him to protect and avoid her. The result is that she is trapped forever in the liminal space between childhood and womanhood. Her most significant memory is of nine dolls that were destroyed in the fire: "I carried them under my heart. Just like little unborn children."[104]

Hilde Wangel is the same Hilde Wangel who found it exciting that Lyngstrand, the would-be sculptor, was going to die without living out his dreams. Ibsen was obviously fascinated with her and after she had grown up he let her leave her father, Dr. Wangel, and her home in the mountains and come down to town to wreck havoc there.

Hilde is a reversed German Gladensvend. German was, as it may be remembered, promised to the "Loathsome Gam" by his parents when the gam had them in his fangs on open sea. The contract was that German should be "collected" by the gam when he came of age. In the ballad, of course, the gam came at the appointed time only to find that German had been hidden by his parents. Eventually German himself left home to find the young woman he loved and met the gam and destruction instead.

Hilde, unlike German, desired the gam or troll to come back and collect her—but he did not. So, Hilde goes out to find her troll. She, like the hero of the ballad, meets the troll on his own turf, but the outcome is different: the troll has forgotten—he is rather a geriatric and fragile troll—and she has to remind him and convince him that he is, indeed, a troll. The outcome is that the would-be troll is destroyed. The intertextual play here is wonderfully imaginative and poignant: Hilde dreams that she is a princess promised to a troll, she then casts Solness as the troll and implants her dream into him. Finally he is destroyed by that dream. She resembles the early Ibsen heroines who have dreamt folklore dreams all their lives. She differs from those early heroines in that she is not just an ordinary girl, destined for a happy end with marriage and church bells. She is dangerous, seductive, and destructive. She seduces and destroys the seducer and destroyer.

Hilde is also a catalyst who pulls all the secret dreams of his being a troll/artist out of Solness, and forces him to test them. She makes him live out his dream of being a lucky and plucky Aladdin and he, as it were, overreaches himself. He is no Aladdin, heights do make him dizzy, and he falls to his death. Solness's dream was a lie, he was no troll, no "devils" were at his command, and only in his dreams could he fly.

Hilde flies in her dreams too. She falls off a cliff and soars amid fear and excitement. She is another Ibsen dreamer, another woman who cannot face reality and prefers to dream instead: "It is so immensely wonderful to lie there and dream."[105] She is against "duty," meaning she's against having to face up to social demands on her. She shares a dream with Solness; she *makes* Solness share a dream with her. The dream is that she is a girl who has been promised to a troll when young. The troll is going to buy her a kingdom and she is going to be a princess. Solness is the troll and she comes to cash in on her abduction and her kingdom. Unfortunately, the troll has forgotten.

And now the troll and the maiden reverse the roles. She becomes the "Loathsome Gam" and he becomes the human victim. In German Gladensvend, the Gam is able to change shape: at one point it is in the ocean where the couple sails; later, when German borrows his mother's bird robe and flies to his fiancée, it is a bird of prey. Hilde too is a bird of prey,

> *Solness:* You are like a wild bird in the forest.
> *Hilde:* Far from *that.* I don't hide under the bushes.
> *Solness:* No, no. More likely there is bird of prey in you.
> *Hilde:* Maybe more of that—perhaps. (With great vehemence.) And why not bird of prey! Why shouldn't *I* too go in search of prey. Take the prey I want? If I can get my claws in it. Overcome it.[106]

Solness is the prey and Hilde gets her psychological tentacles deep into him.

Hilde wants to see her troll, her artist soar and she lives for the excitement that he may fall. When he does she is both desolate and triumphant: she "got her kick" out of Solness and of his fall from the heights. He will from now on be hers because his death was hers: "Hilde (in what seems like quiet disconsolate triumph): But he got all the way to the top. And I heard harps in the air. (Swings her shawl up and screams with wild intensity.) *My—my* master builder!"[107]

Hilde seduces Solness with her dream of a kingdom he is to give to her. She wants to soar, but, being a woman, she has to do so vicariously. She can only dream of flying, she has to get someone else to actually do it. Ironically, she is throughout the entire play dressed for the mountains. She dreams of falling and wants her castle to be way up on the top of the world, but she never entertains the thought that she might actually "fly" herself. So, she seduces Solness, who is marked off as marginal by his own dreams of grandeur, his pride and conviction that he is different. Hilde is the real troll of this play: she is ruthless and willful and seductive. She is youth knocking, like fate, on Solness's door—as he predicts it will—and she destroys him—as he also predicts.

Lille Eyolf

In the modern, realistic, Ibsen plays, the first set is always a cozy, warm, living room populated with cultural symbols such as furniture, pillows and bric-à-brac. But nature is never far away; always visible through windows and glass doors; fjords and *fjelle* ("mountains") are always just beyond the panes, reminding both the audience and the characters that we may be cultural animals who have carved our space and built our buffers, but that we are never distant from nature, neither the one surrounding us, nor the one within. The sets also always carry reminders that we are not living in a vacuum: there are portraits of ancestors and of government officials that place us in historical time and in social space. Nature outside the windows is a reminder of our ultimate provenance: the *fjelle* and the fjords are so typically Norwegian that they serve as reminders to a Norwegian audience of the mythical and distinctly Norwegian demons that used to, and perhaps still do, populate them.

The set for the opening act of *Lille Eyolf* is no exception to the above, although the portraits are missing.[108] In this play one of the protagonists has just emerged from a six- or seven-week foot trip to the mountains. As the play opens, Rita Allmers is unpacking the suitcase of her husband, Alfred Allmers. Alfred Allmers has been "På viddene." He has, like the young man in Ibsen's poem, been in the mountains to have his calling as an artist confirmed. He had to get away from the coziness of the home and from the polluting company of women. Rita's earthy and passionate sexuality has kept him weighted down. Great art and lofty thoughts need fresh air and lack of creature comforts to develop and soar. What Allmers found on the mountain was, as was the case with the man in the poem, death. He had a chance to walk with death as his companion for a stretch and death was a good companion and not a fearful one. He also found inspiration. Or maybe what he found was humility, realization that he was not cut out to write the great book. Allmers comes home ready to start his new project: making a happy human being of his and Rita's son, Eyolf.[109]

Eyolf has to learn to be happy with what he has. And what Eyolf has is less than the average boy. Eyolf is handicapped. Allmers wants to make him happy with what he is and can be. Obviously Allmers is projecting: he found in the mountains that he himself was not cut out to be the great artist. He himself has a "handicap" that keeps him from achieving greatness, and he decides to make it his great achievement to make Eyolf accept his handicap and mediocrity.

The reason Eyolf can never reach greatness, the reason he is handicapped, is that he is the product of a polluted relationship: what Allmers and Rita have or had was only physical, only lust. They never really had—or, for that matter, wanted to have Eyolf:

> *Allmers:* If it is as you think, then we two have never really owned our own child.
> *Rita:* No. Not fully in love.
> *Allmers:* And yet we go here and mourn him so bitterly.
> *Rita* (with bitterness): Yes, isn't it strange. To go here and mourn so for a strange little boy.[110]

Eyolf is, as his name suggests, owned by elves (Norwegian *eie* means "own"; I'm assuming—although the etymology admittedly is a bit far-fetched—that Ibsen was playing on the similarity of *-olf* to *alf*, "elf"). His parents never allowed him to become human because they never loved him for himself. They estranged him: he was "strange" both in the sense of being different and in the sense of not being their child, because they never really loved him.

When the *Rottejomfru*, "Rat Maiden," comes, it is to collect little Eyolf. The scene with her is uncanny in all its insistence that Eyolf is exactly what she has come for. She will remove "all that crawls and swarms," "all those that people hate and prosecute." She talks of the rat children, and when she, at one point, says that she used to lure people, Eyolf asks, "Oh, tell me who that was?" "It was the one I loved, my little breaker of hearts."[111]

In the Allmerses' home there is indeed something that "crawls and swarms," and Rita Allmers thinks it is Eyolf who competes with her for Allmers's love. She talks of his "evil children's eyes," and all but expresses her desire that he were dead.[112] And soon he is—he follows the *Rottejomfru* and drowns in the fjord.

Perhaps Eyolf is symbolic of the great book Allmers is writing, called "Human Responsibility." Eyolf is, of course, his parents' responsibility and they cannot face that responsibility. In Ibsen, the great opus is only created as the result of a perfect union, a union between a man of genius and a woman who willingly sacrifices herself for him. The perfect union is also one which is built on a foundation of a great mutual love unpolluted by sexuality and ulterior motives. The Allmerses fall far short of this ideal. He married her for pecuniary reasons. Her "gold and green forests," a standard Scandinavian expression of "all the riches in the world," which she lured him with are alluded to several times in the play, first in jest, and later on in bloody seriousness. Rita Allmers loves her Alfred but in a stifling and destructive way. She has a voracious sexual appetite and, far from sacrificing herself and her own desires, she cannot even share him with his work or their child.

In *Lille Eyolf* Ibsen plays again with the idea of the artist who is not one. Allmers is a weak and spineless man who, to produce something great, would have to be dependent on the support of a loving woman. But Rita is not a loving woman, in Ibsen's sense, she is an elf, a *huldre*, who seduced her victim by offering him "gold and green forests" and with her physical attractiveness.[113] This is reminiscent of the ballads "Hr. Bøsmer" and "Elveskud," where the knight is stopped by elfin maidens on his way to his wedding. The maidens promise him all the riches he may want and they dance seductively. The young knight is afraid, but he succumbs because of the beauty of the maiden. When Rita and Allmers discuss why he married her, she asks him what he felt for her in the beginning,

> *Allmers:* Fear.
> *Rita:* I can understand that. But how did I win you anyway?
> *Allmers* (quietly): You were so unspeakably lovely.[114]

There are two curious things about the above exchange. Why would she find it understandable that he was afraid of her, and it is most unusual, for the period, that she speaks about "winning him." Possibly he was afraid because of her fervor, but both that and her directness are suggestive of the "child of nature," the elf or huldre. Rita is the elf king's daughter who lured the poor young man into her cave and her bed. One other feature that suggests her demonic nature is that she is tied to one spot. When she at one point suggests that they move away, he rejects it flatly on the grounds that she could never live anywhere else. The elf or *huldre* is always tied to a geographical location, which is her home. If she is moved she perishes.[115]

Once Rita has Allmers, she does not let him go. Much is made of the fact that she has not let him leave the house for as much as one single night since they were married. He is locked in the mountain, like Tannhäuser. In the folklore the human is at one point allowed to leave the mountain to visit family and friends. Allmers is allowed to revisit himself as the aspiring artist he was before. He is allowed to go on a hiking trip to the mountains to finish his book.

When Allmers realizes that he must extract himself from Rita's clinging embrace he looks to his sister Asta. Asta is only a half sister; they have the same father. They have always loved each other in a free and innocent and even *kammeratlig* way, meaning in the way in which two males can love each other. They used to play a game where she dressed up in his clothes from when he was a boy and he would call her Eyolf. In the ballads it is, of course, customary that the abducted human is saved by a fiancé or brother. Allmers expects that Asta will "save" him, let him move in with her again. But there is a complication, recognizable from the "Rosmer" ballad: Asta loves Allmers not as a sister, but as a woman. She knows from some letters she has of her mother's that they are not brother and sister. But even though they are not, after all, genetically related, she feels a union between them would be incestuous and she rejects him. Because she loves him she cannot live with him again.

Once all the various threads are disentangled it becomes increasingly clear how closely the play follows the ballad. If Asta is not Allmers's sister, and since they have always loved each other, then Rita did take him away from the human woman he loved. Allmers is trapped in the elfin maid's lair forever. He has himself become one of the elves and the two of them try to "seduce" Asta to stay with them to take the place of Eyolf, with whom she, in a sense, shares an identity. But Asta manages to escape. When she leaves, Allmers says, "What is this, Asta? It looks like you are fleeing." She answers that it is a flight, she is fleeing from him, and from herself, from his "seduction" and that in her which wants to be seduced.[116] She goes back to the town with the man who saves her, the road builder, Borgheim.

Asta manages to escape back to "culture," the town, because of Borgheim who gives her an alternative to staying with Rita and Allmers.

Borgheim is suggestive of still another folk ballad that we have already seen used in *Bygmester Solness*. Borgheim is a Saint Olav, and builds roads across the mountains, just as Saint Olav sailed his ship right through and across the mountains. And Borgheim's roads serve the same purpose that Saint Olav's churches did: it brings the people together, it unites the nation.

Borgheim and Asta, like Ragnar in *Bygmester Solness*, represent a new generation who forge ahead, full of enthusiasm and idealism. A generation that embodies all the best in the national tradition, they merge all that is good in the heritage with all that is good in youth. Allmers and Rita, on the other hand, represent a dying order, a perverted and aimless idealism that has no use: art for art's sake, and a love that does not lift and give life but that sucks life and kills like a praying mantis.

John Gabriel Borkman

Although this is his second-to-last play, it is the one of all his plays that most clearly epitomizes Ibsen's own theory, expressed in "Om Kjæmpevisen og dens Betydning for Kunstpoesien," with regard to the use of folklore material in writing literature. This is another indication, if one was needed, that Ibsen never abandoned his idea of integrating folklore and literature.

In his essay, Ibsen clearly makes a distinction between the Aryan tribes invading Scandinavia and the resident non-Aryans—Finns and Lapps—they drove further north and further into the *fjelle*. The Aryans are described as tall and blond and full of lust for life, whereas the non-Aryans are described as small and dark and mysterious, full of "secret" knowledge and deceit.[117]

John Gabriel Borkman is representative of the non-Aryans; he shares with these people, as described by Ibsen, the knowledge of how to force the gold out from its hiding places in the mountains. He is, as he puts it, "en bergmanns søn," "a miner's son." In translation is lost, however, the image inherent in the Norwegian that he is a mountainman's son—as in the ballads. His father used to take him with him down in the mines, where "the ore sings . . . when it is chopped loose. The hammerblows that loosen it,—that's the midnight bells tolling and setting it free. That's why the ore sings—for joy—in a way."[118]

Borkman is described as Ibsen describes the non-Aryan races in his essay: he is "of middle height, a firmly and powerfully built man in his sixties . . . keen eyes and greyish-white, frizzy hair and beard."[119] This is interesting also because it matches the description given of Saint Olav in a book by Olav Bø about him, "Many personal features seem . . . to be identical for Olav and Tor [the Nordic god of thunder and war]. They are described as powerfully built ("fat"), with red hair, with penetrating eyes, tough."[120] I shall return to the similarity to Saint Olav below.

The Aryan, although not portrayed as an adversary, in the sense of competing with him, is his son, Erhart Borkman. Erhart is Borkman's opponent in the sense that he is the new generation that is about to take over. He refuses to be dragged down by anything: not by his father's downfall, not by his mother's wish to use him for her own redemption and not by Ella Rentheim's need for his love. Erhart is going to live his life, to shape the world he lives in to his demands and desires. He wants—ruthlessly—to live and love and be happy on his own terms, just as the Aryan tribes ruthlessly drove out the earlier population, disregarding their culture and history.

An interesting image in *John Gabriel Borkman* is that of Borkman, the miner's son. It refers back, not only to Ibsen's essay on folklore, and to "The Miner of Falun" (see Leavy), but also to his poem "Bergmannen" ("The Miner"). I quote the first verse of the poem,

> Mountain wall break with crash and thunder
> from my hammer's heavy blow!
> Downwards I must clear the way
> till I hear the ore resound.[121]

The similarity, both in vocabulary and in imagery to the passage from the play cited above is obvious. The poem describes the thoughts of a man, a miner. He remembers his childhood, lived in the light of day. Then he went into the mine to extract gold and precious stones. He expected to find truth and answers to the mysteries of life in the darkness, but all he found was more darkness. Unable to see by light he keeps on hammering, digging further and further into the darkness and the hopelessness.

There are elements of this in the play. Borkman wanted to penetrate the mountains and to extract the riches that would make humanity happier and richer. He kept digging further and further down, but did not find what he sought. Instead he found the darkness and confinement of jail and the hall in the Rentheim home that he did not even dare leave after dark. Borkman, like the miner in the poem, keeps digging deeper and deeper. He cannot see by the light of day—by allowing himself to face the reality that his dream was a mirage—he keeps believing the answers to all his and life's problems are in the mines. At one point in the play, Mrs. Borkman says, about Erhart, "He shall live his life in purity, loftiness and light, so that your own mine-shaft-life will be as if eradicated up here on earth."[122]

To the image of Borkman the "Bergman's" son is added that of Borkman the king of darkness. He acted like a king in his days of glory. Toward the end of the play, when Borkman and Ella Rentheim take inventory of their lives, Borkman says, "Do you see the mountain ranges *there*—far away? One behind the other. They stand tall. They tower. *That* is my deep, endless kingdom."[123]

Borkman would be a *bjergkonge*, a "mountain king," like the mountain kings of the ballads, who owned all the gold and riches in nature. The would-be *bjergkonge* is also reminiscent of Skule, the would-be king of *Kongsemnerne*, who tries to become king by "stealing" Håkon's, the true king's, great idea of unifying the Norwegian kingdom. Skule, like Borkman, was a pretender who lacked the requisite personal qualities to become what he so desperately desired, a savior of mankind and a great hero. Both Skule and Borkman are modeled after Saint Olav, the man who Christianized Norway.[124] Like Borkman, Olav and Skule were, finally, betrayed by their own men. All three of them, possibly even all four of them, including Thor, the god who was "killed" by his own Nordic "constituents," who gave up belief in him, are unsuccessful in their endeavors because no one believes in them. Ultimately, they are of course unsuccessful because their ambition is too personal, too egotistic, too megalomaniac, too exclusive of those who could lend "soul" and "unselfishness" to their quest and transform merely ambitious men into great ones. The plots of *Kongsemnerne* and *John Gabriel Borkman* show clearly enough the similarities, but that Borkman should be a (perverted) Saint Olav is perhaps less obvious. I quote again from Bø on the personality and quirks of Olav Håkonsson, king of Norway:

From the sagas it emerges that he must have seemed volatile and vengeful, he was hard and commanding and not at all petty. It is obvious from what Snorre [the Icelandic chronicler of the early Nordic kings] says that his men certainly were fond of him but that they also were afraid of him. For they knew that there was a dangerous seriousness in him. He hit hard when something made him angry. To negotiate and haggle was not in consort with his nature and he could not bend or give in.[125]

And later on he is described as "hard, avaricious and mean-spirited."[126] He has a *kongstanke*, "a great ideal": Norway as one united kingdom.[127] Still later on in Bø's book he is described in the following terms: "He was made for the grand style and the goal he had set for himself was attractive but dangerous. . . . [I]t was not an easy matter to unite Norway, to found the kingdom."[128]

That could have been a description of Borkman. He is, like Saint Olav and Skule, hard and mean-spirited, vengeful and convinced of the importance of his "great idea." Like Saint Olav he wants to unite and liberate. Olav wants to unite and liberate the Norwegian people, Borkman wants to "unite" and "liberate" the gold in the mines to create a fortune that will make him the uncrowned king of Norway, because everybody will benefit from his great idea. He will become "king" of a Norway united in admiration and gratitude toward him. But Borkman is a "negative" image of Olav; his kingdom is a cold, dark, subterranean one, as Ella says, in response to his declaration about his kingdom:

> *Ella Rentheim:* Oh, but an icy wind gusts from your kingdom, John!
> *Borkman:* That gust is like a breath of life to me. That gust comes to me like a greeting from subordinate spirits. I feel them, the tied up millions; I feel the ore stretching its winding, branching, enticing arms towards me. I saw them before me like shadows come alive—that night when I stood in the bank vault with the lamp in my hand. You wanted to be released then. And I tried to do it. But I couldn't. The treasure sank into the depths again (with outstretched hands). But I will whisper it to you in the darkness of night. I love thee, there thou lie lifeless but alive in the abyss and the darkness. I love thee, ye life

demanding riches—with all your shining retinue of power and glory. I love, love, love thee.

Ella Rentheim (in quiet but mounting agitation): Yes, down there you have your love still, John. You always had it down there. But up here in the daylight—here was a warm, throbbing human heart which beat for you. And that heart you crushed. Oh, more than that! Ten times worse! You sold it for—

Borkman (shivering; he looks like he is having a cold spell): For the power—and the glory—and the honor,—you mean?[129]

Borkman was convinced that the ore was singing to be released, convinced that he was the man chosen to swing the hammer to release it. He was so sure that he was an Aladdin, the elect, fate's darling, that he felt he had rights others do not have. He had rights to break laws that should not apply to him, the *Übermensch*, the *unntagelsesmenneske*, "exceptional man."[130] He was a Solness without doubts, a Solness who did not get dizzy in the heights. But Borkman was no more an Aladdin than Solness was; he was a *Noureddin*, the prince of darkness and Aladdin's adversary in Oehlenschläger's play. He was a man who wanted to force fate to give him power and glory.

In *John Gabriel Borkman*, Ibsen is playing with the romantic idea of the chosen, nature's darling. But he has a grimmer view of him than did the Danish poet. There are no chosen people and one cannot force fate. Even the counterpart to Borkman, his son Erhart, is perhaps not much better than his father: Erhart chooses to live in the light, but he, like his father is blinded by a false god: he is going to devote his life to sensuality—no matter what the consequences may be. He runs off with his Fanny Wilton[131] to enjoy the pleasures of the flesh.

As Ella Rentheim suggests, Borkman not only ruined his own life, he broke the social rules and with them the social fabric. As I wrote in the second chapter, the one who breaks the rules has to be punished because he destroys the social order: his faux pas is apt to bring down society itself if the culprit is not punished. Borkman is abandoned by all those who knew him and were his friends because he is polluted. The only people who still see him are those who are themselves outcasts and those he pulled down with him in his fall.

When Borkman gave up the woman he loved for the "power and the glory," he destroyed two more lives: those of the Rentheim sisters, Gunhild and Ella. With the female protagonists we are, as the name Gunhild suggests, introduced to another old theme being restated: Gunhild and Ella are reminiscent of Hjørdis and Dagny from *Hærmændene på Helgeland:* they are saga women. The plot of *John Gabriel Borkman* is that of *Hærmændene* in modern setting. Borkman and his best friend—who is like a brother to him, just like Gunnar and Sigurd are fosterbrothers— Hinkel are vying for the same woman's love. They are both in love with Ella. But Borkheim, like Sigurd, relinquishes his claim on the woman so his friend can marry her. In the later play, however, the scenario is slightly changed: Ella does not marry Hinkel, she remains single. And Borkman does not relinquish her out of love for his friend. He does it out of greed and lust for power. He is, after all, the mountain king, or thinks he is, he wants the gold and the power more than he wants human happiness.

In giving Ella to his friend, he destroys her life. And in marrying Gunhild, he destroys her life because he never loved her and never shared his thoughts and feelings with her. Ella says to him "you have murdered the ability to love in a woman who loved you. And who you loved in return."[132] For women, love and their relationships to men are the goals of life, their calling. If a woman marries a man she loves and who loves her, she will be able to blossom as a woman in the love of her children and in being a sweet, gentle, sacrificing and humanizing person. Ella has lost the ability to love; she cannot even feel pity for the poor any more. She has lost her soul. She loves Erhart only because he is John Gabriel's son. But in killing Ella's soul, Borkman has also deprived himself of the chance to obtain one, for men need the humanizing love of a woman to fulfill themselves. Borkman believes that women are interchangeable: if you have to give up one, there is always another to fill in her place. This is why he will never fulfill his quest, as Ella says: "And therefore I predict—John Gabriel Borkman,—that you will never win the prize you claimed for the murder. You shall never have your conqueror's parade into your cold, dark kingdom."[133]

The story of Ella and Borkheim is the story of Hjørdis and Sigurd hin sterke of *Hærmændene* with several twists, but the essence is the same: the two life threads that are rendered because a man gives up the woman he loves. Borkman tore the thread of the norns, the goddesses of fate, and he ruined two lives when he did.

The point of *John Gabriel Borkman* seems not to be still another discussion of the role of the artist and the artist's choice as much as of the Nietzschean *Übermensch*. Ibsen dresses the superman in the garb of the mountain king and paints a stinging psychological portrait of him. For Ibsen there clearly are no supermen, there is no one who can demand special treatment because he is chosen. There are only people who have to live their lives as morally and as "really" as possible.

Når vi døde vågner

In *When We Dead Awaken* Ibsen uses the central metaphor derived from the ballads that he uses throughout his dramatic oeuvre: the image of the artist/troll, who lures the maiden into the mountain where he robs her of her soul. But he uses it as a set of Chinese boxes, one metaphor is hidden within the next one in eternal regress: Ulfheim plays troll to Maja, who has been locked up in Rubek's mountain, where Irene, who is married to the Russian troll (sits in the Ural Mountains, watching his gold ore), used to be, and so on. And as Østerud has pointed out, beyond the ballad material, Ibsen uses in this, his last play, also imagery from Roman mythology.[134]

Når vi døde vågner is Ibsen's last play, and the folklore metaphors are used in dialogue with the themes that fascinated him throughout his career. But the themes are laid out more clearly and with more painful honesty than ever before.

The question that Ibsen struggled with throughout his career was, of course, the question of the interface between art and society, between the artist and the bourgeoisie. The metaphors derived from the folklore that he uses to throw light upon his query are the oppositions between nature and culture, between female and male and between the demonic and the human. The three strands of metaphor are twined together and produce meaning and shades of meaning by illuminating each other as the individual strands merge, take focus, and provide background for each other.

I shall first take the metaphors apart and examine them individually and then look at the fusion of the three.

The opposition between nature and culture is expressed primarily through the two character dyads: Rubek and Irene on the culture side, and Ulfheim and Maja on the nature side. Rubek is the aging and world-weary artist who has become the epitome of cultural sophistication. He is the darling of the bourgeoisie whose portraits he sculpts. But Rubek, like Ibsen—having nature ever present in his sets—knows that culture is but a thin veneer, and he amuses himself by "hiding" animal faces, albeit domesticated, in the sculptures of the idle rich who can afford them. The image is wonderfully ironic and deep: once the cultural veneer is removed the animal nature shines through, but modern humans are even on the animal level tame and docile domesticates.[135] Rubek, the artist, was himself once an exponent of untamed nature, but success and materialism have tamed him and left him with only the bitter taste of knowing that the society he is part of is weak and domesticated.

Irene, the woman who was life and voluptuous nature has become a cultural automaton: a woman who goes through all the motions of being a real, living woman, who dances in the nude on revolving stages and marries exotic millionaires. She epitomizes the bourgeoisie who only feign to live, who live quasi lives of simulated passion and blasé materialism. She has, in fact, become so distant from herself that society deemed her mad and put her in a straight jacket. But Irene also carries within her the knowledge that she was once a real, live, redblooded woman. When she was Rubek's model she was conscious of her potential for living and becoming a full and fulfilled woman, mother, and passionate lover. It was her encounter with the artist-vampire that transformed her into what she has become.

On the other side of the equation, Ulfheim prances and growls his allegiance to nature. He, appropriately for one whose name is Ulfheim (*ulf* means "wolf," *heim*, "home"), feels that his next of kin are his dogs. He revels in the excitement of facing the bear in combat, ferocious carnivore against ferocious carnivore. He is obsessed with blood and the consumption of blood and he only feels at home in the mountains and forests that city dwellers cannot abide. His female counterpart, Maja, is at the beginning of the play trapped in culture, tied as she is to Rubek and the house on Taunitzer See. But once Rubek admits that he has lost interest in her, she grabs greedily the chance Ulfheim offers her to revert to nature. She is scared but also terribly attracted to Ulfheim's obsessions: the bloody bones being wolfed down by the dogs and the wilderness. She never really belonged in Rubek's sphere of sophistication and culture and felt only contempt for his art: *"Maja* (laughs somewhat scornfully): Yes, well you are forever and always the artist."[136]

The opposition between the demonic and the human is expressed, once again in the characters. But the dividing line is the gender line. In other words, the demonic is represented by Rubek, and to a lesser degree, by Ulfheim.

Rubek epitomizes the Ibsen demon, the person who has unusual gifts and powers, but who, like the ballad demon, needs an innocent virgin to give him that which can transform his raw energy and amorphous powers into art and himself into an artist: a soul. Rubek, is aware of this, "You were not a model. You were the source of my creation."[137] Irene herself expresses it even more clearly: "I gave you my young living soul. Then I stood there and was empty inside—soulless. That's what I died from, Arnold."[138]

Like other demons, mermen, and trolls, Rubek has to seduce his victims, drag them away from their home, and isolate them in his "lair." He wanted a virginal woman, and then he found Irene: "You I could use totally. And you were both happy and willing. And you left home and family—and followed me." Her answer is, "It was the resurrection of my childhood that I followed you."[139] This is the "Agnete" ballad: the troll who accosts the child-woman and lures her to follow him, leaving family and home behind. Even the image of Irene's resurrection from childhood fits my analysis of the encounter with the troll as a rite de passage.

Rubek seduces his "victims," in part by promising them that he will take them to a high mountain and show them all the world. This is almost verbatim the promise of the merman in Andersen's *Agnete og Havmanden*.[140] Rubek seduces both Irene and Maja with this promise, and he does not keep it in either case. Maja, incidentally, also followed him, although the decision to do so was less happy and easy for her, away from her home to live with him in Switzerland. But Maja had no soul to offer and Rubek became bored with her—as she became bored with him and his "golden cage."

Ulfheim, like Rubek, is in need of a soul. His whole hunting bravado does little to hide that he is empty and lonely under the surface. He too tries to seduce the maiden, but his seduction is more direct and physical. He too promises a castle, but it is more like an animal's den, a smelly and ugly place where he and Maja can celebrate their animal passions without having to worry about cultural finery.

The opposition between male and female is tied almost inextricably to the image of the artist in his relation to society, but a little can be said about it in isolation. The image of Woman, with capital *W*, in the play is Irene. She is, as Rubek points out, an earth mother, an "earth woman."[141] She was womanhood in all its glory, destined to give birth to children and be happy—until she met her fate, the troll/artist. The male "signifier" in the play is Ulfheim, who is all the frivolous and red-blooded male Rubek could not be in his relationship with Irene. Ulfheim is Rubek's subconscious fleshed out as a lecherous faun, a subconscious that Rubek himself can only connect to by means of sublimation: art.

When Irene follows Rubek to the mountain top to see the whole world, she follows him to her destruction.[142] She loves him and thrives under his eyes and cooperating with him. But she discovers, as did Svanhild of *Kjærlighedens komedie*, that being an artist's model and inspiration is dangerous. In that early play the artist-to-be, Falk is addressing the woman he wants to make his "soul"

> *Falk:* Yes, just that is freedom
> to be all that you can in your calling;
> and you, I know, were consecrated by the Heavens
> as my defence against the fall of beauty
> I must like the bird I am named after
> ascend *against* the wind if I want to reach the heights;
> *you* are the breeze I can ride upon,
> only through *you* will my wings be able to carry me.
> Be mine, be mine, till you become the property of the world,
> when the Heavens fall our roads will part.
> Sing your richness of soul into me
> and I shall give you poem for poem in return;
> then you can grow old by the light of the lamp,

just like a tree turning yellow, without sorrow and complaint.[143]

These words could almost have been the ones Rubek wooed Irene with. As a matter of fact the above passage is almost an outline of the central conflict in *Når vi døde vågner*. Unfortunately Irene was not as wise—or Rubek was perhaps not so direct—as her counterpart Svanhild,

> *Svanhild:* And when you know me by heart, and when I'm empty
> and have sung my last song from my branch,—
> then what?
> *Falk* (looks at her): Then what? Well, try to remember.
> (Points to the garden.)
> *Svanhild* (quietly): Oh, yes, I remember you know how to use a stone.[144]

Rubek "killed" Irene after she had sung her last song, after he had taken her soul. He did not kill her with a stone, he killed her because he did not love her as a man. He created the sculpture he had seen in his imagination, using Irene as his model and inspiration: "*Irene:* And then you were through with me . . . didn't need me any more."[145]

Rubek could not touch her. He was convinced that if he did he would destroy his ability to create. Touching her would have been, in some mystical and mythical sense, polluting.[146] He could not soil his hands that were creating a masterpiece by touching an all too real and earthly woman. But the result was that he destroyed Irene's life, he "killed" her by taking her soul, as she says in the passage quoted above. And he destroyed his own life too: he was never happy after she left him. He never had a life as a man—he just had a short period of ecstatic happiness creating a masterpiece with the woman he loved. After Irene left him he too was dead. The play derives its title from the fact that they together live the dream that their meeting again will be a resurrection for both of them. She will be a living, throbbing woman again, he will be a man of flesh and blood; and they will create together again. It is, of course, a lie, a lie they perish in.[147]

The idea of their resurrection is mapped—with bitter and sad irony—

onto the work of art they created: "The Day of Resurrection." That sculpture has become the metaphor for her life: she sees herself as dead until she meets him again, after which she hopes for a new life with him. But her soul is no longer there and his ability to create is gone too. They are like John Gabriel Borkman and Ella Rentheim: people whose lives were irreparably destroyed by his quest for greatness.

At the very end of the play, Rubek tries, at long last, to make good on his promise to take Irene to the highest mountain and show her "all of the world," but it is too late: they are killed in the avalanche created by Maja's ecstatic song of freedom, "I am free, free!"[148] The irony is evil: Rubek and Irene, locked as they are in the past, are destroyed by the song of freedom of the woman who has escaped from the troll's fangs. Following Rubek and Irene is the strange figure of the nun, who may be an incarnation of Ibsen himself, the observer and spy. The nun expresses Ibsen's own parting greeting to the world: "Pax vobiscum."[149]

Notes

1. Jacobsen 1986a.

2. Heiberg, being a Hegelian, had set up a whole scheme to establish the highest form of literature, eventually choosing drama because it is at once poetic and epic. He has a curious dialectic argument. For the interested, I give a more elaborate analysis of this in Jacobsen 1986a.

3. Ibsen, 1928–57, 1: 253–311. All references to Ibsen in this chapter are to this work and are given in the following way: Ibsen, volume number, colon, page number. If the passage being quoted can be found in the English edition I give volume number, colon, page number in a parenthesis immediately following the reference to the Norwegian edition.

4. Ibsen 1: 167.

5. Paludan-Müller 1899; Schack 1925; Heiberg 1864.

6. Ibsen 14: 400 (the poem in its entirety is pp. 387–400). The following translation is mine, as are all translations in Chapters 2, 3, and 4. The poem does not exist in an English translation. I also use my own translations of passages from the plays, because I find the English translations to be often misleading in the name of poetic license.

> The last of the strengthening juice I drank;
> no longer on the expanses I freeze;
> my sail went under, my life's tree broke,—

but lo, how beautiful her red chimney
among the birches shines.

It goes in a gallop, but lo,
they disappeared where the road turns by the church.
Most beautiful memory, live in happiness!
Now I exchange my last step
for a higher view of things.

Now I am steeled, I feel the bid
that bids me in the heights to wander!
My life in the lowlands is over;
up here in the expanses are freedom and God,
down there the others stagger around.

7. Hans Christian Andersen 1876–80.

8. Oehlenschläger 1852; Baggesen 1816, 1845; Aarestrup 1922; Hauch 1891.

9. Jacobsen 1986b.

10. Ibid.

11. Ibid.

12. Arnold 1856.

13. Kierkegaard 1982: 85–90.

14. Ibsen 3: 128–29.

15. Actually, Ibsen mixed elements from two ballads here: the "Olaf Liljekrans" (Danish "Elveskud") ballad, where Olaf is killed because he refuses to dance with the elfin maidens, and the ballad of "Hr. Bøsmer i Elvehjem." Hr. Bøsmer drinks a potion and forgets his previous life.

16. Gravier 1970–71: 140–41.

17. Another version of the story of the origins of the *huldre* is found in Langset 1948: 51. The major difference is that instead of God, it is Jesus who is wandering about the world. The content of the story is almost identical, except that the version recorded by Langset ends as follows: "It is a tribe who is rejected. They shall grow up around Christians. But they shall have no business with them."

18. Bjørndal 1949: 44–45.

19. Faye 1948: 37.

20. Huld 1937: 27.

21. Bjørndal 1949: 45.

22. Faye (1948: 41) tells the story of a *huldre* ho was "tied" by a young man with a gun pipe. The remainder of the story is as outlined in the text.

23. Ibsen 3: 61 (1: 398–99).

24. Ibid. 3: 163 (1: 485).

25. Ibid. 2: 40 (1: 218).

26. Ibid. 2: 54 (1: 230).

27. Ibid. 2: 55 (1: 230–31).

28. Ibid. 6: 92–93 (*sæterjenter*), 97–107 (*den grønkledte*) (3: 288–89, 292–94). A *sæterjente* is a young girl left in charge of the cattle in the *sæter* over the summer. The *sæter*s are mountain pastures. It was customary in the last century and the early parts of the present one to send the cattle to pasture in the mountains during the summer months because of the scarcity of arable land in the valleys. The young girls would spend the summer isolated in the *sæter*, having only the cattle and the *huldrer* as company.

29. Østerud (1981b: 20) in a discussion of *Rosmersholm*, talks of this play's "symbolic topography. Here sea and land oppose each other. The 'Mølleklop,' you might say, is where sea and land meet."

30. The introductions to the early plays go into detailed and technical discussions of the metric patterns. Readers who are interested are referred to these introductions.

31. Ibsen 3: 46 (1: 384).

> *It was early*, when the bell tolled
> *me felt* like riding to church;
> the *wilden birds* did twitter and sing
> *there between* the willows and birches.
> *There was joy in the air* and the woods
> church was *almost* over;
> for even as I rode along *the shadowy path*
> each *rose-bloom* waved to me.
> I stepped so lightly onto the church floor;
> the priest stood high in the chorus;
> he sang and read; with a solemn mind
> men and women listened to the word.
> *Then a voice was heard over the blue of the fjord;*
> *me thought all the little pictures turned around to listen thereto*
> . . . .
> it was as if a deep, immeasurable bidding
> called me outside the walls of the church
> over hills and vales, through meadows and woods.

32. I remind here of the elf knight's horn in "Elf" and of the proud maid's song in "Nix."

33. Ibsen 6, 2: 388–89 (4: 52–53).

34. Prime examples are *Aprilsnarrene* (*April's Foolery*) and *Recensenten og Dyret* (*The Critic and the Critter*), both discussed in Jacobsen 1986a.

35. See note 31 above and the quotation from the play in the text.

36. Kierkegaard 1982: 86–87n.

37. Since it may be confusing to call Eline the human (culture) and Niels Lykke the demon (nature), let me just add that the story, in a complex way, fits the pattern laid out above in the text. She is the "folklore" personality (listened to Bjørn telling stories and singing ballads when she was a child); he is the

demonic embodied in a slick Dane. Thus she is nature to his culture, since she is the Norwegian maiden seduced by the foreign knight.

38. In *Kongsemnerne* (*The Pretenders*) Skule and Håkon vie for the kingship of Norway.

The subject matter of this play is remarkably similar to Peter Shaffer's *Amadeus*: why are some people—seemingly irrespective of inherent moral qualities—anointed by God to be great, to write divine music or be carriers of "the great idea"?

39. Ibsen 2: 171 (1: 307).

40. Ibid.: 139 (30) (1: 280).

41. Ibid. 6, 2: 471 (4: 128).

42. Ibid. 4: 93 (2: 89).

43. Ibid. 4: 74 (2:72).

44. Ibid. 1: 309 (1: 182–83).

45. See below, Appendix A. The idea that Finns and Lapps were witches and trolls is common in Norwegian popular belief.

Even if the small Lapps were not dangerous because of their strength and fierce bravery, they were still because of their knowledge of the secrets of nature, their cunning and ingenuity dangerous neighbors who could steal away animals, exchange children (from this derives perhaps the many myths of changelings), steal house wares and food, give people narcotic drinks, seduce them into their caves by singing and precious objects, etc., features that give us the key to many a myth about the supernaturals. (Faye 1948: xvi)

46. Freud 1982.

47. Kierkegaard 1982: 86.

48. See note 27 above and the quotation in the text.

49. Gravier (1970–71: 155) points out that Ibsen had read the German physicist Häckel. Häckel said that people ultimately came from the sea—like all other land creatures. In *Fruen fra havet*, Ellida expresses the same theory.

50. Ibsen 10: 345 (6: 293).

51. Ibid. 4: 160 (2: 115).

52. Ibid.: 161 (116).

53. Ibid. 10: 345–72 (act 1) (6: 295–318).

54. Ibid.: 370 (317).

55. Ibid.: 345 (293).

56. Ibid.: 410 (354).

57. Ibid.: 425 (368).

58. I remind the reader of the passage from *The League of Youth* cited above. See note 41 and the quotation in the text.

59. Ibsen 10: 432 (375).

60. Ibid.: 424 (367).

61. Ibid.: 427 (370).

62. Ibid.: 428 (371).

63. Ibid.: 409 (353).

64. Ibid.: 433 (375).

65. Ibid. 5: 23, "Now Inga from Vartejg carries the hot iron for Håkon, the pretender to the throne" (2: 221).

66. Ibid. 10: 436 (6: 378).

67. Ibid.: 438 (6: 380–81).

68. Østerud 1981b: 21–23.

69. Ibid.: 32.

70. Ibid.: 21. Østerud, in his turn, takes his cue from Jørgen Haugan (1977), from whom he quotes the statement that Kierkegaard's treatment of the "Agnete og Havmanden" theme provides a synopsis of *Rosmersholm*.

71. Kierkegaard 1982: 86.

72. Ibsen 10: 426 (6: 369).

73. Kierkegaard 1982: 87.

74. In Gunnar Brandell's *Freud og hans tid*, cited in Henriksen 1967: 129.

75. Ibsen 11: 120–21 (7: 92).

76. Anni Carlsson (1959: 39, 42–43) argues, as I do here, that "die Beziehung des Menschen zu einer in ihm verschütteten Urnatur ist das mythische Thema der 'Wildente.'" She makes the argument with regard to *The Wild Duck*, and she sees the duck as a representative of the ancient, mythic order that does not stand a chance in the modern world. I argue that the female protagonists of both *Rosmersholm* and *Fruen fra havet* are representatives of the mythic *Urseele* who fare just as badly. As can be seen below, I extend the argument—slightly differently expressed—to include also Hedda Gabler.

77. In this regard, it is worth recalling that in some versions of both the "Agnete" and the "Dwarf" ballads, the maid has many suitors whose desirability is made clear—whom she cannot marry because she already is secretly married to the troll.

The following statement from Stuyver (1952: 391–92) also supports my theory that Friman is a troll or witch: "Ibsen scheint die finnische Herkunft gewählt zu haben als Erklärung seiner [Friman's] ruhigen, beharrlichen Entschlossenheit, *aber auch der Zaubermacht wegen, die den Finnländern zugeschrieben wird*" (emphasis mine).

78. Østerud 1981b: 49–50.

79. Nach Koht ist "der altnordische Schiffsname Ellida der Geschichte Fridtjovs des Tapferen (den frøkne) entnommen,—dort ist der Name übrigens ein männliches Wort, das etwa "Sturmpferd" (uvêersgängeren) bedeutet. . . . Ellida in der Saga glich eigentlich einem lebendigen Mehschen." Das wilde heidnische Wesen, das Ellidas männlicher Schiffsname bekundet, hat sie nie erschöpfend ausleben können. Sie ist dagegen äusserlich nachgiebig und zartfühlend und benimmt sich kindlich hilflos und einschmiegsam: in dieser Weise entfloh sie der wilden Heidin in sich selber als "etwas grauenhaftem" (noget grufuldt), um Halt zu suchen bei den Vorurteilen ihres Wortes. (Stuyver 1952: 390).

I have included here Stuyver's interpretation of Ellida because I find it interesting, while I disagree with it.

80. I remind the reader again that once a woman has been secretly married to a troll (e.g., "Agnete" and "Dwarf"), she is not available to marry anyone else, even though she may still be living with her parents like a normal young woman. Ellida has not been able to be Wangel's wife, although she is married to him, because she is already secretly "married" to the Stranger. This supports my theory that the real witch or troll (sea-creature) of the play is the Stranger. Ellida is his victim.

81. The play is in Hans Christian Andersen 1876–80: 467–549. The relevant passages in Andersen can be found on pages 471, 472. The corresponding passage is in Ibsen 11: 63 (7: 38–39).

82. Andersen 1876–80: 472; Ibsen 11:63.

83. Andersen 1876–80: 524–25; Ibsen 11: 88–89.

84. Ibsen 11: 296 (7: 172).

85. Ibid. 4: 38 (2: 37).

86. Ibid. 11: 325 (7: 200).

87. Ibid.: 303 (178–79).

88. Rønning 1973: 498.

89. Ibsen 11: 348 (7: 223).

90. Ibid.: 326 (201).

91. It will be recalled that Marstig's daughter, the maid in "Nix," was busy expressing her pride and love of dancing at a round dance when she was noticed by the nix. Hedda was always the proud queen of the balls she loved to go to. See Ibsen 11: 331 (7: 206). Leavy's contention (see below) that Hedda is indeed a *huldre* is supported by the quotation from Faye above (see note 19 to this chapter and the quotation in the text).

92. Ibsen 11: 331 (7: 206).

93. Ibid.: 330 (205).

94. I may be taking this a bit too far, but in Ibsen's time government officials were like kings of their districts, and the districts, because of topography, were extremely isolated.

95. After taking a nix's or troll's gold, one cannot escape the supernatural. See note 67 to Chapter 3 and the surrounding text.

96. See Bø 1955, esp. ch. 2, "Landekristnaren og kyrkjebyggaren" ("The Christianizer of the Country and the Builder of Churches"), 30–59. Sehmsdorf (1967) compares two myths about Saint Olav to the story of *Bygmester Solness* and finds that the play follows the myths quite closely. In the myths the king is building a church but is having trouble with the tall steeple. A stranger volunteers to help him on condition that Olav shall belong to him unless he finds out the stranger's name before the job is done. Olav manages—he happens to overhear a conversation between the troll's (as he is) wife and child—to find out the name in time to call it to the troll just as he is finishing the job. The troll falls down and is killed when his name is mentioned. Sehmsdorf points out that what triggers Solness's fall at the end of the play is Hilde's calling out his name. The present analysis is more complex, since I assume that Solness is not really a

troll—Hilde is the troll. Hilde *convinces* Solness that he is a troll and then proceeds to destroy him. It might almost be said that in this play Ibsen lets the troll win: that which is vital and strong in the young generation is the aboriginal (the mythic, the *Urseele*), and that which is weak and withered in the old (Solness) is the veneer of culture.

97. Sehmsdorf (1967: 268) says,

it might be of interest . . . to mention a certain passage in a *sagn* noted down by Ibsen. There the phenomenon of "en overordentlig klingende Harpelyd" is associated with the existence of supernatural beings ("huldrefolk"). In *Bygmester Solness* the sound of harps in the air is twice heard by Hilde, namely the two times Solness climbs to the top of a tower.

I refer the reader to Appendix B, where excerpts from Ibsen's field notes from his folklore-collecting trip to the northern parts of Norway are translated.

98. Ibsen 12: 57 (7: 381).

99. Ibid.: 89 (412).

100. Ibid.: 88 (411).

101. The plot of Oehlenschläger's play, reduced to its esssentials, is that Aladdin is a happy and innocent son of nature. He has no education, is lazy and focused on the pleasurable, but he is friendly, gentle, nice, and lady luck's chosen. When he sits around doing nothing, oranges fall into his lap; when he walks, he falls into caves full of riches. His opponent is the studious old Noureddin, who constantly tries to *force* luck to come his way. He sits up nights and studies alchemy, science, and magic to find a way to obtain the riches that come to Aladdin without any effort. Noureddin, like Solness, tries to capture spirits that will work for him. Aladdin has his own spirit who lives in an old lamp he has found and who comes to serve his beloved master at a rub of the bronze. The two contest over the king's daughter and the kingship. Obviously, Aladdin wins, as Noureddin stands turned to stone like the Rosmer of the ballad.

102. Ibsen 12: 60 (7: 388). MacFarlane omits the name.

103. Or perhaps Hilde, the troll—as I argue below—like the nix and the elf knight, was able to recognize in Solness a potential ("marginal") victim.

104. Ibsen 12: 104 (7: 425).

105. Ibid.: 55 (379).

106. Ibid.: 92 (414–15).

107. Ibid.: 123 (445).

108. Ibid.: 199 (8: 39).

109. Ibid.: 213–14 (53–54).

110. Ibid.: 241 (79).

111. Ibid.: 209 (49).

112. Ibid.: 224–25 (64).

113. Ibid.: 245–46 (84).

114. Ibid.: 245–46 (84).

115. There are many indications in the folklore literature that supernaturals are "tied" to one place—for example, Kristensen 1876.

116. Ibsen 12: 258 (8: 96).
117. See Appendix A.
118. Ibsen 14: 297–98.
119. Ibsen 13: 67 (8: 179).
120. Bø 1955: 45.
121. Ibsen 14: 297.
122. Ibsen 13: 101 (8: 210).
123. Ibid.: 124 (231).
124. Although in *Kongsemnerne* (*The Pretenders*), the real Olav is, of course, Håkon Håkonsson, the "Aladdin" of that play, the one who has kingship "in his blood."
125. Bø 1955: 28.
126. Ibid.
127. Ibid.
128. Ibid.
129. Ibsen 13: 124 (8: 231).
130. Ibid.: 79 (190).
131. I keep thinking of *Fanny Hill*. I wonder whether Ibsen knew or knew of that work. Or, perhaps, Fanny Legrand of Daudet's *Sapho*?
132. Ibsen 13: 124 (8: 231).
133. Ibid.
134. Østerud, 1963–64.
135. Ibsen 13: 220–21 (8: 243–44).
136. Ibid.: 245 (264).
137. Ibid.: 239 (260).
138. Ibid.: 241 (262).
139. Ibid.: 238 (259).
140. Hans Christian Andersen 1876–80: 501.
141. Ibsen 13: 238 (259).
142. Interestingly, as we go from act to act we move higher and higher up: the first act is set on a fjord with a beach resort; the second at a mountain resort; and the third so high in the mountains that the characters move among drifting clouds. Aarseth (1969: 76) has also noticed the constant ascending in the course of the play. For him it is symbolic of Rubek and Irene's attempt to travel, once again, to the heights of art and poetry.
143. Ibsen 4: 178–79 (2: 134).
144. Ibid.: 179 (134). Earlier in the same scene Falk has compared her to a bird in the garden they are walking in. He—because of unfounded jealousy—killed the bird with a stone.
145. Ibsen 13: 238–39 (8: 259).
146. For a discussion of the mythic aspects of the nonsexual relation between artist and model, see Fraenkl 1967.
147. They are, in a sense, *already* dead, as Irene keeps insisting.
148. Ibsen 13: 283 (8: 297).
149. Ibid.: 284 (297).

PART
III

Barbara Fass Leavy

CHAPTER 5

John Rosmer and Rosmer Havmand

Like Andersen's Little Mermaid, who for love of a man comes to earth and also gains a soul, Rebecca, overwhelmed by an elemental sexual attraction for Rosmer—"wild and uncontrollable passion" which swept over her "like a storm at sea" (6: 369)—has been spiritualized by a conscience rooted in the Rosmer philosophy of life. In a letter, Ibsen had characterized this ethical sense as "very conservative," having "its roots deep in tradition and in the past generally" (6: 447). But the Rosmer philosophy, dramatized in part by Rosmer's avoidance of the symbolic bridge, an avoidance that Rebecca understands has made her love hopeless, is directed to only one part of the divided psyche. It has therefore the double effect of ennobling the mind but killing happiness for the woman whose origins in the magic north and the sea speak to a sea longing that persists despite the ordinary life that she seeks with obsessive purposefulness.

Critics have frequently noted the affinities between Rebecca and the mermaid.[1] In the play, Brendel calls her his "enchanting little mermaid" (6: 375) an appellation that picks up more importance from Ibsen's urging that particular attention be paid to "what the other characters say about Rebecca" (6: 447). But to call Rebecca a mermaid is to present her as a divided being rather than the enchantress that commentary has focused upon. True, Rebecca's origins in Finmark speak to superstition and witchcraft. But her land longing is as much a part of the folklore as that which produces the siren. In Andersen's sea maiden, all traces of the demonic mermaid have been removed, and it is the mermaid's ethical behavior that characterizes her and lends the story its pathos. But this pathos has been won at the expense of the ambiguity that Andersen explored elsewhere, in his dramatic version of *Agnete*. The ambiguity in *Rosmersholm* comes from Ibsen's having fully developed the dual potential of the mermaid–seal maiden lore. Rebecca West is poignantly aware that she is split between what the land and sea represent, the ethical life on one side, and a world of unbridled will and hedonism on the other. When she confesses the part she played in Beata's death, she describes a painful conflict whose language recalls the agony experienced by Andersen's mermaid as she surrenders her fish tail to gain legs and thus entree to the human world.[2] But whereas the Little Mermaid agonizingly assumes the ethical, Rebecca is moving away from it—a typical Ibsen reversal of the motifs he draws on—in an act that she paradoxically hopes will bring her closer to what both she and her sister mermaid seek:

> I was different then from what I am now, standing here talking about it. And besides, it seems to me a *person can want things both ways*. I wanted to get rid of Beata, one way or another. But I never really imagined it would ever happen. Every little step I risked, every faltering advance, I seemed to hear something call out within me: "No further. Not a step further!" . . . And yet I could not stop. I *had* to venture a little bit further. Just one little bit further. And then a little bit more . . . always just a little bit more. And then it happened. That's the way things like that do happen. (6: 363; first emphasis mine)

The conflicts in the play are immediately introduced in Ibsen's setting for act I, in which, as Jacobsen has argued, the playwright embodies the conflict bewtween nature and culture. The room itself is closed-in space, suggesting the confined Rosmer philosophy of life. The "walls are hung with past and recent portraits of clergymen, officers and officials in their robes and uniforms." But the "window is open" as are the hall and outer doors, and "an avenue of *ancient* trees" can be seen from the room. Moreover, the outdoors, nature, has been brought inside, with *fresh* birch twigs and "*wild* flowers" (6: 293; emphasis mine). The seated Rebecca reflects this duality. Crocheting a shawl, she seems domestic, warranting the approval of the persons whose portraits seemingly observe her. But in this very sedate, womanly task is also a possible link to the magic otherworld: the swan maiden–Valkyries in the *Volundark-vida* occupy themselves during the day with weaving, until they flee the mortal world, once again to engage in combat.[3]

The dual world of *Rosmersholm*, then, is described in its setting, the play then proceeding to explore a series of dualisms. Kroll complains of the political temper of the times, in which "hardly a single idea but what it hasn't been turned upside down" (6: 303). Of Brendel he says that "he's the sort who could turn your ideas upside down all over again" (6: 312). Kroll implacably creates for himself a unified world, and views all duality with alarm, nonetheless recognizing it clearly when forced to confront it. A constant theme early in the play is the unthinkable idea that an irreparable breach could develop between him and Rosmer, and it is Kroll who tells Rebecca that her "background and [Rosmer's] are of course poles apart" (6: 355). The most symbolic image of these dualities is one Ibsen took from the folk ballads, the bridge which Rosmer circumvents rather than cross, until the end when he surrenders to his own alter ego and plays Rosmer Havmand, luring Rebecca into the waters. On a literal level, the bridge is the place from which his wife leapt to her death in a gruesome parody of the bride and her sisters in the "Harpens Kraft" ballad. Thus the bridge is also a symbolic link to the demonic world. That Rosmer has avoided the bridge has long impressed Rebecca as a foreboding that Kroll's view of their irreconcilable differences is correct:

> *Rosmer:* I go with you, I said.
> *Rebecca:* As far as the bridge, yes. You know you never dare go out on it.
> *Rosmer:* Have you noticed that?
> *Rebecca* (sadly and brokenly): Yes. That was what made my love hopeless. (6: 380)

The passage supplies the paradigm for Ibsen's themes in *Rosmersholm:* the tragedy comes in part from his main characters' inability to work out a suitable fit for the disparate elements that define them. Rebecca as mermaid–seal maiden is drawn to Rosmersholm by the very qualities that John Rosmer discards under her influence, finally transformed into Rosmer Havmand, luring to her doom the woman who cannot resist his appeal.

Political radicalism and conservatism, then, are but one set of dualistic elements in *Rosmersholm*. The contrast between the Rosmer way of life and that of the wild country from which Rebecca comes subsumes under it far more than social ideologies. A whole series of dichotomies symbolized by land and sea longing can be traced in the play: they define two worlds that no bridge seems able to join. There is the generalized conflict between nature and culture, between Blakean forms of innocence and experience, between a world of children and adults, between the living and the dead—the latter creating a split of its own, the dead both separate from and determinedly attached to the living. And, finally, a basic duality surrounds Ibsen's treatment of his characters' sexuality, a treatment that resists any placement in a neatly defined dualistic scheme.

Theoretically allied to raw nature is the violent passion whose uncontrolled form is expressed by Beata's supposedly nymphomaniacal advances toward her husband. John Rosmer, a pastor and staunch defender of "culture," is repelled by these excessive sexual demands. But ironically, it is a similar passion that drew Rebecca from a world of pure nature, made her willing to put on humanity, to curb her instincts with temperance (Brendel inquires after a temperance society, 6: 310) and even abstinence. She and Rosmer, to the skeptical surprise of other characters, have not been lovers during the time they dwelt alone at Rosmersholm. Culture requires that sexual instincts be pressed into the service of procreation. It is when Beata knows that she will never be a mother that a pure, acultural sexuality gets hold of her. If this, however, were the end of the issue, it would be possible to define as opposites sexual energy on one side and domestically approved parenting on the other.

But Ibsen shared with his century an understanding that the matter was not so simple. There is in European romanticism a contradictory attitude toward human sexuality. On the one hand the romantics redeemed nature—the senses—from the taint of corruption that in *Rosmersholm* is reflected by generations of dour Christian clergymen. But it is not only Rosmer's deeply embedded prudishness that makes him recoil from Beata and leaves him oblivious to Rebecca's desire. Nor can his behavior be attributed solely to societal values which condemn Mortensgaard for fathering an illegitimate child on a married woman, assuming from the outset, however, that humans will sink to their lower nature whenever the opportunity presents itself. Such a view takes for granted that Rosmer and Rebecca are lovers. The question for the play, however, is why aren't they? Because in addition to the restraints imposed by culture, there is also in rebellious romanticism an idealism that recoils as effectively as Christianity from the earthy as well as the ordinary life. And insofar as sex is associated with gross nature and bourgeois reality, celibacy and virginity represent ideals that define an alternative existence as fully as does the hedonistic life. Ibsen had already been working with these themes in *Brand,* the connection between Brand and John Rosmer and of both to the folklore made more explicit in the earlier epic version (particularly 3: 49–51). But the "Agnete" story is more explicit in *Brand* than in any of Ibsen's other plays, and the young betrothed maiden who leaves her fiancé for Brand—"My eyes / Were fixed upon the ground, but now I see the stars!" (3: 106)—seems an early Rebecca, ecstatically proclaiming her new life in imagery that links ideology and sexuality: "I can feel secret forces stirring, can feel / Floods rising, can see a great dawn breaking" (3: 114). Brand himself recognizes her as the maiden seduced by the merman:

> See how she sits, listening as if to some
> Music in the air—even so she sat, listening,
> In the boat as it cut its way through the raging waves.
> (3: 113)

But if Agnes is Agnete before the call back to earth, and Rebecca Agnete afterwards, the two nonetheless share the same dilemma. Agnes left a "real" suitor to respond to Brand's idealism, and Rebecca has left her sea world to fall victim to the same fanatical purism. Each woman finds herself isolated from the human world, and each suffers the consequences of her own predisposition to scorn it. Thus Rosmer Havmand as idealist is a theme that Ibsen had already a precedent for when he wrote *Rosmersholm.*

The death of Agnes's and Brand's child is also an early example of a theme Ibsen would work with all the way to *When We Dead Awaken,* where the theme of infanticide would highlight the sacrificial use of children in his plays. In the idealistically pure worlds of Brand and Rosmer, children are less the products of earthy and earthly unions than they are disembodied beings, almost supernatural in their symbolic representation of innocence:

> *Rosmer:* If we really think about it, Rebecca . . . we began our life together like two children falling sweetly and secretly in love. Making no demands, dreaming no dreams. Didn't you also feel that way about it? Tell me? (6: 351)

Children, presumably, do not dream because in their innocence they lack the repressed desires or sinful wishes that give rise to dreams. But at Rosmersholm, neither do they cry nor, as adults, laugh: in this they resemble the changeling who makes its appearance in several Ibsen plays, especially—I shall argue—as Little Eyolf. In John Rosmer's view, the worlds of innocence and experience are so irreparably split that the growth to mature but happy adulthood is thwarted. What Blake articulated forcefully in the early period of English romanticism seems applicable as well to Ibsen: human sexuality is an area that points up dramatically the distorted vision according to which experience lacks the joy of the innocent stage of childhood, and innocence is inappropriately clung to by those who will not commit themselves to the adult world, choosing—almost like Thel—not to be born. Rosmer, of course, cannot choose to remain unborn, but he can recoil from the implications of mature relationships expressed in a healthy response to sex. Beata's childlessness and its throwing her back to uncontrolled nature seem less reflections of her than extensions of her husband's character. In this context it is worth remembering Jacobsen's discussion of the Rosmer ballads and their untypical presentation of an apparently asexual merman as kidnapper of a mortal woman.

Rosmer's avoidance of full adult maturity is made quite clear in *Rosmersholm* when Kroll asks him to define his political stance:

> *Rosmer:* In my mind, it is high summer once more. I see with a new youthful vision. And therefore I have taken my stand. . . .
> *Kroll:* Where? Where do you stand?
> *Rosmer:* Where your children stand. (6: 313)

Literally, of course, he means that he agrees with the political and social views of Kroll's rebellious offspring. But Ibsen's repeated references to a world of innocent childhood indicate that a more symbolic meaning is also at work. Rosmer defines for Rebecca his conception of happiness: "happiness is more than anything that serene, secure, happy freedom from guilt" (6: 349).

That such idealism is, again, antithetical to sexual experience is articulated when another character, the writer Brendel, explains why he is reluctant to put into words (that is, in effect, to give flesh to) his ideals:

> I have always felt quite nauseated at the thought of solemnly writing it [his secret fantasies] all out. And anyway, why should I profane my own ideals when I could enjoy them in all their purity, and keep them to myself? But now they shall be sacrificed. In truth, I feel like a mother who gives her young daughters into the arms of their husbands. (6: 310)

This linking of idealism and innocence with the image of marriage confirms what Jacobsen has noted about the role bridges play in the ballads. They reflect not only the healing of the divided spirit, but a kind of rite de passage in which a transition takes place and the individual is carried to a new stage in life: in terms of the play's sexual themes, Rosmer struggles against such a passage. But Brendel's speech also invokes images from "Harpens Kraft" and "Nøkkens Svig" in which weddings play important parts. The brides, such as Beata, who think they are marrying ordinary gentlemen, discover their fatal mistake. And the merman (with perhaps the ironic exception of Rosmer) is, again, as dangerous as an idealist as he is a sensualist.

Although Rebecca is a more interesting character than Rosmer, it is the latter whom Ibsen thought of as his protagonist for *Rosmersholm*. He and Rebecca share the same conflicts—that is why their relationship may be doomed—but it is Rosmer's inability to reconcile them that condemns her, for in coming to the land, so to speak, she seems ready to make the necessary passage to reality despite the price she will pay for leaving behind the freedom of Finmark and the sea. Admittedly, however, Ibsen's description of the central conflict in his play is couched in such a way as to make it applicable to both characters:

> the play deals with the struggle that every serious-minded man must

wage with himself to bring his way of life into harmony with his convictions. The different functions of the spirit do not develop uniformly or comparably in any one individual. The acquisitive instinct rushes on from one conquest to the next. Moral consciousness, however, "the conscience," is by comparison very conservative. It has its roots deep in tradition and in the past generally. From this comes the conflict within the individual. But naturally the play is first and foremost a work about people and their destiny. (6: 447)

In the context of this explanation as well as the multiple dualisms that pervade *Rosmersholm*, it is possible to address one of Ibsen's major ironies in the play, the attribution to his bourgeois hero of the name *Rosmer*, that belongs in Scandinavian folklore to the merman whose underseas-cavern realm would appear to have nothing whatsoever to do with that bastion of conservative respectability, Rosmersholm.[4]

First, as most critics of Ibsen recognize, names per se are very important in his plays: this is a point I will have other occasions to make. In *Rosmersholm* the importance given to his characters' names by the playwright is made part of his dialogue. When Brendel asks for help in obtaining access to the town's meeting hall, Rebecca tells him he must apply to Peter Mortensgaard:

> *Brendel: Pardon, madame* . . . what sort of idiot is he?
> *Rosmer:* What makes you think he is an idiot?
> *Brendel:* Can't I tell straight away from his name that he is nothing but a plebeian. (6: 308)

But the importance of the Rosmer *name* for the play is introduced by Kroll, the character who serves as foil for Ibsen's irony:

> *Kroll:* . . . And on top of all there's the family name and *all that means.*
> *Rosmer:* Oh, the family name. . . . (6: 305; emphasis mine)

It is Kroll who also points up the paradox involved when Ibsen assigns to Rosmer's home the name traditionally associated with the merman's realm:

Kroll: . . . If ever the rumour got about that you yourself had abandoned what I might call the Rosmer tradition, it would lead to disastrous and irreparable confusion. (6: 328)

But, of course, the Rosmer tradition comes from folklore, and represents quite the opposite of what Kroll describes:

Kroll: . . . The Rosmers of Rosmersholm . . . clergymen and soldiers . . . high officials . . . men of the highest principles, all of them . . . the foremost family in the district with its seat here now for nearly two hundred years. (6: 305)

But the deadly merman, according to "Nøkkens Svig," can appear as readily as a gentleman as a radical thinker can be mistaken for a conservative, and that Rosmer was once a clergyman only intensifies the disparity between what he once was and now is. There is a special irony when Kroll says of Brendel that he could turn one's ideas upside down, and Rosmer replies that, "Now I have got all my ideas straightened out" (6: 312). For at this point they speak at cross-purposes, not even the speaker understanding the implications of his own claim—his emergence as the merman who, as idealist, he has actually been all along. Kroll's description of Rosmer's reputation in the community exposes the degree to which Rosmer has deceived the people who mistakenly believe they know him:

You are known as a tolerant and fair-minded man; your fine brain, your indisputable integrity are appreciated by everybody in the district. Then there's the esteem and respect that come from your once having been a clergyman. (6: 305)

It is at this point that Kroll becomes the conduit for Ibsen's irony and reminds Rosmer that it is as clergyman that he had represented the Rosmer name.

It is one of the functions of this irony that it elaborates the theme of illusion and reality that is an intrinsic part of "Nøkkens Svig." As Kroll goes on about the threat to those esteemed virtues that the Rosmer name stands for, Rebecca urges Rosmer to tell the truth:

> *Rebecca:* . . . Go on, do it!
> *Rosmer:* . . . Not tonight.
> *Rebecca:* Yes, do it now! (6: 302)

She herself believes she has helped Rosmer cast off the illusions that had bound him to the repressive philosophy that Kroll advocates, and she boasts that "Rosmer has come to see things with a clearer vision than before" (6: 303). Thus she is willing to "tell [it] straight" (6: 305), that is, reveal John Rosmer as the merman idealist whose mortal danger to herself she has not yet glimpsed.

Paradoxically, both Kroll and Mortensgaard urge John Rosmer to perpetuate the illusion of the revered gentleman:

> *Kroll:* . . . What I say is this: if this madness must go on, then in Heaven's name go ahead and *think* whatever you like . . . about anything under the sun. But see that you keep your opinions to yourself. After all it's a purely personal affair. (6: 328)
>
> . . . .
>
> *Mortensgaard:* . . . we've got plenty of free-thinkers already, Pastor Rosmer. I might almost say too many. What the party really needs is Christian elements—something that everybody has to respect. That's what we're badly short of. So the wisest thing for you to do is keep quiet about any of the things that don't really concern the public. (6: 332)

Ibsen has worked out a complex series of ironies here. Mortensgaard not only articulates but urges Rosmer toward a deception that reflects a popular tenet of Christian belief, that the devil and his henchmen walk freely in the world working their evil on unsuspecting men. Demons may appear as fine gentlemen and even clergymen. This free interchange between the demonic and the Christian realms had impressed itself on Ibsen, and it is a subject in the notes he wrote concerning the folklore he gathered during his travels through Norway.

In another seemingly paradoxical reversal of motifs found in his folk ballad sources, Ibsen initially conceived of an unsuspecting Pastor Rosmer whose enlightenment involved recognizing the siren in Rebecca. In notes written for an early draft, Ibsen created the broad outline of a plot.

> She is an intriguer and she loves him. She wants to become his wife and she pursues that aim unswervingly. Then he becomes aware of this, and she openly admits it. Now there is no more joy in life for him. The *demonic* in him is roused by pain and bitterness. He determines to die, and she is to die with him. This she does. (6: 445; emphasis mine)

It would appear that as his ideas about *Rosmersholm* developed, Ibsen became increasingly aware of the implications of his own plan: the *"demonic"* is roused. But Rebecca does not recognize the demon Rosmer. In his second draft Ibsen wrote some later omitted lines that point up more clearly than in the final play that Rosmer's suicide plan becomes in effect a seduction of Rebecca in the tradition of the merman ballads. Hence once again, the effectiveness of the "true" Rosmer depends upon the illusion of the gentleman. In this early draft, the character Hetman (later Brendel) helps to keep Rebecca off guard:

> *Rebecca:* I am not leaving tonight.
> *Rosmer* (fearfully): Yes! Go! Go!
> *Hetman:* Stay, my fair lady. For you there is no danger lurking. He's not likely to lure *you* into deep water. (6: 422)

To understand the "demonic" Rosmer—that is, the connection between Ibsen's hero and the merman of folklore—it is necessary to return to Ibsen's keen insight into the contradictions inherent in nineteenth-century romanticism. Both raging natural passion and idealism serve the same function insofar as they are both allied *against* the mundane world represented by Kroll and the converted Mortensgaard. Again, in this respect the underseas realm of the merfolk can represent the utopic ideology of a Brand or a Rosmer. It is part of Ibsen's understanding of how the ideas of his time could be expressed through the folklore of an

183

earlier period that he comes to identify the common element that unites all earthly paradises and utopias.

Rosmersholm is sometimes interpreted as the first of those late plays in which Ibsen turned from his customary preoccupation with social issues to concentrate on psychological portraits of individuals experiencing the pressures of culture. He had described Rosmer as experiencing the "conflict within the individual," and he was now as interested in the psychological roots of that conflict as its origins in the environment. *Rosmersholm* was conceived after Ibsen's first visit to his homeland after an absence of eleven years. That politics was very much on his mind can be seen in a speech to a workers' gathering in June 1885:

> Much remains to be done here before we can be said to have achieved real freedom. But our democracy, as it now is, is hardly in a position to deal with these problems. An element of nobility must find its way into our public life, into our government, among our representatives and into our press. Of course I am not thinking of nobility of birth, nor of money, nor of a nobility of learning, nor even of ability or talent.
> (6: 445, 447)

Rosmer's version of this, however, must be contrasted with Ibsen's, for it is based on an unrealistic rendering of the playwright's political aims. Rosmer proclaims: "I will devote my life and all my strength to this one thing: to create a true democracy in this land"; he wishes to "make all my countrymen noblemen" (6: 314). That his utopian vision is unrealistic points to the danger in his new ideology. Sooner or later he would have to confront the collapse of his ideals, and the result was likely to be analogous to Beata's realization that she would remain childless: a reversion to pure nature. The conflict that Ibsen portrays in *Rosmersholm* finds ready-made expression in the folklore of the sea. The dichotomy between sea longing and land longing typifies many nineteenth-century romantic dilemmas. But which of these realms embodies the hopes characterized by Rosmer's supposedly advanced political views? In theory Rosmer's ideology should reflect land longing, since he is committed to the improvement of life in the community. But Ibsen also recognizes the validity of Kroll's charge, "Rosmer, you are a dreamer" (6: 314). More than that, Ibsen understands that Rosmer's brand of political idealism is retrogressive, leading to a yearning for an

Edenlike innocence that, far from benefiting the citizens of the state, represents a kind of sea longing antithetical to any reality principle. The true realm for Rosmer's purist beliefs (not that Ibsen approved of Mortensgaard's accommodation to reality) is the sea, and thus it is actually this free but unrealistic realm that is the true Rosmersholm, that is the place in which the unearthly merman resides. Again, Rebecca's fate is sealed because she does not fully understand the implications of Rosmer's awakening to freedom, and caught in her own illusions of his clarified vision, she names the Rosmer philosophy of life without understanding its real essence.

In believing that the Rosmer philosophy destroys happiness, Rebecca is therefore both correct and mistaken. She is right in that Rosmer's *version* of the liberal ideas she has been encouraging him to adopt involves a regressive element which, in its retreat to childlike innocence, is incompatible with the happiness that adults can hope to achieve in an imperfect but mature existence. She is, however, wrong because, again, she has failed to identify the Rosmer philosophy, to know what it now *is*. She does not recognize therefore the demonic in Rosmer and therefore cannot defend herself against the ultimate seduction to which she will succumb.

Ibsen has introduced Rosmer's political attitudes by means of the sexual themes in the play. His protagonist's longing for purity which he comes close to identifying with virginity, and which in the first draft of the play was focused more exclusively on freedom from moral contamination, has been extended to the utopian and Edenic vision of Rosmer in the final version. When he begins to confront the situation that had created a triangle out of him, Beata, and Rebecca, he is dismayed because he "shall never again know the joy of the one thing that makes life so wonderful to live. . . . Quiet, happy innocence" (6: 340). And when he admits that he had deceived himself—thinks he and Rebecca have deceived themselves—about their friendship, the love he places in its stead is far from the passion that had swept Rebecca: "Even while Beata was still alive," he tells her, "my thoughts were all for you. It was you alone I longed for. It was with you that I found calm, happy, serene contentment" (6: 351). When he asks her if she does not think they began their lives together like children falling in love, she does not know what to answer him, probably because her answer, no, would conflict so painfully with the conception of love that he has created.

185

When Rosmer's idealism collapses, and it is replaced by what Ibsen called the demonic, there is no necessity for a fundamental change in his position vis-à-vis the happiness that Rebecca had hoped to derive from the stability and respectability of Rosmersholm. Rosmer's vision has represented sea longing all the while, and now it has merely shifted to its deadlier form. But in any form, the Rosmer philosophy defeats Rebecca's aims—both in forms that she understands, and in those she does not. Her refusal to be his wife is both a conscious and intuitive realization that a vicious cycle has caught her in an inextricable bind and that any reconciliation of their internal and external conflicts has been inexorably thwarted.

Ibsen drew on another popular element from folk narrative to create the final tragedy that dooms Rosmer and Rebecca. It is a motif which, when it appears in analogues to the seal maiden tales, some folklorists have referred to as the offended fairy theme, and it involves the taboo motif that pervades Type 400 and 425 tales. For general audiences, the motif may be most familiar from the legend adopted by Wagner for his opera *Lohengrin,* which would provide one of the most enigmatic symbols in *When We Dead Awaken.* In most stories of unions between mortal and supernatural beings, the relationship that exists is a tenuous one. It can be disrupted or irrevocably destroyed in two essential ways. In one story pattern, the supernatural partner escapes because she has recovered her stolen animal skin or garment, or flees because the animal covering has in some way been damaged or destroyed. In this way Rebecca comes close to evading her doom when she calls for her sealskin trunk. But in other tales, the earthly partner defies some taboo that has been imposed by the mysterious spouse. The result is usually the departure of the one who had imposed the taboo: thus, Lohengrin must leave Elsa when she disobeys the injunction that she never seek to know his name or origins. The taboo often involves some knowledge on the part of the earthly husband or wife concerning the supernatural mate, for its disclosure would precipitate a catastrophe. In *Rosmersholm* Ibsen combines the folkloristic taboo motif with what today would be understood as the ultimate psychological taboo: incest.

When Rosmer proposes marriage to Rebecca, she at first responds with a cry of joy and then a refusal to marry him. At this point she has discovered that her foster father and lover is also her father. *Rosmersholm* is not absolutely explicit on this point, although only a few critics have challenged it. Indeed, it is worth noting that incest is a strong theme in the Rosmer ballads in the form that seems to have most interested Ibsen, that between brother and sister. But naturally Rebecca will not explain herself to Rosmer, and her warning that he must not ask questions is again consistent with a major folklore theme. Thus she threatens to leave Rosmersholm if he forces an accounting from her:

> *Rosmer:* After today there can be for me only one question: Why?
> *Rebecca* (turns and looks at him): Then that will be the end.
> *Rosmer:* Between you and me?
> *Rebecca:* Yes.
> *Rosmer:* Never can there be an end to things between us. You will never leave Rosmersholm. (6: 343)

The tabooed question in *Rosmersholm* would, according to Freud, who wrote about the incest theme in the play, be a sign of Rebecca's awakening conscience, which could only be fully aroused after the knowledge she has obtained of her own past, a past up until then buried in her unconscious.[5] Hence the taboo motif from folklore has the same significance as the bridge that Rosmer will not, cannot set foot on until he conceives of the final act of reconciliation between him and Rebecca: the bridge must be crossed and the taboo must be defied. But Ibsen's treatment of these themes is closer to those versions of the story in which the loss of the spouse from the otherworld is irrevocable (e.g., *Lohengrin*). This loss would express for the nineteenth century a now recognized split in the individual psyche. That century realized the difficulty, perhaps impossibility, of reconciling opposites without the painful surrender of a longing or ideal whose loss would appear unbearable.

But if the ultimate romantic act of escape is suicide, then even here, Ibsen has perpetrated another irony in portraying Rosmer's resolution to his and Rebecca's dilemma. In *Rosmersholm*, the world of the living and the dead are at one and the same time divided and inextricably connected. This idea is introduced early in the play in a conversation between Rebecca and the housekeeper, Mrs. Helseth:

> *Rebecca:* They cling long to their dead here at Rosmer-
> sholm.
> *Mrs. Helseth:* It's my belief it's the dead that cling to Ros-
> mersholm, miss. (6: 294)

Of course, insofar as Rebecca and Rosmer have died, their part in the
dichotomies that tore Ibsen's world has ended. But in presenting the
living and the dead as he has, Ibsen has effectively conveyed to his
audience his understanding that the romantic dilemma itself remains
untouched. Critics have tended to view his next play, *Lady from the Sea,*
as a more optimistic version of *Rosmersholm,* but some—mimicking Rosmer's and Rebecca's own idealism—have been dissatisfied by Ellida
Wangel's reconciliation to her husband's world. As will be seen shortly,
their complaints are shared by the very instrument for this reconciliation, Dr. Wangel, her husband. Moreover, the dilemma addressed by
these plays persists after Ellida chooses to reject her demon lover in
favor of earthly husband. The essential conflict between land longing
and sea longing survives any individual's choice, and to think otherwise
is but another romantic illusion.

The disparate elements in both Rosmer and Rebecca emerge only to
confront their opposite in the other. When the "demonic" is roused in
Rosmer and he seems ready to accommodate his loss of innocence, at
this point does Rebecca begin to exprience a longing for purity:

> *Rosmer:* Your past is dead, Rebecca. It hasn't any hold on
> you any more . . . hasn't any connection with you . . . as
> you are *now.*
> *Rebecca:* Oh, my dear, these are just empty phrases, you
> know. What about innocence? Where do I get *that?* (6:
> 372)

It is Rebecca the mermaid who invades the world of respectable Rosmersholm, whereas Rosmer the merman exploits the guilt of the ethical
Rebecca. Thus they play out at different times the same role. As the
mermaid-witch—Kroll asks, "Who is there you couldn't bewitch . . .
if you tried? (6: 353)—Rebecca finds herself in conflict with the emerging conscience that stands in the way of her goals. When she first came
to Rosmersholm, the witch had prevailed, and like the mermaid in the

Scandinavian ballads who lured women to serve them in the sea world,[6] so does Rebecca as effectively lead Beata to a watery grave. But as was seen above, the virtual seduction of Beata was accomplished step by step, slowly, as Rebecca experienced the doubts that created hesitation and fear.

Similarly, Rosmer systematically enacts the diabolical seduction of Rebecca that appears to substitute for a true, sexual seduction. As he convinces her, also step by step, to follow him to the bridge over the millstream, he too is partly appalled by what he is doing. With his head in his hands, he confesses to himself that there is a "horrible fascination in this. . . !" (6: 378). But in the meantime, he again reverses their roles and suggests the way out of their dilemma while simultaneously making taboo the answer to the question which would clarify his intentions:

> *Rebecca* (wringing her hands): Oh, but Johannes . . . can't you think of anything . . . anything at all that would make you believe [in his cause].
> *Rosmer* (starts, as if in fear): Don't! You mustn't ask me about that! Please don't go on! Don't say another word!
> (6: 377)

This time it is he, the supernatural lover, who imposes the prohibition, but this time it seems less that he fears disclosure than that he has found a deliberate ploy to lure Rebecca on. And she takes the bait as he taunts her with lacking the will to do what Beata had done—jump into the millstream. In short, he plays the merman who leads to the destructive water the woman whose own conflicts have already predisposed her to follow him:

> *Rosmer:* Yes, Rebecca . . . that is the question that will haunt me . . . after you have left. Every hour of the day my thoughts will keep returning to it. I seem to see you clearly in my mind's eye . . . standing right out in the middle of the bridge. Then you lean out over the railing! . . . You sway as the rush of the water draws you down. No . . . you draw back. You dare not do what *she* dared.
> (6: 378)

The very terms of Rosmer's "seduction" reproduce the interchangeable roles that he and Rebecca have played in their failed relationship. Her hesitation, as he pictures it, mirrors the process she had earlier described in her own hesitant but nonetheless determined destruction of Beata. Meanwhile, his horrified self-awareness coupled with the faltering way in which he verbally lures Rebecca to the bridge, make it difficult to distinguish his manipulations from genuine horror.

Rosmer's seduction of Rebecca echoes another folk motif that Ibsen had already used in *Lady Inger* and would exploit more fully in *The Masterbuilder:* the so-called wonderland motif. Jacobsen has already described the ballad known to English readers as "Lady Isabel and the Elf Knight," and the naturalization of the story in Denmark, where the hero has been transformed from a supernatural abductor and murderer to a quite ordinary man who preys on women for their fortunes. The narrative "idea" of the ballad remains the same, however, involving a villain who "entices a girl away from her home to kill her as he has killed others: she through bravery and presence of mind defeats his design by a ruse; and he, pleading for his life, is destroyed by her."[7] Although the connection of this ballad with the others that we have been looking at has been questioned,[8] it seems clear that Ibsen saw thematic parallels and drew on them.

One of these common strains lies in the "wonderland" theme, which can be understood as a general classification for those supernatural or symbolic otherworlds whose imagined splendors are an integral part of their appeal for the mortal who sojourns there or is kidnapped. That is, the seducer must present the otherworld compellingly. In *Lady Inger,* Denmark itself is the enticement held out to lure Lady Inger's daughter to the fate her sister had already suffered, and this is a point worth stressing, since if Norway's neighbor could be conceived of by Ibsen as a "wonderland," then its ballads on that and related themes would pick up added significance for the playwright.

In any event, the "wonderland" theme involves the verbal seduction of the maiden with promises of an earthly paradise. Of the various inducements offered her by her demon lover, promises of a wonderland are "found scattered in various parts of Denmark," but provide in Norway "the most prevalent form of bait" and were probably the dominant form in earliest versions of the ballad.[9] The language in which Rosmer couches his rehearsal of Rebecca's suicide suggests the wonderland motif, for he depicts a woman hypnotized by the water world which draws her almost as a magnet to the realm below: "you lean out over the railing! . . . You sway as the rush of the water draws you down" (6: 378). In playing on her internal sea longing, he is not only seducer but natural mate, much like the bull seal who both appears to the seal maiden in response to her own dissatisfactions with earthly life, and functions as the symbol of the alternate existence that beckons to her.

Rosmer in other ways fits very well the murderer of the Danish versions:

> It is thus arguable that we have here a supernatural villain whose strange treatment of women has appeared even stranger once his otherworldly nature has been forgotten, and whose acts are therefore with time explained as the result of a combination of perverted sexual drive and a humdrum desire for gold [e.g., the property of the captured maiden].[10]

Even this "humdrum desire for gold" is fulfilled in Ibsen's notes about the "acquisitive appetite" that wars with the moral consciousness of the individual in his time, and it is clear from *Rosmersholm* that the world of the Rosmers is, for all its piety and uprightness, the result of the privileges that belong to rank and acquired wealth. But whereas the rationalized versions of the ballad render more difficult to understand the evil wrought by the male protagonist in the folk narratives, Ibsen has clarified what would otherwise be obscure. By making John Rosmer both the human man—that is, the rationalized form of the otherworld figure—and the merman, Ibsen has covered more ground than either possibility alone would allow him.

But the ballads on which Ibsen drew also reveal, as Jacobsen has demonstrated, that there are some mortals who for one reason or another are marked as potential victims for otherworldly seductions. Child's notes to the "Hind Etin" ballad, which enjoys wide popularity in Scandinavia, describes the analogous German ballad of the "Wassermanns Braut" ("Merman's Bride"), in which a young woman resists her parents' urging that she marry. Instead, she begs for a year in which she will be left to herself. In short, she too seems to be reacting against what in *Rosmersholm* is the Rosmer philosophy of life, stable, secure, socially acceptable, but antithetical to happiness. It is after her refusal of marriage that the merman appears to carry her off, effectively responding to her psychological call. This variant makes explicit what Jacobsen has argued to be inherent in the ballad group to which it belongs.

Thus the young woman who resists marriage and the mermaid who comes to earth precisely to seek worldly husbands are two sides of the same coin, both sides embodied in the "Agnete" ballad and the seal maiden story. Throughout *Rosmersholm*, Rebecca is depicted as both real woman and mermaid. As mermaid, it has been noted, she lured another woman to the waterworld in order to serve her, Rebecca's, ends. In the ballad in which a similar story is told, the young woman—like the maiden kidnapped by Rosmer—is rescued by her brother. Ironically, in Ibsen's play, Kroll plays the role of rescuer-brother only after Beata's death. Nonetheless, he confronts the sea creature who had exercised as uncanny a power over his sister as over him:

> *Kroll:* . . . you had managed to bewitch her as well. Or do you want to call that friendship, the way she came to feel about you? She idolized you, worshipped you. The outcome of it was . . . how shall I put it? a kind of desperate infatuation. Yes, that's the only way to describe it. (6: 354)

Rebecca later admits to this seduction of Beata, guiltily describing herself to Rosmer as a "sea-troll slumped over the ship that is to carry you forward. I must go overboard. Do you expect me to go through life dragging behind me a crippled existence?" (6: 379)

It is interesting to note that the merman's bride in the German ballad asks for a single year in which to indulge her desire for freedom. A year, more or less, of Rebecca's life comes to have great importance in the play. On one level, it helps establish that Dr. West was probably her father, the probable breaking point for the now ethical Rebecca. But that year also helps define in Rebecca the kind of vulnerability that is the focus of a study that contends that her desperation to be Rosmer's wife has to do with her awareness that life offered her few options as a woman.[11] It is a mark of her desperation and of her vulnerability that she tells Kroll that she is actually a year older than she usually admits to being:

> *Rebecca:* When I was twenty-five, and still not married, I thought I was getting a bit too old. So I began subtracting a year. (6: 356)

This passage is also that place in *Rosmersholm* where Rebecca betrays most her potential bourgeoise nature, and she herself is aware of it: "there's always some little thing or other that sticks and you just can't shake yourself free of it. It's just the way we are made" (6: 356). Whether "we" refers to shared humanity or specifically to woman's plight seems to be left deliberately ambiguous.

Rebecca's possession of her sealskin trunk, her ability to choose to stay at Rosmersholm or to leave, is thwarted at that point when, choosing to stay, she becomes a mortal vulnerable to the power of Rosmer Havmand. She is, again, seal maiden and Agnete, torn between land and sea longing, and her death is a symbolic enactment of the impossibility of reconciling her conflict. In essence, she had made the same choice early in the play that Ellida Wangel, whom many see as her counterpart, makes at the end of *The Lady from the Sea*. The two plays are frequently discussed in conjunction with each other. The following analysis of *The Lady from the Sea* will argue that if Ellida resolves her dilemma more successfully than Rebecca, it is because of something that is not ordinarily noticed: her husband, Dr. Wangel, has successfully suppressed his own inclination to be Rosmer Havmand.

Notes

1. Alrik Gustafson notes that the

> symbolistic patterns which Ibsen employs [in *Rosmersholm*] . . . are drawn very largely from primitivistic folkloristic sources—sources which spring directly from man's relationship to land and sea. . . . The central symbolistic patterns are two in number, those which reflect the Rosmer view of life represented primarily by the white horses that haunt the Rosmersholm estate, and those which reflect Rebecca's emancipated views as represented by the mermaid and the sea. (*Rosmersholm*, p. xiii)

There are two problems with this view. First, as we have argued, what is involved in this folklore are four, not two elements: two would allow humans an easier, if not a simple, choice. Second, in folklore, the horses are a common image of the *nökk*, also associated with mythical sea beasts. If the white horses that haunt Rosmersholm represent the dead, it must also be remembered that in myth and folklore there are close ties between the magic otherworld and the world of the dead. (See also note 4 below.) The most significant analysis of merfolk in Ibsen can be found in Gravier's essay on the *ballade magique*. I differ with him on one important point. He argues that Rebecca deserves the name of mermaid because she discovers a kindred spirit in Rosmer (merman) and resolves to save this captive being from the narrowness of the establishment (154). My argument is that the tragedy of the play is that they never interact as similar beings: when she is mermaid, he is mortal; when he is merman, she is mortal. Again, when four rather than two elements are recognized in the folklore pattern, the complexity of Ibsen's view becomes more readily apprehensible.

2. Rosengarten (468) points to similar imagery in *The Lady from the Sea* and also makes the comparison to Andersen's story.

3. See Holmström's introductory chapter.

4. This would be a good place to discuss whether Rosmer can be viewed as a merman. He is "Rosmer Havmand" in Grundtvig's collection, although, as Jacobsen has pointed out to me, nothing in the ballads themselves actually says so. Moreover, Jacobsen notes, in some versions he turns to stone, a fate usually reserved for giants and trolls. In the type index to the Scandinavian medieval ballad (Jonsson et al.), the Rosmer ballads do not appear in the group dealing with the supernatural sea folk. Rather, Rosmer is placed among other giants. Grundtvig's notes suggest that an etymology for Rosmer's name links him to the sea lion, that is, the seal. But Holbek points out to me that Rosmer may be derived from *hross* ("horse"), that is, sea horse, associated with winds and waves, not with the undersea caverns I invoke in my discussion. This would make particular sense of the white horses, of course. But I would argue that the imagery in Ibsen's play invokes so many of the ballads involving the magical sea creatures, drawing on "Agnete," "Nøkkens Svig," and "Harpens Kraft," that Gravier is probably correct in interpreting John Rosmer as Ibsen's merman ("Le drame d'Ibsen").

5. Freud discusses Rebecca West in some detail in his essay "Some Character-Types Met With in Psychoanalytic Work." Elizabeth Hardwick has argued against the incest theme (69–83).

6. See motif index in Jonsson et al. 39.

7. Nygard 319.

8. Ibid. 23.

9. Ibid. 159.

10. Ibid. 320.

11. This is Hardwick's approach to *Rosmersholm*.

When Rebecca comes to Rosmersholm she is in a dangerous state. She is free—

or, rather adrift. She is immensely needy, looking desperately for some place to land, to live. And what can it mean for her, with her high-mindedness and her threatening need? It means she must have a husband, and soon. What else can she hope for? (74)

CHAPTER 6

Ellida as Seal Maiden

That she can reclaim her sealskin trunk at will distinguishes Rebecca from the helpless, land-locked seal maiden, awaiting the return of her magic powers to escape the world. Rebecca is only powerless when she plays mortal woman to Rosmer merman. This alternating relationship makes itself felt as well in Ibsen's next play, *The Lady from the Sea,* which is sometimes read as *Rosmersholm*'s counterpart: the latter, it has been argued,

> has no clear link with the plays preceding it, except that, like all Ibsen's plays, it is concerned with the possibility of freedom, or rather of total independence from all responsibilities of living society. With *The Lady from the Sea* it is linked so closely that the latter play can be seen, if one wishes, as a companion piece, with a positive instead of a negative ending.[1]

Similarly, the heroines of these plays have been compared, particularly their situations at the beginning of the dramas:

> Both have come out of the north, from childhoods shadowed by incest guilt. Both have met men who hold the possibility of deep and fulfilling love and both have adopted projects of the will as defenses against the threat they feel is inherent in this kind of love. Both face the collapse of their projects and try to fight their way free of their past, to achieve a sense of self-unity, and to move into "free and responsible" relationships.[2]

But both plays, I argue, resist the neat, dualistic stuctures attributed to them. Arguments have been made for Ellida's "descent to the underworld of the unconscious" and her "return to light and freedom,"[3] and for the physical setting of the play functioning "as a kind of diorama of the human mind, with the sea corresponding to the unconscious and the land to the conscious portion."[4] The Stranger is both a real person, "un matelot" ("seaman") and "un ondin,"[5] one who inhabits the earth but also speaks as "Ellida's inner voice."[6] Correspondingly, Ellida's problem is either psychological or philosophical, on one side, or she is the "victim of [external] supernatural powers"[7] on the other. An ingenious interpretation of her dead infant holds that it is the "offspring of her selfhood, and hardly of her union with Dr. Wangel."[8] Even the two names given to the Stranger suggest two realms: he is either Alfred Johnston, the ordinary name appropriate to a typical seaman, or he is Friman, determined to live or die a free man ("fri mand"). As Orley Holtan points out, Norwegians would not sound final *d*, and clearly Ibsen intended the Stranger to symbolize the same freedoms Ellida seeks.[9]

But as Alfred Johnston, with a name that hardly evokes images of the demon lover he proves to be in the play, he appears to belong to the ordinary world rather than some magic world which beckons to Ellida. In this sense, he is not so different from her mundane husband, and to recognize this ambiguity concerning the Stranger is also to be struck with Dr. Wangel's admission in act 4 that he never helped Ellida acclimatize to his world, since as a sea lady she was to him what the Stranger was to her. Thus Wangel can be associated with the Stranger's world as the Stranger can be with Wangel's, and thus the two men can interchange roles, together embodying the ambiguity of John Rosmer–Rosmer Havmand, Ibsen once again manipulating the folklore patterns to add another twist to their already potential meaning. It is possible to work out Gravier's inconsistent comparison of Sire Bengt, dull husband of *The Feast at Solhaug*, to the Mountain King if it is understood that *elfarland* and *beijarland* cannot be simply juxtaposed.[10] Margit can hardly bear her husband, and Gravier compares Ellida to Margit, admitting however that Dr. Wangel is more sympathetic than the caricatured Sire Bengt. Both husbands—insofar as they are wed to reluctant wives—can be characterized by the troll-like mountain king.[11]

It is true that a comparison can be made between the woman who follows the troll for the gold he promises her, and the woman who marries in the real world for financial security; but unless the husband proves to be as ambiguously defined as his wife, the ordinary husband and the troll cannot be placed on the same side of the line that divides *elfarland* from *beijarland*. Dr. Wangel, again, proves to be a more ambiguous character than critical studies of the play recognize. Thus Gravier was on the right track, but his emphasis on simple oppositions led him to inconsistences rather than a full recognition of Ibsen's way of handling folklore. In the *Feast at Solhaug* Margit is both ordinary wife and fantasized *huldre* capable of escaping her boorish husband. And so is Ellida both captive wife and seductive mermaid. But whereas Sire Bengt hardly deserves the symbolic status that comes with his association with the mountain king except perhaps as perceived kidnapper, Dr. Wangel reveals a side to himself that is potentially troll-like. Perhaps Ibsen was already working out in the early play the complexity of the seemingly bourgeois husband although he did not bring his theme to real fruition until *The Lady from the Sea*.

Rolf Fjelde extends the usual dualisms to define three elements operating in *The Lady from the Sea*, but stops short of ceding more value to the real world than Ellida herself does. Fjelde contrasts the land and sea worlds, the former a unidimensional place which "by its very meagerness and limitation, necessitates choice," creating an either/or situation, whereas the sea creates at least the illusion of both/and.[12] Conversely, Gravier recognizes the dangers of fairyland, whose human devotees may reject the bigotry of their own world, but revert instead to an amorality that wreaks havoc on those who try to rescue them. The purely illusory nature of the otherworld is part of its very danger. Such is the situation of the Alving (descendants of elves) family in *Ghosts*.[13] But Gravier too stops short of conceding the human world its correspondingly positive elements. What is it, after all, that draws the fairies there or causes them to seek in mortals what their own world lacks. Frequently that lack has been defined, if defined at all, in religious terms: the fairies are either seeking human souls to pay as tithes to the devil or are seeking their own salvation, that soul they may gain in marriage to humans. Thus the world assumes value as passage to a higher kind of supernatural existence in the Christian paradise to which the fairy folk can aspire only if they possess a soul. But many writers who have treated these motifs have not been interested in this religious theme, and it is probably fair to add Ibsen to them.

It is tempting to suggest that it is love that draws beings from different worlds to each other, but surprisingly few writers who drew on folklore found this a self-sufficient explanation. In his poem "The Stolen Child," the Irish poet Yeats was able to avoid that interpretation altogether to focus on the deficiencies of fairyland and the essential warmth of a world otherwise more full of weeping than a child, at any rate, can understand. It is this warmth that the fairies appear to be seeking in the child. But nineteenth- and twentieth-century treatments of folklore themes do not of and by themselves serve to explain folklore. Why the supernaturals seek unions with mortals will remain a more teasing question than why humans seek them. I am inclined to agree with and extend Wagner's explanation of the mythology behind the Lohengrin story, that an essential reality principle has always been present in the stories people tell so that its very absence in fairyland is conceived of as a deficiency in that realm. The Pueblo Indians of North America, for example, tell how their people originally lived below the earth's surface, free of illness and death, but unhappy there. For this reason they emerged from the depths to live in the world.

Gravier understands that in *The Lady from the Sea*, Ibsen has reversed the usual themes of the ballads (but not of the folktales, as we have argued in our introduction). He writes that in this play it is not a matter of a human captive who needs rescue from elves, but rather of a nature spirit, an ondine, who must escape human bondage to find her natural element.[14] To grasp this difference is to recognize how mistaken were the early critics who compared Ibsen's play to Hans Christian Andersen's *The Little Mermaid*.[15] If anything, the comparison would more appropriately apply to *Rosmersholm*, where Rebecca, like Andersen's heroine, has left her magic world for the ordinary, both of them drawn by love of a mortal man, and both willing to sacrifice the amoral freedom of the sea for the ethical existence or, symbolically, a human soul. And both are betrayed: the Little Mermaid because her beloved chooses a woman from his own world, and Rebecca for the same reason rendered paradoxical. John Rosmer, whom Rebecca took to be a real man, proves to be Rosmer merman, who in being one of her own kind, negates her aspirations to be first lady of Rosmersholm.

Differences and similarities between *The Lady from the Sea* and Andersen's *The Little Mermaid* have been drawn but surrounded by seeming confusion: the Little Mermaid is "*inexplicably* fascinated by the terrestrial," and thus Ellida's "dilemma is *curiously* reversed."[16] Clearly, Ibsen intended to invert Andersen's rendering of mermaid lore. He would not know the little statue that now sits in Copenhagen harbor, but would have no difficulty conceiving of a mermaid trapped in the sea, near to shore, but never quite reaching it—yearning toward the human realm that will not accept her. In *The Lady from the Sea*, Ballested paints the reverse situation, a "mermaid lying half dead" because she "has strayed in from the sea and cannot find her way out again. So here she lies dying in the brackish water" (7: 30).[17]

Again, this double perspective is built into the mythology surrounding the merfolk. In a comprehensive study of mermaids (and mermen), titled *Sea Enchantresses*, a Babylonian myth concerning the god Ea or Oannes is recounted. Oannes who emerged from the Erythrian sea, although inhabiting a fish's body, was endowed with reason, voice, and language. Under his fish's head was another, and feet similar to a human's were joined to his fish's tail. Like a Prometheus, this merman gave to the human world such a wealth of theoretical and practical knowledge that no improvement was subsequently required. But at night, when the "sun set, it was the custom of this Being to plunge again into the sea and abide all night in the deep." Oannes faced no conflict between *beijarland* and *elfarland*, but instead illustrates John Keats's wistful claim that "real are the dreams of gods," the English poet depicting in "Lamia" the human need to choose between two worlds. But in most folklore, the merfolk must also choose between two existences. There is also the story of the mermaid whose situation parallels that of Ellida Wangel, having accidentally floated through a broken dike in West Friesland with no ability to find her way out again. Although she is educated by those who discover her, she never fully adapts to human life and lives dumb, alienated from the humans around her, until her death.[18] Her speechlessness echoes a theme in Andersen's fairy tale and, again, what emerges from a comparison are complementary motifs. In one case dumbness reflects a stubborn defiance as well as grief; in the other, dumbness thwarts the Little Mermaid who yearns toward the world but cannot—rather than will not—communicate with it.

When Orley Holtan contrasts Ellida's choice between a "stifling life of security" and a "dangerous life of freedom," he comes perhaps closer than any other critic to the ambiguous pattern on which Ibsen draws.[19] Ibsen was aware of the positive and negative elements that comprised *both* worlds, fairyland and the mortal realm, but would nonetheless find in folklore the difficulty in deciding which corresponded to humans' true nature. As Koht writes in his biography, by the time Ibsen wrote his play, he had heard of the guess "that a fish was the first link in the evolutionary chain which led to the human being, and he asked himself: 'Are there still rudiments thereof in the human mind? In some human minds?' The dream of the sea thus came to rise from the depths of the soul."[20]

In asking whether humans would have been happier had they remained in the sea, Ibsen was in effect addressing the issue embedded in the seal maiden tradition: which is the "real" element of the woman who longs for the sea. Is she a human under enchantment, thus alienated from her own kind, or a captive forced against her will to live among humans as wife and mother? The mermaid as *both* animal and human graphically depicts this dilemma. Ironically, however, both traditional Christianity and psychoanalysis have failed to do justice to this dichotomy insofar as each conceives of the eradication of one side as the resolution to the problem reflected in the duality. Gravier has described these otherworldly beings who both attract and terrify (as both Ellida and Wangel admit to each other), and adds that from the Christian point of view they are the last "avatar des divinités paiennes dechués. Leur puissance est derisoire mais aussi séductrice comme peut l'être le péché pour le paganisme."[21] Esther Harding with like severity secularizes the Christian view to argue that the mythological mermaids are "represented always as concerned only with themselves," that is, as "autoerotic." She details their need to exercise power over men, for which reason they seduce them, seeming to describe Hedda Gabler rather than Ellida Wangel. The mermaid is "cold-blooded, without human feeling or compassion. Instinct in its daemonic form, entirely non-human, lives through [her]."[22] But in the "mermaid" phase of modern woman, Ellida may be found, evidencing "a complete lack of psychological development . . . an animal-like at-one-ness with nature, which has never been broken by any human awareness." Perhaps applicable to both Hedda and Ellida, however, is Harding's admission that modern woman may find herself in "this state because she has found the conventional ways of behaving entirely sterile."[23]

But psychoanalytic criticism of the play usually does not go even this far: Ellida's yearning toward the sea is typically interpreted as a sign of a neurosis threatening to become psychosis if she succumbs to the "black soundless wings" above her (7: 120).[24] Her choice to remain with Wangel, who serves as a healer as well as husband, is a sign of returning health. In short, the psychoanalytic point of view would result in advice to Wangel that he symbolically burn and not merely hide his wife's seal skin, her link to the sea world toward which she yearns. For it is obvious that if any of Ibsen's female characters can be called a seal maiden, it is Ellida Wangel.

Mermaid and seal lore frequently merge in popular legends.[25] If it is a mermaid who is captured, she is deprived not of her animal covering but rather a cap or pouch; and if, as is sometimes the case, she has come to the world of her own free will, she may exchange her tail for human legs. Ibsen's attention to Ellida's walking with her husband has been claimed to take up a larger portion in the play than would be warranted had it not some special significance, significance derived from Andersen's Little Mermaid.[26] (Jacobsen claims that an even stronger influence on this play comes from Andersen's play Agnete.) But it also has to be remembered that Ibsen had altered the original title of his play from Havfruen (The Mermaid) to Fruen fra havet (Lady from the Sea), apparently wanting his sea lore to extend beyond mermaids. Ellida's compulsive bathing in the sea even in poor weather causes her husband to believe she exists for that activity (7: 38). He attributes her strange behavior to years spent living at an isolated lighthouse, which "has left a deep mark on her. . . . The people around here don't really understand it at all. They call her 'The Lady from the Sea' " (7:39).

Wangel's explanation bears an interesting comparison to an Icelandic version of the seal maiden story. After the skin is stolen, the man gave her some human garments and "took her home with him. She grew very fond of him, but did not get on so well with other people. Often she would sit alone and stare out to sea."[27] It is perhaps this alienation from human company that causes Ellida to define herself as well as the Stranger in terms of the many sea creatures that dominated their conversation:

whales and dolphins, and . . . the seals that lie out on the rocks in the warmth of the sun. . . . [When] we talked about such things I used to feel that he was somehow of the same kith and kin as these creatures . . . I too almost felt as though I were one of them. (7: 62)

Insofar as Ellida believes she has married Wangel without free choice, she is like the seal maiden captured by an insensitive man. Wangel admits as much to Arnholm:

Haven't you noticed that people who live out there by the open sea form a kind of separate race? It is almost as though they live the life of the sea itself. Their thoughts and feelings ebb and flow like the tide. And you can never transplant them. . . . Oh, I should have thought of this before. It was sinful to take Ellida away from out there and bring her up here. (7: 92)

And insofar as the Stranger is a fellow sea creature, he—like the bull seal—can assert his prior claim: "she belongs in the first place to me" (7: 79). Even when Wangel accedes to Ellida's plea that she be able to choose freely—"I must be able to let him go away alone . . . or to go with him" (7: 101)—he is acting out another element in folklore, that rare instance which occurs when the animal covering is freely returned to the seal (or swan) bride. Whether or not Ibsen had firsthand contact with such a variant, it remains the case that Ellida's ability to choose can be found in the folklore.

Wangel's hope that his wife will choose him, however, introduces the most paradoxical element in the play. For it has to do with why men marry mermaids. Superficially, of course, there is their reputation for beauty, their exoticism compellingly attractive. And as Wangel says, they both attract and terrify (7: 102); they may even attract the more for terrifying. The world, however, will attempt to domesticate them, as it did the mermaid who found herself trapped *inside* the dykes. But this is precisely what Wangel does *not* do, and he reproaches himself for his failure to help Ellida adapt to his world (7: 92). In preserving that which attracted him to begin with, Wangel has, or so he believes, contributed to her developing emotional illness and he recognizes only too well that the "cure" that will allow him to maintain his hold on her will also deprive him of that which drew him to her in the first place. Either way, then—if she stays with him or leaves with the Stranger—the sea wife will be his no more. That is, either way he in some sense loses.

I choose that formulation because it has its counterpart in Ibsen's early play, *Love's Comedy*, where Svanhild must make a similar choice between Falk, a writer, and Guldstad, a businessman.[28] The confrontation between the two men is not as dramatic as that between the Stranger and Dr. Wangel, but Guldstad, proposing marriage to Svanhild, insists that she be allowed to "make her choice" (2: 187). As he pleads his realistic case in the face of Falk's and Svanhild's romanticism, he conveys to Svanhild that if she chooses him, he will win happiness in having her as his wife; if she chooses Falk, he would still "win a quiet victory all the same, / for you will have won happiness" (2: 192). Perhaps he is indulging in rhetoric at this point, for it is through rhetoric that he persuades her to abandon her dreams and marry him. But there is no verbal ploy in Wangel's attempt to hold his wife; more significant, in this later play a more profound dilemma confronts him. Unlike Guldstad who will, or so he claims, win either way, Wangel is ruefully aware that he will, again, lose either way.

And so act 4 ends on a deliberately ambiguous note: "Mr. Arnholm! Let us go in and drink a farewell glass with . . . with the Lady from the Sea" (7: 105). Michael Meyer's translation makes the point more forcefully; they would drink a farewell *to* Wangel's sea wife. But *with* is the more accurate translation of the play, and it may also be more to the point, for in involving Ellida in her disenchantment—so to speak—he is making her face her responsibilities, not only for behavior in the world in which she chooses to live with Wangel, but also for the part she played in entering that world in the first place. She had always known that she was less than captive bride, but when it suited her to she would ignore the truth: "To put it bluntly," she reproaches Wangel, "the plain truth is . . . that you came out there . . . and bought me. . . . Oh, I wasn't a scrap better than you. I accepted your terms. I went and sold myself to you" (7: 98). But she soon adds, "But I did not come to your house of my own free will. That is what counts" (7:99).

The contradiction of "I accepted your terms" and "I did not come to your house of my own free will" can be resolved in the light of the narrative pattern provided by the folklore. Ellida has reluctantly entered Wangel's world for what a romanticist would interpret as its most crass offering, bourgeois comfort and security. She chooses to remain, however, for that which in folklore draws the sea folk to begin with: an ethical life rooted in warm human relationships. Insofar as the latter represents a higher form of existential choice, it is possible for her to contrast it with her original, materialistic motives. But her decision has not always pleased those romantic critics who believe she has not only accommodated herself to the kindly and loving Dr. Wangel, but to Sire Bengt, and to Guldstad. And, ironically, Wangel would find himself ruefully agreeing with their argument. Hermann J. Weigand has wittily claimed that " 'The Lady from the Sea' stands out among Ibsen's work as the classic of romantic longing,"[29] but it is romanticism's inability to extricate itself from reality that makes the folklore so immediately applicable to nineteenth-century concerns. In any event, to pay closer attention to Wangel's own attraction to a lady from the sea is to realize that the play is something other than an optimistic working out of the dilemma of *Rosmersholm.*

The argument for Ellida as prototypical seal maiden may seem to neglect the background usually cited by Ibsen critics. There are the biographical sources, the experiences of Ibsen's mother-in-law, who broke with her own "demon lover," an Icelandic poet, to make Ellida's choice of a kindly older man with children from a previous marriage. The strong infatuation of the poet Adda Ravnkilde for a similarly inappropriate lover led to her suicide. And then there are the stories that Ibsen heard in his stay at Molde: a person who moved from Finland to Finmark was associated with troll power and convinced a woman to leave her clergyman husband for him. As Koht describes it, "Ibsen became entirely silent as he listened to this story, and sat gazing before him." The story merged with another "about a seaman who was gone for many years, so that they believed him to be dead, but who suddenly came home and found his wife married to another. Thus [in his play] he gave the Finlander a hold from former days upon the woman he would draw away with him."[30]

Other folklore can be added to this account, and many possible sources have been advanced by Pavel Fraenkl, who stresses the revenant theme found in the eighteenth-century ballad "Lenore."[31] To these can be added Holtan's casual mentioning of an "American ballad, found in the hills of Kentucky and West Virginia," which "presents a similar story of a returning lover, though his demonic qualities are more pronounced in the English than the American version. The story also had a wide currency in Scandinavian folklore."[32] Actually, it is difficult to locate precise Scandinavian analogues to this ballad, "The Demon Lover" (Child 243), although the similarities to Ibsen's play are so marked that *The Lady from the Sea* seems to resemble it more closely than any of the analogues suggested by Fraenkl.

There is—besides internal evidence—one striking piece of evidence that suggests Ibsen may have been familiar with Child 243. As analyses of his plays make clear, names and places carry many of his plays' themes. The Stranger who comes for Ellida hails from Finmark, a region traditionally associated with magic and sorcery. His name, "Friman," is consistent with his being called at one time in the play the "American," for as Jorgenson has written about Ibsen in another context, "as a symbol of the world [Ibsen] desired, America could serve him very well," representing to the European imagination that which is "young, fresh, new, unshackled."[33] Therefore, it is noteworthy that when the Stranger comes to claim Ellida, he is wearing a Scottish cap. For where would Scotland figure in the seaman's various attributes?

In his scholarly edition of Danish ballads, Alexander Prior takes up the "Scotch ballads 'James Harries' . . . and 'The Demon Lover,'" which "describe a married lady to whom her first lover returns, and induces her to quit her husband and children and go to sea with him."[34] Prior believes that this story from the British isles tells the same tale as "Agnete og Havmanden." But whether the Scottish and Scandinavian traditions can be linked here as they can in other instances, notably their seal lore, is not certain. Tristram P. Coffin, who cites an impressively large number of American versions of Child 243, argues that there is no specific European analogue, although the Danes have a similar song concerning a treacherous wife.[35] Does he mean Agnete, who betrays her merman husband when she fails to return to the sea as promised (Matthew Arnold picked up, or perhaps introduced this viewpoint, depending on which ballads he had in mind)? In *Folklore in English and Scottish Ballads*, L. C. Wimberly questions any connection between "Agnete og Havmanden" and "The Demon Lover." "Child says nothing to this effect." But he has his own objections to comparing the Scottish and Danish ballads: the "British song is not . . . clear as to the exact nature of the Otherworld lover [as is "Agnete"], nor does it give us a satisfactory idea of the land to which the ghost, demon, or ordinary seaman transports his mistress. [But] It may be that Prior is right."[36] Such vagueness, however, may have suited Ibsen.

Ibsen would have had at least indirect contact with Child 243. For although Grundtvig did not include "The Demon Lover" in his *Engelske og Skotske Folkeviser*, in his notes to "Nøkkens Svig" (#39) in his ballad collection, he specifically refers to the Scottish "Demon Lover," pointing out its similarities and differences. In the Child-Grundtvig index, Child 243 and Grundtvig 39 are linked.[37] Ibsen might have been encouraged by Grundtvig's collection of ballads to track down the reference to Sir Walter Scott's *Minstrelsy of the Scottish Border* or Buchan's collection, or he might have known the Scottish ballad from some other source. And if there is no direct link between his play and the Scottish ballad, then a comparison between them reveals an extraordinary coincidence.

In both ballad and play, the female protagonist is a married woman. In both she had earlier plighted her troth to a seaman, an act more binding than the modern engagement of today, although not as binding as her subsequent marriage. In *The Lady from the Sea* the Stranger tells Wangel that "I admit I have absolutely no claim . . . in the meaning you give it" (7: 80). In both ballad and play she marries an "ordinary" man—a ship's carpenter or a doctor—when her seaman leaves her and/ or is believed dead at sea. In both cases there are children, although Ibsen renders this motif ambiguous through the use of stepchildren. But he has heightened rather than diminished the ethical dimensions of his play. Children cannot be Ellida's sole tie to Wangel and his world, whereas in the hundreds of variants of Child 243 (including American versions), children are the usual explanation for the woman's longing to return to her home after she elopes with her demon lover.

In both play and ballad the seaman returns, an apparition from the past, to be greeted at first with the woman's eagerness to see him and then with her withdrawal and reminder to him that she is another's wife.

> "O where have you been, my long, long love,
>   This long seven years and mair?"
> "O I'm come to seek my former vows
>   Ye granted me before."
>
> "O hold your tongue of your former vows,
>   For they will breed sad strife;
> O hold your tongue of your former vows,
>   For I am become a wife."
>   (Child 243 F; Scott's version)

Ellida (turns with a cry): Ah, my dear one . . . So you've come at last!
Stranger: Yes, at last.

. . . .

Stranger: You know I've come to fetch you.
Ellida (recoils in terror): Fetch me! Is that what you intend?
Stranger: Of course.
Ellida: But you know I'm married!
Stranger: Yes, I know.
Ellida: Yet you still . . . ! Yet you've still come to . . . to fetch me! (7: 76–77)

As in the ballad, domestic reality in the play interacts with supernatural horror.

In many American versions, although not in the two Scottish variants cited by Grundtvig, the wife dresses herself gayly in preparation for joining her demon lover. Interestingly, just before the Stranger reappears, Hilde holds forth on her ways of dressing, on gay colors in contrast to black. And the Stranger himself asks if Ellida is ready, qualifying himself, "I am not asking whether she is dressed to leave. Or whether she has packed her bags" (7: 119). He adds that all she needs will be on ship—also an echo from the ballads, where the unfaithful wife is assured that she will suffer no deprivation (and will, indeed, gain in luxury) if she leaves her husband.

The carpenter's wife goes with her demon lover to one of the many destinations cited by the ballads, but clearly lured away by the freedom he offers her (although only one American version I have found makes "liberty" the explicit goal of the runaway wife and mother). She learns too late the folly of her choice and either sinks with the ship that carries her away or is given a vision of the hell that awaits her. But in *The Lady from the Sea*, Ellida chooses a higher kind of liberty, assuming responsibility for her choice. If Ibsen clothed his Stranger in a Scottish cap in order to link his play to a Scottish ballad it resembles more than either "Agnete og Havmanden" or "Nøkkens Svig," then these alternative endings are consistent with "Agnete," who first runs off with the merman and then chooses the world from which she had come. Ibsen had five more plays yet to write and would continue to work out in them the thematic oppositions between alternative choices embodied in the folk narratives.

Notes

1. Gray 124.
2. Hurt 143.
3. Ibid. 145.
4. Fjelde, *"The Lady From the Sea"* 386.
5. Gravier, "Le drame d'Ibsen" 157.
6. Hurt 144.
7. Holtan 78–79.
8. Raphael 128.
9. Holtan 72–73.
10. Gravier, "Le drame d'Ibsen" 145.
11. Ibid. 157.
12. Fjelde, *"The Lady from the Sea"* 389.
13. Gravier, "Le drame d'Ibsen" 152.
14. Ibid. 155.
15. Egan 249, 251.
16. Rosengarten 468; emphasis mine.
17. Holbek reminds me of a naturalistic explanation for some folklore motifs. Sea animals are frequently stranded on shore, and the painting thus emphasizes the animal nature of the mermaid. Her animal nature, I would add, is itself ambiguous in the context of mermaid lore. It suggests the danger she represents to humans, her own deficiencies and quest for a soul, and an essential rootedness in the real world that impels her to seek an existence in it.
18. Both stories are in Benwell and Waugh 24, 81.
19. Holtan 74.
20. Koht 2: 244.
21. Gravier, "Le drame d'Ibsen" 143.
22. Harding 118.
23. Ibid. 123.
24. It was almost inevitable after Freud wrote on Rebecca West that psychoanalytically inclined critics would turn their attentions to Ellida Wangel. In addition to the general study of Ibsen's women by Lou Salomé, see Faguet, Goitein, Gruenberg.
25. Croker and Lady Gregory include in their collections stories of mermaids clearly patterned on the seal maiden tale.
26. Rosengarten 468.
27. Simpson 101.
28. Brown's essay, "Swan and Mermaid," despite its title, does not include folklore as part of its comparison of *The Lady from the Sea* and *Love's Comedy*. There is the probability that in Svanhild's name is a suggestion of the swan maiden story, which, of course, furthers the comparison to Ellida, a seal maiden. In *The Burial Mound*, the heroine, Blanka, who wishes to escape her life to Northern (i.e., pagan) climes, muses that she could do so, "Had [she] but the

swan's plumage" (1: 158). Holbek has pointed out to me that the feather dress is a commonplace in Northern folktale tradition, and I agree it need not be attached to the swan maiden tale. But I would also argue that the latter was very popular in Scandinavia and that Ibsen appears to have been influenced by it.

29. Weigand 211.

30. Koht 2: 246.

31. Unfortunately, Fraenkl's essay *"Fruen fra havet"* is limited for research purposes by his lack of documentation.

32. Holtan 79.

33. Jorgenson, *Henrik Ibsen* 314.

34. Prior 3: 329–30.

35. Coffin 139. I would like to thank Professor Coffin for his friendly correspondence concerning Ibsen's play and Child 243.

36. Wimberly 136.

37. Hustvedt, *Ballad Books* 312.

CHAPTER 7

Hedda Gabler and the Huldre

In his introduction to *Hedda Gabler*, Michael Meyer contends that the play's chronological place between *The Lady from the Sea* and *The Master Builder* lends it a "curious, almost anachronistic position in the Ibsen cycle." He argues that to date it from internal evidence would be to place it ten years earlier with *A Doll's House*, *Ghosts*, and *An Enemy of the People*. Like these earlier plays, argues Meyer, we feel that *Hedda* is written "simply and directly," from "within an illuminated circle and not, as in the plays of his final period from *The Lady from the Sea* onwards, that he is exploring the darkness outside that circle."[1] This is an ironic view, given that among Hedda's first words in act 1 are "Ugh . . . the maid's been and opened the verandah door. The place is flooded with sunlight" (7: 180). Moreover, in his working notes, Ibsen began to develop the image that would later dominate *John Gabriel Borkman*, that of the dark mines which depict the "subterranean forces and powers" of the human mind. "Women as mine-workers, Nihilism . . . the subterranean revolution in woman's thoughts. Outwardly, the slave-fear of the external world" (7: 488). Both internal and external evidence indicate that *Hedda* belongs just where it is, that the folklore themes and images in the two plays that preceded it are continued in the later play. But whereas the mermaid that characterizes Rebecca and Ellida is well known in world literature, *Hedda Gabler* demands a somewhat more esoteric knowledge, that of the specifically Norwegian version of the fairy temptresses, the *huldre* with her characterizing feature, a hidden cow's tail.

Critics have intuitively turned to folklore and mythology to describe

Hedda's demonic character. She is thus a "Valkyrie in a corset,"[2] or comparable to Faustina or Mesaline, a "human beast domesticated, socialized, and cowed into submission," like Rebecca but without Rebecca's enthusiasm or idealism.[3] McFarlane is more generous, describing Hedda as a "pagan priestess, driven by a vision of Dionysian beauty, whispering of vine-leaves in the hair and the thrill of beautiful death" (7: 14). Put together, these critical comments indicate that like *Rosmersholm* and *The Lady from the Sea*, *Hedda Gabler* shows Ibsen working with the story of a marriage between an ordinary man from the real world and an extraordinary, perhaps demonic woman from another realm of existence.

According to Reidar T. Christiansen, such marriages are the subject of the second most popular folktale group in Norway. In his *Migratory Legends*, the story of the man "Married to a Fairy Woman" (5090) occupies many pages needed to describe variants.[4] Furthermore, in a comparative study of European stories, Norway occupies first place with regard to the popularity of narratives about supernatural or enchanted wives, such tales occurring there "twice as often as those about a supernatural or enchanted husband."[5] The fairy wife in Norwegian folklore usually belongs to a group known as the *huldre*-folk, and two descriptions of them indicate why they would prove symbolically significant for the creator of Hedda Gabler. *Huldre*-folk "generally live at the fringe of an area inhabited by human beings," and the *huldre* woman figures in many traditions "about her marital and other relations to human males."[6] The fairy woman's greatest desire "was to achieve equality with human beings," and the "*huldre* girls tried desperately to marry ordinary men, often flinging themselves at them in the most immodest way." This desire for a mortal husband placed men in a dangerous position. "If a man was unwise enough to jilt a *huldre* she was ruthless in pursuing and punishing him."[7]

It might be going too far to claim that in these descriptions can be found an outline for Ibsen's play, but the *huldre* had filled his imagination from the time of his earliest plays. The *huldre* provides *Olaf Liljekrans* with some of its imagery, and in *Midsummer Night*, as Jacobsen has noted, the *huldre* is a symbol of Norwegian nationalism (also see 2:1). And what I have already cited with regard to *The Lady from the Sea* can be extended to *Hedda Gabler:* in *The Feast at Solhaug*, Margit, whose marriage to Bengt can be compared to Hedda's to Tesman, imagines herself a *huldre* capable of escaping her miserable union. Hedda herself contrasts her dreary marriage to Tesman with the "fairy story" that supposedly describes how it occurred (7: 210). Furthermore, her rival, Thea Elvsted (altered from the earlier, more explicit, Elvstad), is named a lady from fairyland. Nineteenth-century Europe had split the image of the fairy mistress, as I will show, and Norway had followed suit with regard to its *huldre*. Hedda and Thea represent this division. That is, whereas Rebecca and Ellida each embodies within herself both amoral mermaid and ethical human, these qualities have been divided (although, typical of Ibsen, not simply) and assigned to Hedda and Thea respectively.

Thea's married name is, of course, ironic, involving the same inverted perspective that Ibsen had already employed in *Rosmersholm*. Citizen John Rosmer would appear to be the antithesis of Rosmer Havmand, and Mr. Elvsted—according to Thea's description a more unpleasant John Rosmer—offers his wife an existence quite different from what his name would seem to imply. To extend the comparison, Thea can be said in one respect to be a successful Rebecca, having married the man in whose house she worked after his wife died. Critics who compare Hedda to Rebecca have slighted this comparison to Thea, another woman from an ironically conceived of fairyland who must achieve her humanity in a man. Names are, again, very important in Ibsen's plays. Ibsen's use of "Elvsted" is a clue to his audiences and readers that has not received due attention.

In an earlier conception of *Hedda Gabler*, Ibsen named his heroine Hedda Römer, a variant of Rosmer (7: 273). As the daughter of Rosmer, Hedda could be placed directly in the tradition of the demonic *havfru* who lures men to their doom. Therefore it is worth pursuing the possible connection between the names "Hedda" and *huldre*. From Grimm's *Teutonic Mythology*, Ibsen would have found a connection between the Goddess Holda and the Norwegian *huldre*.[8] Hilde Wangel, minor character in *The Lady from the Sea* and major one in *The Master Builder* may perhaps be added to this group. Meyer points out that before *The Master Builder* (which follows *Hedda*) was written, Ibsen had entered into one of those significant relationships with a young girl that marked his late years. This was Hildur Andersen, and Meyer proposes that it was her name that reminded him of Hilde in *The Lady from the Sea* and inspired him to retrieve her from the earlier play to make her a major character in the later one.[9] "Hildur, the Queen of the Elves," it may be noted, is the title of one of Arnason's Icelandic tales, and thus Ibsen might have had another reason to link Hildur to both the *huldre* and Hilde, the Icelandic story one that is both striking and ambiguous in its rendering of the fairy woman as both demon and penitent. To this account it is possible to add that some variation of the name *Hilde* is often taken by the *huldre* after her marriage to a mortal and conversion to Christianity.[10] *Hilde* is also the name of a saga heroine who appears unnamed in the ballad "Kappan Illugen" in Landstad's collection.[11] Finally, Hilde is also a variant form of Hillelil, the name sometimes given to the "Demeter" and sometimes to the "Proserpine" figure in the Rosmer ballads. In any event, the resemblance among a series of names becomes striking to contemplate: Huldre, Holda, Hildur, Hilde, Hillelil, Hedda. Christiansen has noted that *huldre* is the most general term used for the Norwegian supernatural folk.[12] If Hedda were originally thought of as Hedda Römer, then her name, again, reinforces her connection with the supernatural world.[13]

Two aspects of the *huldre* stories prove significant in *Hedda Gabler*. The first has to do with what would appear to be as insignificant a reference in *Hedda* as the sealskin trunk is in *Rosmersholm*. But to catch its significance, it is necessary to recognize how important in the folklore is the mark of the beast that characterizes the *huldre*, who is very beautiful, but possesses a repellent physical characteristic that renders her identifiable: a cow's tail that can often be spied beneath her long skirt. McFarlane has noted, and Jacobsen has already elaborated upon, the ironic tension that arises from this peculiarity in *Midsummer Night*, in which this identifying feature of "'the most national' of all Norwegian fairy creatures" causes great anguish to a character who learns that the *huldre* he falls in love with has a tail: "'I cannot tell you how I suffered,' he cries. 'Aesthetics and nationalism fought a life and death struggle in my breast'" (2: 1).

In his collection of Scandinavian folktales, William A. Craigie includes two versions of "The Huldre's Tail." In one, a young man who glimpses the animal feature tactfully acknowledges what he has seen, and although the fairy disappears, the youth is later rewarded with presents and success in business. In the other version, the man sarcastically jokes about the unfortunate appendage: "that's a rare train you have."[14] She becomes angry and he later dies of a fatal illness.

The cow's tail is a tangible image of the *huldre*'s aberrant nature, and in many stories, it falls off as she enters or leaves the church in which she marries a human. Like the mermaid, then, she wins through marriage to a mortal a soul and the possibility of eternal salvation. But in addition, the Norwegian tales take their place among a universal group of stories in which a supernatural woman's abnormal physical shape (e.g., the serpent tail of Melusine) speaks of some essential evil that threatens her human husband or from which she pathetically longs to be freed. Sometimes she demands a regular interval during which she must not be seen by her husband, for during this time she assumes her beast form. When he betrays her and learns her secret, she usually leaves him. In Craigie's version of "The Huldre's Husband," the wife inadvertently betrays not her animal form but nonetheless her "nature," again, characteristically repelling the man who had never before glimpsed her true essence. The two had

lived very well together and had a child, but suddenly one evening as the child was playing on the hearth, where the woman sat and span, while the husband was doing something else, something of her wild nature came over her, and she, in a savage mind, said to him that the child would be splendid to spit and roast for supper. The man was scared, and the woman, who noticed that she had made a bad mistake, checked herself and entreated him to forget it; but he didn't. The frightful words were always in his ears; he got by them an ugly glance into his wife's true nature, and the peace of the home was destroyed.[15]

The *huldre*'s tail both symbolizes that which reveals her as a being living only on the fringe of society, as well as that which makes it difficult or impossible for her to adapt to it. Her marginal position also emphasizes the peril of the mortal men who encounter her: "mortals and *huldre*-folk may be closely related, but they are essentially different. Every contact with them involves a risk."[16] Conversely, however, the existence of her tail also defines the *huldre*'s vulnerability when she attempts to move securely within human society, for if this tangible proof of her deviant personality is glimpsed, her position is jeopardized and her goals threatened. There is a special joke in the choice of words used by the critic who inadvertently employed an English idiom to speak of Hedda's being "cowed" into submission.

In the context of the *huldre*-tail motif, it is striking to note Hedda's description for Judge Brack of her dreary honeymoon trip and her sense of being trapped in a compartment for two with a companion she already finds unutterably boring:

> *Brack:* Well, then you jump out. And move around a little, my lady.
> *Hedda:* I'll never jump out.
> *Brack:* Are you quite sure?
> *Hedda:* Yes. Because there's always someone there who'll . . .
> *Brack* (laughing): . . . who'll look at your legs, you mean?
> *Hedda:* Exactly. (7: 208)

Ibsen could hardly provide Hedda with a cow's tail. But he seems to have come close. The exposure of her legs beneath the long skirt symbolically compromises her desire to live respectably in society as effectively as the disclosure of the *huldre*'s tail compromises hers. It is important to both that they not be fully known.

The Melusine type to which the *huldre* story can be related contains within it a strong antifeminist tradition consistent with the themes of *Hedda Gabler*. The fairy's nature is an exaggerated version of an inherent feminine evil that is at no time so apparent as when a power struggle for dominance ensues. The serpent tail of Melusine has been interpreted by one critic as a phallic image, and her husband's dismay at discovering his wife's secret as an inability to cope with the masculine strength she thus evidences.[17] Interestingly, one of the legends concerning the origin of the *huldre* is that they are descended from Lilith, the first wife of Adam, who departed from Eden because she could not maintain there her equality with her husband. About Hedda, Ibsen specifically says in his notes that she wants to live fully as a man. In the play these masculine tendencies are symbolized by the guns she plays with, offers to Lövborg for his supposedly glorious suicide, and finally turns on herself.

Significantly, guns and other iron objects play an important role in *huldre* narratives. In his early play, *The Grouse in Justedal*, Ibsen evidences familiarity with this theme, and one of his characters, who fears the influence of the fairy folk as he enters their terrain, notes with relief that he is carrying an iron object with him that is his protection (1: 438). Christiansen designates as motif A5a that the human man catches the *huldre* by "throwing iron over her" (*Migratory Legends*). In the variant contained in the collection of legends by Andreas Faye, a collection Ibsen had in his library,[18] a gun replaces the iron object. Craigie uses this version in "The Huldre's Husband": in Nordland the story is told that a "smart fellow got hold of a huldre in the wood" by laying the barrel of his rifle over her. She was baptized, and became his wife.[19] In other stories, men conversely discourage male *huldre* suitors who court their women, or themselves escape from the supernatural folk, by aiming guns directly at them or shooting over the dwellings in which the *huldre*-folk attempt to attach themselves to mortal mates.[20]

Guns and analogous iron objects are thus symbols of male power and dominance. In an early version of *Hedda Gabler*, Judge Brack is as frightened as Tesman of Hedda's use of guns, but in the final version of act 2, he takes out of her hand the pistols which she has been aimlessly shooting. This scene follows the conclusion of act 1, when Tesman begs his wife not to touch the lethal weapons but makes no move to remove them from her possession. Of course, Brack's superior strength of will foreshadows the end of the play, when one of the pistols becomes the means by which he will blackmail Hedda, threatening to expose the knowledge that it was her gun that Lövborg used in the events that led to his death.

It is a mark of Hedda's cowardice that although she possesses guns, she does not really use them until her suicide, and even this act has been provoked by the threat of male will. In folklore, the *huldre*'s power to manipulate iron is something she can hide or reveal according to the role she wants to assume in her marriage. Both Craigie and Christiansen tell of the *huldre* who weds a human, is baptized, or loses her cow's tail, and submits to ill-treatment by her husband until she is pushed beyond endurance. "Olav was not nice to his wife. He was quarrelsome and ill-tempered and scolded her from morning till night. She kept quiet and never made a fuss about it." Finally, one day she saw him in a foul mood, attempting to fit a horse with a shoe. "Then she took the horseshoe and wadded it up with her bare hands. Then she straightened it out again, fitted it to the hoof, and bent it a little more at the ends."[21] Impressed, or frightened, because it was the forebearance not weakness of his wife that caused her to submit to his misuse of her, Olav reforms and becomes a good husband. In Craigie's version of this story, the wife's power is more straightforwardly expressed:

> So things went on for a time, while the woman suffered and sorrowed. One day she went to the smithy in all friendliness to look at her husband working, but when he began as usual, and they finally came to blows, she, to give him proof of her superiority, caught up an iron rod and twisted it like steel wire round her husband, who had then to give in and promise to keep the peace.[22]

The first reference to guns in *Hedda Gabler* comes at the end of act 1 when Tesman's wife similarly believes herself to be ill-used. That is, she learns that she will not soon have what she hoped marriage would bring her: the ability to entertain lavishly, a male servant, and a saddle horse. She tells Tesman in what has to be interpreted as a threat that she has "one thing at least that [she] can pass the time with" (7: 201). At first he is ecstatic with relief, and asks what that might be, to which she answers, "looking at him with concealed contempt," "My pistols" (7: 202). And like the husbands in the *huldre* stories, he is reduced to abjectness: "No, for the love of God, my darling, Hedda . . . don't touch those dangerous contraptions! For my sake, Hedda!" (7: 202).

So long as she had wished to play woman's traditional role, the *huldre* had refrained from demonstrating her potential power to use iron as she could, and the man who captured his fairy bride with his own iron or gun might never have known her might had he not abused his position. Her concealment of strength is a gesture acknowledging her willingness to play her husband's game with his rules. But in *Hedda Gabler*, the heroine's failure to more than toy with her guns indicates not conciliation but cowardice. That she might have used guns to impose her will on the men in her life is revealed in an exchange between Hedda and Lövborg, during which they reminisce about their past and about a relationship that seems never to have advanced beyond teasing provocation:

> *Lövborg:* Oh, why didn't you play it out! Why didn't you shoot me down, as you threatened!
> *Hedda:* I'm too much afraid of a scandal. (7: 223)

The scene is reminiscent of that point in the folktale when the *huldre* wife has succeeded in shoeing the horse by twisting the iron by hand:

> "You're more than a woman, Torgun," said Olav. "As bad as I've been to you more than once, and you haven't hauled off and given me a thrashing! I think that's strange." "I've got better sense," said Torgun.[23]

In both cases the man wonders at the woman's constraint, and in both she responds by indicating a reluctance to abandon her traditional role. This is also true when Hedda later confesses that another, softer emotion had staid her hand. In the end, Ibsen characteristically provides his traditional themes with a twist of their own. Judge Brack "uses" the gun against Hedda as he had earlier taken it away from her, enacting the beginning of the *huldre*-wife tale by in effect capturing his woman with iron or, in this instance, a gun. But instead of using the iron weapon back against the aggressive male, Hedda turns her gun against herself. Yet, symbolically, it is his—Brack's—hands that can be imagined as holding the weapon, and his finger as pulling the trigger. Those who find something heroic about Hedda's final act have not contrasted it with the *huldre*'s demonstration of power, although insofar as gender relationships constantly define the way guns are presented in the play, Ibsen has remained faithful to his folklore.

So long as the *huldre* type was believed (in world folklore) to be a descendant of Lilith or a daughter of Eve, she was also conceived of as part of a malevolent group of female demons who lured men to their doom, kidnapped and destroyed other people's children out of jealousy or spite (*Hedda:* "Now I'm burning your child, Thea! . . . Your child and Ejlert Lövborg's" [7: 250]), and generally posed a threat to a world which found embodied in her all that was evil. But as the centuries passed, two other sets of beliefs arose to color the folklore and affect the literature that grew out of it. The first was that the unfortunate fairy, deprived of God's grace, sought it, and that she longed for salvation. But another view held that rather than being an evil, succubuslike creature without a soul, the fairy was one of the nature spirits that inhabited the visible world, and that like nature itself, she was not malevolent, but benign. Thus her redemption lay not in the church, but in the human mind itself. Moreover, it was she who held out to the mortal world promise of a different kind of salvation, a release from the imprisoning forces of culture. In the nineteenth century, stories such as Andersen's "The Little Mermaid" depicted the otherworldly females as pathetic creatures more often betrayed by men than dangerous to them.

This new view of the supernatural woman arose during the nationalistic resurgence of folklore that was taking place during the nineteenth century. In Norway, too, a "new" *huldre* had made its appearance, and she was, according to Oscar Falnes, formally introduced to the reading public in a review of Landstad's collection of Norwegian ballads. In his study *Norwegian National Romanticism,* Falnes describes a creature who can hardly be recognized as a relative of the dangerous Lilith-like fairy:

> nature's dreamier aspects—the undulating hills of the south and east with their leafy thickets of birch and their shady forests of deep green pine—were symbolized in the wood-nymph, *Huldren.* She was a dainty sprite, refreshing and alluring, delicate and diaphanous, with golden hair set off by eyes of deep blue. . . . Her temperament was melancholy and those who listened to her song and stringed music were moved to sadness and tears. The most striking thing about her (suggesting the gap between Man and nature) . . . was lack of a soul and the circumstances that she had grown a cowtail. The romanticists became thoroughly infatuated with her and she assumed a central place in their nature symbolism. More vividly than any other figure she personified national traits (in nature symbolism there was postulated an intimate relationship between folklore, natural phenomena and national character).[24]

In short, the *huldre* evolved as a national romantic muse, and her soul would have to be won not merely through union with a mortal man but through the *artist,* a theme that would take on explicitness in Ibsen's later plays.

It is possible to see in Ibsen's portrayal of Thea Elvsted an ironically modified version of the new *huldre:*

> Mrs. Elvsted is a slight woman with soft, attractive features. Her eyes are light blue, large, round, and somewhat protruding, with a scared, questioning expression. Her hair is strikingly fair, almost whitish-

yellow, and unusually rich and wavy. She is a couple of years younger than Hedda. (7: 185)

As the *huldre* is transformed into the romantic muse so does Thea find her salvation in inspiring the men in her life: as Lövborg tells Hedda after learning that his book was burned, "Thea's soul was in that book" (7: 249).

But the nineteenth-century writer was too sophisticated to reduce to simplistic dimensions the double aspect of the fairy woman, and he usually exploited the ambiguity that surrounded her to express his own relationship to the world of art. In his notes, Ibsen gave Thea, his lady from fairyland, attributes as much at odds with the traditional *huldre* as John Rosmer was with Rosmer Havmand: "Thea Elfsted is the type of conventional sentimental, hysterical petty bourgeoise" (7: 483). He was to alter the spelling of her name, and he may have softened his conception of her. But what nonetheless emerges from *Hedda Gabler* is consistent with other nineteenth-century literature, for to transform the *huldre* into the benign nature spirit is in effect to deprive her of her own symbolism and reduce her to philistine proportions. Heine had so treated the goddess of the Venusberg as a hausfrau in the last part of his "Tannhäuser"; Jean Giradoux had poked fun at a modern world that would pave over a brook to rid itself of mermaids, and his Ondine, forced back to her underseas world, promises her earthly husband to live there as a bourgeoise; and Thomas Mann found in Andersen's Little Mermaid the worst danger the artist could face, pressing art into the service of an everyday world (*Doctor Faustus*).[25]

Ibsen depicts the simultaneous difference and similarity between Hedda and Thea. He wrote in his notes that "Mrs. Elfsted, who forces [Lövborg] into respectability, runs away from her husband. Hedda, who eggs him on beyond the limits, flinches from the thought of scandal" (7: 484). The two women emerge as closely related, if antagonistic classmates, just as the two aspects of the *huldre* had once coexisted:

> *Mrs. Elvsted:* . . . since then . . . we've grown such miles apart. We don't meet the same sort of people at all.
> *Hedda:* Well, we must try to bridge the gap again. (7: 190)

Both women prove to be in the end ambiguous characters. Like Hedda, who is both aggressive and cowardly, Thea is also split. She wins where Rebecca West and the Little Mermaid fail and gets her man. But like the seal and swan maidens, she seizes the opportunity to flee both husband and children as soon as the former is absent: "I just packed up a few of my belongings. The essentials. Without letting anyone see. And then I left" (7: 193).

McFarlane points out the "almost indecent haste" with which Thea abandons her family to run after Lövborg (7: 17). Seeking to realize her "soul" through union with the artist, Thea does seem to display an almost contemptible lack of self. But this view must be posed against the argument that Hedda is an emptied-out version of such Ibsen heroines as Rebecca West and Ellida Wangel. Without Thea's interest in the goals pursued by the men in her life, lacking any other kind of altruism, Hedda is an otherworldly being whose longing for a place in the real world is without the ethical component explicit or implicit in the folklore. Those who defend her on feminist grounds and claim Ibsen as an ally have to ignore Ibsen's own notes, which create a nature-culture conflict along gender lines: "A woman's imagination is not actively and independently creative as is a man's. It needs a little bit of reality to help it along" (7: 482).

The folk traditions on which Ibsen drew have their own discouraging message. The mermaid needs marriage to a man to win a soul; conversely, the woman from the real world, an Agnete, risks her soul when she abandons her own people for the freedom of the otherworld. These stories describe the need for sacrifice, and as Ibsen's next play would make absolutely clear, the sacrifice for art's sake would be exacted from the woman. Perhaps only Kierkegaard paid sufficient attention to the price paid by the merman in the same struggle to unite two disparate modes of existence. But to the extent that it is woman who must choose, to that extent is Hedda Gabler victim, robbed of the sympathetic traits of the new *huldre* and deprived as well of the spiritual quest of the old *hundre*—and thus trapped within a much older tradition of the evil and demonic fairy than the nineteenth century ordinarily remembered.[26]

Notes

1. Meyer, *Plays* 2: 3.
2. Lavrin 113.

3. Heller 263, 261.

4. Christiansen, Folktales xliii; *Migratory Legends* 113–23.

5. Boggs 10. Holbek has pointed out that a more thorough corresponding study of the Danish and Swedish traditions would alter these statistics. Fairy wives and husbands are plentiful and ubiquitous throughout Scandinavia. The place that Boggs gives Norway, however, is nonetheless striking for the purpose of studying Ibsen and the *huldre*.

6. Christiansen, *Folktales* 260.

7. Marwick 197.

8. Grimm 3: 946–47, 968.

9. Meyer, Plays 3: 270.

10. Feilberg 92. The name Hildegunne is specifically mentioned; this is striking in the context of Ibsen's use of Gunhild in *John Gabriel Borkman.* Gunhild's association with the supernatural woman will be discussed below when I treat the play.

11. Liestøl and Moe 3: 171.

12. *Folktales* 260.

13. Sandstroem discusses the name symbolism in *Hedda Gabler* (368) but does not deal with folklore associations. She does, however, find significance in Hedda's being called at one point "Lille fru Hedda," which I find noteworthy because of the resemblance, admittedly remote, to the "Hillelil" of the Rosmer ballad, but perhaps less remote because in *The Master Builder,* Ibsen's next play, Hilde is called at one point "Lille Hilde." Holbek has pointed out to us that etymologically *huldre* is derived from the verb meaning "to conceal" *(hylja),* whereas "Hilde" may be traceable to the Scandinavian names Svanhild, Gunhild, Alfhild, where -*hildr* means "battle." He notes the association with the Valkyries, without, however, arguing that Ibsen interested himself in these old etymologies. We find the etymological distinction itself striking, since the folklore concerns the *hidden* power of the *huldre* to do *battle* of a sort, her might displayed in her skill in manipulating iron objects. Several scholars have pointed out the connection between the swan maidens and the Valkyries, and we might point out that in the European tradition, the earliest swan maidens appear to be those Valkyrie-like fairies in the saga of Wayland the Smith (see note 20 below).

14. Craigie 168.

15. Ibid. 168–69.

16. Christiansen, *Folktales* xxxvii.

17. Markale 92, 108. The peculiar characteristics of fairy women from culture to culture is itself a fascinating study. As both Jacobsen and Holbek have told me, the Swedish fairy has a back like a tree trunk, which I interpret as evoking a negative—that is, rough and unyielding—link to nature, whereas the Danish fairy is usually hollow. The Danes would seem to have been less concerned about the gross nature of the fairy than about her ephemeral, illusory, or delusory qualities and would therefore seem to have anticipated a much later symbolic interpretation of her existence in the life of men. My own studies of the fairy woman in the world's folklore have caused me to link the *huldre* most

closely to the French Melusine and oriental Fox Wife traditions. Also see Lederer, *Kiss of the Snow Queen*, 250–51.

18. For the contents of Ibsen's personal library, see *Ibsenårbok 1985–86*.

19. Craigie 168.

20. Christiansen, *Folktales* 102–03, 115–17, 133–34. Jacobsen has pointed out above that although iron objects represent culture (as Holbek has reminded us), iron is itself rooted in nature, and in some societies—African, for example—the blacksmith is thought to possess magic power or to be a shaman. The *huldre's* power with iron objects is thus a complex rendering of her ambiguous relationship to both nature and culture.

21. Christiansen, *Folktales* 113.

22. Craigie 169; see also a comparable story from Denmark, "The Bergman's Daughter of Dagberg-daas," Craigie 110–11.

23. Christiansen, *Folktales* 113.

24. Falnes 221.

25. I have treated these themes in these works: Fass [Leavy], *La Belle Dame sans Merci and the Aesthetics of Romanticism*.

26. The interpretation of the fairy is part of the history of folklore, and frequently misunderstandings arise among those not familiar with the changes that took place. In the summer of 1986, a London production of *Giselle* was accompanied by program notes indicating that the vampirelike qualities of the willis were being restored to eliminate the confusion between these demons and sylphs. But this idea apparently was not communicated to the costume designer, who added the usual small gossamer wings to the willis' costumes.

CHAPTER 8

Halvard Solness: The Reluctant Troll

The term *huldre* means "the hidden people" or "the invisibles."[1] Compared to the use of supernatural imagery in *Rosmersholm* and *The Lady from the Sea*, the employment of similar images in *Hedda Gabler* is submerged, almost lost to sight. But in Ibsen's next play, *The Master Builder*, the supernatural visibly emerges again, as the world of the trolls becomes the symbolic realm in which Solness and Hilde confront each other. The troll is as characteristically Norwegian as the *huldre*, but the similarities and differences between the two have to be understood. As a generalization, it may be said that the troll makes fully visible that which is symbolized by the hidden cow's tail. Fjelde quotes from Muriel C. Bradbrook to argue that the "troll [is] humanity minus the specifically human qualities," that is, the "animal version of man, the alternative to man; he is also what man fears he may become."

He is primeval and remorseless, permanent as rock in the nature of things. From another viewpoint, he may appear unreflective, irresponsible, purposeless—in other words, the animal that man remains if he fails to act upon his self-discovery.[2]

Peter Watts similarly argues that trolls "have a lot in common with the *id* of the Freudians—an embodiment of the primitive urges of mankind."[3] And W. Edson Richmond has argued that in the course of their development, ballads, as compared to folktales, present trolldom as "an inner state. We might even discover, along with Peer Gynt, that we ourselves have been trolls among men without ever recognizing the fact and that ballad trolls have been created in our own image."[4] He claims that "Ballad trolls, in brief, though hardly handsome creatures, may easily be confused with human beings, at least with thralls, pagans, and other non-establishment types; they may (so similar are they to human beings) even be confused with Christian folk."[5]

According to Christiansen, the troll is an "ogre of superhuman size and strength," and in the Type index to the Scandinavian medieval ballad, Rosmer is placed among such giants.[6] But Christiansen adds that the term "troll" can denote any kind of demon. "This is particularly true in international usage where the word *troll* has come to stand for all types of Norwegian supernatural beings."[7] Yet the description of the troll as a particular kind of unsocialized being is apt for *The Master Builder*, where the pull between self-realization and an ethical obligation to others provides the dramatic tension.

Some of Ibsen's conception of this tension may be traced back to Kierkegaard, specifically the philosopher's treatment of "Agnete og Havmanden." The Kierkegaardian influence is immediately apparent in *Brand*, where Agnes is asked to choose between her fiancé Einar and a "grim suitor / And his dark demands" (3: 126). Recognizing the "boundless ocean" (3: 125) that lies between her and him, on one side, and Einar and her mother, on the other, she chooses Brand, and hence "the way of death," hoping to find beyond, "the crimson dawn of day" (3: 126). The name of her son, Alf, is testimony enough to the world she has chosen. That Kierkegaard's reading of "Agnete" makes itself felt in *Rosmersholm* has been argued by Eric Østerud,[8] whose claim suggests how persistent an influence on Ibsen was Kierkegaard's reading of the ballad. Jacobsen has already described Kierkegaard's changes in the story: what he altered was the depiction of Agnete, whose innocence arouses in the merman a conflict that makes it impossible for him to carry out his plans to seduce her. But Kierkegaard wittily suggests that in the legend, Agnete was not without the taint of the seductress. According to Jacobsen's analysis of the ballads, the philosopher's interpretation is consistent with any reading of the ballads that picks up the theme that under certain circumstances, the female is predisposed to welcome the merman's advances. Again, the German "Merman's Bride" ballad makes this point explicit, the demon appearing as a projection of the maiden's rebellion.[9] Some young women, that is, want trolls rather than human men for husbands.

Direct influence or not, Kierkegaard's reading helps define the role of the seductive Hilde in *The Master Builder*. For if the *huldre* or mermaid who wants a bourgeois existence can only achieve her ends by marrying a mortal man, the obverse is that the woman who wishes to flee the bourgeois world has to find a troll. Discovering and encouraging the troll in Solness is what Hilde sets out to do, and in her reproach that he has not come to fetch her for the past ten years as he had promised, she in effect tells him he has failed to play merman to her Agnete. In analyzing *The Master Builder*, it is important to remember that Solness has gone through stages in his life, from an ethical builder of churches to one who has realized selfish aims by demanding sacrifices from others. In the interim he has become a philistine, building ordinary houses for people to live in. In his last stage, inspired by Hilde to be the artist-troll, he must again confront the conflict between the ethical and the aesthetic. Kierkegaard had similarly altered the story of Agnete to provide the merman with a prehistory in which he had abandoned a conscience to become the seducer. Solness's fall from the tower may parody Kierkegaard's leap into faith, for it corresponds to Solness's attempt to fulfill Hilde's demands that he go beyond the ethical obligations of human beings to each other and be *purely* artist.

Those who study *The Master Builder* stress Ibsen's friendship with the young woman, Helene Raff, who, as Russell has noted, "mentioned [to him] the legend of the master builder who had thrown himself off the tower of St. Michael's Church there. Ibsen thought the legend must have come from Scandinavia, since he had heard it there,[10] but Helene replied that every famous cathedral in Germany had such a legend. This is, of course, a widespread tale, perhaps related to foundation sacrifices."[11]

If these legends influenced Ibsen, it may have been in part because of the connection he could make between them and the Rosmer ballads, where a castle that is also a tower plays a role that the playwright seems to have expanded and transferred to *The Master Builder*. For in one of the ballads, the opening stanza provides what for the play is a central image, the second stanza adding an ambiguity on which Ibsen was able to draw for his themes.

> In Denmark once a lady dwelt,
> Hellelil the name she bore;

A castle new that lady built,
It shone all Denmark o'er.

Her daughter dear was stolen away,
She sought for her far and near;
The more she sought the less she found,
To her great distress and care.[12]

In the ballads the name "Hellelil" is sometimes given to the mother and sometimes to the daughter stolen by the merman, Rosmer. In *The Master Builder*, Hilde plays both roles to the extent that she wishes to be stolen by the trolls, and in that she simultaneously wants to inspire the building of a tower.

Again, it is her reproach to Solness that he has not fulfilled his promise to carry her away. When she reminds him of what took place ten years earlier when he promised to return for her, she expresses resentment that despite his bending her back and kissing her over and over—an event he seems not to remember—he treated her as a child instead of the kind of woman trolls kidnap:

> *Hilde:* Don't you remember? You called me Hilde yourself. The day you—misbehaved.
> *Solness:* Did I also do that?
> *Hilde:* But that time you said "Little Hilde." And that I didn't like. (7: 388)

In the Norwegian text, "Little Hilde" is "Lille Hilde," an inverted, "Hellelil," the name of the woman who built the castle that looks over all of Denmark.

Hilde will insist that Solness build her a similar edifice. But even more significant is that while she makes this demand on him, Hilde imagines it as her castle, and as she begins to describe it, it becomes *her* creation:

> *Hilde* (slowly): My castle shall stand on high ground. Very high it must stand. And open to all sides. So I can see into the far, far distance.
> *Solness:* With a high tower, I suppose?

Hilde: A tremendously high tower. And at the very top of the tower there's to be a balcony. And out up there I shall stand. . . . (7: 431)

When questioned about how she could bear the height without dizziness, she responds, "But of course! That's where I shall stand looking at the others—at those who build churches. And homes for father and mother and the children. And you can also come up and have a look" (7: 431).

The passage is susceptible of two readings. On the one hand, Hilde's castle is the kind of castle in the air she later insists Solness build for her, and it is with*out* his firm foundations—the churches that stand for the "duty" to which Aline is bound, or the homes in which families will be happy on the world's terms. But on the other hand, the passage suggests that although Hilde can imagine herself a Hellelil, who built a castle that looked over all of Denmark, she, Hilde, must watch the "others," the master builders without whom she cannot—perhaps because she is a woman—realize her dreams. And it is with this realization that she seeks her troll, must become the daughter, the other Hellelil who is stolen by Rosmer.

Hilde's desire to be stolen is spelled out in her response to Solness's questions about her knowledge of the saga literature; indeed it is spelled out so clearly that it is possible to wonder if Ibsen feared that otherwise the theme he was developing in his play would remain obscure:

Solness: The sagas are all about the vikings who sailed to foreign lands and plundered and burned and killed . . .
Hilde: And carried off women . . .
Solness: And held them captive . . .
Hilde: Took them home with them in their ships . . .
Solness: And behaved towards them like . . . like the worst of trolls.
Hilde (staring straight ahead with half-veiled eyes): I think that must be exciting.
Solness (with a short, gruff laugh): Taking women, you mean?
Hilde: Being taken. (7: 413–14)

In her desire to be taken, and in what we will see is Solness's reluctant acquiescence to playing troll (he has the potential, but cannot without Hilde's goading fit the part), the roles of Hellelil the kidnapped and Rosmer the kidnapper are in effect reversed.[13]

Such reversals also involve significant inversions of other folklore patterns. In one popular story type, a parent or parents unwittingly promise their young child to a troll, who will return at some future date when the child is grown to claim what has been promised. During this time the parents try to forget the promise, hoping that the inevitable will not occur, or in some way contriving to stave off the catastrophe. Sometimes the child is handed over to the demonic being; sometimes, as in the Rumpelstiltskin story, the demon is outwitted. (Jacobsen has described this motif in some of the ballads. And, of course, it is central to the legends of Saint Olav.) But in *The Master Builder* there occurs what the parents of these narratives pray for: the troll does not appear as threatened. Hilde views this good luck as a betrayal; therefore, she has been forced to seek out her captor.

> *Solness:* . . . Why did you leave [your father], then.
> *Hilde* (half serious, half in jest): Aren't you forgetting again that the ten years are up?
> *Solness:* Oh, nonsense! Was there something wrong at home? eh?
> *Hilde* (utterly serious): Something inside me forced me, drove me, here. Drew me, tempted me, too.

Solness responds to this eagerly. "There you are, Hilde! There's a troll in you, too. Just as in me. And it's the troll in us, you see, that calls on the powers outside" (7: 413).

This had been Kierkegaard's interpretation of the role Agnete played in her own seduction. In *The Master Builder*, ironically, the demonic in Hilde is raised almost in proportion to the extent that Solness shrinks from being the troll. He has his own memories of the fateful day ten years earlier, when he had climbed the tower with the wreath, endangered because of a "little devil" in white who below "was shouting and yelling" so much. He recalls that at the sight of the waving and flapping white flag, he "almost grew dizzy," and Hilde responds: "That little devil—was *me*" (7: 381).

In his introduction to *The Master Builder*, Michael Meyer recounts another "tower" anecdote which may have fed Ibsen's conception of Hilde as a devil:

> Ever since childhood, Ibsen had been fascinated by towers. . . . Ibsen had mentioned that the house in which he was born "stood exactly opposite the front of the church, with its high flight of steps and its conspicuous tower" from which the watchman used to proclaim the hour at night. A poodle also lived in the tower; "it had fiery red eyes, but was rarely visible. Indeed, so far as I know, he was never seen but once." One New Year's morning, just as the watchman shouted "One" through the opening in the front of the tower, the poodle appeared behind him and looked at him with his fiery eyes, whereupon the watchman fell down into the market place and was killed.[14]

This description of the poodle with its "fiery red eyes" and its fatal effect on the watchman in the tower evokes—as is often the case in Ibsen's plays—more than one motif from folklore narratives and popular beliefs. In legends concerning Saint Olav the Masterbuilder, it is Saint Olav who causes the troll to fall from the tower, and in a parallel sense, the dog plays its role as guardian spirit of the church (according to a common belief throughout Scandinavia), and the watchman assumes the role of the intruder in, again, a reversal that is common in Ibsen's plays.[15] The anecdote does indeed anticipate the character of Solness, who is both masterbuilder and troll.

But given the use of werewolf and animal bride and groom motifs in Ibsen's late plays, the poodle with its "fiery red eyes" can also invoke the popular idea of the witch's familiar, the animal who is actually a devil in disguise and accompanies the witch as she works her spells. Witches abound in the later works. Not only is the Rat Wife a witch-like creature, but she is accompanied by a dog; Fanny Wilton in *John Gabriel Borkman* is described as a witch. Heller, who believes there is something of a "vampire nature in [Hilde], the promise of a fiendish wrecker of strong men," has certainly described nothing if not a witch. He finds in the Hilde of *The Lady from the Sea* the promise of a "full-fledged Hedda Gabler,"[16] and to accept his argument is once again to confront in Ibsen's plays a *huldre* type emptied of any yearning for a soul, that is, a witch. But again, as witch, devil, troll, Hilde is none-

231

theless dependent upon Solness's playing his demonic part for her to achieve her ends. She cannot have her wonderland unless Solness is willing to kidnap her.

As Jacobsen has shown, in some versions of the magic ballads, the kidnapped maiden has been lured by her demon lover's promise of material riches, although, of course, these are symbolic of more complex motives for her willingness to follow him. "He gave me silver, he gave me gold, / And sprigs of coral my hair to hold," says Agnete in one of these ballads. In short, the wonderland motif common to the "Heer Halewijn" ballads can also be found in other "troll" narratives.

As was seen in the discussion of *Rosmersholm,* the wonderland motif involves the promise by a diabolical otherworldly suitor that the stolen maiden will experience with him an existence far beyond anything her own world could offer. It will be remembered that according to Nygard's study the wonderland motif is not only the earliest form of enticement in the ballads, but is particularly prevalent in Norway. In *The Master Builder,* not only does Hilde remind Solness that he failed to keep his promise to come for her in ten years, but she must also remind him of the wonderland he had offered her:

> *Hilde:* And then you said that when I grew up I should be *your* princess.
> *Solness* (laughs a little): Well, well . . . Did I say that, too?
> *Hilde:* Yes, you did. And when I asked how long I had to wait, you said you'd come back in ten years—like a troll—and carry me off. To Spain or somewhere. And there you promised you'd buy me a kingdom. (7: 383)

She is insistent on this point.

> *Solness* (looks searchingly at her): Did you honestly think in all seriousness that I'd come back?
> *Hilde* (with a half-suppressed roguish smile): Of course! I expected *that* much of you.
> *Solness:* That I'd come to your home and carry you off with me?
> *Hilde:* Just like a troll—yes!

232

> *Solness:* And make you a princess?
> *Hilde:* That's what you promised.
> *Solness:* And give you a kingdom too?
> *Hilde* (looks up at the ceiling): Why not? It didn't actually have to be an ordinary, real kingdom. (7: 386)

Solness's realistic interpretation of her "wonderland" is one that Hilde rejects, although she herself had already talked of his *buying* her a kingdom (an ironic economic metaphor but consistent with the "Heer Halewijn" ballads), for it resembles the world in which he had already from her point of view built too many houses.

> *Solness:* Yes, indeed. Princess Hilde of . . . of . . . What was to be the name of that kingdom?
> *Hilde:* Pah! I don't want to hear any more about *that* stupid kingdom. I'm going to want a very different sort. (7: 388)

But to the end, Solness ignores the implications of her magic realm:

> *Solness:* After today we two will build together, Hilde.
> *Hilde* (with a doubting smile): A *proper* castle in the air?
> *Solness:* Yes, with a real foundation. (7: 432)

The "Heer Halewijn" ballads involve stories of a seducer destroyed by his potential victim, and effectively describe the relationship between Solness and Hilde. This is true even if she has had to rouse in him the sleeping troll, for again, this involves Ibsen's reversal of the folk themes. First Hilde imagines Solness in the role played by the elf knight in the ballads, and then, when he does her bidding, he plunges from her symbolic tower to his real death.

Very important to Ibsen's themes and to the reversals that he has worked on the ballad material is another point that Nygard makes concerning the ballad's development in Denmark where the elf knight was substituted for by an ordinary human being: "the incident was no longer conceived of by singers as a maid's contention with a being of the otherworld, but instead was thought of as a human drama, a story of two human beings."[17] It will be remembered from the discussion of *Ros-*

233

mersholm that according to Nygard the villain's acts are explained as coming from perverse sexual drives and the rather ordinary quest for riches.

The development of the ballad in Denmark, then, thematically corresponds to some important elements in *The Master Builder*. Solness's desire for gold is what, of course, has driven him on to success as a master builder who has turned from building churches to constructing homes for families who will pay handsomely for his work, and has caused him to exploit those around him to insure that those fees continue to come in. His wife believes he is constantly unfaithful to her, but whether he displayed some kind of perverse sexual drive—to retain Nygard's description of the Danish elf knight—when he bent back and kissed a child over and over again as if she were a woman is not quite so clear, since its truth is questionable. Hilde's imagination may be constructing that which never in reality occurred. In any event, like the villain in the "Heer Halewijn" ballads, Solness is destroyed by one of his "victims." But not because she outwits him. Rather, it is because she has pushed him back to the demonic nature that was latent in him but might have been controlled had she not appeared in his life. By forcing him to confront the struggle between the ethical and the natural, Agnete has destroyed the merman.

Whether or not Solness is an autobiographical portrait of Ibsen, it seems clear that in *The Master Builder* as well as in *Hedda Gabler*, Ibsen was dealing with the plight of the romantic artist. It is a critical commonplace to compare Hedda and Hilde. But once again, the relationship of the new *huldre* to nineteenth-century art has to be considered, as well as the Hedda-Thea split. Thwarted as Thea is in playing romantic muse to Lövborg and uncertain as her final role in Tessman's life is, Thea's position does not force the critical question that must be answered. Again, Kierkegaard's treatment of "Agnete og Havmanden" is significant. One study of the philosopher surveys the options that the merman has once he retreats from his original intentions to seduce Agnete. He can confess, receive what would surely be her forgiveness (since she loved him), and build with her a relationship based on honest communication.[18] And here the philosophical explanation of a philosophical problem concludes. But then what? Are Agnete and the merman to settle down in one of the homes that Solness builds for those who will live happily ever after? If so, so much the worse for them: "*Solness:* Because now I see that people have no use for these homes of theirs. It doesn't help them to be happy" (7: 439).

It seems clear that Kierkegaard had rejected the life such homes represent, for his own broken engagement is a biographical element stressed in studies of his philosophy. Similarly, the nineteenth-century artist abhorred such a resolution to his dilemma, for he knew that "happily ever after" probably meant the death of art. Solness had understood too well the kind of sacrifice demanded of the artist, and although he is able to exact it of his wife, he cannot do so without guilt and, more important, he cannot go the whole way himself in negating the ordinary life lived by those people for whom he builds houses. But when he describes his predicament, he glorifies what he has bought with his supposed sacrifice. The tragedy of the artist has become the pathos of the mere contractor:

> *Solness:* No. To be able to build homes for other people, I have had to renounce . . . for ever renounce . . . any hope of having a home of my own. I mean a home with children. Or even with a father and mother. . . . That was the price of "happiness" people are always talking about. (7: 405)

Neither true artist nor contented philistine, Solness's only recourse seems to be building for Hilde her precious castle in the air, one remote from bourgeois reality. And she, with her hitched-up skirts, rucksack, and refusal to do secretarial work, is an Agnete who needs to realize herself in a place where "duty" is a word as abhorred as she abhors it. She hates it that Aline will shelter her and buy her clothes out of moral obligation rather than spontaneous feelings. And when she, Hilde, responds ethically to Aline's grief over the losses that she has had to endure to be Mrs. Solness, she reacts by picking that time to demand more vehemently than ever that Solness deliver her wonderland:

> *Hilde:* . . . Time's up! Ten years. And I'm not waiting any longer. So—bring out the castle, master builder!
> *Solness:* It's no easy matter owing *you* anything, Hilde.
> *Hilde:* You should have thought of that before. Now it's too late. So! (Beating on the table). Out with the castle! It's *my* castle! I want it at once. (7: 430)

As Agnete who seeks the troll, Hilde rejects the ethical soul at the very moment it has been most aroused in her. She must, however, live as vicariously through Solness as Thea must through Lövborg and Tessman. Hilde's utter selfishness, like Hedda's, suggests the danger that explodes as women are forced to create through men, living life indirectly. But as Hilde demands from Solness the purely aesthetic life, her uncompromising ruthlessness also points up the dilemma faced by the artist in the nineteenth century. As a demonic "Agnete" in search of her "Rosmer," Hilde allows Ibsen to portray one side of a coin the other side of which Thomas Mann would treat years later. If the Little Mermaid symbolized Adrian Leverkühn's dangerous desire to create an art that served the world, Solness, in trying to act out Hilde's troll, stands for the equally destructive temptation of the artist to turn his back on that same world and to create castles in the air, a fall from which, again, portends a real, not a fancied, death.

Notes

1. Christiansen, *Folktales* 260.
2. Fjelde, Introd. xvii.
3. Watts 14.
4. Richmond 311.
5. Ibid. 307.
6. Jonsson et al. 261.
7. Christiansen, *Folktales* 262. Holbek reminds me that the word *troll* is cognate to *trylle*, to perform magic, specifically to transform through magic power, to enchant (*forttrylle*). This only reinforces my sense of Ibsen's irony in this play, where the question is—as Jacobsen puts it with regard to *Rosmersholm*—who is enchanting whom?
8. "Den rosmerske adelighet."
9. Child's notes to "Hind Etin" 365–66.
10. The story of Saint Olav the Masterbuilder is widespread in Norway. See Jacobsen's discussion and Sehmsdorf.
11. Russell 18.
12. Borrow 7: 133.
13. Sehmsdorf has analyzed the relationship between the troll motif and the widespread folklore concerning Saint Olav the Masterbuilder, as well as Ibsen's use of both in *The Master Builder*. But on two points he and I differ. The first is his belief that, beginning with his social plays, Ibsen stopped drawing heavily

on legends, sagas, myths, and ballads: "elements from the older literature and popular lore become relatively rare" (269). Second, in analyzing the troll symbolism in the play, he neglects Ibsen's characteristic twisting of folklore motifs to achieve an ironic counterpoint. Solness is sometimes a troll and sometimes one who resists that role mightily. That is what thwarts Hilde.

14. Meyer, *Plays* 3: 274.

15. I am particularly appreciative of Holbek's drawing to my attention the popular beliefs concerning the animal guardian of churches, since I had originally perceived only a demonology theme in the anecdote.

16. Heller 276.

17. Nygard 115.

18. Taylor 174.

CHAPTER 9

Little Eyolf as Changeling

Little Eyolf was written before *John Gabriel Borkman* and *When We Dead Awaken*. Some of its folklore themes harken back to the earlier plays: for example, the "mystery" Ellida insists characterizes the eyes of her dead child, the same eyes as her demon lover, becomes a recurrent theme in *Little Eyolf*. But other narrative elements point to the two plays, Ibsen's last, to follow. The werewolf motif, which I will argue plays a significant role in *John Gabriel Borkman*, is introduced when Allmers says of the Rat Wife that her "real name is said to be Wolf, I believe, Miss Wolf," and Eyolf responds that therefore there *"might* be some truth after all in the story that she turns into a werewolf by night" (8: 45). Similarly, the figure of Rita as "white lady," the folklore character who is in some manner betrayed by a man and therefore develops murderous feelings about their child, is more fully developed when Irene, a more obvious "white lady," develops fantasies about infanticide. Moreover, there is slight but striking evidence that the legend of the mines at Falun that, it has been argued,[1] influenced *John Gabriel Borkman* was already a part of Ibsen's conscious working out of his themes in *Little Eyolf*. In E. T. A. Hoffmann's short story "Die Bergwerke von Falun," a passage in which it is possible to find an analogy between the sea and the mines as representing a mysterious otherworld has a parallel in *Little Eyolf*. In Hoffmann's story, his hero looks down into the waves of a body of water and sees instead a "crystal floor."

Impelled by some mysterious force, he stepped forward, but in that instant everything about him began to move, and like curling waves, beautiful flowers and plants of shining metal rose about his feet. They shot forth their leaves and blossoms from the depths, and in a graceful way became intertwined. (148)[2]

The mines claim Hoffmann's Elis as the sea claims Little Eyolf and Asta consoles Allmers by offering him some flowers.

> Asta: . . . You see these water-lilies?
> *Allmers* (nods slowly): They are the kind that grow up to the surface . . . from deep down below.
> *Asta:* I gathered them from the lake. Where it flows out into the fjord. (Holds them out.) Would you like them, Alfred? . . . They are like a final greeting to you . . . from little Eyolf. (8: 88)

In *Little Eyolf* as in so many of Ibsen's plays, there is a contrast between the ordinary world in which Rita's claims for exclusivity in her relationship with Allmers signals the stifling narrowness from which he had tried to escape, and some otherworld, natural realms conceived of as supernatural because they hold out the possibility of such escape. When Allmers and Rita contemplate the sea into which Eyolf seems to have been lured by demonic forces, Allmers affirms their own place in their own world: "No. This earthly life is where we—the living—belong" (8: 82). He had already experienced his "wonderland" in the mountains in which he sojourned alone—and can appreciate the attraction held out by the Rat Wife: "I can understand something of that compelling power of attraction [of the sea] she talked about. The solitude up among the mountain peaks and on the great desolate open spaces has something of the same power" (8: 50).

If Ibsen had been influenced by Hoffmann's story, he might also have been familiar with one of its sources, Ludwig Tieck's "Der Runenberg," in which a young man is torn, as is Allmers, by the conflicting pull of the mountains, on one side, and the plains in which family relationships define reality on the other. German romanticism supplied at least two traditions on which Ibsen could and seems to have drawn: the contrast between the mountains and the flatlands, the former a kind of "wonderland," the latter a place of domestic relations; and the mountains, the sea, and the depths of the earth (i.e., mines) as symbolic otherworlds.[3]

Allmers' decision to commit himself to the flatlands, that is to devote himself to his role as father of Little Eyolf, involves Ibsen's exploiting in *Little Eyolf* a theme that exists in others of his plays but moves to the foreground in this one. It is arguable that Allmers' decision itself reverses an event that can be traced back as far as *Brand* when Ibsen, strongly influenced by Kierkegaard, implies an analogy between the death of Brand's and Agnes's infant and the sacrifice of Isaac. The child as sacrificial victim is found in many of Ibsen's important plays, notably *Ghosts, The Wild Duck,* and *The Master Builder.* The kinds of substitutions or sacrifices that go on in these plays invoke another very popular folklore motif that has already been introduced with regard to *Rosmersholm,* that of the changeling. As Christiansen's *Migratory Legends* makes obvious by the number of pages devoted to the changeling story in Norwegian lore, it virtually rivals the *huldre* tales in popularity. To understand Little Eyolf as a changeling is to find an important clue to the narrative and thematic pattern of the play.

The definition of a changeling is "the child of a non-human race left in place of a human child which is stolen away from its mother by members of that race."[4] Many "changelings are so called merely because of some bodily deformity or because of some abnormal mental or pathological characteristics capable of an ordinary rational explanation . . . [but] other changelings who exhibit a change of personality, such as is recognized by psychologists, are in many cases best explained on the Demon Possession Theory."[5] That is, changelings are paradigms for children maimed or emotionally disturbed, or for offspring who have in one way or another caused their parents significant distress. At one point, Aase tells Peer Gynt that she wished he had "gone up the chimney like a changeling" (3: 266), referring to a folklore belief that allowing the child to be blown up the chimney is a way of getting rid of it.[6] And in *Ghosts,* the vision of Oswald Alving (translated, "descended of elves")[7] in the throes of paresis, "turned into a helpless child . . . [having] to be fed" (5: 418), suggests Christiansen's motif of the changeling as a child resembling an old man, evidencing a voracious appetite.[8]

It appears that Ibsen had already had the changeling motif in mind when he wrote *The Master Builder.* Hilde, a difficult child in *The Lady from the Sea,* comes to Solness's home and asks for shelter. As Mrs. Solness sets out to prepare a guest room, Solness suggests their nurseries instead, effectively substituting this preternatural young person for his own dead children:

> *Hilde* (stops and looks at him): Do you have more than one nursery, then?
> *Solness:* There are three nurseries in this house.
> *Hilde:* That's a lot. You must have many children.
> *Solness:* No. We have no children. But now *you* can be the child while you're here.
> *Hilde:* For tonight, yes. I won't cry. I'm going to try and sleep like a log. (7: 378–79)

Although some changelings never cease crying, the opposite is true of others,[9] and Hilde's promise not to cry may recall the children of Rosmersholm who neither laugh nor cry. Sometimes changelings are abused precisely to the end of forcing them to weep.[10] And when Hilde says she will sleep like a log, the English idiom into which Ibsen has been translated ironically recalls the changeling motif, for in some folklore, a wooden effigy is left in place of the human stolen by the otherworld. The more accurate "stone" is, however, equally significant in the folklore Ibsen knew, for one way in which the troll is defeated by human forces is to become petrified (this happens in the Rosmer ballads). Hilde, who seeks a troll as a compatible partner, is troll-like in that she chooses to remain outside the moral boundaries of culture, and her invasion of the Solness household is like that of the changeling from the otherworld. Hilde may even owe some of her character to a popular literary figure from German romanticism, the model for Andersen's Little Mermaid, Undine. She is a changeling left by her merman father on earth so that she may win a human husband and hence a soul. The creator of this enormously popular and influential character,[11] Fouqué, begins his novella by describing the trial this troublesome changeling is to her worldly parents until, indeed, marriage results in her reformation—a transformation that has drawn the same kind of regret from readers as Ellida's reconciliation with her husband and his world.[12]

The changeling belief suggests, on a literal level, a rationalization for damaged children: the "changeling was ill-favoured or deformed . . . and was, to all appearance, imbecile."[13] As Christiansen has noted, the idea that beings from other worlds steal human babies and substitute their own "explains the birth of abnormal or deformed infants, or the disappearance or premature deaths of some young person."[14] But a reading of changeling tales, with their grisly descriptions of how to test for the otherworldly substitution, or of how to retrieve the stolen human child from the fairies, is to find a terrible record of child abuse. "The stories of how the right child might be recovered take numerous forms; and some of these stories suggest how weak and sickly children become the objects of systematic cruelty at the hands of even their own parents."[15] Thus, on a symbolic level, the changeling becomes the focus of family pathology, and not only the child but the parents are involved in the narratives of strained or abnormal husband-wife, parent-child relationships.

Little Eyolf has been analyzed in the context of the "family romance," a term extended beyond its original meaning by some contemporary psychologists to describe a disturbed situation in which a child becomes the focus of the family's abnormal relationships.[16] The original Freudian sense of "family romance" and its contemporary modified usage by advocates of family therapy suggest some provocative ideas both about the changeling legends and Ibsen's *Little Eyolf*. As Bruno Bettelheim describes the family romance in *The Uses of Enchantment*, it centers "on the idea that one's parents are not really one's parents, but that one is the child of some exalted personage, and that, due to unfortunate circumstances, one has been reduced to living with these people, who *claim* to be one's parents."[17] The family romance then reverses what appears to be a central theme of changeling stories, the fantasy of parents that their malformed or emotionally troubled child is not really theirs, that their own, true child had been taken from them and that an impostor has taken its place. That a child who grew up with such parents might develop corresponding fantasies would not be surprising—hence the need to treat the family and not just the individual, and to extend the concept of child abuse to the emotional rather than the exclusively physical mistreatment of the child. In any event the folklore theme involving the reclaiming of the changeling by the otherworld is one that could express the fantasies of both child and parents.

But those who practice family therapy today commonly report that families are even more resistant to change than individuals, particularly when the child's problems deflect attention from the parents' relationship. That this is part of what is going on in *Little Eyolf* is clear. But, strikingly, a similar situation seems to exist in a variant of the changeling story that Ibsen could have found in Landstad; indeed, it so closely parallels *Little Eyolf* that Jacobsen and I are prepared to argue for it as a major source for the playwright. In the story, a changeling grows up sickly and *crippled* in a family that does not want him. He, in turn, cares only for one member of it, his sister Anne (e.g., Asta). When, at one point, he wanders away from his family, he meets an old woman (e.g., the Rat Wife) who with lines of verse lures him to follow her, after which his family never sees him again. But the story is less about the changeling than about his earthly father, a minister who does not believe in the supernatural otherworld and thus ignores his wife's entreaties that they baptize their infant immediately before he is changed, that is substituted for by a changeling. That this happens seems the father's punishment for denying the existence of the otherworld.[18]

The father who does not believe in the supernatural otherworld may parallel the parent who cannot accept the reality of troubled but intangible emotional states, and the condition of the child reflects his obduracy. His ignoring of his wife's entreaties that their child be baptized quickly reflects the pair's conflicts as well as their disagreements over the welfare of their offspring, a common enough phenomenon. It would be difficult to say how much intuitive folk understanding of family pathology is reflected in changeling stories although two points can be made about the folklore motifs. First, as already indicated, changeling stories often describe behavior that suggests emotional rather than physical symptoms of the child's abnormality. Second, as has been commented on by those who study folk and fairy tales, they usually present a nuclear family structure whose symbolism has been explored by the commentator.[19] In any event, changelings remain a striking paradigm for contemporary family problems and may even help explain (as I argue in a work still in progress) the recent popularity in novels and films of the demon child.

As in psychology, so in folklore does the mother play a particularly crucial role in changeling stories, and thus woman's role becomes a significant element in understanding the tales: "stories of changelings, wherever found, show that the act of [theft] took place when the human child had been left unguarded for a moment, or through the helplessness of the mother, or by some trick on the part of fairy thieves, or because

243

the usual precautions against them [e.g., baptism] had not been taken."[20] In some stories the mistreatment of the changeling by the human parent often induces the otherworld being to reclaim the child.[21] For *Little Eyolf* this suggests the integral relationship between the Rat Wife and Eyolf, and may even anticipate the theme of the good and bad mothers in *John Gabriel Borkman*. The Rat Woman appears to have enticed Eyolf to enter the otherworld to which he is conceived of as belonging. For "in general, the changeling may be the child of fairies . . . of dwarfs, elves, or under-earth folk . . . of various nature-spirits— water sprites [etc.]" or "of a witch or some other demoniac creature."[22]

It is interesting to compare *Little Eyolf* to the story of "The Sickly Changeling," one of the legends in Christiansen's collection *Folktales of Norway*. In the story, parents of a changeling are advised by a pastor to christen the child. They proceed to set out by boat for the place where this religious ceremony will take place:

Halfway between Tjotta and Skotsvar, another boat with three sets of oars came rowing up . . . [and] the head man on the other boat wanted to know where they were going. Up to now they had never heard this child [the changeling] speak, but now it suddenly answered before any of the others could say anything: "We're on our way to Hellepung to drop fiddle dung!" which in their language meant "We're on our way to Tjötta to be christened!" And when he had said that he dived right into the sea, and at the same moment the strange boat was gone.[23]

It has already been argued that the changeling story in Landstad resembles Ibsen's play beyond what coincidence would account for, and no special connection is being made here. Yet this legend and others like it might have appealed to the playwright who described himself as an "ugly and undersized boy who felt cut off by his temperament from the other village children,"[24] and might therefore be drawn to the changeling tales. Nor is the gentle if tortured Eyolf being compared to the crude changeling whose gross language is a sign of what he is. But similarities between the folktale and Ibsen's play emphasize the role of the changeling in *Little Eyolf*. The Rat Wife, who describes the compulsion that lures the rats to an underwater realm, and seems to have similarly lured Eyolf there—Allmers insists that she "drew him down into the deep. That's certain" (8: 68)—seems to have an affinity to the strange passengers in the boat come to fetch the unchristened child from the world. And Eyolf's initial fascination with the Rat Wife suggests the same basic affinity that links the changeling in the folktale to the beings who come to fetch it back to the sea, to that same realm in which the rats "sleep a long sleep, a sweet sleep—they who are hated and persecuted of men" (8: 49).[25]

The child's christening becomes an irrevocable link to such persecution, while, conversely, the mark of the fairy folk causes the human beings marked by them to be rejected by their own world. There are seal folk stories in which baptism makes it impossible for the otherworldly beings to return to the sea. And in an Icelandic folktale, an adult woman taken by the fairies, and who could have been reclaimed by her father, is left by him with the supernatural folk because he is repelled by a blue mark on her forehead that speaks to her intimate contact with the otherworld.[26] Folklore, that is, provides a double perspective: under some conditions, a human must be rescued from the fairies; under others, the changeling, often substituted for a person taken to the otherworld, must be taken back from a culture to which he cannot or does not wish to adapt. That the two patterns may prove complementary is suggested by Ibsen's play itself, which treats the rescue motif.

Allmers's decision to devote himself to Eyolf suggests such a rescue, as does his demanding to know how Rita interprets the description of Eyolf, drowned, on his back in deep water, with "his eyes wide open" (8: 77):

> Allmers: . . . Were they evil, those eyes, Rita?
> Rita (turns pale) Evil?
> Allmers (goes close up to her): Were they evil eyes staring up from the depths?
> Rita (shrinks back): Alfred!
> Allmers (follows her): Answer me! Were the child's eyes evil? (8: 77)

In this scene, Ibsen appears to have reversed the situation in *The Lady from the Sea*, in which Ellida speaks of the mysterious eyes of her dead child, which linked him both to the sea (to which Eyolf returns), and the seaman,

How could you not see it? [she asks Wangel]. The child's eyes changed colour with the sea. When the fjord was calm and sunny, his eyes were the same. The same when it was stormy. Oh, I saw it well enough, even though you didn't. (7: 68)

But whereas Wangel attempts to allay his wife's fears, Allmers is angry enough at Rita to provoke her guilt: "There must always be a wall between us from now on. . . . Who knows whether a child's eyes, opened wide, will not watch us night and day" (8: 83).

It would be interesting to know if Ibsen was familiar with Matthew Arnold's "The Forsaken Merman," whose translation into Danish would have been available to him before he wrote *The Lady from the Sea* and *Little Eyolf*—as we noted in our Preface. For while demonic eyes are by no means a novelty in folklore and literature (Jacobsen has already noted the demonic eyes that characterize the deceitful merman in one version of *DgF* 39), and while the "evil eye" constitutes a widespread folk belief,[27] the English poet had introduced into the Agnete ballad an element that—while doubtlessly more reflective of nineteenth-century concerns than folklore—suggests another way of looking at Ibsen's use of dead children's strange eyes. For the "strange cold eyes" of Margaret's mermaiden daughter is one of the strongest clues the poet offers concerning the inadequacy of the otherworld for mortals who hope to find in it an alternative to a world of grey churches and white-walled towns. And it is precisely at the moment when Margaret has completed the productive, joy-producing tasks of her day and has turned yearningly to the sea and memories of the mermaiden that this image of the strange eyes is introduced. Ellida Wangel also equates her dead son's eyes with the sea—they change as the sea changes—and for this reason she believes he was the son of the stranger, a demon, and not of Wangel. Similarly, Eyolf's eyes staring up from the depths of the sea become the focus of the tensions between Allmers and Rita, as well as the sign of her final redemption, her gaining the ethical "soul" that Agnete and Margaret seek, a soul that symbolizes the health of Ellida when she rejects her sea demon. Rita will devote herself to the children of the town in order to win the approval "of those big staring eyes" of her dead son (8: 105), which she no longer thinks of in terms of "children's evil eyes" (8: 64) that have separated her from Allmers. What is being argued here is that for Ibsen (as for Arnold) a child's strange or demonic eyes may be a projection of the parents—perhaps of an ethical commitment that the child in life had not enjoyed or that excludes the world from which the child is imagined to come.

To return to "The Sickly Changeling" and its parallels to Ibsen's play, it is striking to note that in both the legend and the dramatic work, the abnormal child is claimed by the sea at that very point where he is about to be redeemed on the world's terms. In "The Sickly Changeling," the substitute is about to be christened and gain a soul. In *Little Eyolf*, Allmers laments that it is precisely at the point when he was about to devote himself to helping his son that the Rat Wife had come for him:

> There is Eyolf on the very threshold of a new and fuller sense of life. There are endless possibilities open to him. Rich possibilities, maybe. Was about to fill my existence with pride and joy. Then all it needs is for some crazy old woman to come along . . . and produce a dog in a sack. (8: 68)

Whatever the direct sources of Ibsen's conception of the changeling, the folklore pattern proves significant in his play. It is possible to identify four stages in the folk narratives. First, because of some mishap or parental neglect, the substitution is made and the strange, otherworldly child is substituted for the normal, healthy infant. Second, the parents of the changeling are now beleaguered by the problems attendant on having the strange being in the family. Whether the child is treated very well or, to the contrary, is abused, the otherworld will, third, be motivated to reclaim its own. And sometimes, fourth, the human child is returned to the family.

With regard to the first of these motifs, that the transformation from a normal to a maimed child is caused by parental neglect, involves one of the play's major themes, the precipitating cause of the catastrophe involving the relationship between the parents. It is because of Rita's sexual attractiveness for Allmers and because of her strong sexual appetite that their baby is left alone, vulnerable to harm:

> *Allmers:* . . . It was you who left that little baby on the table unattended.
> *Rita:* He was lying so comfortable on the cushions. Sleep-

> ing so soundly. And you had promised to keep an eye on
> him.
> *Allmers:* Yes, I had. (Lowers his voice.) Then you came—
> and tempted me to come to you.
> *Rita* (looks at him defiantly): Why don't you say you for-
> got all about the child, and everything else.
> *Allmers* (with suppressed fury): Yes, that's right. (Lowers
> his voice.) I forgot the child . . . in your arms.
> *Rita* (agitated): Alfred! Alfred! That's disgusting of you!
> *Allmers* (in a low voice, raising his fist to her): In that
> moment you condemned little Eyolf to death. (8: 80)

Significantly for the changeling-returned-to-the-sea motif, he had earlier
phrased it that her neglect made her "to blame for [Eyolf's] not being
able to save himself in the water" (8: 80).

The theory that, after the terrible accident, they effectively had another child than their own is supported by a critic whose analysis of
Little Eyolf does not, however, involve folklore: "Eyolf is, so to speak,
born twice, or rather conceived twice, the second time as a cripple."[28]
In the play, Rita suggests that neither of them had loved Eyolf, accusing
her husband of hypocrisy in claiming that he had. At this point both
admit that at least symbolically, he was in fact not theirs:

> *Allmers* (looks thoughtfully at her): If what you think is
> right, our own child never really belonged to us.
> *Rita:* No. There was no real love.
> *Allmers:* Yet here we are bitterly mourning his death.
> *Rita* (bitterly): Yes. Curious, when you think about it.
> That here we are mourning a little stranger boy. (8: 79)

About the second point in the changeling pattern, that the parents of
the strange child are beleaguered and tortured by its presence, there is
no need to make an argument. For this is what the play hinges on, the
conflict between Rita and Allmers over Eyolf. His very birth torments
Rita, who denies any need to nurture the little stranger boy. E. S. Hartland, who has written a detailed account of changeling legends, says
about one group of them what probably can be extended to all, what
suggests that the changeling motif does represent a reversal of the "fam-

ily romance," and what seems specifically to define the relationship between Rita and Eyolf: "the apparently human babe is an impostor [and]
it belongs in fact to a different race, and has no claim on the mother's
care and tenderness."[29]

> *Rita* (in a low trembling voice): . . . I could wish I'd
> never borne him.
> *Allmers* (starts up): Rita! You don't know what you're say-
> ing!
> *Rita* (shaking with emotion): I gave birth to him in un-
> speakable pain. But I endured it gladly and joyfully for
> your sake.
> *Allmers* (warmly): Yes, yes. I know that.
> *Rita* (firmly): But that's past and done with. I want to
> *live.* Together with you. Wholly with you. I can't go on
> just being Eyolf's mother. And only that. Nothing else. I
> won't, I tell you! I can't! (8: 59–60)

It is their difference with regard to their now damaged child that
brings the third motif into play, the treatment of the "changeling." Allmers' decision to translate his book, the "Responsibility of Man," into
what he conceives to be his true responsibility, to help Eyolf to transcend
his misfortune and achieve a fine life, contrasts with what might be called
verbal child abuse, analogous to the kind of treatment afforded the changeling in legends. Rita had hated the book, and now she hates the action
implied in the title and about to be transformed into Allmers's day-to-
day life.

> *Rita:* . . . Only now you are caught up by something
> worse.
> *Allmers* (outraged): Worse! You call our child "something
> worse"?
> *Rita* (vehemently): Yes, I do. As far as it affects our re-
> lationship, I do. Because, on top of everything else, the
> child . . . the child is also a living being. (With rising
> passion.) But I won't stand for it, Alfred! I won't stand
> for it, I tell you!

> *Allmers* (looks steadily at her, then speaks quietly):
> Sometimes you almost frighten me, Rita.
> *Rita* (darkly): I often frighten myself. For that reason,
> you mustn't rouse the evil in me. (8: 59)

Meyer has translated "worse" into "hateful," less accurate in terms of the play's denotative language, but perhaps more accurate in terms of its connotations. Rita, who dresses herself in white to seduce her husband and learns how irrevocable is the effect on them of Eyolf's injury, is in her rage only second to Irene, who, as the white lady, carries similar anger toward Rubeck as far as verbalized expressions of infanticide against, however, another kind of "child."

Changeling stories involve abusive acts directed against the child in the name of some test or in order to lure the otherworldly parents to come to reclaim their child. That the latter effectively happens in *Little Eyolf* draws a parallel between the original "substitution" of the Allmers child and the retrieving of Eyolf by the Rat Wife. For if the initial event had to do with the lovemaking of the parents, the second episode comes when lovemaking proves impossible and Rita's hatred of Eyolf becomes pathological. It is at this point that she learns that Eyolf has drowned.

The fourth step in the folklore pattern sometimes involves the return of the human child once the changeling has returned to the otherworld. Again, this may happen because the human parent has been kind to the changeling. It is perhaps for this reason that Allmers, who was determined to help his son overcome his handicap, is afforded at least a vision of his son in the state before the substitution—that is, the fateful accident:

> . . . I dreamed of Eyolf last night. I thought I saw him coming up from the jetty! He could run, like other boys. As if nothing had happened to him. Absolutely nothing. This crushing reality was only a dream, I thought. Oh, how I thanked and praised . . . (8: 81)

For Rita, a symbolically "restored" Eyolf demands her repentance, and her decision to adopt the unfortunate children of her village causes the play to end on a note that has drawn complaints from audiences and critics. What happens, however, is consistent with folklore. Because of her philanthropy, Rita effects the second substitution and gets back the child originally lost—if only symbolically. She tells Allmers that when he leaves her, she shall "go down to the waterfront and bring all those poor deprived children up to [their] house. All those uncouth boys."

> *Allmers:* What will you do with them here?
> *Rita:* I'm going to look after them.
> *Allmers:* You what?
> *Rita:* Yes, I am. The day you leave they'll all move in here—as if they were mine.
> *Allmers* (agitated): In our little Eyolf's place?
> *Rita:* Yes, in little Eyolf's place. They shall live in Eyolf's room. Read his books. Play with his toys. Take turns at sitting in his place at table. (8: 103)

But the passage and the conclusion to the play suggest that like many other Ibsen characters, Eyolf is of both this world and the next. As a child of this world, he has been the sacrifice necessary for his parents' redemption. As the changeling, he must return to the world from which he came because his "otherness" marks him as an outcast. Eyolf is, that is, both victim of the family pathology and symbol of it.

John A. MacCulloch, whose folkloristics is often based on theories no longer accepted, or on premises for which no sound evidence exists, has nevertheless written so frequently and compellingly on fairy lore that he remains a valuable source for ideas about it. With regard to the changeling, he has attempted to account both anthropologically and psychologically for the belief that substitutions of children belonging to different worlds took place, and that although adults were also taken by the fairies, children were particularly liable to be kidnapped:

> Nor can we omit from a consideration of the changeling belief the possibility of its containing an element of actual fact, which did not originate, but served to strengthen, the superstition. When the territory of an aboriginal people was invaded by a conquering race, before the two finally came to terms, the former may have lived in seclusion, venturing forth by stealth to harry and raid their conquerors. Women and children would fall victims to them and would be stolen away; nor is it altogether impossible that, when a child was taken, a deformed or weakly child of the aborigines would be left in its place, perhaps

with a view to its being benefited by the care of members of the superior race. Many of the fairy and dwarf legends of northern Europe are eminently suggestive of actual fact, and in this sense fairies may once have been a real race hostile to and tricking the invading folk.[30]

Jacobsen has already argued that such a pattern defines the confrontation between paganism and Christianity, an element in the folk ballads important both to Ibsen's conception of the ballad (in his essay) and to his use of folklore themes in his plays. It is only necessary to substitute a marginal young person trapped between two cultures for the changeling to supply a link between *Little Eyolf* and other Ibsen plays. But the divided world of paganism and Christianity reveals itself in *Eyolf* in another form, a form that may tell much about its potential symbolism for Ibsen.

Ibsen's conception of Christianity and paganism as a paradigm for the conflict between life and art would not have been unique among nineteenth-century writers. To invoke Matthew Arnold again, his treatment of an ideologically conflicting Hebraism and Hellenism was derived in part from German romantic writers such as Heinrich Heine. What Ibsen may have done that was unique, however, was to equate the child who would be the prize of rival cultures to the work of art. For whether art was to exist in its own, exclusive sphere (symbolically Hellenic or pagan), or serve humanity (ethical Hebraism) was a reiterated concern in Ibsen's time. When Allmers chooses to give up his book to devote himself to his son, and Asta asks him if he cannot work both for himself and Eyolf, he replies:

No, I can't. Impossible! I cannot divide myself in this. So I shall make way. Eyolf shall achieve the consummation of the family line. And my new life's work shall be that of bringing him to that consummation. (8: 54)

It is ironic that his life's work should be entitled "Human Responsibility," and that he will do no more work on it: "No, never," he tells Asta. "I told you I cannot split myself between two tasks. But I shall carry through the concept of human responsibility—in my life" (8: 54).

Eyolf, then, is both the object of Allmers's commitment to life, and a symbol of the sacrificial victim. For the theme of the destroyed work of art as a murdered child and its effect on the couple that destroys it was one that Ibsen had begun to develop in *Hedda Gabler* and had worked a variation on in *The Master Builder*, where Aline Solness is a kind of Clytemnestra mourning the loss of her children but robbed of her vengeance against the father who has sacrificed them for his own ends. Again, these literary motifs would reach their climax in Ibsen's final play, *When We Dead Awaken*, in which the sacrifice takes another form; and art is conceived of as a substitute child—again, an idea already introduced in *Hedda Gabler*.

Thematically, *Little Eyolf* continues the motifs of these earlier plays. For if it is true that in his late plays, Ibsen had shifted away from social concerns to the psychology of the individual, so does it seem the case that from *Hedda Gabler* on, this preoccupation with the individual is focused on the artist torn between the personal gratification he receives from his art, be that greatness or financial reward, and an obligation to do the world some good—through art, he hopes, and if not, through social action. *Little Eyolf* plays an ironic variation on a dilemma from which few nineteenth-century writers escaped. The sympathetic concern of Allmers's family (outside of Rita) is itself a problem for him. If, traditionally, the artist is torn between the demands of his art on the one side, and his family on the other, then his family's invasion of his artistic space with their concern confuses what for the nineteenth century was at least a definable problem.

Only Rita stubbornly refuses to concern herself with Allmers's book. Ironically, neither will she stand for his ethical commitment to a world of human obligations. Indeed, she rejects not only both sides of her husband's dilemma but his sense of himself as a split being who must choose one of those sides, for neither of them corresponds to her requirement for his exclusive attention. Thus she will not tolerate Allmers's claim that he "must divide [himself] between Eyolf and [her]" (8: 59). She "threateningly" promises revenge, after the ominous warning, "If you parcel yourself out between me and anybody else" (8: 62). Rita's role as the demonic enchantress in *Little Eyolf* is to substitute one kind of "wonderland" (the pure aesthetic realm) with another (a sexual paradise). As soon as the claims of the real world are advanced, however, then art itself is a changeling, an ugly exchange for the child who has been sacrificed to it. These themes had made themselves felt in the plays that preceded *Little Eyolf*, and they would be perpetuated in the final two plays to follow.

Notes

1. Fleck.

2. Fleck does not claim to have direct evidence that Ibsen read Hoffmann's story; she relies on internal evidence (which I find convincing). Since her essay, the contents of Ibsen's library have been published. A book by Hoffmann is cited, but it was published in 1897, too late to have served as a direct influence. I think it is nonetheless a fair inference to claim that Ibsen knew Hoffmann. The following is the German text and Ibsen's Norwegian.

> Von unbekannter Macht fortgetrieben, schritt er vorwärts, aber in dem Augenblick regte sich alles um ihn her, and wie kräuselnde Wogen erhoben sich aus dem Boden wunderbare Blumen und Pflanzen von blinkendem Metall, die ihre Blüten und Blätter aus der tiefsten Tiefe emporrankten, und auf anmutige Weisse ineinander verschlangen. (*Serapions* 178)

> *Asta:* Ser du disse vannliljene her?
> *Allmers:* (Nikker langsomt): Det er av den slags som skyter opp,—dypt nede fra bunnen.
> *Asta:* Jeg plukket dem i tjernet. Der hvor det flyter ut i fjorden. (Rekker dem frem). Vil du ha dem Alfred?
> *Allmers* (Tar dem): Takk.
> *Asta* (Med tårefylte øyne): De er som en siste hilsen til deg fra—fra lille Eyolf.

3. I have treated the opposition between the mountains and flatlands in Ludwig Tieck and Thomas Mann in *La Belle Dame sans Merci and the Aesthetics of Romanticism*.

4. MacCulloch 358.

5. Evans-Wentz 491.

6. Watts 36.

7. See Gravier, "Le drame d'Ibsen" 144: his interpretation of names such as Gudmund Alfson as "fils d'elfe" is derived from the work of Clara Stuyver.

8. Christiansen, *Migratory Legends* 109.

9. MacCulloch 359.

10. Ibid.

11. See my discussion of *Undine:* Fass [Leavy], *"La Belle Dame sans Merci and the Aesthetics of Romanticism."*

12. This transformation of the enchantress into the hausfrau was part of my discussion of *Hedda Gabler;* see Chapter 7.

13. MacCulloch 359.

14. *Folktales* xxxvii.

15. Evans-Wentz 136.

16. See Ericsson, passim.

17. Bettelheim 68.

18. Landstad, *Mytiske* 69–73.

19. See Lüthi 20; Fischer 246; Bettelheim 50, 83, 97.

20. MacCulloch 359.

21. Ibid. 359.

22. Ibid. 358.

23. Christiansen, *Folktales* 94.

24. Meyer, *Plays* 4: 433.

25. Holbek has reminded me about the Pied Piper motif, adding that rats can be understood as otherworldly beings, a supernatural or infernal plague. The Rat Wife as Pied Piper is a commonplace in *Little Eyolf* criticism, and I omitted mentioning it deliberately to focus on the changeling and related themes, which are not. Nonetheless, the idea that Ibsen's play might exist on the fringes of the body of plague literature remains an intriguing one. As an added point, Christiansen (*Studies in Irish and Scandinavian Folktales*) tells of a subgroup of the animal bride tale in which a particularly repulsive bride is a rat: "While getting on very well with the tiny lady and with the toad and mouse, up to his last visit to the rat [the hero] is obsessed by the idea of how to get away from her" (110). Similar folklore is implied in a study of *Little Eyolf* in which the Rat Wife is seen as an archetypal seductress, "a cruel distortion of Rita herself. . . . In Norwegian she is literally the 'Rat-Maid' (*Rottejomfruen*)" (Jacobs 606).

26. Craigie 151.

27. Holbek rightly points out that in pursuing my own interpretation of the children's strange or demonic eyes, I had omitted the obvious and widespread belief in the "evil eye." The belief Holbek describes—that unless the eyes of the dead are closed, they will be looking for companions to follow them in death—suggests an apt metaphor for the pull of the otherworld. Many romantics were already half in love with easeful death, and this folklore is consistent with literary themes.

28. Roed 75.

29. Hartland 117.

30. MacCulloch 363.

CHAPTER 10

John Gabriel Borkman: The Miner and the Werewolf

As in *Hedda Gabler,* the folkloristic elements in *John Gabriel Borkman* are not immediately apparent. Seeming hints at folk themes appear at times: Mrs. Wilton, who in act 4 of the poem elopes with Borkman's son, Erhart, appears as a witchlike seductress in act 1—even if a facetious one:

> *Mrs. Wilton* (in the doorway, with a dismissive gesture): . . . But beware now, Master Borkman—I am warning you!
> *Erhart:* Why should I beware?
> *Mrs. Wilton* (gaily): Because as I go down the road—all alone and abandoned, as I said before—I shall try to cast a spell over you.
> *Erhart* (laughs): Oh, that! You want to try your hand at *that* again.
> *Mrs. Wilton* (half seriously): So watch out. As I walk down the road I shall say to myself—summoning together all my will-power, I shall say: "Mr. Erhart Borkman, pick up your hat!" (8: 174)

And John Borkman himself is linked to the image of a sick and howling wolf whose emergence into the world and the day-to-day existence of his family terrifies some of its members. In turn this image evokes the werewolf popular in Scandinavian (indeed European) lore. Again, the

256

werewolf had already appeared in *Little Eyolf* and would adhere to the figure of Ulfheim ("wolf's home") in *When We Dead Awaken*.

Were this all, however, there would be little reason to seek in *John Gabriel Borkman* the influence of folklore themes that figure prominently in the five plays that precede it, and the one—Ibsen's last—that would follow. But there is more, and what there is can be focused on the images in the play that cluster about the figure of the mine. Jacobsen has already demonstrated in our earlier discussion how crucial to Ibsen's concept of folklore was the ambiguous figure of the *bergmann*, who is either miner or troll (and in Ibsen's play, effectively both). And in notes to *Hedda Gabler*, as I earlier noted, Ibsen was already thinking of the mine as a symbol for the demonic recesses of the human mind. In a poem written in his youth, Ibsen had treated a theme that, as will be seen, was popular among the German romantics, that of the mine as escape from the ordinary life (although his image of reality is an ambiguous one): "I forgot the glory of day in that dark as midnight shaft, forgot the sounds and songs of the hillside in the cloisters of my mine" (8: 340).

Not long ago, the argument was made that an influence on Ibsen's play was the legend of the mines at Falun, particularly as rendered in a short story by E. T. A. Hoffmann, "Die Bergwerke von Falun." The legend enjoyed great popularity in Germany, and in the hands of romantic writers, the idea of the mine as another kind of wonderland developed as a literary motif. Drawing on it would allow Ibsen to continue to work out themes that he had begun at least as far back as *Rosmersholm*: "the Falun story falls into the category of humans attracted by the 'other world' and consequently enchanted in it."[1]

The legend itself concerns a Swedish miner killed in a mining accident. Fifty years later his body, preserved in vitriol water, is recovered and recognized by his now aged fiancée, Ulla, who had mourned him all her life. The tale enjoyed more popularity than the study of its influence on Ibsen suggests. Among the German romantics who exploited its potential themes, Achim von Arnim introduced the idea of an enchantress, the Queen of the Mines, who lures the miner, Elis Fröbom, from his fiancée, Ulla. In Hoffmann this supernatural figure remains in the background, more symbolic than active, but it is clear that she is nonetheless a rival of Ulla since Fröbom feels torn between them.[2] In both Hoffmann's story and Ibsen's play, it has been argued, the two women—Gudrun and Ella—who vie for the Borkmans' (both father's and son's) love represent two worlds: the everyday world of "happiness, love, and marriage," on one side, and a magic realm of riches and power with the exacting price of "loneliness . . . coldness, darkness, and social isolation," on the other.[3] The line that would establish Gudrun as Mine Queen, however, is not quoted in this study: at one point Borkman tells Ella that Gudrun is as "hard as the iron [he] once dreamed of quarrying from the rock" (8: 204).

While there is no question that Ibsen's plays can be placed in a romantic tradition that contrasts two realms of existence, it should be clear by now that he avoided any simple confrontation between the two. Just as John Rosmer is a conservative pastor turned political radical *and* Rosmer Havmand, so is Gudrun Borkman both wife *and* mine queen. Similarly, Frida, who is more than a minor character in *John Gabriel Borkman,* is both passive victim of her family and society, and, as a musician, allied to what in German romanticism was one of the most powerful wonderlands of all: pure music. Frida, I will argue, is another incarnation of Agnete, torn between two kinds of existence, and finally "kidnapped" and carried away to the otherworld. In any event, in *John Gabriel Borkman* as well as in his other late plays, Ibsen had avoided what for him was a simplistic juxtaposition of two worlds, one of them conceived as an alternative to the place in which people live out their mundane existences. It may be that Hoffmann's portrayal of his Mine Queen was uniquely adaptable to Ibsen's purposes, for unlike the otherworld temptresses of most romantic literature, she is a shadowy figure, hardly Ulla's active rival. As a projection of the miner's own striving for an ideal the world seems to have denied him, she provides Ibsen with a more malleable character than a clearly defined *huldre.*

I have written elsewhere at some length of the legend of Falun, in particular on the supernatural elements in Hoffmann's rendering of it.[4] It is important to understand that there is a tradition surrounding mining in German romanticism that *contradicts* any argument that as magic otherworld, the mines represent riches, power, and loneliness. True, it is his connecting of the mines with material wealth and position that has helped to destroy Borkman. As for loneliness, it is also true that it represents a powerful force that may drive the miner to seek a real as well as symbolic light in the world of human interaction. Ibsen's early poem spoke of the "glory of day" and the "sounds and songs of the hillside" that were forgotten as he retreated into the mine, symbolic of what Coleridge would call the "caverns measureless to man." Ibsen's words would also find their counterpart in German romanticism: "[I] thought how [the miners] had worked all day in lonely and secret places in the mines, and how they now longed for the blessed light of day, and for the glances of wives and children."[5] To be denied this return to earth would be to experience what Ibsen describes in the closing lines of his poem, "Hammerblow on hammerblow until life's final day. No ray of morning shines; no sun of hope rises" (8: 340).

But this loneliness might also be the price that the romantic-as-miner would have to pay for the imaginative life. It was the writer Novalis who perhaps described most fully the symbolic meaning of the mines. More important, he establishes in his writing the very principle that Borkman fatally violates:

The miner is born poor and he dies poor. He is content to know where the metal powers are found and to bring them to the light of day, but their dazzling glamor has no power over his pure heart. Uninflamed by perilous frenzy, he takes more delight in their peculiar structures and their strange origin and habitat than in their possession which promises so much. They have no charm for him any more once they are turned into commercial articles, and he had rather look for them within the strongholds of the earth amid a thousand dangers and drudgeries than to follow their call into the world and to strive after them up on the surface by means of deluding, deceitful arts.[6]

Thus it is not merely a matter of why Elis Fröbom or Borkman fail to get their treasure, or even of the illusory nature of the treasure,[7] but of Borkman's greed, which was anathema to the romantic. And Borkman, who has much of the romantic in him, is trapped in his own inconsistencies.

Like Novalis's ideal miner, content "to know where the metal powers are found and to bring them to the light of day," so does Borkman imagine that the iron ore sings for joy: "It wants to come up into the light of day and serve mankind" (8: 180). But his quest for self-realization leads him to those very "commercial articles" that according to Novalis should lack all charm for him.

> *Borkman:* When I think . . . how close I was to my goal.
> If only I'd had another eight days to make certain dispo-
> sitions. Every deposit would have been covered. All the
> securities I had so boldly used would have been back in
> place. Gigantic companies were within a hairsbreadth of
> being established. Nobody would have lost a penny. (8:
> 186)

It is because he perverts the aims of the romantic miner that the bank
vault becomes an inverted, parodic image of the mine whose ore is to
serve humanity.

Ibsen actually provides Borkman with four enclosed places that correspond to each other and spell out both his inconsistencies and the
prices he must pay for them. These places are the mine, the bank vault,
the prison, and the room in which he imprisons himself. To understand
the relationships among these four is to understand better how Ibsen
has used folk motifs for the themes in his play.

The mine is ideally a place of imaginative contemplation:

> How tranquilly . . . the poor, contented miner works in his deep sol-
> itudes, withdrawn from the restless tumult of the day and inspired
> only with desire for knowledge and love of concord. In his solitude he
> thinks of his companions and family with hearty affection and feels
> ever anew the interdependence and blood kinship of all mankind.[8]

But this is not what Borkman ultimately responded to as the mines
beckoned him:

> *Borkman* (vehemently): I had the power! And the indom-
> itable sense of ambition! All those millions lay there, im-
> prisoned, over the whole land, deep in the mountains, and
> called to me! Cried out to me for release! But nobody else
> heard it. Only me. (8: 207)

As will be seen, it is ironic that he describes his response in terms of
prisons and imprisonment.

In his greed to obtain the profits mining yields, Borkman not only
violates the romantic ideal but sins against what Keats calls the ties of
humans to each other, although he reminds Ella that he had spared her:

> *Borkman* (flaring up): . . . As the last decisive battle ap-
> proached . . . when I could spare neither family nor
> friends . . . when I had to take, and did take, those mil-
> lions that had been trusted to me . . . I spared everything
> that was yours, everything you possessed . . . though I
> could have taken and used it all, in the same way I had
> used everything else! (8: 195)

The bank vault in which he left her fortune intact becomes, again, an inverted image of the mine. He who had imagined the ore singing for joy as it is taken to earth to serve humanity can no longer separate his own ambitions from his supposedly worthy goals. Probably every embezzler has fantasized about the temporary use of funds not his to use. And so the jail in which Borkman is imprisoned by law is the realistic justice exacted by society, whereas Novalis's miner pays a psychic price if he betrays the mines.

Borkman's betrayal of the self that belonged to the mines exacts its own price, and the imprisonment that society imposes on him is followed by his self-imprisonment in a lonely room, cut off from all of the outside world save those he chooses to let in. And here the folklore of the werewolf proves to fit the narrative and symbolic pattern of Ibsen's play. But to relate the wolf image to others in the play, it is first necessary to consider Gunhild Borkman's structurally ambivalent role in *John Gabriel Borkman* as both wife and metal queen. In the last two of Ibsen's plays, the thematic strands that he borrowed from folklore appear to have become more difficult to separate, and the task of interpreting his use of folk patterns even more complicated. Yet it is a task that must be undertaken, since Ibsen's borrowings from popular tradition are woven into the increasingly complex patterns of his drama.

Insofar as *John Gabriel Borkman* follows Hoffmann's "Mines at Falun" in depicting the opposition between two realms, Ibsen is still exploring the concept of the wonderland versus the culture that requires the individual to fulfill responsibilities to society. The question that can be asked is, to what extent can the dichotomies between reality and fantasy correspond to the opposition between nature and culture? Or perhaps the question should be not how nature and culture oppose each other, but how their very ways of interacting create human dilemmas. In a simple way the realm of domestic relations stands for culture, and the wife or husband (especially when rival of a fairy or demon lover) epitomizes the demands of the "real." The wonderland can then correspond to the realm of pure nature insofar as both allow for total freedom from the real. But that the matter was not so simple impressed itself on the nineteenth-century mind. In that nature as procreative power also finds expression in domestic life, nature and culture form a synthesis, any retreat from which would take two possible directions. On the one hand, the opposite of warm, procreative nature is the sterile, inorganic matter represented by the mined ore that instead of serving humanity becomes the source of strife. That man's first digging in the earth for its metals constituted another Fall is a theme sometimes encountered in Western literature. But for the romantic nineteenth century, images of metal and precious stones also represent escape from a mutable world. Drawing on one of Andersen's fairy tales, William Butler Yeats wrote in "Sailing to Byzantium" that once out of nature he would never submit to natural processes again. Instead, in his next life, he would take

> such a form as Grecian goldsmiths make
> Of hammered gold and gold enameling
> To keep a drowsy Emperor awake;
> Or set upon a golden bough to sing
> To lords and ladies of Byzantium
> Of what is past, or passing, or to come.

And in Ludwig Tieck's short story "The Runenberg," there is a similar conflict between organic and inorganic nature, the hero torn between what each signifies, his dilemma supplying the story's tragic conflict.

The second retreat from a nature-culture synthesis is a more common one, in which a human being who for one reason or another seeks to evade the human condition takes on an animal body. One might say that the person having in some way offended against nature, he experiences nature's vengeance by being transformed into a purely natural form. In folklore, his return to the real world is a matter of disenchantment. Ibsen would amplify this theme through the images of the animal groom in his next and last play, *When We Dead Awaken*, where the bear hunter can be seen as a rationalized form of the bear husband who appears in the well-known Norwegian variant of Tale Type 425, "East of the Sun, West of the Moon." In such tales, the civilizing influence of a woman effects the hero's transformation. But Gunhild Borkman cannot play that role, because she is not *only* Borkman's wife and the mother of his son, that is, representative of the most positive elements in nature as well as of its alliance to culture, but also the mine queen, antagonistic to both. In *John Gabriel Borkman* inorganic nature (the mines) and organic nature (the animal) create a fatal paradigm in that both resist an accommodation to culture.

In widely disseminated groups of folktales the animal skin and human clothes both imprison in and release from their animal forms those persons whose shapeshifting powers are associated with their covering. Seal and swan maidens retrieve their skins and feather garments and escape the human world, or they lose them and are forced to become wives. (The importance of the dress in which Nora will dance the tarantella in *A Doll's House* can be recognized in this pattern.) Or the animal skins of enchanted beings are burned and the donning of human garments symbolizes the full human status of the disenchanted being. In *When We Dead Awaken* these themes will be more explicit: Irene wears a swansdown cloak, and the Lohengrin story whose taboo motif I earlier discussed in the analysis of *Rosmersholm* plays an important thematic role. But in *John Gabriel Borkman*, Ibsen employs these folklore motifs in seemingly innocuous images that easily escape notice.

As betrayed wife, Gunhild Borkman views her husband from the perspective of culture and finds in his iniquity his reversion to the beast. It is this perspective that endows the room in which he secludes himself with its correspondence to the mines, to the bank vault, and to the literal prison that expressed the way in which culture enforces its values:

> *Mrs. Borkman:* Many a time I feel as though I had a sick wolf pacing his cage up there in the great room. Right above my head. . . . Listen, Ella! Listen. Backwards and forwards, backwards and forwards goes the wolf. (8: 163)

But unlike the submissive heroine who kisses the frog prince and restores him to humanity, or the heroines of other folktales who destroy the animal skin in order to rescue enchanted men from the curse of their aberrant natures, Gunhild will not "liberate" Borkman: "After all that he's done to me! No, thank you! Let the wolf keep to his prowling up there" (8: 163). The first act ends as she muses on how the "wolf howls again. The sick wolf" (8: 178).

It is at this point that Borkman's human garments come to resemble Rebecca's sealskin trunk (that the former represents the "real" world, and the latter the potential for escaping it, does not alter the analogy). In the nature-culture conflict, animal skin or human garment provide escapes from the opposite realm. Thus, when Borkman emerges from the room in which he pads as a sick wolf, his ordinary clothing plays a significant if seemingly innocuous role:

> Mrs. Borkman: He never goes out.
> *Ella Rentheim:* Not even in the dark?
> *Mrs. Borkman:* Never.
> *Ella Rentheim* (with emotion): He can't bring himself to?
> *Mrs. Borkman:* I suppose not. He still has his cape and his felt hat hanging in the hall cupboard.
> *Ella Rentheim* (to herself): The cupboard we used to hide in when we were little. . . .
> *Mrs. Borkman* (nods): Occasionally . . . in the late evening . . . I've sometimes heard him come down . . . as though he was on his way out. But then, halfway down the stairs, he stops . . . and turns back. And then he goes back to his room. (8: 163–64)

And at the end of act 3, when Borkman makes the decision to come out of his isolation, even if it is to face the storm alone, he announces his transformation with "My hat! My cape!" (8: 220).

Once again Ibsen has inverted the folklore he was using. The werewolf tradition ordinarily involves a human who emerges from his home and prowls the neighborhood until he finds the victim he tears apart. Instead, Borkman the "wolf" prowls his room and occasionally makes a gesture toward assuming human form (that is, wearing socially approved clothing) to go outside. Borkman's lonely room for all of his isolation occupies the space ordinarily filled by culture. Instead it represents his reversion to pure nature. But to read a large number of folktales about shape-shifting animal-humans is to understand that the themes work in either direction without necessarily altering the basic conflict. Indeed, the human garments that traditionally spell the "release" of the animal-man can also be conceived of as the opposite, the imprisonment *by* culture of the human "animal" through repression. In *John Gabriel Borkman* this is made clear in the way that Erhart Borkman's clothing plays a thematic part in his seduction by Mrs. Wilton.

In her role as good, that is "natural," mother, Gunhild Borkman faces the rivalry of the "witch," Mrs. Wilton; but in her role as the "bad" mother (e.g., metal queen), Gunhild effectively reverses Mrs. Wilton's role as well. The latter is now conceived of as Erhart's rescuer. As Ella says to Gunhild, "I'd rather she [Mrs. Wilton] had him than you" (8: 178). The deliverance of Erhart from the unnatural world of the mines, from, in short, the world that corresponds to pure nature, is once again conceived of by Ibsen in terms of the character's clothing, his theme, however, rendered ironically as Mrs. Wilton, in her threat to place a spell on Erhart, says only half seriously (therefore, half jokingly), "I shall say to myself—summoning together all my will-power, I shall say: 'Mr. Erhart Borkman, pick up your hat!'" (8: 174).

> *Mrs. Borkman:* And you think then he'll pick it up?
> *Mrs. Wilton* (laughs): Bless you, yes. He'll snatch up his hat at once. And then I'll say: "Put on your overcoat, Erhart Borkman! And your galoshes. Don't forget your galoshes! And follow me! Good boy! Good boy!" (8: 174)

Of course, Mrs. Wilton is parodying the mother-son relationship, but the full significance of her imagery, as will shortly be seen, goes beyond parody.

In juxtaposing the animal skin symbolic of nature against human clothing representative of culture, Ibsen raises the same question posed by Hoffmann in "The Mines at Falun." For in any dichotomy involving the real world of human interaction opposed to purely free organic and inorganic nature, the real question concerns how these antithetical realms correspond to a human being's conception of a "higher" and "lower" self. In "The Mines at Falun," Hoffmann's hero confronts this dilemma on the eve of his marriage and believes himself to be making the wrong choice:

> He felt split in half; it seemed to him that his better, his true being, was climbing down into the center of the earth and was resting in the

Queen's arms, while he was seeking his dreary bed in Falun. When Ulla spoke to him of her love and how they would live together happily, then he began to speak of the splendor of the shaft, of the immeasurably rich treasures which lay concealed there, and he became entangled in such strange, incomprehensible speeches that fear and anxiety seized the poor child and she did not know at all how Elis could have changed so suddenly into a quite different person.[9]

The idea that a man's lower self belongs to his wife, who in consequence of this realization is to be sacrificed to some higher ideal, was a theme already employed by Ibsen in *The Master Builder*, where Aline Solness is immolated on the altar of her husband's egotism. Of course, the most powerful expression of this theme occurs in *Brand*, but it is like other Ibsen motifs, a recurrent one in his plays. And so like other Ibsen characters, and like Elis in Hoffmann's story, Borkman excuses his behavior by an appeal to a higher self.

He had married Gunhild instead of Ella because the latter was coveted by a man Borkman believed necessary for his realizing his ambitions. By marrying Gunhild, he thus connivingly left the road to Ella open, although she had not cooperated and had rejected the unwelcome suitor. When Ella accuses Borkman of having betrayed her, he responds,

> *Borkman:* Broken faith, you say? You know very well it was higher motives . . . well, other motives, then . . . that forced my hand. Without *his* support I couldn't get anywhere.
> *Ella Rentheim* (controlling herself): So you broke faith from . . . higher motives? (8: 196)

She recognizes only too well the symbolic correlation between the mines (the site of his so-called higher self) and the bank vault: "Yet you made me part of your cheap bargain, all the same. Traded your love with another man. Sold my love for a bank directorship!" (8: 196). Ibsen has, of course, rendered Hoffmann's themes ironically. Elis Fröbom leaves Ulla to go to the Queen of the Mines because he associates his higher self with the underground realm; Borkman leaves Ella to go to Gudrun for what he claims is an attempt to realize his higher being—but this, again, has been perverted to pure greed.

And this is not the end of Borkman's arrogant rationalization. Not only had he sacrificed Ella to what he still half defends as superior motives, but he reproaches her for having failed in the role she should have played—to save him. If Gunhild cannot redeem the animal-man because of her deep sense of betrayal, Ella, according to Borkman's twisted reasoning, had equally failed him because she was not willing to play her role as sacrificial victim: "Is that so, Borkman . . . ! So when it comes to the point, it seems *I* am the one who has to make it up to *you*" (8: 194).

Ella and Gunhild may indeed stand on opposite sides of Borkman's life, but it is also true that each is a flesh-and-blood human being he has been willing to use for his own ends. Unlike the Mine Queen, who corresponded to the higher nature of Hoffmann's hero, neither of Ibsen's women can stand for the superior goals to which the other is to be sacrificed. And yet it is also true the parallel between Gunhild and the Mine Queen can be sustained. As was earlier suggested, Gunhild Borkman is queen of the mines in much the same way that John Rosmer is Rosmer Havmand. Rosmer, it was earlier argued, was committed to a political idealism so pure in conception that it spoke of an Edenic innocence. In this sense Rosmersholm is as much of a wonderland as is the merman's underwater realm. Similarly, Gunhild Borkman is obsessively committed to a return to an imagined Eden, to a time and place before the Borkmans' personal fall. She is fixated on the point when the life she had known "all collapsed. Everything. And all the glory was over" (8: 159). And like fallen humanity, she looks for her deliverer, "somebody who will wipe the record clean of every stain left by that man" (8: 159). This is to be her son, Erhart. "He'll find a way to restore the family, the house, the name. All that *can* be restored" (8: 159). For it is no spiritual redemption she seeks, but the restoration of the earthly paradise. And insofar as she dwells emotionally in her dreams of this wonderland, she rules over a domain in which her son will be trapped if he cannot escape her. In short, as the Queen of the Mines was to Elis Fröbom in Hoffmann's story, so is Gunhild to her son, Erhart Borkman, in Ibsen's play.

It is in light of Gunhild's paradoxically conceived idealism and the way in which it corresponds to the dual world of *John Gabriel Borkman* that the subplot concerning Frida takes on significance. From his early plays—*Brand* is a significant example—Ibsen had been acutely aware of the symbolic potential in the story "Agnete and the Merman." Brand's wife is thus both the image of pure female love, and also one of those marginal girls willing to turn away from the ordinary life she would live with her fiancé Einar (although he is an artist, a character probably borrowed from Andersen's play *Agnete*, as Jacobsen notes, an artist whose transformation to fanatical preacher is consistent with Ibsen's themes) to follow Brand to a place so remote from social reality that ordinary humans cannot survive in it. Agnes's story in *Brand*, as I have contended all along, reflects a narrative pattern that, like the seal maiden folklore, is often split although complete only when the two sides are juxtaposed. It is probably not merely a matter of common folklore that led Andersen to write a play about Agnete, the human drawn to the merman, and a story about a mermaid who longed for the world of men and hoped to win a human soul. To recognize the way these motifs are worked out in *John Gabriel Borkman*, it is important to understand the significance of Frida, the musician who longs to dance and is barred from this communal activity as effectively as the mermaid who had a beautiful singing voice instead of the requisite legs.

When I wrote elsewhere on the mines at Falun, I quoted from Ibsen's friend, Georg Brandes, on the difficulty of analyzing German romanticism because its ideal is not a clearly defined figure (as the French romanticists produced) so much as "a melody, not definite form, but infinite aspiration."[10] Frida's music, which she plays to Borkman as the two seclude themselves in his room, is thus appropriate to his isolation. He has, that is, turned his private domain into a bizarre version of those wonderlands that figure in romantic literature, be they mines, a pre-Fall earthly paradise, political utopias, the habitat of the *huldre*-folk, or the sea world of Rosmer and Agnete.

In pursuing the analogy between Agnete and Frida, it is important to note not only that she plays her music in Borkman's isolated room, but that for her to develop her talent, she must be taken from her parents' home and must live with the "witch" Mrs. Wilton, who will eventually take her along on her wedding trip, grooming the young girl as her eventual replacement. At this point two familiar themes are joined. First, Frida's final departure involves the same kind of wonderland images associated with the ballad variant in which luxury and precious metals lured Agnete to the merman's realm. (As Jacobsen has argued, it is clear in the ballads that these material gains symbolize more deep-seated motives. Ibsen exploits both the literal and symbolical meanings of the ballads.) Second, there is the loss experienced by the young woman's mother. Just as Hillelil grieves when her daughter is taken by Rosmer, and Agnes's mother mourns the marriage of her child to Brand in a play that seems to draw on the Agnete ballad both directly and as interpreted by Kierkegaard, so does Frida's mother react to her daughter's departure from her home. But Frida's mother is never heard from directly; how she reacts to Frida's departure is conveyed by Foldal, who does not grieve at all.

> *Foldal:* . . . I'll go home now and comfort her mother who is sitting in the kitchen crying.
> *Borkman:* Crying?
> *Foldal* (smiling): Yes, would you believe it. She was sitting there crying her heart out as I came away. (8: 227)

Impressed by the wealth his daughter will have, he does not even mind that he has been run over as she sojourns to the "otherworld."

> *Foldal* (claps his hands): My little Frida in that magnificent sleigh!
> *Borkman* (nods): Yes, yes, Vilhelm. Your daughter is not doing too badly. And Erhart Borkman too. Did you notice the silver bells?
> *Foldal:* Oh yes, . . . *Silver* bells, did you say? Were they silver bells? Real genuine silver?
> *Borkman:* You may be sure they were. Everything was genuine. (8: 227)

As yet, he has not turned his thoughts to his wife and her loss of their child:

> *Foldal* (with quiet emotion): How strange are the workings of fate! There's my . . . my modest talent for poetry been transformed into music in Frida. So after all's said and done I haven't been a poet for nothing. Now she's got the chance of going out into the great wide world which I once used to dream so passionately of seeing. Little Frida

traveling in a grand sleigh. With silver bells on the harness. . . ! (8: 227)

But by now Borkman, having achieved some insight into how devastating an impact his own distorted values have had, wryly adds, "And running over her own father" (8: 227). But in vain. Like the avaricious father in "East of the Sun, West of the Moon," Foldal is willing to relinquish his daughter to a life in which silver bells command all his heart's desire.

Just as Borkman's idealism descends to his greed, and Foldal sees his poetry as the means by which his daughter will experience luxury, so must Frida play her music for money. The analogy between the mines and music holds. Each represents in the play inert, dead matter. That Frida plays "Danse Macabre" for Borkman points up how remote are both his existence and her art from real life. In contrast is the music she plays for those who wish to dance at their social gatherings, for that music is related to the "sounds and songs of the hillside" that Ibsen, in his poem "Bergmannen," contrasts with the "cloisters of [the] mine." It is finally Frida, then, who embodies in *John Gabriel Borkman* the theme of the artist and society. It is on her, perhaps more than on either Gudrun or Ella, that the folklore themes that Ibsen had been employing in his plays converge. For as was already suggested, in the end, Frida is another Agnete.

Both Agnete and Andersen's Little Mermaid can be conceived of as living a cloistered existence in the sea: the former longs to rejoin the world she now has misgivings about abandoning; the latter wishes to enter it for the same reasons. Similarly, Frida yearns toward the world from which her music effectively isolates her:

> *Borkman:* . . . Do you like playing for dancing? In various houses?
> *Frida:* . . . Yes, when I can get an engagement. I manage to earn a little money that way.
> *Borkman:* . . . Is that what you think about as you sit there playing while they dance?
> *Frida:* No. I generally find myself thinking it's pretty hard I can't join in the dancing myself. (8: 180)

Once again Ibsen seems to have picked up a theme from an early play and rendered it less obvious but thematically more complex. In *Olaf Liljekrans*, Alfhild likens herself to the fairy in the ballad who has stolen Olaf from his bride and from the world, and also to a bewitched princess herself, waiting for her deliverance: "And now I am free, and I know what I want! I want to take part in the great game of life!" (1: 498). The "dance" and the "great game of life" are positive representations of earthly reality, but both are aesthetic images as well. Hence they suggest the ambiguity that surrounds the conflict between art and life.

Matthew Arnold's "The Forsaken Merman" provides an example of how the "Agnete" ballad could be used to portray the split between life and art. When Margaret returns to the land, she equates "joy" with the spiritual values attached to work, children, and the religious life. In contrast to warm humanity, her mermaiden daughter's eyes are not only strange but cold. But the land is also walled in and gray, and it offers her no solace for those nights when she yearns for what only the sea can offer. Frida, paradoxically, resembles the forsaken merman more than she does Margaret. Her contact with the world merely shows her that she is excluded from the dance, from the game of life.

The separation of life from art also provides a theme in *John Gabriel Borkman*. The story of Agnete and its cognates was important to the nineteenth century precisely because it embodies the double pattern of the sea maid whose struggle is to decide which is her true element. Thus she provided the artist with a paradigm for his own existence. It would only be necessary to make one change in the ballad story to make the analogy between Agnete and Borkman as appropriate as Thomas Mann would later make the analogy between Andersen's Little Mermaid and Adrian Leverkühn in *Doctor Faustus*. That is, if Agnete's motivation for coming to earth is confused, and the desire for spiritual salvation or service to humanity is mixed—perhaps perverted—by a greed for worldly riches and power, then her story becomes Borkman's. And this, perhaps, is Ibsen's special twist to a theme that reverberated through nineteenth-century literature. For what Ibsen contributed to a motif already popular in his time was a new metaphor: the artist as embezzler.

The artist, like Agnete and like the Falun miner, conceived of the wonderland as a projection of the creative imagination. But like the miner and his raw ore, "joy" came not from the artist's retreat from the world so much as from the use of art for the betterment of the world. But to push art into such servitude was also to push it into the world of mundane relations and moral responsibility, and to do that was to threaten the very nature of the aesthetic realm. Thus the artist, like Solness and Borkman, would sacrifice human needs to what they conceive as a higher purpose, but in so doing would also endanger their souls.

But the artist's problem was compounded by an economic necessity Ibsen would have known but too well. The starving artist experienced a plight more dire than the one willing to give up the world for an aesthetic wonderland. Thus the meaning of the Falun mine disaster became in *John Gabriel Borkman* an important depiction of a literal reality not unknown among other romantic writers. It is noteworthy that when he wrote his poem "Lamia," John Keats was drawing on the same folklore patterns as those provided by the "Agnete" ballads. (He knew Fouqué's *Undine* very well, and he may have been familiar with the Rosmer ballads in Robert Jamieson's collection.) In any event, he wrote in "Lamia" that

> Love in a hut, with water and a crust,
> Is—Love, forgive us!—cinders, ashes, dust;
> Love in a palace is perhaps at last
> More grievous torment than a hermit's fast:—
> That is a doubtful tale from faery land,
> Hard for the non-elect to understand.

This might very well be read as an ironic response to Novalis, who urged the laborer to turn an income-producing mine into a symbolic otherworld.

But in the "real" world, the line between economic need and greed is very fine. Borkman, like Arnold's Margaret, finds potential joy in productivity, but Borkman cannot extricate himself from the vision of personal gain. He tries, but cannot succeed in excusing his embezzlement on grounds of the ultimate good he would do the world. Ibsen, again, had personal reasons for recognizing early on that the desire for fame and financial success would drive the artist as effectively as any creative force. When he added to this bitter understanding the dilemmas he inherited from the European romantic tradition, he was able to add to the folk and literary tradition on which he drew unique twists that make *John Gabriel Borkman* one of those enigmatic works that marked

Ibsen's late career. But the folklore and the literary tradition that grew up around it show that in this play, Ibsen continued to explore the relation of the writer to the "wonderland" of art on one side and, on the other, to the mundane world that seems to make him choose between a soul and worldly success.

Notes

1. Fleck 455. Fleck errs in separating folkloristic materials from the Falun legend. For even if it is true that the latter provided the "model for the metal and mine imagery" (444) in *John Gabriel Borkman*, the treatment of the legend by German romantics makes it clear that they recognized it as an analogue to a large body of folklore.

2. Since Fleck's essay, Ibsen's reading of Hoffmann has been demonstrated by the published list of books he owned. With regard to the folklore surrounding the miner, Holbek informs me that Swedish folklore tells of the *gravra*, a female spirit who guards (reigns over) the mine, and suggests that von Arnim may have known this.

3. Fleck 445.

4. Fass [Leavy], *La Belle Dame sans Merci and the Aesthetics of Romanticism:* the chapter "Demonic Gems" treats Hoffmann's story and Ludwig Tieck's "The Runenberg," which, I have already suggested, may have provided a theme in *Little Eyolf*.

5. Heinrich Heine. Quoted in Fass [Leavy] 94.

6. Novalis 100.

7. Fleck 11.

8. Novalis 70–71.

9. Hoffmann 209.

10. Fass [Leavy] 93.

CHAPTER 11

The Wild Men and Wild Women of When We Dead Awaken

The father willing to give up his daughter for material gains, and the silver bells that symbolize her good fortune appear in "East of the Sun, West of the Moon," one of the most popular stories in Peter C. Asbjørnsen's and Jørgen Moe's collection of Norwegian folktales. "East of the Sun" also belongs to one of the world's most widespread folktale types, "The Search for the Lost Husband" (Type 425), best known in the classical account of Cupid and Psyche; related tale types involve a variety of animal groom stories such as "The Frog Prince." The story, whose motifs had already shown up in *John Gabriel Borkman*, provides a more central theme in *When We Dead Awaken*. Maja and Ulfheim tell each other stories. His is about a girl he had lifted out of the gutter and carried "so that she shouldn't ever again bruise her foot against a stone. Her shoes were worn right through when [he] met her" (8: 290). The shoes provide a common motif in Type 425 tales, where frequently the heroine does not win back her lost spouse until she has performed the requisite tasks and has traveled long enough for her shoes to wear out. As usual, Ibsen plays his own games with his folk material: here the shoes are worn out before the story gets under way. But Maja has her own version of the tale:

Once upon a time there was a silly little girl. She had a father and a mother, but they were rather poor. Then into this life of poverty came a splendid gentleman, and he lifted the little girl up in his arms—just like you—and carried her far, far away. (8: 290)

274

In "East of the Sun, West of the Moon," it is not a splendid gentleman who carries the girl away, but an animal who must be disenchanted to become one. And, significantly—given that this exchange of fairy tales occurs between Maja and Ulfheim, the bear hunter—the animal in the Norwegian tale is a bear. Bears, in turn, are featured in a number of widespread Norwegian folktales,[1] although in ways that will be shown to be paradoxical. It has already been noted that Ulfheim can be translated as "home of the wolf," and that the werewolf motif could be found in the two plays that preceded *When We Dead Awaken*. It can be added now that "werewolf" can be understood as a generic term and that one form that the shapeshifting human-animal can take is the bear.[2]

The bear hunter, Ulfheim, who—again, paradoxically—also displays characteristics of the animal he hunts, does not, however, allow for as focused an analysis as the John Rosmer–Rosmer Havmand duality made possible. For Ulfheim cannot be characterized by a single folklore actor. If this last play was, as Ibsen claimed, a dramatic epilogue to the works beginning with *A Doll's House*, so does *When We Dead Awaken* appear to be a summary of folk themes that Ibsen had been using all along. It is not merely that his last play is replete with folk material, but that as his main characters form and reform alliances with each other, so does the interlocking quality of the folk motifs reveal the deadlocks that they experience in an attempt to reconcile opposites or fulfill themselves through each other. As will be seen, one way that Ibsen achieves his effects is to juxtapose patterns from Type 425 tales with those from its corresponding Type 400 ("The Search for the Lost Husband"), the type to which the seal and swan maiden tales belong.

As Ibsen approached the composition of *When We Dead Awaken*, a German edition of his works was in progress, and not wishing to be distracted by attention to the project, he wrote his editor to stop sending him the proofs of *The Vikings at Helgeland* (8: 353). It is noteworthy that in that play a bear had to be slain in order for some hero to win Hjördis as his wife. Another link between Ibsen's early and last play can be inferred in the notes to the Norwegian edition, Irene likened to a Valkyrie,[3] a description perhaps more appropriate to Hjördis than any other female character in Ibsen's plays. In both *The Vikings at Helgeland* and *When We Dead Awaken*, there is an implicit or explicit bear hunter, and a woman set apart by temperament and behavior from the ordinary mortal woman—that is, one who with varying degrees of conformity accepts the role woman is expected to play. Theoretically, the action of *The Vikings at Helgeland* might have concluded happily had Hjördis and her "bear hunter" wed: that at the end of the play Sigurd's Christianity challenges her paganism reveals the extent to which Ibsen wished to deny even such a theoretical premise. In *When We Dead Awaken* the impossibility of such a union is pushed even further, since the pairing of Irene and Ulfheim is the only relationship that Ibsen omits from the shifting alliances in the play.

But these images—bear, bear hunter, Valkyrie—are but a few of the folklore motifs that cluster about the characters in *When We Dead Awaken.* Erik Østerud, who emphasizes classical myths as Ibsen's sources, divides his study of the mythical background to *When We Dead Awaken* into isolated sections: Ulfheim as faun; Irene as one of the Horae, goddesses of the seasons and fertility; although treating as well such Teutonic legends as those of Lohengrin and Tannhäuser.[4] The following analysis of the play will turn to folk material closer to Ibsen's home than Greece and Rome—although it will not be denied that he would have recognized analogues in classical myth. There is a paradoxical element in folklore gathering. On the one hand, collecting of popular traditions is often nationalistic in spirit (and was particularly so in the nineteenth century); but on the other hand, the folklorist knows very well that, to cite Dorson again, folk characters often form an international family,[5] and that folklore themes recur throughout the world. For the sake of order and clarity in this analysis of *When We Dead Awaken,* the two characters who most obviously embody folk motifs, Ulfheim and Irene, will be analyzed as examples of the wild man and wild woman. In folkloristic studies, wild man and wild woman are both specific characters and generalized designations for a host of other beings from popular narratives: werewolves, mermen, trolls, mermaids, *huldre*s, swan maidens, and the ghostly white lady who seems to have provided Ibsen with a model for Irene.

Richard Bernheimer describes the wild man as "a literary and artistic figure whose imaginary character is proved by its appearance: it is a hairy man curiously compounded of human and animal traits, without, however, sinking to the level of an ape."[6] Representing man living outside the boundaries of culture, the wild man responds to a "persistent psychological urge," that is, "the need to give external expression and symbolically valid form to the impulses of reckless physical self-assertion which are hidden in all of us, but are normally kept under control."[7] Such a description of the wild man and his artistic function corresponds to Fjelde's description of the Norwegian troll as unsocialized man and to Watts's of the troll as pure id. That Ulfheim fits the physical description of the wild man can be seen in Ibsen's description of him: "Ulfheim is in shooting costume, with top-boots and a felt hat with a feather in it. He is a tall, lean, sinewy man, with matted hair and beard; and loud-voiced" (8: 250). That he is a wild man is confirmed in a conversation between Rubek and Maja:

> *Maja:* . . . What an ugly man he is! (Plucks a sprig of heather and throws it away.) So ugly, so ugly! Ugh!
> *Rubek:* Is that why you feel so safe going off with him . . . into the wilds? (8: 265)

Bernheimer himself makes the connection[8] between the erotically conceived wild man and the folklore actors that parade through Ibsen's plays when he notes that in ballads that tell of young women kidnapped by supernatural beings, "the identity of the kidnapper may vary from what appears to be a well-defined wild man to that of dwarf king, elf king, hill king or merman. All these variants occur in the North German and Scandinavian versions of the ballad of 'Hind Etin.'"[9] Add to this tradition the faun of classical antiquity, and the cast of folklore figures who qualify as wild men is nearly complete:

> *Maja:* . . . Do you know what you are like, Mr. Ulfheim?
> *Ulfheim:* I imagine I'm mostly like myself.
> *Maja:* Absolutely right. You are exactly like a faun.
> *Ulfheim:* A faun?
> *Maja:* Precisely.
> *Ulfheim:* A faun—isn't that some kind of monster. A wood-demon or something?
> *Maja:* Yes, just like you. With a beard like a goat and legs like a goat. And horns as well. (8: 288)

In notes to "Hind Etin," Child points to the link in Scandinavian lore between elf and mermen,[10] and between Bernheimer and Child, it is therefore possible to see in the wild man figure a link between Ulfheim and Rosmer. But whereas the latter is associated with the sea, the former's dwelling connects him even more closely to the wild man, for, according to Bernheimer, it is in mountainous regions that the concept of the wild man has best survived, "partly because such areas offer an excellent defense for archaic modes of thinking against modern depredations, partly because there is a kinship between the raw grandeur of the mountains and the indomitable strength of the wild man."[11]

Bernheimer's study covers not only the wild man but also the wild-man hunts, thus making possible an understanding of two features of *When We Dead Awaken*. First there is the association between the wild man on one side, and the troll and bear on the other; the second has to do with how Ibsen could use his folklore to create a character who is both "bear" and bear hunter. As to the first of these features, in the ritualized wild-man hunts that took place in some regions of Europe, the "wild man's closest associates were bears . . . and devils."[12] This correspondence between wild man and bear can be substantiated in the new Tale Type Index to Norwegian folktales, where a separate designation is given to "The Wild Man" (502. *Villmannen*): "A prince/boy is tricked into setting free a white bear or a wild man."[13] Bears, again, are often the animal form of werewolves in England and Iceland. And still another link between bear and troll can be found in the scholarly literature on the bear son tales considered to be among the sources of *Beowulf*. The hero of bear son narratives is frequently born of the union "of a human being and an animal, most often a bear. Later variants present the non-human parent as a giant(ess) or a troll."[14]

With regard to the second feature, it may commence from the reminder that Ulfheim is the bear *hunter*, not the hunted bear. But the theme of the hunt in folklore also has a paradoxical relationship to the wild-man theme. Bernheimer has noted that the "capture of the wild man is one of the most frequent stories in his mythology."[15] The hunter would thus appear to be the antagonist of the hunted, except, of course, that the hunt and capture of the wild man can be understood to symbolize an internal process projected outward and ritualized so that the hunter and hunted need not be distinguished. It is worth noting that in Norwegian folklore, the bear can be located on both sides of the boundary that separates the stalker from its prey. The bear is, again, sometimes the troll-like figure of the wild man not yet civilized or the animal groom awaiting disenchantment (the capture and disenchantment of the bear have analogous meanings). But also in an extremely popular story that Ibsen utilized in *Peer Gynt*, the bear is the figure before whom trolls retreat in panic. As Tale Type 1161 ("The Bear Trainer and His Bear"), it is known in sixty-four variants in Norway.

A wayfarer with a (white) bear has a night's lodging with a farmer who is much troubled by ogres. When the ogres come and discover the bear, they think it is a cat and try to feed it. The bear gets angry and chases them all off. Later they ask the farmer whether he still has the big white cat. He answers that it now has many kittens. The ogres then promise never to come again.[16]

In short, in Norwegian lore, the bear is both troll-equivalent (by analogy to the wild man theme) and troll-antagonist. Ulfheim plays both roles.

Again, the wild man himself often appears as a hunter, the leader of those "marauders known as the Wild Hunt or the Wild Horde—that spectral chase known also as the Furious Host—which races in certain winter nights through the valleys and deserted villages, destroying every living thing it meets in its way."[17] In his *Teutonic Mythology*, Grimm devotes much attention to the "Furious Host," and one story he relates contains within it two elements significant for Ibsen's play. He tells of one wild hunter who "makes the peasants hold his dogs": when Ulfheim appears at the lodge he similarly orders a servant to "Go and see to your fellow-creatures" (8: 250). In the same account Grimm tells that the wild hunter stalks as prey a merwoman, and that one man saw him return with the dead sea creature laid across his horse.[18] But the symbolic slaying of the mermaid, who would seem to be the hunter's natural mate (Østerud, who interprets Maja as a kind of wild woman, believes she is thus suited to Ulfheim the faun), demands some intricate untangling of folk motifs and their inherent symbolism. Once again, Ibsen's earlier plays make his intentions more obvious than do his later dramas. When Sigurd slays the bear at Hjördis's door, he is effectively taming the Valkyrie (i.e., wild woman), thus winning her, although a substitute groom actually claims her. It is the conflict-laden and often paradoxical relationships among wild man and wild woman types on the one hand, and more civilized men and women on the other, that form the quadrangles that provide many of Ibsen's plays with their dramatis personae. The hunter who slays the mermaid and the one who merely slays the symbolic bear that guards her door, like the mortal maiden who in turn disenchants the bear, are performing similar acts in defense of culture. That the hunter himself can also appear as wild man only shows how complex the folklore patterns themselves are that Ibsen exploited. In *When We Dead Awaken*, he seems to have allowed this complexity free reign, making less attempt than in the previous plays to untie the threads himself. It was their very tangle that seems to have served his thematic ends.

Wild woman is as inclusive a term as wild man, and it has been invoked by folklorists and literary critics to cover a wide variety of supernatural and powerful women: Valkyries;[19] heathen goddesses who may also lead wild hunts;[20] mermaids;[21] Scandinavian elf women;[22] lamias;[23] and the Norwegian *huldrer*.[24] Bernheimer identifies three main classes of wild women, including libidinous ugly hags or less loathsome but still hairy wood and moss damsels. His third species is "plainly conceived as revenant ghosts," creatures who "were said to appear wearing beautiful flowing white robes."[25] Without naming her, Bernheimer has described the white lady, a character who has drawn to herself special attention by folklorists.

That Irene is a white lady is immediately apparent once the tradition surrounding this mysterious folklore character is recognized. Ibsen can be assumed to have been familiar with this tradition—from Grimm's *Mythology* and Scandinavian folklore. Indeed, one summary of a white lady story pattern seems virtually to define the plot surrounding Irene and Rubeck:

a) A girl of humble origin is ruined and abandoned by a young aristocrat; b) she murders her bastard infant(s); c) she goes insane and dies violently; d) she returns as a malign ghost, sometimes a beckoning temptress; and e) those unfortunate enough to meet her die shortly afterward.[26]

In *When We Dead Awaken*, the aristocrat and girl of humble origin are replaced by an artist and his model. Irene affirms that she has been abandoned (rather than the reverse, as Rubek protests) by recalling that after his sculpture was complete (that it is later referred to as their child sustains the analogy to the white lady tradition), he was thus "finished" with her. As she puts it, he "had no further use" for her (8: 259). She also insists that she was "nothing more than an episode in [his] life" (8: 295).

But where the white lady murders her children, Irene only expresses the wish that she had murdered their offspring (the art work):

> *Irene:* I should have killed that child.
> *Rubek:* Killed it, you say!
> *Irene* (whispering): Killed it . . . before I left you.

She adds that since then, "I've killed it countless times. By day and by night. Killed it in hatred, in vengeance, in torment" (8: 254). Later, when Rubek asks her if she had married and had children, she responds,

> *Irene:* Yes, I have had many children.
> *Rubek:* And where are those children now?
> *Irene:* I killed them.
> *Rubek:* (sternly): Now you are lying to me again!
> *Irene:* I killed them, I tell you. With murderous passion. As soon as they came into the world. Oh, long, long before that. One after the other. (8: 256)

Like the white lady, she had become insane and—according to her own symbolism—had died: for her the image of a strait-jacket is also that of a shroud:

> *Irene:* I was dead for many years. They came and bound me. Tied my arms behind my back. . . . Then they lowered me into a tomb with iron bars over the opening. And with padded walls . . . so that nobody above ground could hear the shrieks from the grave. . . . But now, I'm half beginning to rise from the dead. (8: 257)

Just as the white lady returns as malign ghost and sometimes temptress, so is Irene a self-proclaimed revenant, always on the verge of completing the white lady legend by killing her betrayer. She tells Rubek that she had killed her second husband with the "fine, sharp dagger" she always keeps in bed with her (8: 256). It is her insanity that makes her not only white lady but wild woman, and Rubek tells her to put her "wild

ideas" behind her (8: 257). As it turns out, however, it will be as temptress, that other aspect of the wild woman, that she will effect the re-
union that is also a kind of revenge—eventually enacting the final
episode of the white lady story and leading Rubek to his death, gaining
his acquiescence to her plea that he go up the mountain with her:
"Come, come, Arnold! Oh, please come to me. . . !" (8: 260).

The white lady tradition, like that of the wild woman, however, is a
varied one. Strikingly, most patterns comprised by it show up in *When
We Dead Awaken:* (1) the revenant theme; (2) the redemption or deliverance theme, (3) the infanticide theme, (4) the shapeshifting animal
theme. That is, Ibsen's play resembles not only the summarized variant
above but other parts of the tradition not included in the summary.

Again, the white lady is commonly a victimized woman, "a returning
dead woman, who has met her untimely demise usually at the hand of
a murderer."[27] The revenant signifies a ghoulish form of resurrection
consistent with themes Ibsen had begun to develop in previous plays.
The artist as murderer, one who steals the soul of what McFarlane has
called a "human sacrifice" (8: 28), applies not only to Rubek but to
Solness, and Irene seems in many ways an extension of the beaten and
morbid Aline. For each couple, not only the women but their children—
real or symbolic—have been the price paid for the artist's endeavors.
As earlier argued, Brand's Agnes had similarly paid for her husband's
unworldly ambitions, and the resemblance among these women reinforces the argument that their men may also be linked, all of them one
version or another of the wild man or Rosmer Havmand turned ascetic.
Children had been from Ibsen's early plays the sacrificial victims of their
parent's or parents' incapacity to adapt to the demands of the ordinary
world. But when works of art become substitute children—in themselves
changelings—the infanticide motif becomes the extreme and brutal
expression of the artist's life as a substitute existence.

The revenant motif is not only linked to murder but to the central
theme of Ibsen's play, resurrection, and leads as well to the idea of
redemption. Irene has an alter ego in the mysterious nun who follows
her around, the latter also a figure described in the folklore surrounding
the white lady. Grimm describes this character as appearing sometimes
as "half-white, half-black," and suggests that one could find this characteristic in the "garb of a nun." He traces the origins of the white

women to Germanic antiquity: "Elfins and swan-wives appear in white shining garments; among goddesses may be named three in particular, of whom the 'white woman' and finally the 'nun' might be the outcome."[28] Irene, whose role as swan maiden will be discussed shortly, is inextricably bound to the nun who accompanies her. Before he recognizes her, Rubek knows her only as a lady behind whom was "another figure. And it was quite dark. Like a shadow" (8: 247). Irene calls the nun a witch: "Do you know, Arnold . . . she's changed herself into my shadow!" (8: 274). The nun may also be conceived of as a version of the loathly lady of folklore, often capable of transforming herself into her beautiful counterpart, sometimes needing—as does the white lady—the hero's kiss to be transformed.

In Germany, a specific legend connects the white lady to a nun. One Kunegonde of Orlamunde, a widow anxious to remarry, learns that the man she desires had stated that he would wed her were it not for the "four eyes" by which she was encumbered. Believing these to be a reference to her children, she pitilessly murders them by plunging a long needle into them (cf. Irene's long, pointed knife), only to learn that her would-be suitor meant her parents. In an act of repentance, Kunegonde walks on her knees between two cities and enters a convent. Many white lady stories are believed to be derived from this legend.[29] It is interesting to note that Irene tells Rubek how "for our child's sake . . . I have undertaken this long pilgrimage" (8: 277).

The infanticide theme, however, probably predates the story of Kunegonde. Grimm likens the Norwegian Huldra to the German goddess Holda because the former "takes unchristened infants with her."[30] According to Bernheimer wild women are "prone to eat human children," or to steal human children. Among the varieties of wild women is the lamia, "the child-devouring ghoul from Greek antiquity."[31] The prototype for these supernatural child-slayers is probably Lilith, a figure from Hebrew lore apparently borrowed by Norwegians for one explanation for the origins of the *huldre*-folk. She, Lilith, was believed to prey on other women's children because her own died as her punishment for abandoning Adam when he refused her equality with him in Eden. (In some accounts, her children live, the demons or nature spirits who inhabit the universe.) Thus Lilith is also the yearning mother, just as Irene who fantasizes about infanticide is surrounded in act 2 by a crowd of children who instinctively respond to the maternal in her. Like the white lady and Lilith, that is, she not only is the child-murderer but the mournful mother: "I should have borne children," she tells Rubek, "Many children. Real children. Not the kind that are preserved in tombs. That should have been my calling" (8: 280). A complex of themes can be found surrounding these various white ladies, strikingly connected by Grimm with the *huldre:* a destructive relationship between man and woman resulting in the latter's murderous impulses toward her own and other's children, culminating in remorse and a quest for redemption.

Ibsen's original title for *When We Dead Awaken* was *Resurrection Day.* Themes of resurrection and redemption are closely allied to the folk motifs surrounding the wild man and wild woman. About the hunt for the wild man, Bernheimer speculates that its meaning might inhere in a "fertility ritual bringing with it the promise and assurance of immortality after death," or the "removal of a personified obstacle to the return of spring, a winter demon [having] to be killed so his icy breath would not impede the sprouting of greenery."[32] Rebirth motifs are thus important in the folklore surrounding the wild man and the wild woman; they provide a narrative pattern in white-lady tales as well.

Indeed, one of the important narrative traditions attached to the white lady has to do with what was frequently her thwarted quest for deliverance from some enchantment she was suffering, forced to assume a loathly animal shape—snake, dragon, toad—in which she was trapped unless her deliverer could summon the courage to kiss her three times. In this analogue to stories in which a woman can similarly disenchant a man forced to take on a loathly form ("Frog Prince" tales, or the British ballad of "Tam Lin"), the male deliverer frequently fails. Stories of the white lady frequently tell of men unable to summon the courage for any or sometimes only the last of the kisses,[33] and thus the narratives join a larger group of folktales and ballads. Grimm explains the theme in terms of ancient goddesses, "Banned and longing for release":

> the pagan deities are represented as still beautiful, rich, powerful and benevolent, but as outcast and unblest, and only on the hardest terms can they be released from the doom pronounced upon them. The folktale still betrays a fellow feeling for the white woman's grief at the attempted deliverance being always interrupted and put off to some indefinitely distant date.[34]

The loathly form, then, is a shape the outcast is forced to assume as punishment, and/or is a projection outward of some internal drives or values that must be brought under control.

In *When We Dead Awaken*, the failure of the hero to disenchant the white lady with a kiss is worked out through the distance Rubek had maintained between himself and Irene when she was his model, thereby denying her the fulfillment that in the folklore is allied to salvation. As usual, however, Ibsen has given the folk motif his own twist. Whereas in the folktales and ballads, the failure of the man to bestow the needed kiss may speak to some terror (perhaps symbolic of the fear of woman studied by Wolfgang Lederer), Irene claims that although her naked beauty was capable of driving other men wild, he, Rubek, "kept better control" of himself (8: 255). Nonetheless, the *fier baiser*[35] theme is developed in Ibsen's play. Irene plays the loathly lady—again—in her wildness: her fearsomeness is revealed in her admission that he would have been endangered if he attempted to touch her: "I think I'd have killed you on the spot" (8: 258). Yet she reproaches him, "I offered myself wholly and completely to your gaze. . . . And never once did you touch me" (8: 258). She had given him her "young living soul" and was "left standing there, all empty within. Soul-less" (8: 262). She professes to hate "the artist who calmly and casually took a warm living body, a young human life, and ripped the soul out of it—because you needed it to make a work of art" (8: 276).

Whether or not white ladies originated in folklore (in Mexico they are part of folk belief, even if originally imported from Europe, as Kirtley hypothesizes), they frequently became attached to motifs common in animal bride and animal groom tales, particularly by way of the disenchantment and redemption theme. Again, this resurrection theme provides the symbolic focal point of Ibsen's play. Animal motifs pervade *When We Dead Awaken*. Not only is Ulfheim bear hunter and (as wild man) bear, but—to return to the beginning of this analysis—it is he who alludes to the story of "East of the Sun," in which a bear depends on the love of a young maiden to be released from his animal form. Ibsen has extended the folklore motif (or perhaps exploited its inherent symbolism) to include the beast's dwelling in the description of the loathly being in need of deliverance. When Ulfheim suggests taking Maja to his house, she rejects it not only as a potential castle, but him as the prince charming who supposedly inhabits it:

Maja: . . . That old pigsty there?
Ulfheim (laughs into his beard): That has housed more than one King's daughter in its day.
Maja: Was that where that awful man you told me about came to the King's daughter in the form of a bear? (8: 289)

Maja has begun with the less romantic version of the story that will follow, commencing, that is, with a variant closer to "East of the Sun, West of the Moon," in which the more than willing father sells his daughter to the bear. Moreover, the exchange with Ulfheim invokes echoes of animal groom tales in which more than one girl has been the object of the animal's pursuit (in some stories the father duplicitously sends the wrong daughter; or perhaps the Bluebeard or Isabel and the elf-knight theme have been combined with the more benign folktale). But Maja's more romantic version may also have to do with her attraction to the bear rather than the handsome gentleman who lurks beneath the animal skin—much the reverse of the animals that lurk beneath Rubek's portrait busts. Maja does not at this point want to tame the beast, for to do so would undermine the very object of her desire. When her husband tells her how he cleverly hides beneath the likenesses of his clients "simple-minded donkeys, . . . lop-eared low-browed dogs, . . . overfed heavy-jowled pigs," as well as "a few dull-eyed thick-skulled bullnecks thrown in," she responds indifferently, "All the dear old barnyard" (8: 244). Perhaps their dialogue involves Ibsen's own invitation to the reader to look for the animals hidden beneath the characters in this play, to distinguish the wild from the tame, and to recognize their thematic value for his play. For Maja, Rubek's animals are too timid. Her husband was himself emptied of the animal, and as Hilde sought her troll, so would Maja seek her beast in the wild man, Ulfheim.

Irene, as white lady, is also swan maiden,[36] wearing at the end of the play a swansdown hood as she leads Rubek to that remote world from which the swan maiden comes, enacting in this final scene those versions of the Type 400 tale in which the fairy wife allows her earthly husband to follow her to the otherworld. Once again, it is possible to see this final piece of the pattern as the equivalent to the man's death in white lady legends.

It is perhaps in light of these different kinds of resurrections and disenchantments (or failures at disenchantment) as well as Ibsen's use of the swan maiden tale that the playwright's use of the Lohengrin story may be understood. Among all of Ibsen's borrowings of figures from myth, saga, legend, this evocation of the swan knight tale remains one of the most elusive—perhaps the most elusive. But certain points might be made about the legend and its relationship to other folklore motifs in *When We Dead Awaken*. First, the Lohengrin story is about deliverance, and if Elsa is thought of as a type of white lady in need of such deliverance, then her rescuer has not failed her. To the contrary, he is another Sigurd conquering the enemies that stand between him and his woman. But Lohengrin also duplicates the bear–bear hunter dichotomy in Ulfheim. For the swan knight is both deliverer and an animal lover dependent on the obedience of his woman for the perpetuation of their relationship. The swan knight legend, that is, belongs to the same group of tales that includes "East of the Sun, West of the Moon," although *Lohengrin* forms a variant in which the heroine who breaks the taboo imposed upon her has no hope of winning back her lost spouse. But insofar as their separation is final, so too is his "redemption" thwarted.[37]

That the "swan maiden" Irene had played a game with Rubek in which they pretended that he was Lohengrin reveals both the mutual need that draws them together and the betrayals that will separate them. In any event, the white lady as wild woman cannot be delivered by another, if benign version, of the wild man. Each needs his or her complement from the ordinary world. Rubek understands the principle, although in his egotism he distorts it to fit his own needs, the artist's needs: "I need to live with somebody who can fulfil me . . . make me complete," to "be as one with me in everything I do" (8: 268). Recognizing that he must find his counterpart, he argues instead for an alter ego, what the English romantic poet Shelley would call his epipsyche. Thus Irene was never Elsa but rather an extension of himself, the swan that pulled the swan knight's boat. Not only because of his egotism, but because he does not understand the significance of the story he plays at, Rubek is a failed Lohengrin, unable to be the deliverer hero.

It will be recalled that to achieve her own redemption, Agnete had to leave her "wild man" beneath the sea to respond to the call of church bells. In his borrowing from the Danish ballads, Matthew Arnold extended the implications of these bells, and his Margaret returns to her world at Easter. The holiday is an appropriate one for what Agnete experiences as a personal resurrection. But her dilemma, as Jacobsen has shown, is not thereby resolved. Like the seal maiden she resembles, she lives a marginal existence, unable to commit herself to either of the worlds that pull at her. Similarly, the borderline existence of the wild man (and by analogy, the wild woman) creates a discomfort comparable only to that experienced by any human beings aware of their unique position on the chain of being. The "wild man holds . . . a curiously ambiguous and ill-defined position in God's creation, being neither quite man enough to command universal agreement as to his human identity, nor animal enough to be unanimously classified as such."[38] Embodying the conflict between nature and culture, the wild man

> enjoys none of the advantages of civilized sex, regularized social existence, or institutionalized grace. But, it must be stressed, neither does he . . . suffer any of the restraints imposed by membership in these institutions. He is desire incarnate, possessing the strength, wit, and cunning to give full expression to all his lusts.[39]

It is the ambiguity of the wild man's situation that creates his marginality—as it does that of the wild woman. Forced, ultimately, to choose their world, such marginal beings would seem constrained to decide which part of themselves to sacrifice: either way, completion is only possible when, having chosen one existence over another, they can somehow take as mate one from the opposite realm. (This would be the basis of my differing with Østerud concerning the natural alliance of Maja and Ulfheim.)

Wild Man and Wild Woman cannot be happily matched: each is incomplete, and neither can "disenchant" the other. Both are marginal, although seemingly closer to nature than to culture, and thus each must seek a deliverer from the "real" world. (It will be remembered that the *huldre* is a being conceived of as ruthless in her pursuit of a mortal husband, union with whom demands, however, that she pay the price exacted by culture, her surrender of her cow's tail as well as her repression of the force that allows her to manipulate iron.) The associations among fairy women, wild women, and Valkyries seem consistently to have invoked in Ibsen an effort to resolve the conflict between nature and culture. As early as *The Vikings at Helgeland*, Ibsen appears to have been working toward some solution of a seemingly insoluble dilemma. In killing the bear that guards Hjördis, Sigurd is in a sense conquering (i.e., delivering) Hjördis. But, symbolically and paradoxically, to slay Hjördis's animal watcher is also to kill within himself that which the beast represents. This perhaps explains what seems a gratuitous element introduced at the end of the play, that Sigurd is a Christian. Hjördis's situation is totally deadlocked. The man for whom Sigurd slew the bear is unable to subdue her; and had she married her true bear-slayer, he—as Christian—would be something other than what she sought, having already subdued himself.

Mutual conversion, that is, has its own penalties, as Dr. Wangel was only too ruefully aware. Again, the marginal being seems unable to tolerate its uncomfortable position, requiring some resolution to its dilemma. The wild man needs an ordinary woman, and wild woman seeks an ordinary man. But this is not satisfactory either. They will remain unsuited unless one takes on the attributes of the other, leaving the other once again incomplete. And so the unsatisfactorily vicious cycle continues to spiral—at least in Ibsen's plays. The human who disenchants the beast may come to miss the beast, as the beast itself experiences, in turn, difficulty in adapting to the world, experiencing the discontents of civilization. The irony of the situation is alluded to in an interchange between Ulfheim and Maja at that very point when each is ready to abandon the realm of the wild folk. Indeed, Ibsen may be hinting that Maja is a *huldre* seeking a place in the real world without relinquishing her cow's tail.

Maja had already taunted the bear hunter with being a faun, and he does not deny it:

> *Ulfheim:* Then we'll stand . . . free and unafraid. As we really are!
> *Maja* (laughs): You with your goat's legs, eh?
> *Ulfheim:* And you with your . . . Well, let it pass! (8: 291)

This exchange may well parallel that between Hedda and Judge Brack, when he cites her reluctance to have her legs spied beneath her clothing. Ulfheim, earlier responding to Maja's designation of him as faun, had asked her if she could "see [his] horns" (8: 289), implying that they were hidden. But just as the *huldre* must lose her cow's tail to achieve her ends, so must he relinquish those attributes of the wild man. What lends an added bite to Ibsen's conception of these themes is that Ulfheim may have to lose his goat's legs not for his own but for Maja's ends.

As possible *huldre*, then, Maja is not so much Irene's opposite as a version of her rival. Østerud's description of their mythological ancestresses, indeed, reveals them to be very close in kind. Maja's very name suggests the wild woman, not only because—to cite Østerud again—she is a Roman goddess who is frequently the erotic partner of Faunus, but because *maja* is also a Spanish word and invites some speculation concerning Ibsen's intentions. It will be remembered that Spain was a country that supplied one of the wonderland motifs of *The Master Builder* as Hilde demands that Solness carry her away to their earthly paradise. A connection between Hilde and Maja is reinforced in the description of Maja's dress in act 2 of *When We Dead Awaken:* "She is wearing a flat travelling bonnet, a *short skirt hitched halfway up her legs*" (8: 263; emphasis mine). A wildness in both women is suggested by a defiant revealing of what Hedda wished to keep hidden, her legs. Maja's name, her link to Hilde and thus a play in which Spain represents a wonderland, and her half-undressed state make it difficult not to think at least of the clothed and naked Majas of Goya's paintings: the properly attired bourgeois woman, and the erotically naked temptress. Ibsen's Maja, bored with her husband, finds her wildness aroused in her, and like Hilde Wangel, she seeks her troll, her equivalent. And like Hilde, Maja reproaches Rubek for not delivering the wonderland he had promised her: "You said you'd take me up with you to the top of a high mountain and show me all the glory of the world" (8: 244). She ruefully understands that she has perhaps been brought up the mountain, but still denied the vision she had hoped for.

And so Maja seeks her mountain man, her wild man, but, like Ingeborg in *Olaf Liljekrans*, she also wants her servants and her social life. That is, Maja cannot have Ulfheim unless she tames him sufficiently so that he fits into the world she insists on living in. But to tame Ulfheim, Maja must tame herself. So there is irony in her final song as she and her disenchanted mate descend to the real world. By analogy with the quadrangle of the early *Olaf Liljekrans*, Maja's song would appear to make her an Alfhild (part wild woman), ready to join the game of life. But in truth, she is only Ingeborg, unwilling to give up the comfort of life in the flatlands. Thus it is almost inevitable that she reverses Hilde's demand for a castle:

> *Ulfheim:* I can offer you a castle. . . .
> *Maja* (points to the hut): On the style of *that?*
> *Ulfheim:* It hasn't collapsed yet.
> *Maja:* And all the glory of the world perhaps?
> *Ulfheim:* A castle, I said. . . .
> *Maja:* No, thank you! I've had enough of castles. (8: 292)

But Maja's is a philistine reality. Ironically, however, she nonetheless fulfills her mythic role and disenchants the beast. But what this means in Ibsen's play is quite different from the outcome of "East of the Sun, West of the Moon": for what Maja has done is turned Ulfheim into Hemming. In Jacobsen's formulation, she has taken the folklore out of the character and rendered him once again ordinary. But the disillusionment she is bound to experience in her day-to-day life with her tamed beast is in the end no less devastating then the avalanche that buries Irene and Rubek.

As artist, Rubek too is part wild man, and the animals who lurk beneath his portrait sculpture are like the naked Maja beneath the properly clothed one. In themselves, animals suggest the natural creative energy upon which the artist must draw to create a masterpiece. But Rubek, like Solness, has sacrificed real art for worldly success. He has effectively denigrated the wild animal to produce the tame—a parody of the disenchantment motif. But this reduction of art's value, its insignificance within the framework of culture, is not the only tragedy of the nineteenth-century artist. Rather, it was that even were he to create his masterpiece, there was no place save a museum (in this play a sterile repository of work that "culture" deems great) in which it could be contained. Life and art are as irrevocably split as nature and culture appear to be. For it is striking that both women in his life, Irene and Maja, hate his work—one because she has been sacrificed to it, the other because she is indifferent to it.

Like four chess pieces moved about a board in different relationships to each other, the antithetical couples Ibsen frequently uses in his plays suggest that he was constantly seeking a resolution to some inevitable mismating. McFarlane speaks of how in the last three plays Ibsen explores "the complex interactions, the interdependencies, the shifts and dislocations, the endless conjoining and disjoining of multiple relationships" (8: 4). But this was true in the early plays as well: these multiple structures were built into the folklore on which Ibsen drew throughout his career as playwright. But late in that career, Ibsen developed more fully the implications of this folk material for the nineteenth-century writer. Rebecca returns with her wild man, doomed to the sea; Rubek similarly follows Irene to the ice palaces whose coldness suggests their remoteness from worldly concerns, for the artist a symbol of the purely aesthetic realm. In effect, Rubek as Rosmer has climbed to Hillelil's tower, and it proves only the counterpart to his own magic realm as Irene beckons him "through the mists . . . right to the very top of the tower, lit by the rising sun" (8: 297). Ellida and Dr. Wangel only appear to supply a more optimistic reconciliation with reality, for Wangel himself knows that whether he loses Ellida to the Stranger or retains her, he has lost his wild woman, and as a result, that wild part within him which needed her as she was would disappear altogether. Paradoxically, for the artist the supposedly happy ending may prove the worst debacle of all. For it may be the final irony of Ibsen's plays that the worst plight that could befall the artist-merman is not to be excluded by what Matthew Arnold depicted as the "shut" door of the "little grey church" in the "white-wall'd town"—but rather to be let in.

Notes

1. On bear lore, see Bø, "Bjørnen"; and Mysterud.
2. Jordan 57.
3. Norwegian edition 9: 203.
4. Østerud, "Når vi døde vågner på mytologisk bakgrunn."
5. Dorson, *Folklore Research* 1.
6. Bernheimer 1.
7. Ibid. 3.
8. Bernheimer makes distinctions with which I would not agree concerning folklore characters who inhabit the wild and those associated with the world of the dead. Folklorists do not always agree about the degree to which the supernatural otherworld is to be distinguished from mythical hells—if at all.
9. Ibid. 128.
10. Child 361.
11. Bernheimer 23.
12. Ibid. 59.
13. Hodne 113.

14. Pizzaro 266.
15. Bernheimer 52.
16. Hodne 219.
17. Bernheimer 24.
18. Grimm 3: 944. I have found no specific evidence that Ibsen read Grimm, but given the playwright's interest in folklore gathering as well as his living in Germany for long periods, and given the attention paid to the Grimm brothers in the nineteenth century, it would be surprising if Ibsen were not acquainted with his writing.
19. Norwegian edition 9: 203.
20. Grimm 3: 932.
21. Bernheimer 40.
22. Keightley 234.
23. Bernheimer 39.
24. Grimm 3: 962; Beck 300.
25. Bernheimer 33.
26. Kirtley 158–59; his notes provide a useful bibliography of white lady sources.
27. Beck 293.
28. Grimm 3: 968. For the figure of the nun, also see the study by Mary G. Wilson on a painting by Edvard Munch and its influence on Ibsen.
29. Kirtley 157–59. Again, Ibsen may have become acquainted with white lady legends while living in Germany.
30. Grimm 3: 4.
31. Bernheimer 35.
32. Ibid. 55–56.
33. I treat this motif in *La Belle Dame sans Merci* 35, 278 n. 27. Danish ballads usually involve successful disenchantments; Child, in contrast, usually provides unsuccessful ones (e.g., "Allison Gross").
34. Grimm 3: 968.
35. Translated as "fearful kiss," this folk motif is often studied in medieval literature and as one of Chaucer's sources in "The Wife of Bath's Tale."
36. Grimm links them: see quotation in my discussion above.
37. I would argue against Swahn's exclusion from his study of Cupid and Psyche of those tales that do not involve the quest for the lost husband. Swahn, of course, discourages interpretations of Tale Type 400 of the sort that it has received. But if Cupid and Psyche folktales and legends that resemble them are to be interpreted (and I think they should be), those versions that end in the breaking of a taboo, making reconciliation impossible, should be analyzed as part of the group. That Ibsen perceived the relationship of *Lohengrin* to "East of the Sun, West of the Moon" would suggest that some folkloristic distinctions might surprise him.
38. Bernheimer 6.
39. White, "The Forms of Wildness" 21.

PART IV

Per Schelde Jacobsen

APPENDIX A

I have translated Ibsen's essay as faithfully to the original as possible without attempting to make it more elegant or easy to read. The original Norwegian is heavy and a bit clumsy, with many "Germanic" constructions and sentences embedded in sentences ad infinitum. My choice has been to capture the spirit of the original as closely as possible.

"On the Folk Ballad and Its Significance for the Literary Arts," by Henrik Ibsen

About the art of former times the folk ballad is almost the only monument that down through the ages, with all their changes, has continued a fresh and vital existence in the consciousness of the people. Orally transmitted, the folk ballad has for centuries been passed from generation to generation. Certainly, it has, as might be expected under such circumstances, been distorted, yet its fundamental tenor has been preserved. The people itself who, here as elsewhere, has not been influenced directly by literary poetry, has in its ballad poetry found a satisfactory expression for its inner life. It has in this poetry an artistic form that lays its spiritual content bare for all to see. The folk ballad was not written by one single individual, it is the sum of the poetic powers of the people in its entirety, it is the fruit of its poetic gifts.

This objectivity, which is a basic trait of the folk ballad, and which thus is a measure of the desires of the people in this regard, is perhaps one of the reasons that the masses until now have been estranged from most of our national literary poetry. Artistic subjectivity has no meaning to the people. The people do not care about the poet—only about his work and only insofar as it recognizes in it something peculiar to itself. The people are not like those people today who visit the theatres, going there only when they have an opportunity to be titillated by a new situation or excited by a new intrigue. If something new is to appeal to the people it has to be, in a certain sense, at the same time old. It should not be *found* but found *anew*. It should not be perceived as unfamiliar and strange with regard to the conceptual world that is the inheritance of the people and wherein the national energy to a large extent rests. It should not be donated like a foreign kitchen utensil, the use of which is unknown and which does not fit with the familiar service. It should be transmitted as an old family heirloom that we have forgotten, but that we remember as soon as we lay eyes upon it because all manner of memories are attached to it—memories that, in a way, were resting within us and were fermenting in the dark—until the poet came and lent them words.

By this is not meant of course that the poet should not be concerned with the education of the people, on the contrary, but he must leave room for its need to be part of the creative process, he must take the raw material from the people itself, then he can forge from it what he desires. The need for poetic expression is a trait particular to the Germanic tribes. This is the reason that only certain forms of artistic expression are truly of the people in these tribes, whereas the other forms, through civilization, have become the property of the educated alone, and even today seem dead and strange to the people proper. It was different among the Greeks and the Romans, and it is still different among the Romance peoples; Italians, Spaniards, and Frenchmen. None of these nations owns a national poetry like our folk ballads. These southern peoples did not produce their own poetry, they had their poets and bards; the southerner let himself and his past be extolled through his artists; the northerner, on the other hand, extolled himself; the southerner let himself be sung about, the northerner was himself both poet and bard. Ariosto, Tasso, Cervantes, Calderón, etc. stood above their countrymen and, in a certain sense, also above their own time. The northern poetry, however, burst forth as a natural fruit of the overflow of the time—it became an expression of the richest and the best that the people carried inside—and herein lies the great difference. In those poets of the south it was as if the entire poetic gift of their nations were concentrated, and the people were, measured against them, but receptacles, audience, not collaborators. In this passive relationship to art in the southern peoples is also to be found, among other things, the reason that the plastic arts emerge as so important. The sculptor and the painter give almost a total, a manifest expression of the thought they had; they demand, to be understood, more so by contemplation than by actual creative effort on the part of their audience. This largely holds true also for the dramatic arts. None of these art forms have, then, really become national property with us. The Scandinavian is not quite at home within these confines where he cannot, according to his own desires, add on to what is already there. He does not want to see the products of his own imagination, his concepts and beliefs, rendered in finished form from the hand of someone else. All he demands is an outline of the drawing—he will finish the work according to his own demands. He does not, like the southerner, want the artist to point to his work and show where the core is, he wants to look for the core himself and not via any predetermined route, but through that radius which his individual expression of the national character points to as the shortest.

Since the people are the source of the ballads there also is a greater intensity in the act of appropriation. The ballads are to us not just a gift; they are not something that has come from outside. They are an edifice to which each one of us feels we have contributed a stone, insofar as we each one of us feel within us a spark of the spirit that gives soul to it all. The folk ballads are not, like the troubadour-poetry, an independent, limited part of the nationality to which it belongs. It is an important component in all the expressions of our popular life; it has colored them all by its peculiar light, has grown to be part of them all and has thus stayed fresh for a relatively longer period, whereas the troubadour-poetry withered and disappeared along with the conditions that gave rise to it.

There is, however, something strange about this as there is about all products of the people's spontaneous poetic desire; it seems as if oral transmission were the only form under which it could freely develop and live a constantly fresh life in the people. It seems as if the fossilized, written-down form is detrimental to its transmission, as if there in this form were erected a barrier against the adding on and rewriting that the folk ballad needs to be handed on from generation to generation, ever fresh and young. If the folk ballad becomes part of the world of books it will at the same time and in the same measure stop living in the mouth of the people and be put before us in a new light. In print the folk ballad becomes old and grey, yes, even old-fashioned, if you will. On the lips of the people it has nothing to do with the concept of age. The living word is for it what the apple of Ydun was to the "Aser" [Nordic gods], it not only nourishes, it renews and rejuvenates.

It is, however, lucky that these notations have been made, and it would be well if more were to be made while there still is time. The period of poetic productivity of the people may be said to be over, and if the summer is gone, a dried collection of herbs is better than nothing at all. With the increase of civilization, the national peculiarity, which is a precondition for a popular poetry, disappears. To be able to write poetry the people further needs a powerful, active and dramatic period, rich in events and outstanding personalities, rich in men in whom many or some of its [the people's] peculiarities have manifested themselves. For as the people writes from itself, it also basically writes *about* itself. It only sings when it in its bosom carries more than it knows what to do with, more than it needs to meet daily needs. All of these preconditions for a living popular poetry, the times and circumstances can no longer procure; and thus the folk ballad has to stop being the property of the people in the same sense as before. The necessity of and the need for a continuing production is no longer there and thus ballad writing is cut off by its roots. Individual products can be stored in memory, but even so they are like a bouquet of flowers in a glass of water: it can seem to stay fresh for a long time, but the life-thread has been cut, the ability to procreate is gone. The ballad was a fruit of the people's overflow, henceforth it can only be an object of knowledge.

But as with all things that carry a germ of spiritual life, so also with the folk ballad: it dies not in death. As popular poetry in the strict sense it may be said to have stopped existing, but it contains within it the preconditions for a new and higher existence. The time will come when the national literary poets will find in the ballads an inexhaustible gold-mine. Purified, taken back to its original purity and elevated through art it will set roots once more in the people. The beginning has already been made with the sagas. The genius of Oehlenschläger saw the necessity for a national foundation for the national literature and his entire opus is based on this principle. That Oehlenschläger chose the saga and not the folk ballad was a natural outcome of the conditions when he first emerged. The importance of the sagas was recognized; scholarship of no little merit had been produced on that topic, the work of Saxo [Grammaticus] was widespread in translations, and as a counterpiece to the taste that had to be opposed, the sagas were more fitted than the folk ballads. To be sure, these latter were also, via the editions of Anders Vedel and Peder Syv [early Danish ballad publishers] available to the public, from which Sandvig and Nyerup already in 1780 and 1784 had published a couple of pamphlets. But, firstly, a change in tastes as that beginning with Oehlenschläger was needed to make the importance of the ballads obvious and to elevate them to more than just "pleasant pastime," and, secondly, and especially, their particular poetic keynote became obvious to us only after the romantic school had developed in Germany and began to influence also the Scandinavian artistic consciousness—something that did not happen until after Oehlenschläger's emergence. It is true that he already in his early poetic production took material for a couple of his best dramatic works, *Axel and Valborg*, and *Hagbarth and Signe*, from the folk ballads, but it seems as if he did not take into account the special treatment the ballads demand as distinct from the sagas. Certainly those two tragedies are masterpieces, but they are also quite different from what the corresponding ballads give us. That those two works became what they are must (in addition, of course, to the genius of the poet) be ascribed to the fact that the folk ballad to a much higher degree than the saga is suitable for dramatic treatment. The saga is a big, cold, complete and confined epos, by its innermost character objective and foreign to the lyrical. And it is in this cold, epic light that the saga period stands before us; it is in this grand, plastic beauty its figures pass review before us. Such and not in any other way can and must the saga period be seen by us; for each period is mirrored in the eyes of posterity according to the nature of the remnants through which it is known.

If, now, the writer is to create a dramatic work from this epic material he must by necessity bring a foreign element into it: he must infuse it with poetry—as it is a well-known fact [to the followers of Heiberg] that the drama is a higher synthesis of the poetic and the epic. But by so doing he dislocates the original relationship of the material vis-à-vis the spectator. The period and the events that had represented themselves to us in an abstract, plastic beauty of form, the writer now renders as a painting with colors, with light and shade and we have trouble relating to the content that we had gotten used to observe through a totally different medium. Through dramatic treatment the saga period enters into a closer relationship with reality. But this is exactly what it should not do: the statue does not gain by being given natural skin, hair, and eye color.

The problems coming from the above have left not unnoticeable traces in the dramatic works of Oehlenschläger. It remains a question whether not much of this could have been avoided if the poet had chosen a different linguistic form that better matched the material. A *Hakon Earl* in prose should, thanks to Oehlenschläger's pen, presumably have been just as poetic as one in verse. It will, at least, one day be recognized that the iambic pentameter is in no way well fitted for the treatment of Scandinavian topics of the past; this meter is totally foreign to our national prosody and it is, certainly, only through a national *form* that a national *material* can be done justice.

The sagas are, as already mentioned, entirely epic; in the folk ballads, on the other hand, the poetic is present, to be sure in a different measure than in the drama, but it is present. The dramatic writer who takes his material from the ballads does not need to submit his material to the kinds of changes that are necessary when using the sagas. This fact is a considerable advantage; it allows the writer to more closely and intensely absorb into his work the image of the time and the events he is dealing with. He can thus (if, indeed, he is capable of it) put his heroes before the spectator in the form in which he already knows them from the folklore itself. To this can be added that the elasticity of the prosody of the ballads allows for many licenses that are of great importance to the dramatic dialogue. It is thus without doubt that this poetic source in the near or distant future will be used diligently by poets to come; poets who build on the foundation laid by Oehlenschläger. For that his work should be regarded as but a foundation for works to come is obvious enough and in this is in no way suggested a reduction of his laurels: it is a mark of all that is good and beautiful that it is not complete in itself, but holds within it the germ of a higher perfection. The national poetic literature in Scandinavia began with the sagas, now the turn has come to the folk ballads. Oehlenschläger's treatments of the sagas are the variations of a genius composer upon a popular theme. The dramatic treatment of the folk ballads can be the folk melody itself, artistically treated and executed.

Even though the writing down of the sagas falls within the Christian era in Scandinavia, their poetry is essentially heathen. For this reason they present themselves much more comfortably as material to be treated

Appendix A

in the ancient Greek style than in the style which is called the modern Christian. Undoubtedly this is also the reason that Oehlenschläger's *The Death of Baldur* is more successful than any other of his dramatic works. When I have used the expression "the sagas" above, I must point out that under that term I understand to be listed not only historic traditions, but also the mythic tales and songs. As opposed to these the folk ballad must be considered in all essentials Christian. It does, for sure, contain a heathen element but this is present in the ballads at a quite different and higher level than in the mythic tales and it is through this that the poetic child of Christianity, romanticism, shows its influence on the ballads. The worshipper of the Nordic gods who did not know the power of belief—where the intellect is shut off—construed a world in which the laws of common sense were totally abolished. In this world *all*—and thus also *nothing*—was supernatural, and thus he helped himself, thus he knew how to reconcile belief and sense. The romantic view of life, however, takes another course, it holds to be true Shakespeare's phrase: that "there are more things in heaven and earth than are dreamt in your philosophy." It gives common sense its due, but along with it, above and through it, is the mystery, the enigmatic, the inexplicable, the Christian, if you will. For Christianity is itself a mystery; it preaches belief in those things "that could not be understood." [Kierkegaard quotation? If so, it is from *Fear and Trembling*.] In this the mythic tale differs in its very tenor from the folk ballad. The tale relates to the ballad as the fable to the fairy tale. The fable knows nothing of the miraculous, the fairy tale is rooted in it.

It is this at once real and surreal world the folk ballad shows to us. In many of the ballads the heroes and events of Nordic mythology present themselves as the basic content, but then always in a newer form, always under a more or less Christian appearance. Thor and his fight against the *Thurser* [mythic giants], Sigurd Fafnersbane and his exploits, the "Tyrfinger" myth, etc., are all recognizable in their medieval guises and names. From being gods and mythic heroes the characters have descended to being giants and fierce knights. But it is certainly a mistake to try to locate the reason for this change in the religious feelings of the people or in some political or religious coercion from those in power. Probably the myths continued their life among the people long after the advent of Christianity and it is dubious whether the understanding of the new religion was clear and pure enough to kill the belief in the gods of the ancestors. On the contrary, the many apparent points of similarity between the old and new teachings make it likely that the two for a long time coexisted in and with each other and that the Christian teachings worked more by their civilizing force than as religion in the proper sense. Not even the priests, the preachers of the new religion, had clearly understood the crucial issue; not even they were able to detach themselves from the inherited traditions. Instead of preaching the imaginary existence of the Nordic gods, instead of preaching their eradication through the faith that replaced them, they represented them as evil, hostile powers, dangerous to the new teachings and their adherents. No wonder, then, that the old *Vætter* [a type of supernaturals] were tenacious—they had a good foothold. Holy Olav could as much as he wanted change them to stone until the Day of Judgment—they stayed alive in the consciousness and beliefs of the people, and they have remained so to our days.

It is thus not from the outside that the myths have received the imprint with which we find them in the folk ballads. Outer influence could perhaps have subdued, indeed destroyed, the spiritual inheritance from the ancestors, but no force is strong enough to change their shape to fit its own desires. The people does not let itself be *forced* to write and sing in riddles and murky metaphors, whose real meaning would soon have been lost. Thus the press can, for a time, be influenced by oppressive censorship, but a people can never be.

No, what lead the people onto the course suggested in the ballads was not an outside influence but a prompting from its own artistic sense of tact. It was not the religious but rather the esthetic feeling, and this latter is never faulty in the people as it may well be in an individual. The people did not dress its mythic heroes in medieval finery because through Christianity it had lost the true understanding of Nordic mythology—its spirit and teachings—but rather because the romantic view of art, which through Christianity entered the popular consciousness, did not allow any continued poetic production in the ancient heathen direction. Thus the material had to be changed, thus it had to be made supple as material for the new artistic form.

Now just a few words about the lyrical in the folk ballad. Besides being present in the epos of the ballad in the same strange way as metal is in metallic salts, it is also there in the chorus as a special element which is distinct from the rest of the makeup of the ballad. The chorus is to the folk ballad what the overture is to a piece of music; it sets the mood in which the ballad is to be received. But this lyricism is not of a personal nature, it is not rooted in the peculiarity of the poet. The poet is not through it conveying to the audience any of his own spiritual abundance, he only brings into conscious life that which lay dreaming and fermenting in the people itself. His poetic gift is mostly in a certain clairvoyance with regard to what the people wants to have said and in a certain ability to give what is to be said the form in which the people most easily recognizes it as its own.

From the above it should be clear that I in no way have entangled myself in a self-contradiction by having above mentioned the folk ballad as written by the people itself, and now distinguishing between the people and the poet. The case is here the same as with the sagas; they too owe their first notation to an individual, but this notation, the form in which it has reached us was in close harmony with the view of the people. The folk ballad, however, has during the long time it has lived in the mouths of the people never been written down and therefore it is not as easy as with the sagas to determine what is original and what later periods have added or removed. This, however, is sure, that the folk ballad even in its present shabby shape, gives witness to a pure and particular artistic form; that a correct meter through a somewhat changed word order usually can be established; and that, as Professor Petersen has shown in his literary history, the same is the case with the rhymes.

The strongest proof of a spiritual relatedness between the individual branches of the great Germanic tribe is to be found in the folk ballads. The Scandinavian, the German, the English and the Scottish ballads all have the same basic character although this character emerges in different shades among the different people dependent on local circumstances and the way the ballads were treated in individual countries. In Germany the ballads seem early to have become the property of a privileged class. Through wandering troubadours they became a literary poetry that was only heard in the castles, whereas the unfree estates, commoners and farmers in silence fought to make ends meet, suppressed and subdued and, as it seems, robbed of the ability to sing. Changing times worked, however, a return to an earlier state, and it seems that the ballads descended once more from the castles to the humble dwellings of the people, it seems that the people absorbed once more its paternal inheritance, that ballad writing became once more a true national property—but then only at second hand. Roughly the same was probably the case in Denmark and Sweden, but not in Norway. Norwegians have never, as have their brethren peoples, known sharply defined castes; with us farmer and knight were never opposites but only different spheres of activity. This, in connection with the isolated position of the country, the people's comparatively limited contact with the rest of the world, and, finally, the natural surroundings that suit so well the spirit of Scandinavian mythology and the influence of this latter on the ethos of the people, are all reasons that easily explain why the Norwegian folk ballad has kept its ancient flavor while, for instance, the Danish and Swedish ballads suffer from having had—for many different reasons—their original character in language and tone erased and thus seem to belong in a comparatively much more recent period.

But just as the *basic tenor* of the Germanic ballads in the essentials is the same, so also the *material* is taken from very closely related conceptual universes. In the Scandinavian ballads we find, among other things, the heroes of the German national epos *Niebelungenlied* in more or less recognizable form, and also from *Rolandslied*, etc. The expeditions of knights, the abduction of women and its revenge, fighting against dragons and *lindorme* [see above in Chapter 3], fantastic travels to the home of the trolls, which is thought to be far to the north, war with trolls and dwarves who live in mountains and hills and possess huge treasures— these and many more seem to have been favorite subjects of popular writing. Strictly historical characters and events are treated much more sparingly, and, in the Norwegian ballads, hardly at all.

In the form in which we have them before us today, the folk ballads have, as already remarked upon, a strongly medieval flavor and it seems that our scholars of times past for this reason agree in assuming that the ballads were composed between the end of the saga period and the Reformation. There seems also to be some agreement as to how to explain the diffusion of identical, or at least similar, ballads among all the Germanic peoples. This shall have happened through translations from one langauge to the other, but none of these explanations seem to me to have any inner probability.

If the folk ballads *over time* had taken over from the saga literature they should also have taken over their *spirit* and *content*, but greater opposites cannot be imagined. The saga literature as it was in its last period, i.e., just before the growth of the folk ballads, had, as is well known, sunk into a state of empty formalism, a shell without a kernel. For the writer of scaldic poetry it was not a question of having a poetic gift but only of having a roomy container for storing inherited, traditional turns of phrase, expressions and images. His poetry was only a ghost from the past, the empty holster of a spirit that had long since departed, that no one believed in anymore and no one understood. In France a similar situation is found with the imitated antique tragedies; but as it went in France, so it went with the scaldic poetry here: to a certain extent both art forms were disseminated within particular layers of the population. But neither one was capable of setting roots deeply and fervently in the people, of gaining access to its way of thinking. The scaldic poetry was an artifice, the folk ballad a powerful, living fruit; the scaldic poetry was *fabricated* the folk ballad was *composed*.

Of the petrified formulas that constituted the conditio sine qua non of the scaldic poetry there is nothing left in the folk ballads. To be sure, they too have their recurrent expressions and images, but anyone can with the greatest ease convince himself that these do not originate in the scaldic poetry. In the scaldic poetry there is no trace of the lyrical. Events treated therein are not really meant to have an impact via the way they are expressed—that was mostly and greatly always the same—what the scald had in mind seems to have been solely to take care to, in the prescribed way, neatly and according to rule, carry forth his praise of this or that hero, whom the poem was to glorify and whose generosity, by the by, often was what particularly inspired him.

And the fresh, vibrant bloom of the folk ballad is to have grown from this withered tree! Never! At least that would have been an instance of a reproductive act without precedent. From an insipid literary poetic tradition could never spring a vigorous, popular literature. It is much more reasonable to assume that the two art forms existed together in prehistoric times. Then the period when the folk ballad changed, its transition to the romantic form in which we know it, would coincide with the last days of the scaldic poetry, i.e., with the period which commonly (and certainly erroneously) is taken to be the first childhood of the ballad poetry. For it can hardly be doubted that the folk ballads have not reached us in their original form. Much internal evidence from the ballads themselves suggests a close relationship to the Edda poems, which presumably are not available in the original form either. The intense relationship between the ballads and the mythic renders it not unlikely that the entire mythology was once, long ago, way back in antiquity, commonly expressed among the people in ancient lays that, so to speak, constitute a skeleton for our folk ballads. When Christianity was introduced and when writing made the transition to the romantic art form and, finally, as the tenor of the times changed, these ancient lays have undergone some or many changes until at last, as "folk ballads," they stop at the time of the Reformation, after which time they do not seem to have been influenced much. This seems to be the case even with the so-called historical ballads; even these are perhaps only rewritings of older mythic lays. All of this is, especially in the Norwegian ballads, clear enough, but any particular proof would take us too far. I shall therefore restrict myself to referring to Landstad's collection where what has been suggested here will certainly be confirmed.

If we then assume that the ballad poetry, in changing forms, has lived in the mouths of the people from prehistoric times, this assumption is in no way weakened because the sagas do not mention such a tradition. The scaldic poetry, which developed along with the older (heathen) ballads, was a literary tradition, the ballads, on the other hand, were a popular tradition. So, that the saga writer took notice only of the former tradition and ignored the latter should not surprise any of those of us who know that the same type of thing has been repeated almost in our own time. Further, it should not be forgotten that because of their, at that time no doubt, totally heathen content, the ballads could not in propriety have pleased the educated and learned saga writer even if the people found pleasure in them. That also the *sagas* in their *poetry*, were heathen escaped, of course, the notice of the writers, since the *topic* had nothing to do with the glorification of the Nordic gods or mythic heroes—as in the folk ballads. Using the scaldic poetry as sources could offend his conscience even less although these too were heathen both in form and in content. The difference was that while the mythology in the folk ballads continued to live a fresh and spirited life, the scaldic poetry had even then, as noted above, sunk into being just formulas and empty phrases that certainly could not give offense to anybody. This is especially true of the younger scaldic lays. As for the older and better ones, they—as products of art—had in the world at the time a certain reputation that can be presumed to have outweighed other considerations.

Appendix A

If it is true that the folk ballads are to be regarded only as a newer form of the ancient mythic writings, we do not have to turn to assumptions about translations to explain the diffusion of the same ballads among all the Germanic tribes. That explanation seems tortured and is, on many points, far from enough to throw light on the phenomenon. First of all there is little internal probability in claiming that a poetic form that, as was the case with the folk ballads, had been able to set roots in the innermost life of the people, should not have germinated there but, on the contrary, have been grafted on after having been plucked from foreign soil. During which period of the past should, for example, the Norwegians have felt the desire to glorify events that had nothing to do with their own lives or praise men who were known to them only from hostile clashes, through Danish, Swedish or German ballads? And how would even the existence of such ballads have come to the notice of our forebears? The intercourse between the nations in those days was certainly not such that the exchange of spiritual treasures would be furthered by it. Add to this that what have been called translations can not really be so denominated. Rather, we are dealing with parallel, mutually independent treatments of the same material. Apart from the absurdity in claiming that a rich, oral literature finds its source of life in the people's own creative urge—it has to be considered that the historic ballads practically have not been translated at all, and where they have, it is more than dubious whether the translations were ever popular. In Norway, where the written notations are firsthand, there are no such translated ballads; they are to be found, to be sure, in the Danish and Swedish collections, but as these collections are created largely on the basis of old written ballad books [mentioned in chapter 3 above], this does not constitute certain proof that those translations should, to any appreciable degree, have been widespread among the people. They more likely derive, as also the language seems to suggest, from a relatively recent period when the ballad tradition in Denmark and Sweden was in the hands of the nobility and thus had stopped being nourished by and in the people. The so-called Eufemia ballads that were translated from the French around year 1300 here in Norway do not in any way constitute a weakening of this claim. For one thing, these poems do not belong with the folk ballads proper, and for another, it can be said with certainty that they have never been popular among the people, but at most in that part of the nobility who adopted Queen Eufemia's idea of introducing the troubadour poetry in Scandinavia. This was, however, an idea that was killed at birth.

For all of these reasons it seems to me unreasonable to assume that the ballads spread as a result of translations. Besides, a more probable explanation is close at hand. For if it is admitted that the first origin of the folk ballads can be found in mythic times, then there is no reason not to go back as far as possible, namely to a time that *precedes* the entry of the Germanic tribes into Europe, that is, to a time when the great tribe was a whole.

The worldview within which the folk ballad operates seems to suggest strongly such a point of view. On the vast plains at the foot of the Ural mountains, the Germanic tribe—then already powerful and warlike—romped. The Chudic peoples who inhabited the mountains stretching north all the way to the White Sea, and whose brethren, the Finns, were roving the Scandinavian plateaus, were the natural enemies of the Germanic tribe. They were fought and subdued and thus had to defend themselves as best they could through cunning. This tribe is, then, the original dwarfs of the folk ballad who live in the mountains and who knew how to forge weapons and artful jewelry from metal. Dwarfs are described as small, cunning and malevolent. This all fits well to describe the Chuds and the Finns, and their homes among the Ural mountains must have given them the reputation for being people who, through secret arts, knew how to extract riches from the stones. This was an art our forefathers did not know but in which the Chudic tribe, according to the testimony of history, was well versed. It is not possible to imagine that a notion of hidden treasures in the mountains could have emerged after the migration to Scandinavia, for here the mountains must have seemed to be the abodes of barren poverty. Nor do the travels to the home of the trolls, mentioned in the ballads, fit a people who themselves live in Scandinavia. Firstly, the original inhabitants (the trolls and dwarfs of the ballads) remained living on the plateaus of Norway for a long time; there could thus be no idea of seeking them in the *north*, but that is what is constantly said in the ballads. Secondly, a hardy people, accustomed to our climate and circumstances, could not have been so overwhelmed by the hardships and dangers involved in traveling to the far north—but this is the case in the folk ballads. This home of the trolls far to the north is described as icy cold and dominated by constant darkness. But as it seems that the actually undertaken travels from southern Norway to the north only took place in the summer, it can be seen that the above description could not be taken from personal experience but only from vague stories that are in part misinterpreted, embellished and rewritten. It is true, for sure, that it is mentioned that the travels to "Trollbotten" were undertaken on water, but one might here imagine equally well a trip up the great rivers of Russia as a sea voyage along the Norwegian coast. On the whole it has to be remembered that our ballads give evidence to all manner of adjustments that clearly are the work of more recent times. Nor could the travels to Bjarmeland [Norwegian region] could have given rise to these notions; for in other places is mentioned a huge "iron forest" that has to be passed. This makes one think of the pine forests of northern Russia, which were unknown to our ancestors during their sojourn in the east, but which they had to pass through on their migration north and which could be seen by them as iron forests. It is also strange that the very fauna of the folk ballads suggests more southern regions. With the exception of wolves, none of the wild animals of Scandinavia are, to my knowledge, mentioned in the ballads, whereas, on the other hand, the *Lindorm* ["Lindenworm," mentioned above in Chapter 3] or the Dragon [although this is considered to be derived from the mythic *Midgardsorm* [a mythic creature that enveloped the entire world of the Nordic mythological universe] make one think of the huge remains of the animals of primeval times that are still found in eastern Russia and that, it seems, were much more frequent in those times and which could well have awakened in our ancestors the first notion of those fantastic monsters which, through the folk ballads, have become so popular. It is further worth noticing that even though the Germanic tribes, after their migration to Scandinavia, developed into a *seafaring* people, whose heroic deeds were mostly performed at sea, the folk ballads have nothing whatsoever to say on the topic of *sea-battles* or on travel or deed *aboard ships*, but so much the more on battle on land and that as good as always *on horseback*, despite the fact that this method of fighting was foreign to our forebears. This too suggests the period in the east: that the localities there did not allow for warfare at sea is obvious, while it is most probable that the Germanic people then were an equestrian people just as is still the case with the tribes who inhabit those areas today.

It is not valid here to object that the universe of the ballads is only a fictionary one that thus has nothing to do with reality. The literature of the people is at the same time its philosophy; it is the way in which the people expresses its intuition that there is something of the spirit in the concrete. This literature finds, like all artistic products, its point of departure in real life, in history, in things experienced, and in surrounding nature. So it can, for instance, not be doubted that the myths of Thor and his fight against the *Jøtuner* [mythic giants] is symbolic of the proto-Germanic power and its hostile skirmishes with foreign opponents. Overall a people must always to a certain extent have a history before it can make a religion for itself, and this has been the case also with our forefathers. The fictional glorification of the exploits of the original ancestors, their attempt to forge their way north, etc., have given material to mythic accounts and these, in turn, are the foundation for the folk ballads.

The testimony to the origin of the Germanic ballads during the sojourn of the tribe in the east, here but touched upon, could be extended ad infinitum, were it my intention to supply exhaustive proof in this matter. This, however, is not the case, all I have intended to do is register a protest against the claim that the folk ballads were spread via translations, a claim that would deny our aboriginal ownership to a great and important part of the spiritual inheritance from our forefathers. For the so-called Icelandic saga literature attempts have been made to take the authorship away from us, but scientists have in that matter demonstrated our rights. Should not the same be worth our while with regard to the folk ballads? Should not one of our scholars of ancient times feel urged to say the final word in this matter? If there in these lines be an incitement to do so, I feel they have more than served their purpose, whether the final judgment be for or against the point of view I have dared put forward in the preceding.

APPENDIX B

Henrik Ibsen: Diary, June 24–July 17, 1862

Henrik Ibsen was always interested in folklore. When he was still a student he went on a two-month field trip to Hardanger and other areas in northern Norway to collect folk ballads and folklore in general. He had received, by a royal resolution of May 24, 1862, a stipend to perform this "fieldwork." After he came back, Ibsen contracted to publish his findings in book form, but the book never materialized. What is translated in edited form below are Ibsen's diaries from the trip. The principle behind my editing has been to give a flavor of the folklore notes and to select individual stories and tales that seem to have found their way into Ibsen's later writings in one form or another.

Diary, June 24–July 17, 1862

Tuesday, beautiful weather at departure. In the morning we heard thunder[?]. Nervous. Drank a cup of Rostock. Amongst others in my compartment was also a Swede—I strongly suspect he is the poet Snoilsky. Heavy rain in Hamar. In Næs a girl came aboard about whom the captain told that when she last winter from [J . . .] the day before went to L. a young man jumped into the fjord after her. Long boring trip to Lillehammer. In the sun Mj: is wonderful—drab in rain. Bitterly cold. Fredrik's hotel is a good one—nice woman, he is somewhat of a "Tværpeis"[?]. 25th, left Lillehammer around ten thirty—met a man from Lom who told, with some pride, of his trip to Lillehammer to go on bread and water for illegally burning coals. To Moshus (Aronsveen) at 21/4—good place—no woman—went fishing. In the meantime a Swede changed horses, suspect him too of being Snoilsky, for the man onboard "Dronningen," I think, I falsely accused.

Took the boat up over Losna to Losnæs . . . the man who rowed the boat could tell about the sea monster which in former times had appeared there. . . . Of myths and fairy tales there is not much left in Gudbrands-dalen. The kid who took us from Skiftet above Listad to Vik told us some things but all was known and had already been written down except for one story about one Ole Kløvstuga who, some years ago, disappeared in the mountains and was later found lying unconscious in the stalls of a summer cowshed without having any idea how he had gotten there and what had happened to him. He was for a long time "låk" ["strange?"], because of the experience and still hasn't totally recovered. On Thursday, the 3d of July, I traveled from Svee by boat across the Vaagevand to Gardmo; still rainy. The people on the ferry told of a little girl at the farm of Nørnæss in Lom (or Vaage), the farm right on the water, to whom it had happened several times that she disappeared for long periods without anybody being able to make her explain anything with the exception that she once said that she had been with many children and had played with them. One time she was watching her mother scrubbing wood cups and then she said: "I know a place where the cups are whiter than here at mother's." She has not yet been confirmed. There is also a man there by the name of Erik, once he was in the mountains looking for horses, then the mountain wall opened like a gate and he saw enormous amounts of wonderful things and it was as if it would lure and pull him in, but he started running as fast as he could, and when he at long last dared look back, the mountain had closed and there was nothing to see. Then there was Sivert Sannæs who was a "reader" and of very strong faith, but who emphatically denied the existence of supernatural beings. Once he drove up through the Vaa-geruste and from there into the Jøn valley on an errand (looking for horses) and came to a rock called "Svartskulen" and there he suddenly saw a beautiful girl and a flock of tabby cows and big black beautiful horses, but as he was wondering who that might be, it was all gone as if it had sunk into the ground. Since that time he has believed in both huldrer and all manner of other things, but he gave up the reading, and this, his former companions in the faith believed, as the ferry man said with a sarcastic smile, was due to the power of the devil. I got some lies to boot, e.g., one about a sea monster which was said to have been caught in the Lysterfjord and to have been bought by an Englishman for 300 Daler—but that money he got back, for he knew of the place inside the monster where it hides all the precious things—both gold and silver—that it swallows—and those he took after having opened it.

Tales told by Peder Fylling

On P.(eder) Str.(øm) The aforementioned Mr. P.S. had, while he was studying to become a minister at the Wittenberg School, made the acquaintance of the King who, while still a Prince, was also at the school. The acquaintance was made on the following occasion. It was at the time recognized custom at the Wittenberg School that to become a minister five years were needed. After this some students, chosen by lot, had to continue studying the Black Book. For this study another five years were needed. The lot, it is said, fell that year on, among others, the Prince. He could, however, not continue his studies at the school because affairs of government demanded his presence at home. Mr. Peder, who already before had acquired a taste for those things, took it upon him to stay in the Prince's stead. He performed his studies well, so well, in fact, that it is said that there was only one who was a match for him. It was also obvious here, in his work as minister of Borgund, that Peder had learned more than his catechism. It was told that the people then were stubborn and would not listen to the minister's admonitions and would not go to church or take communion or pay the church taxes. Thus the minister was forced to use artful tricks that seemed to them to be supernatural and were believed to derive from some higher being. This was often more effective than ordinary punishment. It is thus told, among many other stories, that there was a farmer at the Molær farm on the Sul Island who was not on good terms with the minister. The reason was that he did not want to pay the minister his due. The minister rebuked him but in vain. The man was plain and simple stubborn. At last Peder talked the man into coming over to Borgund one day—on the pretext that he then would be forgiven the entire debt. The man came. The minister had watched out for him and went out to the eastern corner of his garden. The man came from the sea dressed in leather, for it was ugly weather. The minister asked him to stop a while, the man stood for a moment and suddenly it seemed to him as if he was sinking into the very road. He threw his arms open and screamed and begged of God and the minister to help him. The minister went up to the man who seemed to have sunk so low that only his head and arms were above ground. The minister asked him if he would not now ask forgiveness and act like a man of Christian faith and give the minister his due, etc. To the minister's question, the man answered yes. The minister gave him his hand and suddenly the sinking stopped. It is also told that the same Mr. P. had a servant who was a true church-shirker—he went neither to church nor to communion. The rebukes of the minister had no effect on him either. At last the min. convinced him to go with him to Borgund church. It was already dark, but the weather was quiet and mild. They both went to the southern side of the chorus. He asked the servant to put his ear to the wall and asked him if he heard anything. The boy answered no. The minister said, hold my left hand and put your ear to the wall again. The minister asked if he heard anything, yes, the boy answered, now I hear all kinds of things. The minister asks, what do you hear? I hear pleasant singing voices, I can hardly tell the Minister what I hear, but it all seems so pleasant and beautiful. Yes, says the minister, now you have heard the home of the saved. All who go to church and communion and who live according to the words of the minister, go there after death. Now follow me to the other side of the church, here he asked the servant to put his ear to the wall,—the servant says no. Then take my hand again, said the minister. The boy did this. The minister asked if still he didn't hear anything. Yes, says the boy. What do you hear? I hear a pitiful lament and crying and sorrow. The minister said, now you have listened to the home of those who are condemned. That's where all those have gone who will not believe in what the minister says and will not go to church and communion. This is said to have had such an effect on the servant that he from that day on lived a Christian life. In Søndmør there was at the same time the belief that when a man was taken by insanity or what is called madness he must be possessed by the devil. Of course people then came to the minister that he should exorcize the evil spirit. Now it was the good fortune of the people at Søndmør that Mr. Peder in Borgund well knew how to get rid of the devil. He is to have often—on many occasions—have shown the Devil the door. People have often, so it is said, seen and heard that what we here say is true. Once a woman at the Dyrø farm in Skøi became half mad. The minister had to be sent for. He came and performed, in the presence of people, some operations with the woman—wherein they consisted the tale has forgotten—but this much is remembered that it was seen how the Devil through the power of the minister was driven out of the woman. It looked like a black crow that jumped right from the woman's bed, via the dining table and shot out through a hole in the wall that the minister had made there before. And the woman was well after that.—In Søndmør as well as in other places, existed until that time the belief that there among the peasant women were a not unsubstantial group who were sorceresses or witches. Mr. Peder was also energetic in finding out which women in his parish were said to be witches. He admonished them to stop their magic. This had but little effect: no one wanted to of their own will admit that they were witches. Neighbor wives often accused them of being the cause that their cattle dies, that they get no milk from the cow, that they can't get butter from the milk. This all, they say, is caused by this or that sorceress. The lore has it that Mr. Peder had a way in which he commonly ascertained who was a witch and who not. So, when he went about his parish and food was set before him, he would never touch the food until he had called the mistress of the house to stand by the table. He then asked her if it were true what the neighbors' wives said of her that she was a witch. The woman of course denied this. But the minister rejoinders that they soon shall see. Stand still, he says to the woman, now I'm going to take my knife and stick it in the butter—which mostly has been set out especially for the minister—if blood runs from the cut when I take the knife out, then the one who has churned the butter is indeed a witch. Mr. Peder knew how to arrange it so that blood only ran when the woman was one of those profligate women who always wish evil on their neighbors. So, it is told that Mr. Peder came to make such a visit at a farm in Vatnesogn. The woman set food out for the minister. The entire family, man and wife and children had a bad reputation and it was held that the wife in particular was the worst of witches. Before the minister began to eat, he asked the woman, who always wore a red sweater (which in Sundmøre is a sign of a witch), if she was a witch as people said. She absolutely denied this. Well, the minister said, we shall see, come here old girl, if blood runs from your butter when I stick my knife in it then your denials are to no avail. Mr. Peder now took the knife and stuck it into the butter and all those present saw the truth, for blood ran not only from the butter but all over the table cloth. No one could say any more. The minister castigated them with a lecture and the wife in particular left the room.

On the Thingfjord farm in Vatne parish there is a hillock formed by the river and nature. Its name is Harpehøj ["Harp Hill"] and it is situated north of the river which is east of the buildings of the farm. The name Harpehougen it is said to have gotten because from time immemorial an extraordinary singing music harp-sound has been heard. It is almost like the beautiful string music the huldre-people perform. It is said that people often talked to Mr. Peder about this but he always dismissed them, saying that it was just nonsense and without any reality. Once he came to Thingfjord himself. Those present suggested Mr. Peder a trip to the hillock to observe the sound for himself. The minister was curious and went. When he and the others came to the hill the sound was heard even more solemnly than ever before. The minister was embarrassed since he had before refused to believe what the people told him. He was quite surprised and went up on the hill and addressed the inhabitants of the hill. He asked them to stop the music and noise which was apt to confuse people. Immediately as the minister had left the hill, bypassers heard from it a terrible mourning, wailing and screaming, all damning the minister who had upset them in their happiness. Now they had to go to Mr. Peder again and tell him what had happened. He arrived, after having been told, at the place, shall himself have heard a pitiful mourning from inside the hill, held a speech in which he blessed the hill and its inhabitants. Since that people have not heard anything and the inhabitants of the hill must have moved to another place.—The Black Book is, according to the lore, a book which is not found in everybody's house and if someone takes it in the hand and of carelessness reads the passage in it that sets Old Erik [the Devil], as it's called, free, then it is most dangerous. He comes forever and asks the reader to give him work to do. If the reader is not imaginative enough to give him real work then it becomes dangerous. Again you have to turn to the minister. It is thus told that a young woman at the farm by the name Strømmen in Skaue parish, one Sunday afternoon when the people were at church, took the Black Book and was so unlucky as to come upon the passage mentioned.

Erik came and demanded work but she was clever enough and said that he must go down to the river and empty it. Erik went and began to scoop the water out, as it turned out, he was strong. The lake was about as high as the mountains. In the afternoon, Peder Strøm came from the church, when he came to the river he realized what was going on. No one could get through the river as long as Erik kept on working. The minister grasped what had happened, he told the ferry-man to row as close to Erik as possible, then he stood up in the boat and commanded Erik to stop and all of a sudden both Erik and his lake were gone.

Margrethe Stud, also called M. Hanken (after a small island in Bgd parish) lived as a widow on Hankø in Borgund parish. She had been married to (see Søndmøre description, part two). Lore has it that she in her day was an authoritative, proud, industrious and extremely wealthy woman. Each time she came to Borgund church everybody noticed her and everybody had great respect for her. She was always, so it is said, wearing as a cape a large shaggy black skin of a mare. She wore it so that she had the horse's behind over her shoulders and let the mane drag on the ground. There was always much to-do when she was seen entering the church with the long mane dragging after her. The lore has it that those who had the good fortune of being close to her, such as her office clerks, etc., suddenly became wealthy men—for she was not particular with them.

Among the sons of Paul Olsen the lore mentions one Mads Abelset who lived at Sliningen in Borgund parish and one Jørgen. This Jørgen is said to have had a great desire when he was young to travel abroad. But his parents were against it. His mother, it is told, came out with a trough filled with silver coins—money from the find at Sundsbakken. These coins she would give him if he would give up his travel prospects. Jørgen now declared that he would stay at home. But no sooner had he received the money than he left anyway, taking with him both that and much more money. He lost it all, was gone seven years and came back almost naked.

About Saint Olaf's pig. Olaf the Holy is said, on his last trip through Sundmøre, while he was camped in Stenvaagen inside the borders of A[a]lesund, that he convinced a man at the Godø farm to take care of his pig until further notice. The reason for this was that he had realized that he would have to go through the mountains to get to the area he was aiming for and that it would be difficult for him to transport a pig. The man took the pig, it is said. It did fine after the king left, but after rumor went abroad that he had fallen at St:, the pig thrived less each day. He was so destroyed by disease that he finally became stone. He is still found as a rock on the Godø.

It is likely that *Olaf The Holy* once must have travelled through the area called Strømmene into the Ellingsfjord, past the Vemø through Strømmen into the Skaue Bay, from where he dragged his ships via land to Folden in Højemsvik. In support of this contention is a popular myth in which it is told that when a sudden big seastorm arises it is customary to say: this is heavy, I cannot think that it looked worse when Saint Olaf sailed up Straumane.

Olaf the Holy once came, en route from Trondheim, and wanted to enter the Romsdalsfjord. When he came as far south as Hustadviken between Bud and Fagrevik evening fell so that he with his ship had to anchor for the night. At midnight, the King was suddenly attacked by enemies and had to cut the cables and flee. Afterwards the cables drifted to the shore at the Guldberg where they can still be found, although they have become rock. The anchors themselves are still left untouched on the bottom of the sea where the buoys still are visible although they too have turned into three little skerries. Once O.t.H came sailing through the Romsdalsfjord, when he came to Oxen in Rødven parish the east wind became so hard that he had to go ashore there although it was not a good place to land and the ship turned back. The King intended to cross the mountain to the Rødven Valley. He had to leave his suitcase with his travel money on the beach where it still is, turned to stone. (There was snow on the mountains where the King went, he had expected this and had brought a pair of skis.) He came to a steep mountain, called Horungen in the parish of Grytten. At first he found it to be hazardous to ski down this mountain, but at last he dared attempt it and arrived on the beach in good shape. There is still a deep furrow in the mountain after that ski run.—King O.t.H. once landed on Bolsø in the Romsdalsfjord, here he decided to build a church where ordinary people could worship the Lord and convinced the people to pay for a builder. This rumor spread wide and far. A female troll who lived on the mountain of Skaala, one mile from Bolsø in Vedø parish, also heard of his plans to build a church. She did not like the idea of having a church near her abode and decided to stop the building. She did not act with any haste, though, but waited until the church was almost finished, then, one day, she took her bow, put an arrow on the string and shot. The arrow did not manage to reach the church but hit the ground a ways from the cemetery where it remained and where it can still be seen. It looks like a menhir, it is twelve to fourteen feet high.

Stories are told about a minister who long ago is said to have been the minister of Nordfjord parish. He had studied theology at the Wittenberg School for five years, which is what it takes to learn the ordinary things ministers have to know, and then five more years to study the Black Book. He learned this latter thoroughly. When he was through, Old Eric came and wanted to get him, calling him by name, "Jon." Master Jon was prepared for this and had to this end placed bowie knives at all four corners of the room. The knives answered Eric in Jon's name. Master Jon had to get out of the room hidden in the chimney which he was climbing up through. Eric discovered this and stepped up into the fireplace to hold on to the minister's legs. He got a hold of one of Jon's boots and kept the heel while Jon got away without hindrance. Now Jon came home and became minister at Indviken. He had not been there long before his wife raised a suspicion that he had unlawful intercourse with a farm girl. He was accused of this, a case was made against him in court, and he was found guilty. The verdict was that he was to be executed. He asked the king's pardon and the king pardoned him, but at the insistent bidding of the minister's wife, the king had to promise to go through with the execution. While the case was being tried, Jon had to give a service at the church of Opstroyen. En route to get there, by the so-called Risøjer, a great snake came hurrying across the road and hissed loudly. The minister noticed it and said, "You know it too?" The minister rode the entire day, his guard asked whether the snake said anything, the minister answered: "It says that this will be the last time I ride here." This turned out to be true, for before long the verdict was spoken and executed. He was beheaded at a place near the Indviken rectory which is still called the Mordskog ["Murder Wood"]. Before Jon was executed he said: "If I am innocent, my blood will run up the hill"—and so it did. At this place grass can still not grow. After this his wife was struck by disease, withered away, and became so small that people while she was sick carried her to church in a small basket until she died.

Long ago there was at the farm of Hole in Breheim's parish in the *præstegjæld*, [another word for] "parish" of Gloppen in Nordfjord a woman by the name of Kari Hole who was the worst witch. She was accused of her evil deeds and found guilty and admitted that she had committed evil acts against both people and cattle. She was burned alive on a small islet, called the Haneholm in Gloppen's parish. What she repented most when she was prosecuted was that she had stolen the milk of a cow in Nedstryen parish, although neither she personally nor anyone in a natural form for her had performed the milking, or, for that matter, been to Ned-Stryen. Yet the cow was so ill-treated that it died. Kari Hole declared that the milk of this cow gave her the very best butter. She had promised that when she came to the stake she would make it so that in the future no plant should be able to grow or thrive as far as she could see. It was therefore seen to be necessary to blindfold her.

A story is told of a boy by the name of Lars [first written as Jakob] Thormodsen Medlid[?] in Skaue parish. He once came, on his way home from the *sæter*, to a place where [there was] a round hill, formed by nature, which had already been said to be the home of Haug-dwellers or *Huldre*-people. Into this hill, which is close to the road, Jakob was taken, as he said, before he knew what was happening. He seemed to have entered a roomy stable where a collation was arranged almost the way it was customary in the villages. He thought it strange that there were so few people to be seen; just one girl was in the house the entire time he was there. She was dressed in blue [as *huldres* often are], had hair as beautiful as silk which hang down over her back. She put the food before him, but he was so confused because of his unacquaintedness with the place that he was not able to eat of the food. The aforementioned girl comforted him and encouraged him in all kinds of ways to be of good courage. She assured him nothing would happen to him if he would just take it easy. But however much she caressed him, he seemed as dumb as he was befuddled. She brought out a beautiful violin [*fedle*] and asked him to take it and play on it. She told him that she knows you are good at playing the violin and how come you cannot play on this

322

violin? He seemed to be aware of and able to remember that he many times had played his violin at home but it was incomprehensible to him how much distaste he now had against taking it, not to mention playing on it. He seemed to see many strange things, such as wood carvings and such, and all he could think of was if he might not be able to make similar things. He himself did not know how long he was in the hill, and he was not aware either how he had gotten either in or out again. He was gone from his home for forty-eight hours. He had been wearing a little hat when he left home, this had returned to the farm after the boy had been gone twenty-four hours. When his parents found that hat and the body did not return they suspected that something had happened and realized he must have been taken into the hill. Therefore they rang the bells and used other means employed in such cases to convince the supernaturals to let those in their power go. Whether this worked or not, Jakob came home to the farm in good shape. Yet he was somewhat disoriented and taciturn. When people asked him where he had been he said little or nothing in reply. Seldom could he be made to work around the farm after that time. All he wanted to do was try to copy everything he had seen in the hill. Thus he made violins like the ones he had seen in the hill and that were different from what had been seen before. He made a doll that, especially dressed, is said to have looked like the girl he saw in the hill. He now lived at home in a small loft where could always be found partially finished or unfinished models of objects no one but he knew what were to be. After that time he also became more proficient at playing the violin. He did not like much to remain in the area and therefore he went to Bergen and since then no one has heard news of him.

At the very bottom of Storfjord is a farm called Korsbrække. On the same plot stood once the old church of the Sunelv, but an avalanche came and destroyed the church down to the foundation. To avoid such things a new church was built in a different place, out by Hellesylt. Nothing is left of the old church building, but of the church wall most is left standing, just as signs of graves or barrows can be shown inside the walls. There stands also a tall, narrow stone without any inscription. Lore has it that this stone was erected as a memory of the first preachers of Christianity who landed at this spot. Others say that the Norwegian crusaders met in this place to plan new crusades. Both stories conclude that this is how the farm of Korsbrække got its name [*Kors*- means "cross"].—At almost the same place is a strange indentation in the mountain. It averages a depth of a foot with sides that are polished quite smooth. How deep it is cannot be determined as it is almost filled with gravel. The common people tell that Saint Olaf churned butter here and still call the indentation Saint Olaf's churn, but they do not know the precise circumstances under which this is to have happened.

As for the story of the black death in Stordal[?] and of Jens Jamt and Saint Olaf's boatride in the Storfjord more information has to be obtained from Ludv. Daae.—

Bibliography

Aagaard, Anton. *Syv berømte folkeviser: En approksimation til urformen.* København: G. E. C. Gads Forlag. 1964.

Aarestrup, Emil. "Flodpigens Vise." In *Samlede Skrifter.* Vol. 1. København: : H. Koppels Forlag. 1922–25: 134–36.

Aarne, Antti, and Stith Thompson. *The Types of the Folktale.* Helsinki: Suomalainen Tiedeakatemia. 1961.

Aarnes, Sigurd Aa. "Ibsens Hedda Gabler som sosial type og tragisk helt." *Edda* 81. 1981: 303–09.

Aarseth, Asbjørn. "*Når vi døde vågner*—myte og symbolikk. In Noreng 1969.

Aasen, Ivar. *Norske Minnestykke.* Kristiania: Norsk Folkeminnelag. 1923.

Andersen, Flemming G., et al. *The Ballad as Narrative.* Odense: Odense University Press. 1982.

Andersen, Hans Christian. "*Agnete og Havmanden.*" In *Samlede Skrifter.* Vol. 11. København. 1876–80.

———. "Den lille Havfrue." In *Samlede Skrifter.* Vol. 13. København. 1876–80: 65–89.

Andersen, Lise P. "The Development of the Genres: The Danish Ballad." *Sumlen* 1981: 25–35.

Anderson, Marilyn A. "Norse Trolls and Ghosts in Ibsen." *Journal of Popular Culture* 5. 1971: 349–67.

Ardener, Edwin. "The Problem of Women." In Shirley Ardener, ed., *Perceiving Women.* London: Malaby Press. 1975: 1–29.

Arnason, Jón. *Islandske folkesagn of æventyr.* Trans. Carl Andersen. 2 vols. København. 1864.

Arndal, Vibeke. *Heksen i håret: Kvindelig personlighedsudvikling i eventyr.* København: Lindhardt og Ringhof. 1985.

Arnold, Matthew. *Poems.* ed. Kenneth and Miriam Allott. 2d ed. New York: Longman. 1979.

Asbjørnsen, P. Chr. *Norske Huldreeventyr og Sagn.* 2 vols. Oslo. 1832.

Bibliography

————. *Norske Folkeeventyr.* Stockholm. 1845–47.

————, and Jørgen Moe. *Norske Folkeeventyr.* 2d ed. Kristiania. 1852.

Bachofen, Johannes Jakob. *Das Mutterrecht.* Frankfurt: Suhrkamp Verlag. 1975.

Baggesen, Jens. *Trylleharpen. Originall Syngespil.* Kjøbenhavn. 1816.

————. "Agnete fra Holmegaard." In *Danske Værker.* Vol. 2. Kjøbenhavn. 1845–47: 88–97.

Bang, Jørgen. *Synspukter på folkevisen.* København: Munksgaard. 1972.

Barranger, M. S. "Ibsen's 'Strange Story' in *The Master Builder:* A Variation in Technique." *Modern Drama* 15. 1972: 175–84.

————. "Ibsen's Endgame: A Reconsideration of *When We Dead Awaken.*" *Modern Drama* 17. 1974: 289–300.

————. "*The Lady from the Sea.*" *Modern Drama* 21. 1978: 393–403.

Barthes, Roland. "Le mythe aujourd'hui." *Mythologies.* Paris: Éditions du Seuil. 1965.

————. *S/Z.* Paris: Éditions du Seuil. 1970.

Bascomb, William R. "Folklore and Anthropology." In Alan Dundes, ed., *The Study of Folklore.* Englewood Cliffs, N.J.: Prentice-Hall. 1965: 25–35.

Beck, Jane. "The White Lady of Great Britain and Ireland." *Folklore* 81. 1970: 292–306.

Bekker-Nielsen, Hans, et al. *Oral Tradition. Literary Tradition: A Symposium.* Odense: Odense University Press. 1976.

Benwell, Gwen, and Arthur Waugh. *Sea Enchantress: The Tale of the Mermaid and Her Kind.* New York: Citadel Press. 1965.

Berg, Anne Margrethe, Lis Frost, and Anne Olsen, eds. *Kvindfolk: En danmarkshistorie fra 1600 til 1980.* København: Gyldendal. 1984.

Bergstøl, Tove. *Atterljon: Folkeminne fraa Smaadalana kring Lindesnes.* Oslo: Norsk Folkeminnelag. 1930.

Bernheimer, Richard. *Wild Men in the Middle Ages: A Study in Art, Sentiment, and Demonology.* Cambridge: Harvard University Press. 1952.

Bettelheim, Bruno. *The Uses of Enchantment: The Meaning and Importance of Fairy Tales.* New York: Alfred A. Knopf. 1976.

Beyer, Edward. "*When We Dead Awaken.*" *Ibsenårbok* 1970–71: 26–42.

————. "Henrik Ibsens *Rosmersholm.*" in *Noreng* 1979.

Bjørndal, Martin. *Segn og tru: Folkeminne frå Møre.* Oslo: Norsk Folkeminnelag. 1949.

Blind, Karl. "Scottish, Shetlandic, and Germanic Water-Tales." *Contemporary Review* 40. 1881: 399–423.

————. "New Finds in Shetlandic and Welsh Folk-Lore." *Gentleman's Magazine* 252. 1882: 353–57, 469–86.

Bø, Olav. *Heilag-Olav i norsk folketradisjon.* Oslo: Det Norske Samlaget. 1955.

————. "Bjørnen i folkediktning og folketru." *Norveg* 23. 1970: 80–99.

Boggs, Ralph. "A Comparative Survey of the Folktales of Ten Peoples." *Folklore Fellows Communications.* 33. Helsinki: 1930.

Borrow, George. *The Songs of Scandinavia and Other Poems and Ballads.* Vol. 7 of *The Works of George Borrow.* London: Constable. 1923.

Bibliography

Brandes, Georg. *Main Currents in Nineteenth-Century Literature.* New York: Boni and Liveright. 1923.

Brown, Lorraine A. "Swan and Mermaid: *Love's Comedy* and *The Lady from the Sea.*" *Scandinavian Studies* 47. 1975: 352–63.

Buchanan, Robert. *Ballad Stories of the Affections: From the Scandinavian.* New York. 1869.

Buchholtz, Peter, and Iørn Piø. "En publikumsorienteret visegenre. Lidt om markeds-, gade- og skillingsvisesang." *Folk og Kultur* 1980: 19–30.

Bugge, Kristian. *Folkeminne-optegnelser: Et utvalg.* Oslo: Norsk Folkeminnelag. 1934.

Bugge, Sophus. *Norske Eventyr og Sagn.* Kristiania: Gyldendalske Boghandel Nordisk Forlag. 1909.

Burmeister, Tereza, et al. *Heks, hore, ærbar kone: Kvindeliv på landet i 1800-tallet.* København: Chr. Erichsens Forlag. 1987.

Burston, Daniel. "The Cognitive and Dynamic Unconscious: A Critical and Historical Perspective." *Contemporary Psychoanalysis* 22, 1984: 133–57.

Bynum, David E. *The Damon in the Wood: A Study of Oral Narrative Patterns.* Cambridge, Mass.: Harvard University Press. 1978.

Carlsson, Anni. "Aspekte des Mythos im neunzehnten Jahrhundert: Andersen und Ibsen." *Wirkendes Wort* 1. 1959: 36–43.

———. "Andersenspuren in Ibsens '*Vildanden.*'" *Ibsenårbok* 1977: 46–51.

Carlsson, Marvin. "Patterns of Structure in Ibsen's *Rosmersholm.*" *Modern Drama* 17. 1974: 277–88.

Carmichael, Alexander. *Carmina Gadelica.* Vol. 4. Edinburgh: Oliver and Boyd. 1941.

Child, Francis J. *The English and Scottish Popular Ballads.* Vol. 1. New York: Dover Publications. 1965.

Christiansen, Reidar T. *Norske Folkeminne: En veiledning for samlere og interesserte.* Oslo: Norsk Folkeminnelag. 1925.

———. *Eentyr og Sagn.* Oslo: Olaf Norlis Forlag. 1946.

———. *The Migratory Legends.* Helsinki: Suomalainen Tiedeakatemia. 1958.

———. *Studies in Irish and Scandinavian Folktales.* Copenhagen: Rosenkilde and Bagger 1959.

———, ed. *Folktales of Norway.* Trans. Pat Shaw Iversen. Chicago: University of Chicago Press. 1964. Reprinted by permission.

———. "Some Notes on the Fairies and the Fairy Faith." *Bealoides* 39–41. 1971–73: 95–111.

Coffin, Tristram P. *British Traditional Ballads in North America.* Rev. ed. Philadelphia: American Folklore Society. 1963.

Craigie, William A. *Scandinavian Folk-Lore.* 1896; rpt. Detroit: Singing Tree Press. 1970.

Croker, Thomas L. *Fairy Legends of the South of Ireland.* London. 1862.

Crow, Brian. "Romantic Ambivalence in *The Master Builder.*" *Studies in Romanticism* 20. 1981: 203–23.

Bibliography

Cucchiari, Salvatore. "The Gender Revolution and the Transition from Bisexual Horde to Patrilocal Band: The Origins of Gender Hierarchy." In Sherry B. Ortner and Harriet Whitehead, eds., *Sexual Meanings: The Cultural Construction of Gender and Sexuality*. Cambridge: Cambridge University Press. 1981: 31–80.

Curtin, Jeremiah. *Tales of the Fairies and of the Ghost World: Collected from the Oral Tradition*. Boston: Little, Brown. 1895.

Danmarks gamle Folkeviser. Vols. 1–12. København. 1853–1976.

De Lauretis, Teresa. *Alice Doesn't: Feminism, Semiotics, Cinema*. Bloomington: Indiana University Press. 1984.

Dorson, Richard. "Print and American Folk Tales." *Western Folklore* 4. 1945: 207–15.

———. *Folklore Research Around the World*. Bloomington: Indiana University Press. 1961.

Downs, Brian W. *Ibsen: The Intellectual Background*. Cambridge: Cambridge University Press. 1948.

Dudley, Edward, and Maximillian E. Novak, eds. *The Wild Man Within: An Image in Western Thought from the Renaissance to Romanticism*. Pittsburgh: University of Pittsburgh Press. 1972.

Duerr, Hans Peter. *Traumzeit: Über die Grenze zwischen Wildniss und Zivilisation*. Frankfurt a.M.: Suhrkamp Verlag. 1985.

Dundes, Alan. *Interpreting Folklore*. Bloomington: Indiana University Press. 1980.

Durbach, Errol. "The Apotheosis of Hedda Gabler." *Scandinavian Studies* 43. 1971: 143–59.

———. "The Geschwister-Komplex: Romantic Attitudes to Brother-Sister Incest in Ibsen, Byron and Emily Brontë." *Mosaic* 12. 1979: 61–73.

———. *Ibsen, the Romantic: Analogues of Paradise in the Later Plays*. Athens: University of Georgia Press. 1982.

Eco, Umberto. *A Theory of Semiotics*. Bloomington: Indiana University Press. 1976.

Egan, Michael. *Ibsen: The Critical Heritage*. London: Routledge and Kegan Paul. 1972.

Eliade, Mircea. "Some Observations on European Witchcraft." *History of Religions* 14. 1974: 149–72.

Elliot, Kari. "The Master Builder: Houses Built on Rock and Sand." *Edda* 79. 1979: 365–73.

Ericsson, Kjersti. "Lille Eyolf og familiemyten." *Samtiden* 81. 1972: 8–19.

Evans-Wentz, Walter Y. *The Fairy Faith in Celtic Countries*. N. pl.: University Books. 1966.

Faguet, E. "The Symbolic Drama." *International Quarterly* 8. 1904: 329–41.

Falnes, Oscar J. *National Romanticism in Norway*. New York: Columbia University Press. 1933.

Fass [Leavy], Barbara. *La Belle Dame sans Merci and the Aesthetics of Romanticism*. Detroit: Wayne State University Press. 1974.

Bibliography

Faye, Andreas. *Norske Folkesagn.* Oslo: Norsk Folkeminnelags Skrifter. 1948.

Feilberg, H. F. *Bjærgtagen: Studie over en Gruppe Træk fra nordisk Alfetro.* København: Det Schønbergske Forlag. 1910.

Fergusson, Francis. *"The Lady from the Sea." Ibsenårbok.* 1965: 51–59.

Fischer, J. L. "The Sociopsychological Analysis of Folktales." *Current Anthropology* 4. 1963: 235–95.

Fjelde, Rolf, ed. *Ibsen: A Collection of Essays.* Englewood Cliffs, N.J.: Prentice-Hall. 1965.

————. *"The Lady from the Sea:* Ibsen's Positive World-View in a Topographic Figure." *Modern Drama* 21. 1978: 379–92.

————. Introd. to *Peer Gynt.* By Henrik Ibsen. Minneapolis: University of Minnesota Press. 1980.

Fleck, Eva Maria. *"John Gabriel Borkman* and the Miner at Falun." *Scandinavian Studies* 51. 1979: 442–59.

Foucault, Michel. "Sexuality and Solitude." In Marshall Blonsky, ed., *On Signs.* Baltimore: Johns Hopkins University Press. 1985: 365–72.

Fraenkl, Pavel. *"Fruen fra havet* og Nordisk Folketro." *Ibsenårbok* 1954: 7–18.

————. "Tabu og drama i *'Når vi døde vågner':* Et bidrag til den etnologiske dramaturgi." *Nordisk Tidsskrift* 43. 1967: 340–63.

Frandsen, Ernst. *Folkevisen: Studier i Middelalderens poetiske litteratur.* Aarhus: Universitetsforlaget. 1935.

————. "Middelalderlig lyrik." *Danske Studier* 1954: 75–108.

Freud, Sigmund. *Totem and Taboo.* New York: W. W. Norton. 1950.

————. "Some Character-Types Met With in Psychoanalytic Work." *Psychological Works.* Trans. and ed. James Strachey. Vol. 14. London: Hogarth Press. 1957.

————. *Introductory Lectures on Psychoanalysis.* Trans. James Strachey. New York and London: W. W. Norton. 1965.

Gamle Norske Folkeviser. Kristiania. 1858.

Geijer, E. Gustav, and A. August Afzelius. *Svenska Folk-wisor.* 3 vols. Stockholm. 1814–16.

Goitein, P. Lionel. *"The Lady from the Sea." Psychoanalytic Review* 14. 1927: 375–419.

Gravier, Maurice. "Le drame d'Ibsen et la ballade magique." *Ibsenårbok* 1970–71: 140–60.

————. "La conversion de Rebekka." *Ibsenårbok* 1978: 120–37.

Gray, Ronald. *Ibsen: A Dissenting View.* London: Cambridge University Press. 1977.

Gregory, Lady Isabel. *The Kilkarton Wonder Book.* Dublin: Maunsel. 1910.

Greimas, A. J. *Sémantique structurale.* Paris: Larousse. 1966.

Griffith, Lee Ellen. *The Tale of the Mermaid.* Philadelphia: Philadelphia Maritime Museum. 1986.

Grimm, Jakob. *Teutonic Mythology.* Trans. James S. Stallybrass. 4 vols. New York: Dover Press. 1966.

Bibliography

Gruenberg, Sidonie. "*The Lady from the Sea.*" *Psyche* 9. 1929: 84–92.

Grundtvig, Svend Hersleb. *Engelske og Skotske Folkeviser.* København. 1842–43.

———. *Prøve på en ny Udgave af danmarks gamle Folkeviser. Med Aftryk af "Planen" samt nogle Tillægsbemærkninger.* København. 1847.

———. *Danmarks gamle Folkeviser.* Vols. 1–5. København. 1853–90.

Grüner-Nielsen, Håkon. "Den danske Folkevise." *Nordisk Kultur* 9. 1931: 14–37.

Gustafson, Alrik. "Some Notes on Theme, Character, and Symbol in *Rosmersholm.*" *Tulane Drama Review* 1. 1955–56: 3–13.

———, ed. *Rosmersholm.* By Henrik Ibsen. Trans. Ann Jellico. San Francisco: Chandler Publishing. 1961.

Haakonsen, Daniel. "Henrik Ibsens *Brand.*" *Edda* 41. 1941: 350–78.

———, ed. "Ibsens private bibliotek og trekk ved hans lesning." *Ibsenårbok* 1985–86.

Haalund, Arild. *Seks studier i Ibsen.* Oslo: Gyldendal Norsk Forlag. 1965.

Hannay, Alastair. *Kierkegaard.* London: Routledge and Kegan Paul. 1982.

Hansen, Adolf, trans. *Oversatte Engelske Digte: Shelley, Tennyson, Arnold, Swinburne.* Kjøbenhavn. 1884.

Hansen, Børge. *Folkeeventyr: Struktur og genre.* København: Munksgaard. 1971.

Hansen, Ib Fischer, Jens Anker Jørgensen, et al., eds. *Litteraturhåndbogen.* København: Gyldendal. 1985.

Harding, M. Esther. *Woman's Mysteries: Ancient and Modern: A Psychological Interpretation of the Feminine Principle as Portrayed in Myth, Story, and Dreams.* New York: G. P. Putnam's Sons. 1935.

Hardwick, Elizabeth. *Seduction and Betrayal: Women and Literature.* New York: Random House. 1974.

Harris, Marvin. *Cultural Materialism: The Struggle for a Science of Culture.* New York: Vintage Books. 1980.

Harrits, Flemming. "Folkeviseproblemer—med særlig henblik på Villy Sørensen." *Kritik* 10. 1969: 286–311.

Hartland, Edwin Sidney. *The Science of Fairy Tales.* London. 1891.

Hartmann, Ellen. "*Fruen fra havet:* En psykologisk analyse." *Samtiden* 77. 1968: 320–30.

Hauch, Johannes Carsten. "Den Bjergtagne." In *Samlede Digte.* Vol. 1. Kjøbenhavn. 1891: 291–93.

———. "Bjergpigen." In *Samlede Digte.* Vol. 2. Kjøbenhavn. 1891: 89–95.

Haugan, Jørgen. *Henrik Ibsens metode: Den indre utvikling gjennom Ibsens dramatikk.* København: Gyldendal. 1977.

———. *Diktersfinxen: En studie i Ibsen og Ibsenforskning.* Oslo: Gyldendal Norsk Forlag. 1982.

Heiberg, Hans. *Ibsen: A Portrait of the Artist.* Trans. John Tate. Coral Gables, Fla.: University of Miami Press, 1969.

Bibliography

Heiberg, Johan Ludvig. *Elverhøj*. In *Johan Ludvig Heibergs Poetiske Skrifter*. Vol. 3. Kiøbenhavn. 1862.

———. *En sjæl efter døden*. In *Johan Ludvig Heibergs Poetiske Skrifter*. Vol. 10. Kiøbenhavn. 1864.

Heller, Otto. *Henrik Ibsen: Plays and Problems*. Boston: Houghton Mifflin. 1912.

Henningsen, Gustav. "'Kvinderne udefra': Feer, hekse og fattigdom på Sicilien i det 16. og 17. arhundrede." *Norveg* 23. 1980: 60–67.

Henriksen, Aage. "Freud og digterne: Omkring Gunnar Brandells Freudstudie." *Kritik* 1. 1967: 123–34.

Hildeman, Karl-Ivar. *Tilbaka till balladen: Uppsatser och essäer*. Stockholm: Svenskt Förlag. 1985.

Hodne, Ornulf. *The Types of the Norwegian Folktale*. Oslo: Oslo University Press. 1984.

Hoffmann, E. T. A. *Die Serapions-Brüder*. München: Winkler-Verlag. 1963.

———. "The Mines at Falun." In *Selected Writings of E. T. A. Hoffmann*. Trans. Leonard J. Kent and Elizabeth C. Knight. Chicago: University of Chicago Press. 1969.

Holbek, Bengt. "The Ballad and the Folk." *Arv* 29:30. 1973–74: 5–25.

———. "Nordic Research in Popular Prose Narrative." In Lauri Honko, ed., *Trends in Nordic Tradition Research*. Helsinki: Suomalainen Kirjallisuuden Seura. 1983: 145–62.

———. *The Interpretation of Fairy Tales*. Helsinki: Suomalainen Tiedeakatemia. 1987.

Holmström, Helge. *Studier över svanjungfrumotivet*. Malmö: Förlag Maiander. 1919.

Holtan, Orley I. *Mythic Patterns in Ibsen's Last Plays*. Minneapolis: University of Minnesota Press. 1970.

Holzapfel, Otto. *Det balladeske: Fortællemåden i den ældre episke folkevise*. Odense: Laboratorium for Folkesproglig Middelalderlitteratur. 1980.

Horton, Robin. "Ritual Man in Africa." *Africa* 34. 1964: 85–104.

Huld, Ruth. *Østfjorminne*. Oslo: Norsk Folkeminnelag. 1937.

Hull, Myra E. "The Merman Lover in Ballad and Song." *Studies in English* (University of Kansas Humanistic Studies) 6. 1940: 65–80.

Hulme, F. E. *Natural History Lore and Legend*. London. 1895.

Hurt, James. *Catiline's Dream: An Essay on Ibsen's Plays*. Urbana: University of Illinois Press. 1972.

Hustvedt, Sigurd B. *Ballad Criticism in Scandinavia and Great Britain During the Eighteenth Century*. New York: American-Scandinavian Foundation. 1916.

———. *Ballad Books and Ballad Men*. Cambridge: Harvard University Press. 1930.

Ibsen, Henrik. *Samlede Verker*. Ed. Francis Bull, Halvdan Koht, and Didrik Arup Seip. Hundretårsutgaven. 21 vols. Oslo: Gyldendal. 1928–57.

———. *The Oxford Ibsen*. Ed. James W. McFarlane. Trans. McFarlane et al. 8 vols. Oxford: Oxford University Press. 1970–77.

Bibliography

Illich, Ivan. *Genus.* Frankfurt am Main: Rowohlt Verlag. 1982.

Jacobs, Barry. "Ibsen's *Little Eyolf.*" *Modern Drama* 27. 1984: 605–15.

Jacobsen, Per Schelde. "Johan Ludvig Heiberg." *Critical Survey of Drama: Foreign Language Series.* Pasadena, Calif.: Salem Press. 1986a: 897–909.

―――. "Arnold, Andersen, Kierkegaard and the Demonic." Unpublished paper given at the Victorian Society of the Department of English, CUNY Graduate Center. New York. 1986b.

Johansen, Jørgen Dines. "Om sammenhængen mellem religiøs, sexuel og social tematik i Ibsens *Bygmester Solness.*" *Tekst/Historie.* 1980: 39–60.

Johnston, Brian. "The Dialectic of *Rosmersholm.*" *Drama Survey* 6. 1967: 181–220.

―――. *The Ibsen Cycle: The Design of the Plays from* Pillars of Society *to* When We Dead Awaken. Boston: Twayne. 1975.

―――. "The Demons of *John Gabriel Borkman.*" *Comparative Drama* 33. 1979: 17–32.

―――. *To the Third Empire: Ibsen's Early Drama.* Minneapolis: University of Minnesota Press. 1980.

Jonsson, Bengt R., et al. *The Types of the Scandinavian Medieval Ballad: A Descriptive Catalog.* Stockholm: Svenskt Visarkiv. 1978.

Jordan, James William. "Wereanimals in Europe and Africa." *Ethnos* 42. 1977: 53–68.

Jørgensen, Aage. "Some Recent Contributions to Danish Ballad Research." *Folklore* 87. 1976: 186–91.

Jørgensen, Jens Anker. *Jorden og slægten: En indføring i folkevisens univers.* København: Tabula/Fremad. 1976.

Jørgensen, Peter A. "The Two-Troll Variant of the Bear's Son Folktale in *Hálfdanar saga Brönufóstra* and *Gríms saga Ioðikinna.*" *Arv* 31. 1975: 35–43.

Jorgenson, Theodore. *History of Norwegian Literature.* New York: Macmillan. 1933.

―――. *Henrik Ibsen: Life and Drama.* Northfield, Minn.: St. Olaf Norwegian Institute. 1945.

Kapferer, Bruce. *A Celebration of Demons.* Bloomington: Indiana University Press. 1983.

Keightley, Thomas. *The Fairy Mythology: Illustrations of the Romance and Superstition of Various Countries.* 1850; rpt. New York: AMS Press. 1968.

Kierkegaard, Søren. *Frygt og Bæven.* In *Samlede Værker.* Vol. 5. København: Gyldendal. 1982.

Kirtley, Basil F. "'La Llorona' and Related Themes." *Western Folklore* 19. 1960: 155–68.

Kittang, Atle. "Realisme som mytekritik i *Bygmester Solness.*" In Noreng 1969: 100–13.

Koht, Halvdan. *The Life of Ibsen.* 2 vols. New York: W. W. Norton. 1931.

Krane, Borghild. "*Bergmannen i John Gabriel Borkman.*" *Ibsenårbok* 1967: 14–26.

Bibliography

Krappe, Alexander H. "Scandinavian Seal Lore." *Scandinavian Studies and Notes* 18. 1944: 156–62.

Kristensen, Evald Tang, ed. *Jyske Folkeminder*. 12 vols. København. 1871.

———. *Danske Folkeæventyr*. Viborg. 1888.

———. *Danske sagn som de har lydt i folkemunde. Udelukkende efter utrykte kilder samlede og tildels optegnede af Evald Tang Kristensen*. Vol. 3. Århus and Silkeborg: Zeuners Bogtrykkeri, Silkeborg ny Bogtrykkeri. 1892–1902.

———. "Bjørnemanden." In *Festskrift til H. F. Feilberg*. Stockholm: Svenska Landsmålen. 1911: 456–65.

———. *Danske Sagn*. København: Forlaget Cai M. Woel. 1931.

———. *Danske Sagn som de har lydt i folkemunde*. 6 vols. København: C. A. Reitzels Forlag. 1936.

Landstad, Magnus B. *Norske Folkeviser*. Christiania. 1853.

———. *Mytiske sagn fra Telemarken*. Oslo: Norsk Folkeminnelag. 1926.

Langset, Edvard. *Segner-Gåter. Folketru frå Nordmark*. Oslo: Norsk Folkeminnelag. 1948.

Lavrin, Janko. *Ibsen: An Approach*. 1950; rpt. New York: Russell and Russell. 1969.

Lederer, Wolfgang. *The Fear of Women*. New York: Grune and Stratton. 1968.

———. *The Kiss of the Snow Queen: Hans Christian Andersen and Man's Redemption by Woman*. Berkeley: University of California Press. 1986.

Lee, Richard B. *The Dobe !Kung*. New York: Holt, Rinehart and Winston. 1984.

Lévi-Strauss, Claude. *Mythologiques I: Le cru et le cui*. Paris: Plon. 1964.

———. *The Elementary Structures of Kinship*. Boston: Beacon Press. 1969.

Lewis, Brian. *The Sargon Legend*. Cambridge, Mass.: American School of Oriental Research. 1980.

Liebgott, Niels-Knud. *Danmarkshistorien: Middelalderen*. 3 vols. København: Sesam. 1984.

Lien, Asmund. "Hulemotivet hos Aksel Sandemose: Om 'Manden fra Hulen' og trollet som ikke sprakk." *Samtiden* 79. 1970: 431–40.

Liestøl, Knut. "Scottish and Norwegian Ballads." *Studia Norvegica* 1. 1946: 3–16.

———, and Moltke Moe. *Norske Fokevisor*. 3 vols. Kristiania: Jacob Dybwads. 1920–24.

Lorentzen, Jørgen, ed. *Et Hundrede udvalgte danske viser*. 2 vols. København: G. E. C. Gad. 1974.

———. "Danmarks gamle Folkeviser 1853–1976." *Danske Studier* 72. 1977: 5–18.

Lucas, F. L. *The Drama of Ibsen and Strindberg*. New York: Macmillan. 1962.

Lund, Niels, and Kai Hørby. *Samfundet i vikingetid og middelalder: 800–1500*. Vol. 2 of *Dansk socialhistorie*. København: Gyldendal. 1980.

Lüthi, Max. *The European Folktale: Form and Nature*. Trans. John D. Niles. Philadelphia: Institute for the Study of Human Issues. 1982.

MacCormack, Carol, and Marilyn Strathern, eds., *Nature, Culture and Gender*. Cambridge: Cambridge University Press. 1980.

Bibliography

MacCulloch, John A. "Changeling." *Encyclopedia of Religion and Ethics*. New York: Charles Scribner's Sons. 1925–32. 3: 359–63.

McFarlane, James W., ed. *Ibsen: A Critical Anthology*. Harmondsworth: Penguin Books. 1970.

———, ed. *The Oxford Ibsen*. See Henrik Ibsen.

MacGregor, Alasdair A. *The Peat-Fire Flame: Folk-Tales and Traditions of the Highlands and the Islands*. Edinburgh: Moray Press. 1937.

MacRitchie, David. *The Testimony of Tradition*. London. 1890.

Markale, Jean. *Melusine; ou, L'androgyne*. Paris: Éditions Retz. 1983.

Marwick, Ernest W. "Creatures of Orkney Legend and Their Norse Ancestry." *Norveg* 15. 1972: 177–204.

Meisling, Peter. "Folkevisernes univers—bemærkninger om og til Jens Anker Jørgensen: 'Jorden og Slægten' (1976)." *Kritik* 43. 1977: 72–97.

Meyer, Michael. *Ibsen: A Biography*. Garden City, N.Y.: Doubleday. 1971.

———, trans. and ed. *The Plays of Ibsen*. 4 vols. New York: Washington Square Press. 1986.

Middelfort, H. C. Erik. "The Social Position of the Witch in Southwestern Germany." In Max Marwick, ed., *Witchcraft and Sorcery*. Harmondsworth: Penguin Books. 1970: 174–90.

Mossin, Steffen. "Folkeviser: Et led i en historisk rekonstruktion af en kulturarv." *Pædagogiske Arbejdsmapper* 2. 1974.

Motz, Lotte. "Of Elves and Dwarfs." *Arv* 29–30. 1973–74: 93–127.

Müllenhof, Karl. *Sagen, Märchen und Lieder aus Schleswig-Holstein-Lauenburg*. Kiel. 1845.

Mysterud, Ivar. "Bjørn og bjørneforskning." *Norveg* 23. 1980: 101–23.

Nergaard, Sigurd. *Hulder og Trollskap*. Vol. 2. Oslo: Norsk Folkeminnelags Skrifter. 1925.

Nettum, Rolf N. "Den åpne og den lukkede verden: En kommentar til noen av Henrik Ibsens samtidsskuespil." *Ibsenårbok* 1980–82.

Nicolaisen, Claus M. *Sagn og Eventyr fra Nordland*. Kristiania. 1887.

Noreng, Harald, ed. *Ibsen på festspilscenen*. Bergen: J. W. Eide Forlag. 1969.

———, ed. *En ny Ibsen? Ni Ibsen-artikler*. Oslo: Gyldendal Norsk Forlag. 1979.

Novalis [Friedrich von Hardenberg]. *Henry von Ofterdingen*. Trans. Palmer Hilty. New York: Frederick Ungar. 1964.

Nygard, Holger O. *The Ballad of "Heer Halewijn": Its Forms and Variations in Western Europe. A Study of the History and Nature of a Ballad Tradition*. Knoxville: University of Tennessee Press. 1958.

Oehlenschläger, Adam. "Agnete." In *Digterværker og Prosaiske Skrifter*. Vol. 17. Kjøbenhavn. 1852: 97–100.

———. "Bjergtrolden." In *Digterværker og Prosaiske Skrifter*. Vol. 17. Kjøbenhavn. 1852: 4–14.

———. "Rosmer Havmand." In *Digterværker og Prosaiske Skrifter*. Vol. 17. Kjøbenhavn. 1852: 56–68.

———. *Aladdin eller den forunderlige lampe*. København. 1878.

Bibliography

O'Flaherty, Wendy Doniger. *Women, Androgynes and Other Mythical Beasts.* Chicago: University of Chicago Press. 1980.

Olrik, Axel. *Nordens Trylleviser.* København: J. H. Schultz. 1934.

———, and Ida Falbe-Hansen. *Danske Folkeviser i Udvalg: Udgivne for Dansklærerforeningen.* 2 vols. København: Gyldendalske boghandel nordisk forlag. 1927.

Ortner, Sherry. "Is Female to Male as Nature Is to Culture?" *Feminist Studies* 1. 1972: 5–31.

Østerud, Erik. "Når vi døde vågner på mytologisk bakgrunn." *Ibsenårbok* 1963–64: 72–97.

———. *Det borgerlige subjekt: Ibsen i teorihistorisk belysning.* Oslo: Novus. 1981a.

———. "Den rosmerske adelighet og dybdepsykologien. En studie i Henrik Ibsens *Rosmersholm.*" *Norskrift* 34. 1981b: 1–45.

Paludan-Müller, F. *Adam Homo—et Digt.* København. 1899.

Piø, Iørn. "Overnaturlige væsner i nordisk balladetradition I. DgF 33 German Gladensvend og DgF 60 Valravnen." *Danske Studier.* 1969: 48–71.

———. "Overnaturlige væsner i nordisk balladetradition II. DgF 38 Agnete og havmanden." *Danske Studier* 1970: 24–51.

———. "Svend Grundtvig og hans folkloristike arbejdsmetode." *Danske Studier* 1971: 91–120.

———. "On Reading Orally Performed Ballads: The Medieval Ballads of Denmark." In Bekker-Nielsen et al. 1976.

———. *Nye veje til Folkevisen.* København: Gyldendal. 1985.

Pizzaro, Joaquin Martinez. "Transformations of the Bear's Son Tales in the Sagas of the Hrafnistumenn." *Arv* 32–33. 1976–77: 263–81.

Poestian, Joseph C. *Lappländische Märchen.* Wien. 1886.

Prior, R. C. A. *Ancient Danish Ballads.* 3 vols. London: 1860.

Propp, Vladimir. *Morphology of the Folktale.* Austin: University of Texas Press. 1979.

Qvigstad, Just. *Lappiske eventyr og sagn.* 4 vols. Oslo: Institutet for Sammenlignende Kulturforskning. 1927.

Ragland-Sullivan, Ellie. *Jacques Lacan and the Philosophy of Psychoanalysis.* Urbana: University of Illinois Press. 1986.

Raphael, Robert. "Illusion and the Self in *The Wild Duck, Rosmersholm* and *The Lady from the Sea.*" In Fjelde 1965: 120–30.

Richmond, W. Edson. "From Edda and Saga to Ballad: A Troll Bridge." In Kenneth S. Goldstein and Neil Rosenberg, eds., *Folklore Studies in Honor of Herbert Halpern: A Festschrift.* St. Johns, Newfoundland: Memorial University of Newfoundland Press. 1980: 303–13.

Roed, Arne. "The Crutch Is Floating." *Ibsenårbok* 1974: 64–88.

Rosengarten, David. "The Lady from the Sea: Ibsen's Submerged Allegory." *Educational Theater Journal* 29. 1977: 463–76.

Russell, W. M. S. "Folktales and the Theater." *Folklore* 92. 1981: 3–24.

Bibliography

Rønning, Helge. "Könets fånge og klassens: Om Ibsens *Hedda Gabler*." *Ord och Bild* 82. 1973: 491–93, 495–99.

Saari, Sandra E. "Of Madness and Fame: Ibsen's *Bygmester Solness*." *Scandinavian Studies* 50. 1978: 1–18.

Salomé, Lou. *Ibsen's Heroines*. Ed., trans., and introd., Siegfried Mandel. Redding Ridge, Ct.: Black Swan Books. 1985.

Sandstroem, Yvonne L. "Problems of Identity in *Hedda Gabler*." *Scandinavian Studies* 51. 1979: 368–74.

Schack, Hans Egede. *Phantasterne*. København: Holbergselskabet. 1925.

Seemann, Erich, et al. *European Folk Ballads*. Copenhagen: Rosenkilde and Bagger. 1967.

Sehmsdorf, Henning K. "Two Legends about St. Olaf the Masterbuilder: A Clue to the Dramatic Structure of Henrik Ibsen's *Bygmester Solness*." *Edda* 54. 1967: 263–71.

Simpson, Jacqueline. *Icelandic Folktales and Legends*. London: B. T. Bratsford. 1972.

Simrock, Karl. *Die deutschen Volksbucher: Die deutschen Volkslieder*. Frankfurt am Main. 1851.

Solheim, Svale. *Norsk sætertradisjon*. Oslo: H. Aschehoug. 1952.

Sønderholm, Erik. "Nogle folkevisebetragtninger." *Danske Studier* 77. 1982: 114–23.

Sørensen, Villy. *Digtere og dæmoner: Fortolkninger og vurderinger*. København: Gyldendal. 1959.

Streiber, Whitley. *Communion: A True Story*. New York: William Morrow. 1987.

Sturtevant, A. M. "*Olaf Liljekrans* and Ibsen's Literary Development." *Scandinavian Studies and Notes* 5. 1918–19: 110–32.

Stuyver, Clara. *Ibsens dramatische Gestalten: Psychologie und Symbolik*. Amsterdam: North-Holland Publishing Company. 1952.

Swahn, Jan Öjvind. *The Tale of Cupid and Psyche*. Lund: C. W. K. Gleerup. 1955.

Swire, Otta F. *The Highlands and Their Legends*. Edinburgh: Oliver and Boyd. 1963.

Tammany, Jane Ellert. *Henrik Ibsen's Theatre Aesthetics*. New York: Philosophical Library. 1980.

Taylor, Mark C. "Sounds of Silence." In Robert L. Perkins, ed., *Kierkegaard's Fear and Trembling: Critical Appraisals*. Alabama: University of Alabama Press. 1981.

Thiele, Just Mathias. *Danske Folkesagn*. København. 1820.

———. *Danmarks Folkesagn*. København. 1843–60.

Thomas, David. "'All the Glory of the World': Reality and Myth in *When We Dead Awaken*." *Scandinavica* 18. 1979: 1–19.

Thompson, Stith. *The Folktale*. New York: Dryden Press. 1951.

Thomson, David. *The People of the Sea: A Journey in Search of the Seal Legend*. London: Barrie and Rockliff. 1965.

Bibliography

Tieck, Ludwig. "The Runenberg." Trans. Thomas Carlyle. In F. E. Pierce and
Carl F. Schreiber, eds., *Fiction and Fantasy of German Romance: Se-
lections from German Romantic Authors, 1790–1830.* New York: Oxford
University Press. 1927.

Tinker, C. B., and H. F. Lowry. *The Poetry of Matthew Arnold: A Commentary.*
London: Oxford University Press. 1929.

Turner, Victor. *The Ritual Process: Structure and Anti-Structure.* Ithaca, N.Y.:
Cornell University Press. 1969.

Vaa, Dyre. "Ibsens lesning og Rebekka West." *Ibsenårbok* 1959: 187.

Valency, Maurice. *The Flower and the Castle: An Introduction to Modern Drama.*
New York: Grosset and Dunlap. 1963.

Vedfelt, Ole. *Det kvindelige i manden: En beskrivelse af den moderne mands psy-
kologi.* København: Gyldendal. 1985.

Voigt, Vilmos. "Folktale or Tale of Folk." *Arv* 36. 1980: 77–84.

Wähler, Dr. Martin. *Die weisse Frau: Vom Glauben des Volkes an den lebenden
Leichnam.* Erfurt: Verlag Kurt Stenger. 1931.

Watts, Peter. Introd. to *Peer Gynt.* By Henrik Ibsen. Harmondsworth: Penguin.
1985.

Weigand, Hermann. *The Modern Ibsen: A Reconsideration.* New York: E. P. Dut-
ton. 1960.

White, Hayden. "The Forms of Wildness: Archaeology of an Idea." In Dudley
and Novak. 1972: 3–39.

Wiingaard, Jytte. *"Bygmester Solness.* En semantisk analyse." *Ibsenårbok* 1977:
180–208.

Wilson, Mary G. "Edvard Munch's *Woman in Three Stages:* A Source of Inspiration for Henrik Ibsen's *When We Dead Awaken."* *Centennial Review* 24. 1980: 492–500.

Wimberly, Lowry C. *Folklore in the English and Scottish Ballads.* 1928; rpt.
New York: Frederick Ungar. 1959.

Index

Index

Index

Index

iron (guns, weapons, metals),
50 n. 24, 137, 164 n. 22, 216–19,
224 n. 20, 256–73
journeys, 63, 66–69, 71–76, 83, 84
offended fairy, 186
parents promise or give child to
troll, 50, 146, 230, 286
redemption, 21, 251, 267, 284,
285, 286, 287–89. See also disenchantments
revenant returns to claim mate, 5,
205, 207–8, 281, 282
runes, 41–42, 54, 75–76, 93 n. 5,
127
search for the lost husband or wife,
14, 274, 275, 286, 287, 293 n. 37
supernaturals seek human soul, 21,
36–37, 39, 43, 125–26, 173–74,
176, 198, 199, 215, 219, 220,
222, 231, 246, 247, 268. See also
redemption, disenchantments
taboos, 186, 187, 263, 287
wild hunt, 279
wonderland, 190, 232, 233, 235,
239, 257, 258, 261, 262, 267,
268, 273, 290
Folktales (as subject), ix, 10
Folktales (by title)
"Bergman's Daughter of Dagberg-
dass, The," 224 n. 22
"Boy Who Was Promised to the
Mermaid, The" ("Gutten som
var lovet til havfruen"), 50 n. 22
"Cupid and Psyche," 274, 293 n. 37
"East of the Sun, West of the
Moon," 262, 270, 274, 275, 285,
286, 287, 291, 293 n. 37
"The Frog Prince," 274, 284
"Hildur, the Queen of the Elves,"
214
"Huldre's Husband, The," 215,
217
"Huldre's Tail, The," 214
"Human Soul Has the Shape of a
Bumblebee, The," 97 n. 65

"Mer-king and the Earth King,
The" ("Havkongen og landkon-
gen"), 50 n. 22
"Merman's Lament, The" ("Hav-
kongens klage"), 93 n. 3
"Sickly Changeling, The," 244,
247. See also 243
"Tom Moore and the Seal Woman,"
15
Foucault, Michel, 45–46, 69, 94 n. 8
Fouqué, Friedrich de la Motte: Un-
dine, 241, 272
Fraenkl, Pavel, 170 n. 146, 205
Frandsen, Ernst, 31
Freud, Sigmund, 52 n. 34, 69,
98 n. 65, 122, 187, 194 n. 5,
209 n. 24, 225, 242
Frykman, Eric, xiv n. 7

Geijer, E. Gustav, 48 n. 10
Gennep, Arnold van, 67
Ghosts, 198, 211, 240
Giraudoux, Jean: Ondine, 221
Giselle. See Folklore characters, willis
Goethe, Johann W.: Faust, 142
Goitein, P. Lionel, 209 n. 24
Goya, Francisco de, 290
Gravier, Maurice, 5, 6, 16, 20,
22 n. 3, 27, 105, 166 n. 49,
194 nn. 1, 4, 197, 198, 199, 201,
209 n. 5, 254 n. 7
Gray, Ronald, 209 n. 1
Gregory, Lady Isabel, 23 n. 29,
209 n. 25
Grimm, Jakob: Teutonic Mythology,
213, 279, 280, 283, 284,
293 nn. 24, 34, 36
Grouse at Justedal, The, 11, 216
Gruenberg, Sidonie, 209 n. 24
Grundtvig, Svend Hersleb: Danmarks
gamle Folkeviser (aka DgF), 3, 27,
28, 30, 58, 60, 87, 105, 194 n. 4,
206–7, 208; Engelske og Skotske
Folkeviser, 87, 206
Gustafson, Alrik, 193 n. 1

345

Index

Index